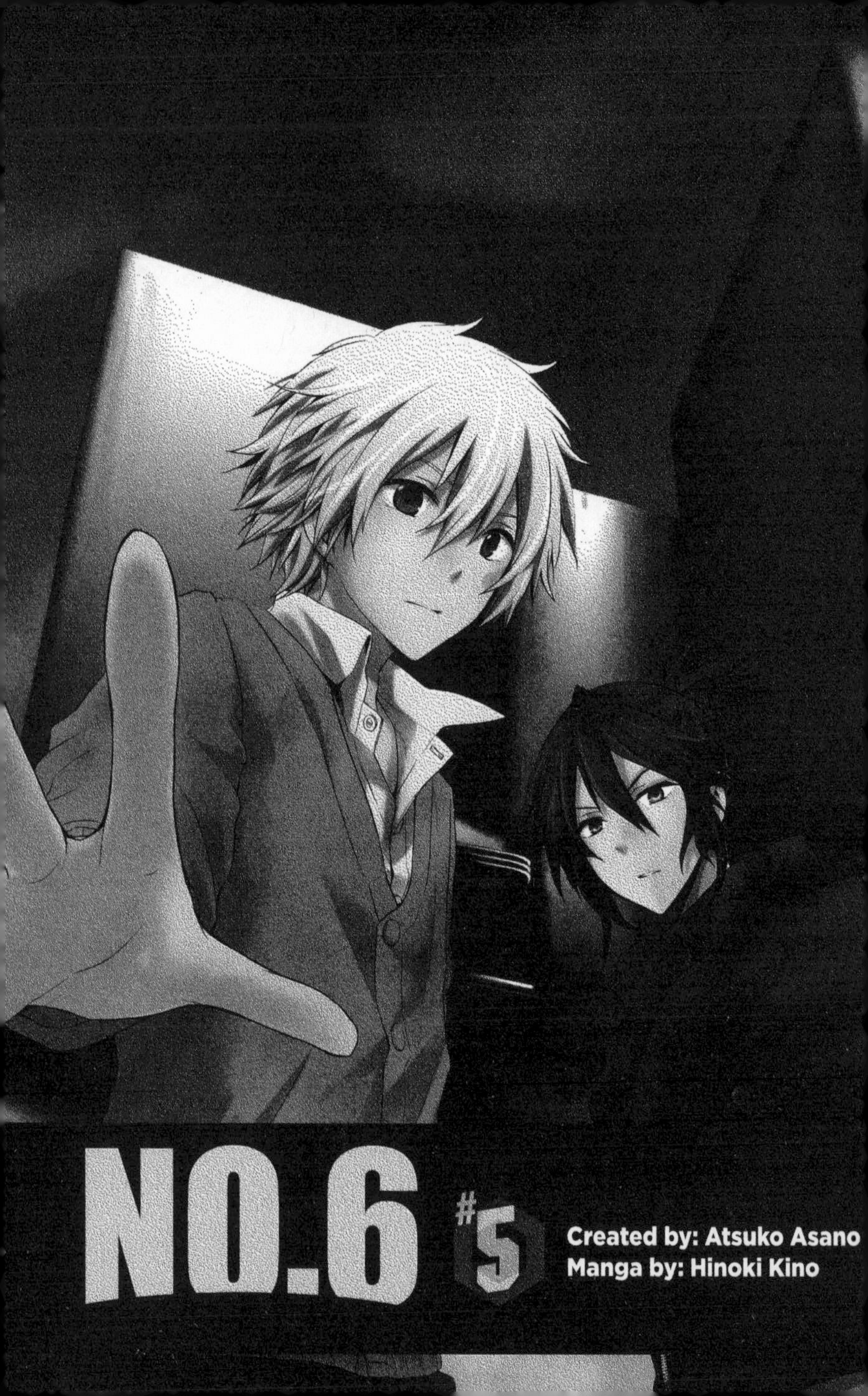
NO.6
#5
Created by: Atsuko Asano
Manga by: Hinoki Kino

NO.6 STORY and CHARACTERS

Shion was raised as a privileged elite in the holy city of No. 6. But after sheltering Rat, a fugitive on the run, Shion was stripped of his elite status and forced to live in Lost Town. Just as he was being arrested by the Security Bureau on suspicion of murder, Rat—the fugitive from four years earlier—came to Shion's rescue, and together they escaped No. 6 for the violence and despair of West Block. After his body was mysteriously transformed by a parasitic bee, Shion decided to stay with Rat in West Block.

But then Shion learned that his childhood friend Safu had been abducted and taken to the correctional facility. He and Rat decided to free her, and they developed a scheme to break in. With the help of Dogkeeper and Rikiga, they learned that "the Manhunt" will soon come to West Block.

SAFU

A childhood friend with feelings of love for Shion. An elite researcher specializing in neuroscience.

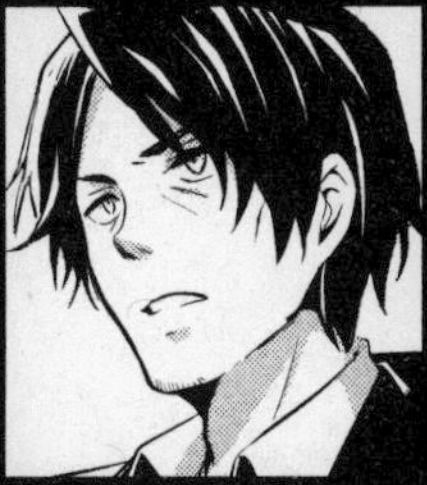

YOMIN

Harbors doubts about No. 6 since losing his wife and child.

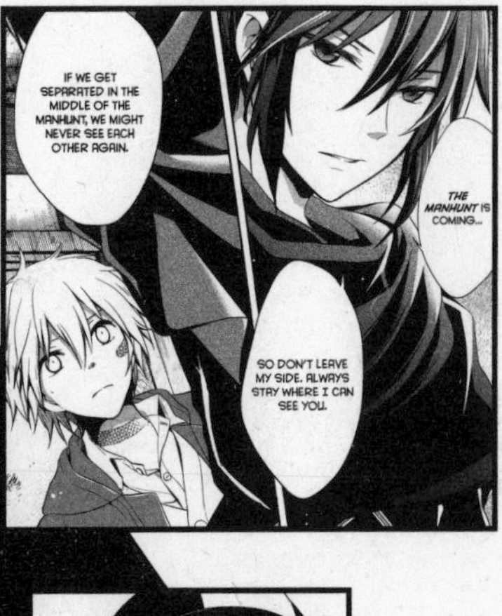
THE MANHUNT IS COMING...
IF WE GET SEPARATED IN THE MIDDLE OF THE MANHUNT, WE MIGHT NEVER SEE EACH OTHER AGAIN.
SO DON'T LEAVE MY SIDE. ALWAYS STAY WHERE I CAN SEE YOU.

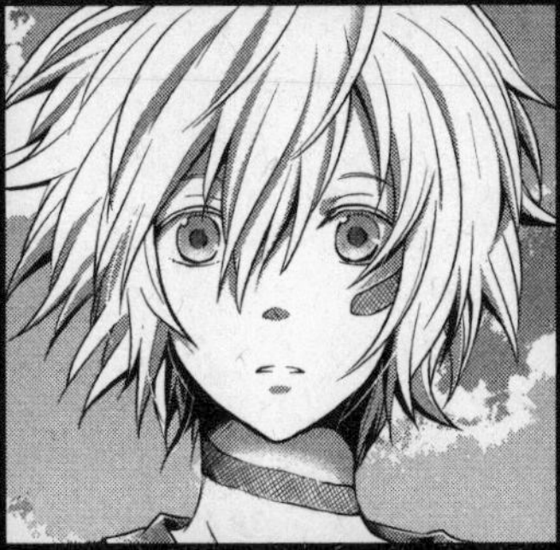

SHION

Fallen from the elite, he escaped to West Block. He was infected by a parasitic bee, but survived.

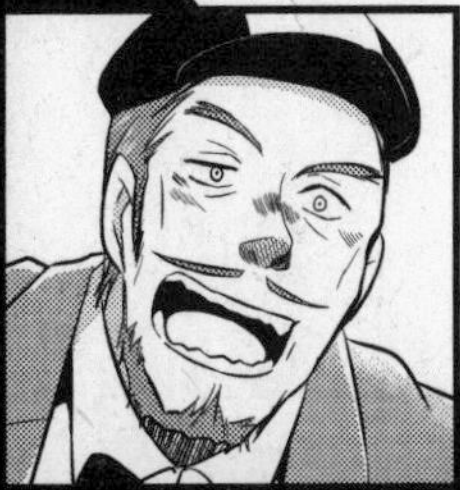

RIKIGA

A former journalist who now publishes a porno magazine in West Block. An old friend of Karan.

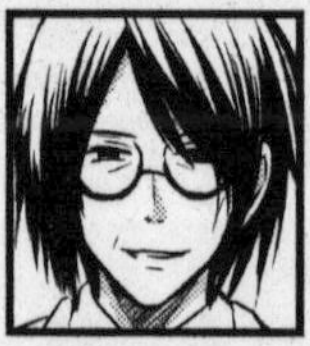

The Man in White

An ambitious research scientist.

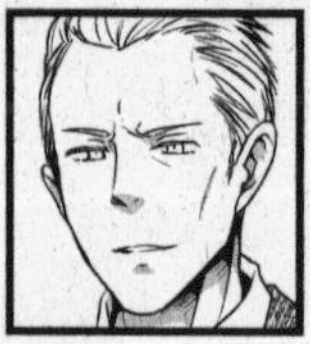

The Mayor

The most powerful man in No. 6.

Inside No. 6

Upper Class

The center of the city, with the Moondrop (City Hall) at its apex.

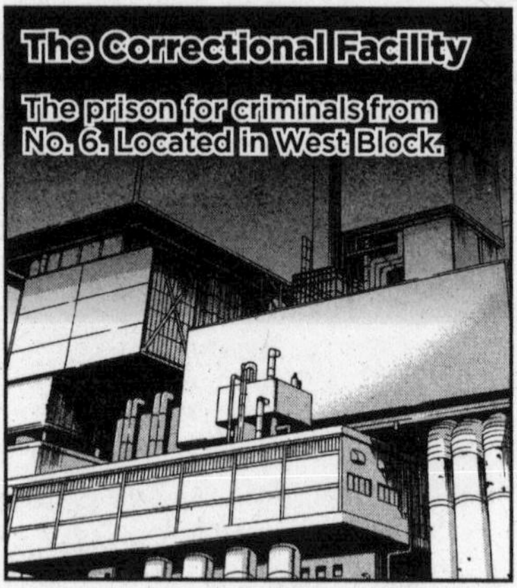

The Correctional Facility
The prison for criminals from No. 6. Located in West Block.

Chronos

The top-class residential area, open only to special elite citizens.

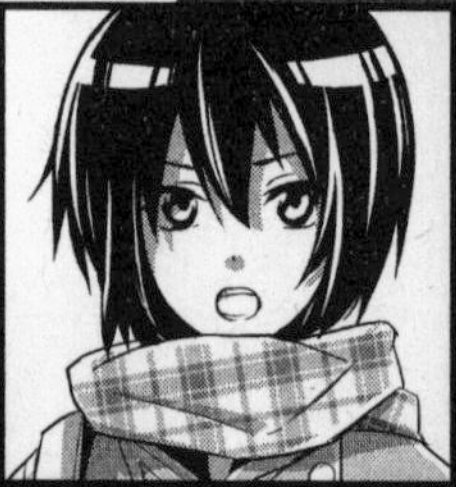

Arrested

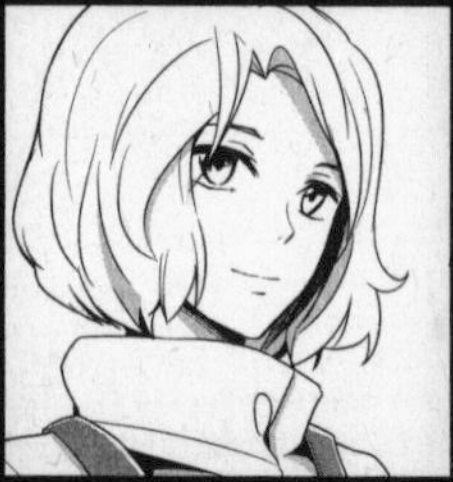

KARAN

Shion's mother. Operates a bakery in Lost Town.

Lost Town

The lower-class residential area for the city's disenfranchised.

The Outskirts

West Block

The dangerous special zone outside the walls of the city. A criminal correctional facility is located there.

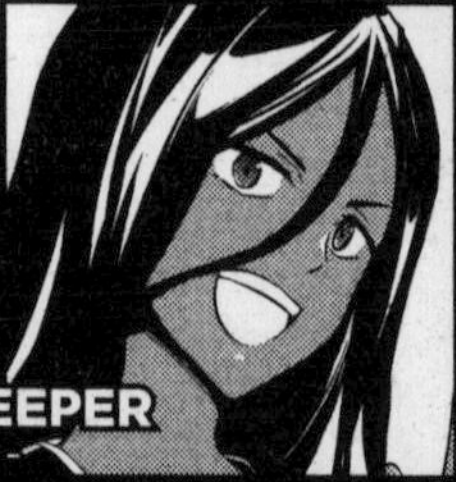

DOGKEEPER

Lives with dogs and operates a dilapidated hotel. Also gathers information for a price.

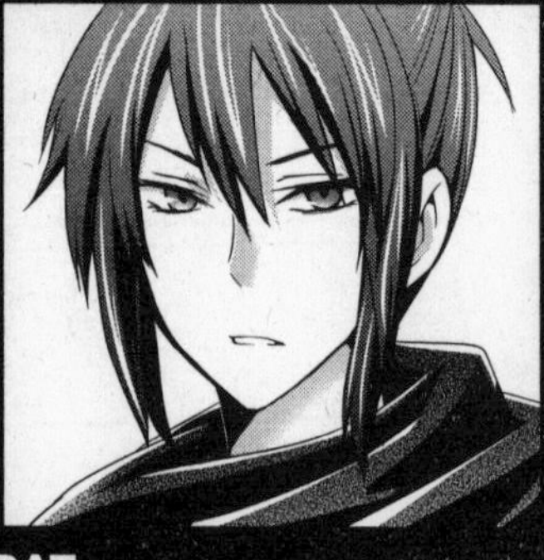

RAT

Four years ago, Shion saved his life in Chronos. In return, he helped Shion escape from No. 6.

NO.6

Chapter 16: Stage for Disaster

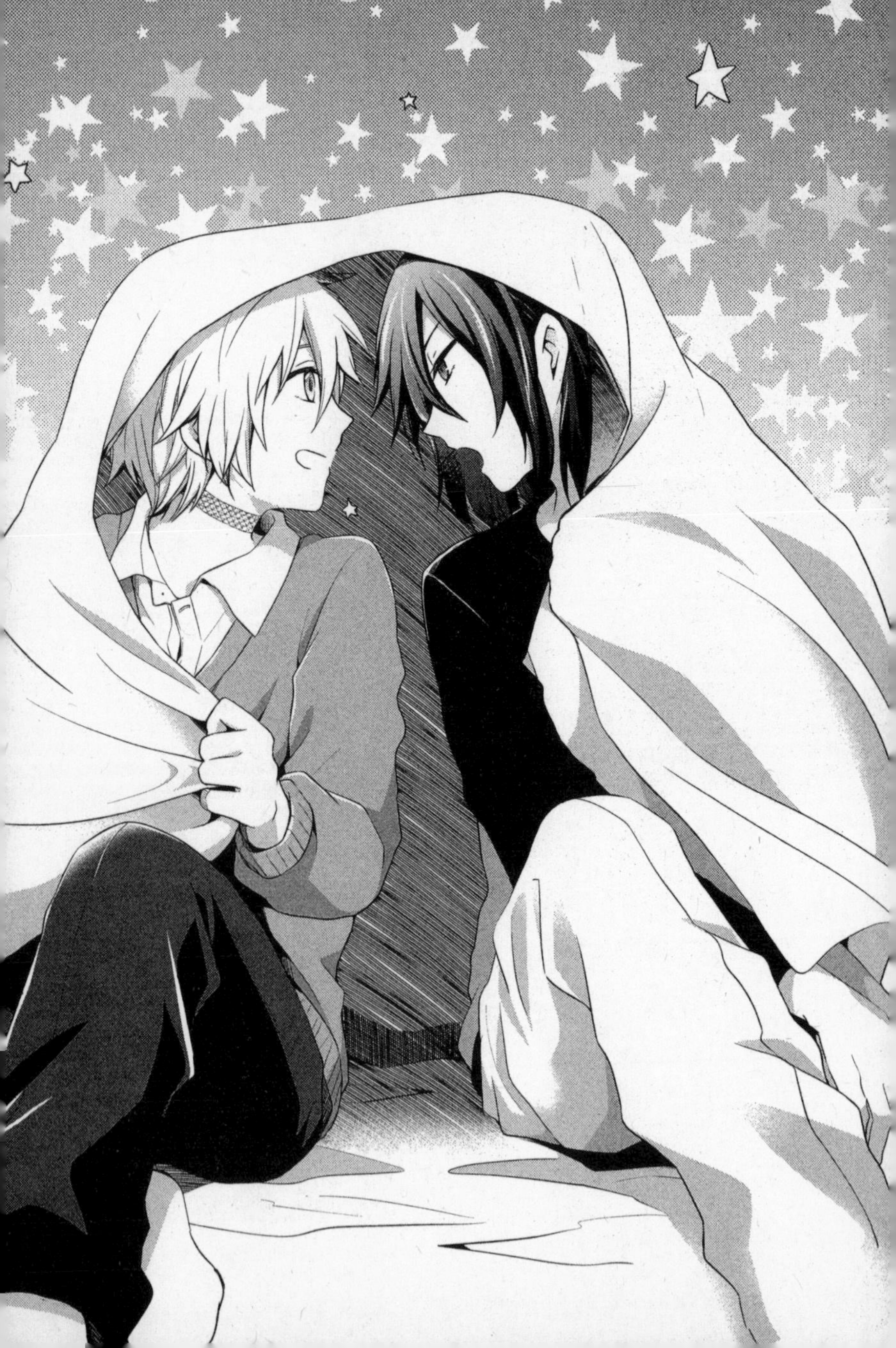

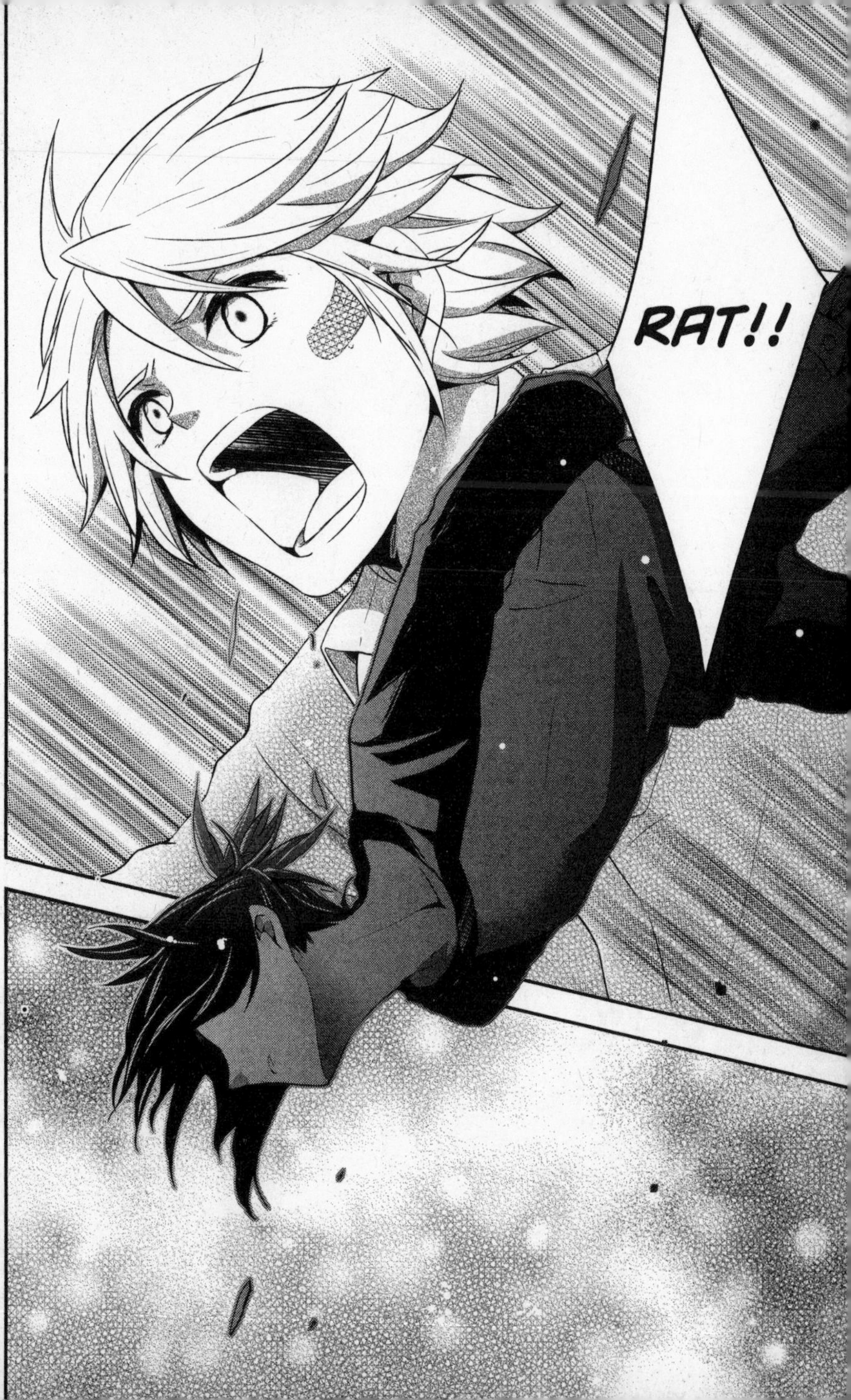
RAT!!

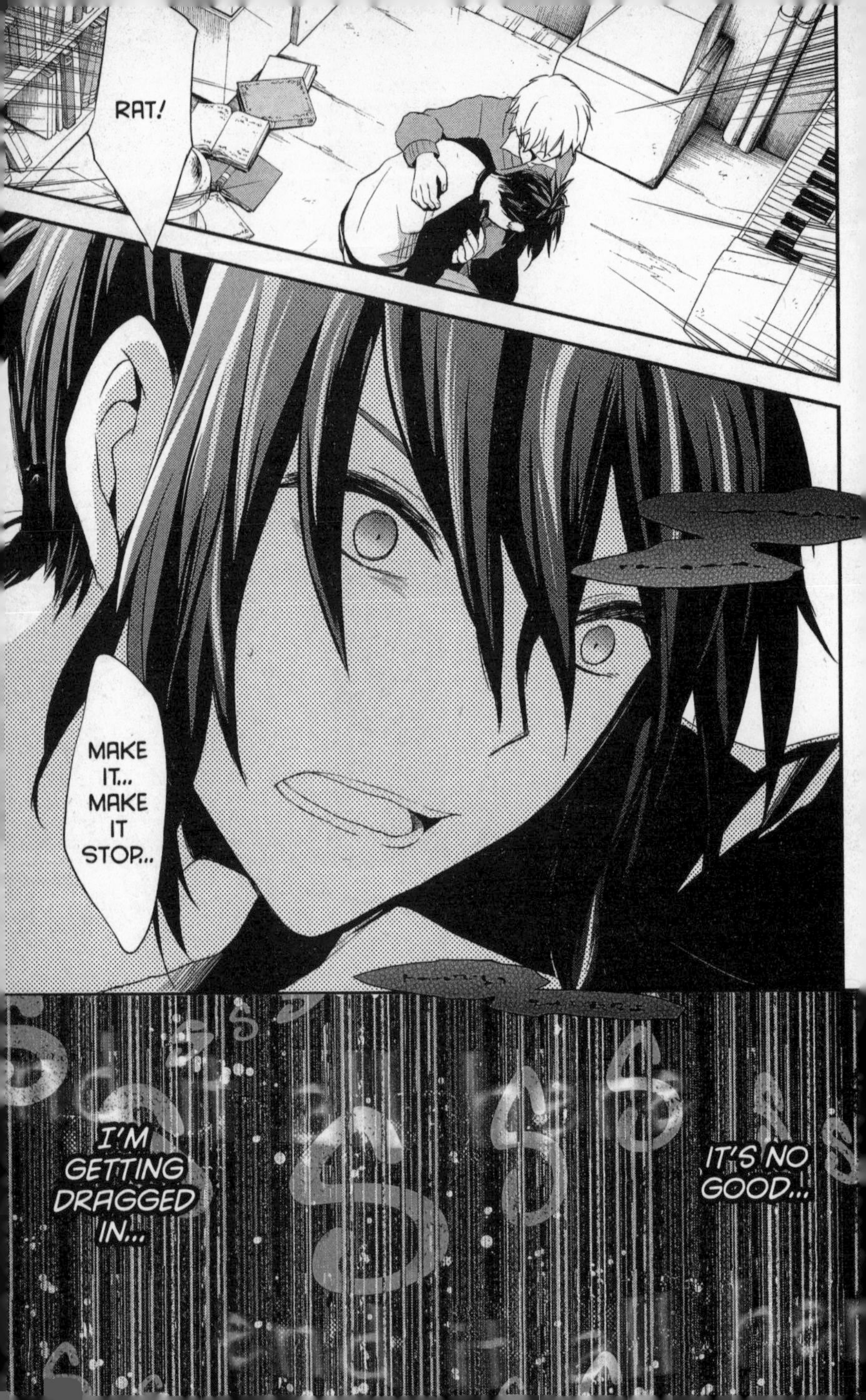
RAT!
MAKE IT... MAKE IT STOP...
IT'S NO GOOD...
I'M GETTING DRAGGED IN...

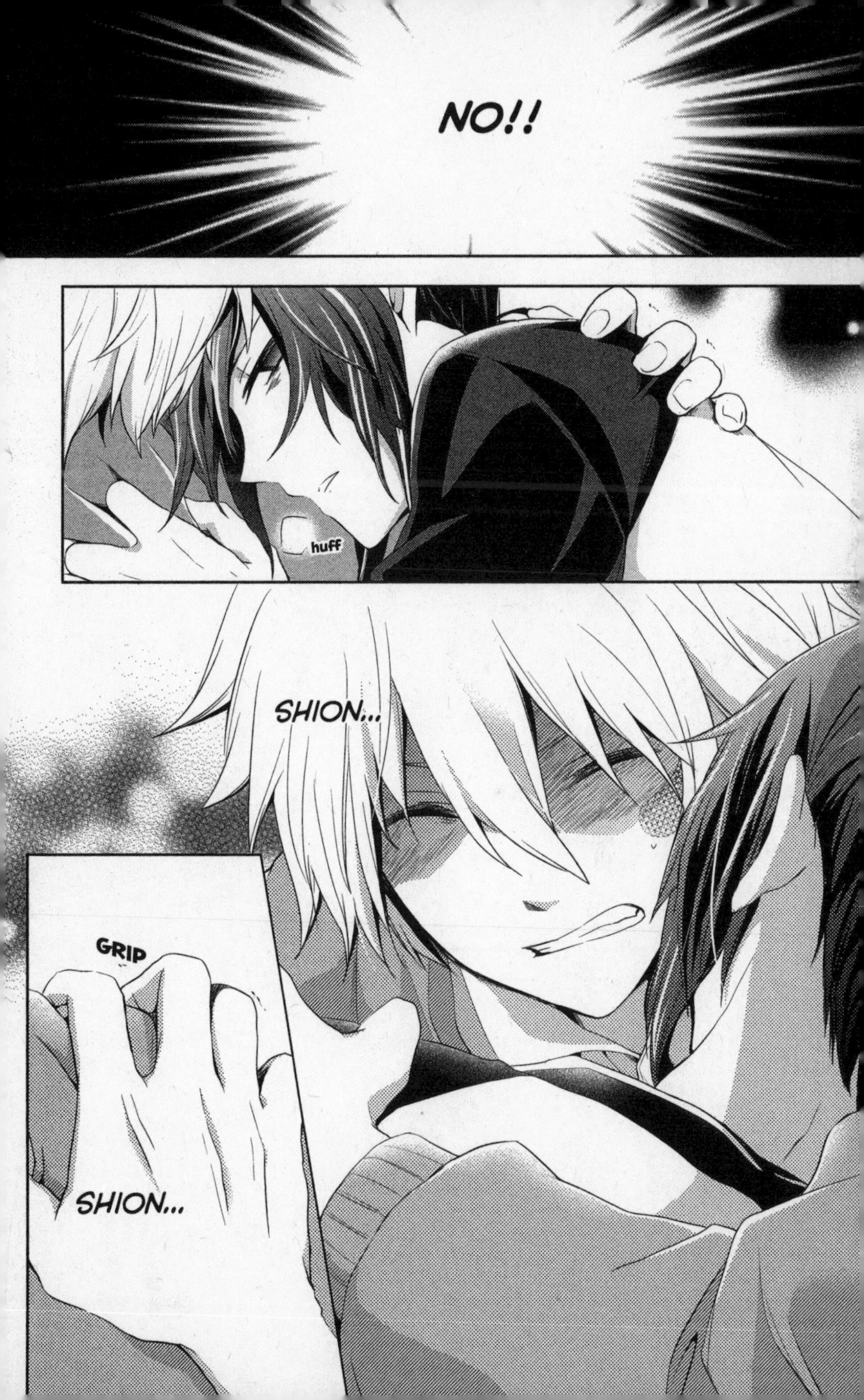
NO!!
huff
SHION...
GRIP
SHION...

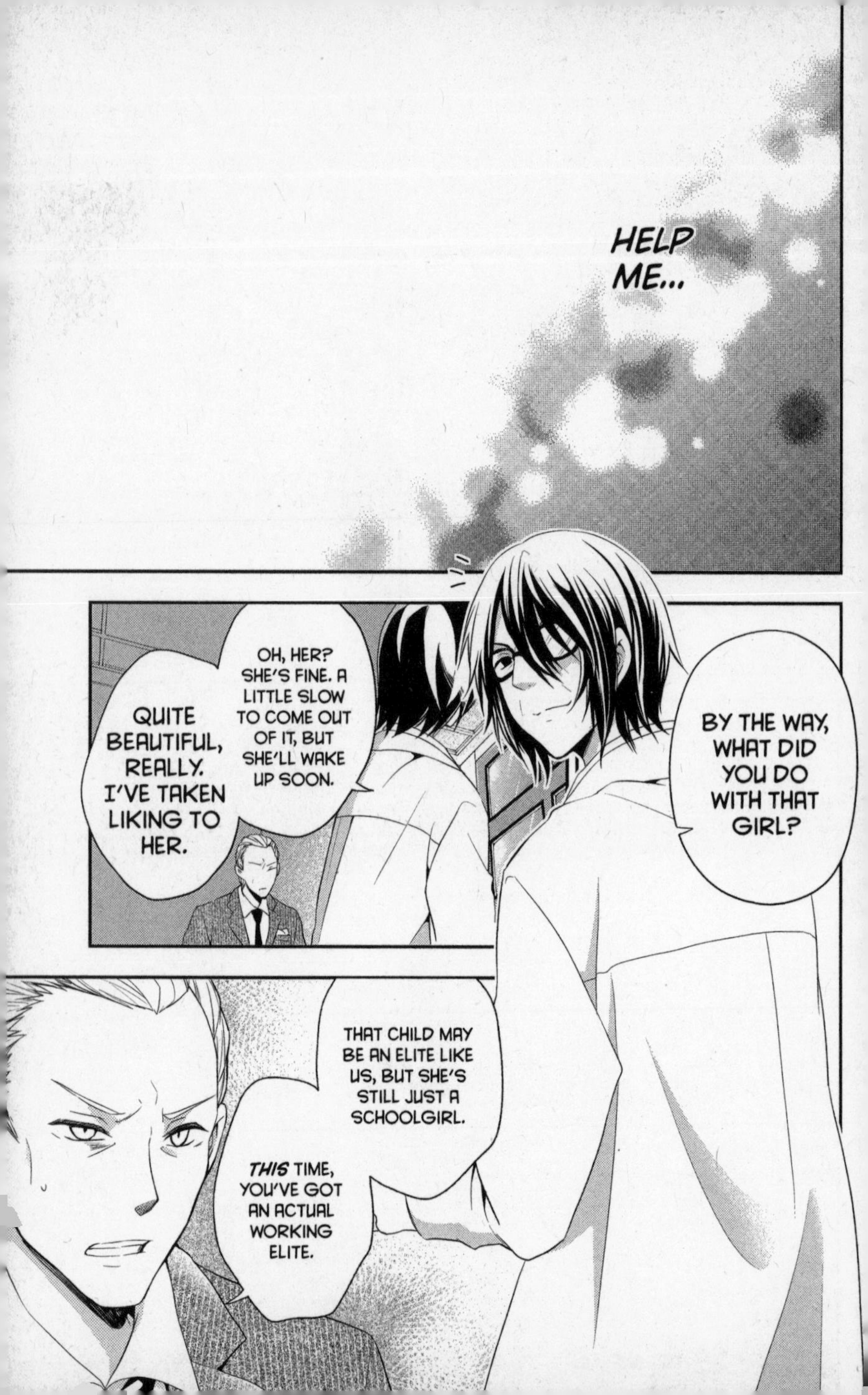
HELP ME...
BY THE WAY, WHAT DID YOU DO WITH THAT GIRL?
OH, HER? SHE'S FINE. A LITTLE SLOW TO COME OUT OF IT, BUT SHE'LL WAKE UP SOON.
QUITE BEAUTIFUL, REALLY. I'VE TAKEN LIKING TO HER.
THAT CHILD MAY BE AN ELITE LIKE US, BUT SHE'S STILL JUST A SCHOOLGIRL.
THIS TIME, YOU'VE GOT AN ACTUAL WORKING ELITE.

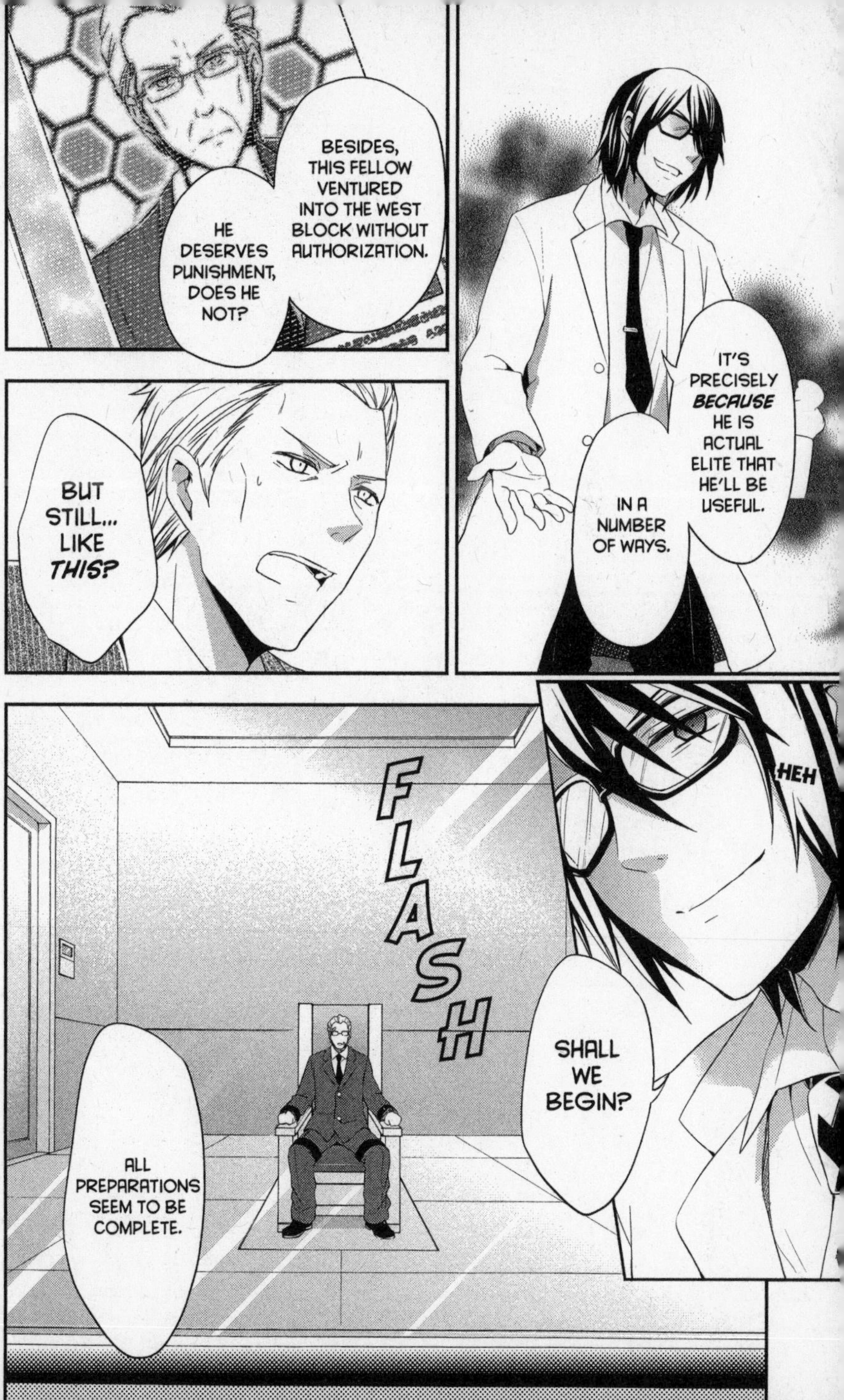
IT'S PRECISELY *BECAUSE* HE IS ACTUAL ELITE THAT HE'LL BE USEFUL.
IN A NUMBER OF WAYS.
BESIDES, THIS FELLOW VENTURED INTO THE WEST BLOCK WITHOUT AUTHORIZATION.
HE DESERVES PUNISHMENT, DOES HE NOT?
BUT STILL... LIKE *THIS?*
HEH
SHALL WE BEGIN?
FLASH
ALL PREPARATIONS SEEM TO BE COMPLETE.

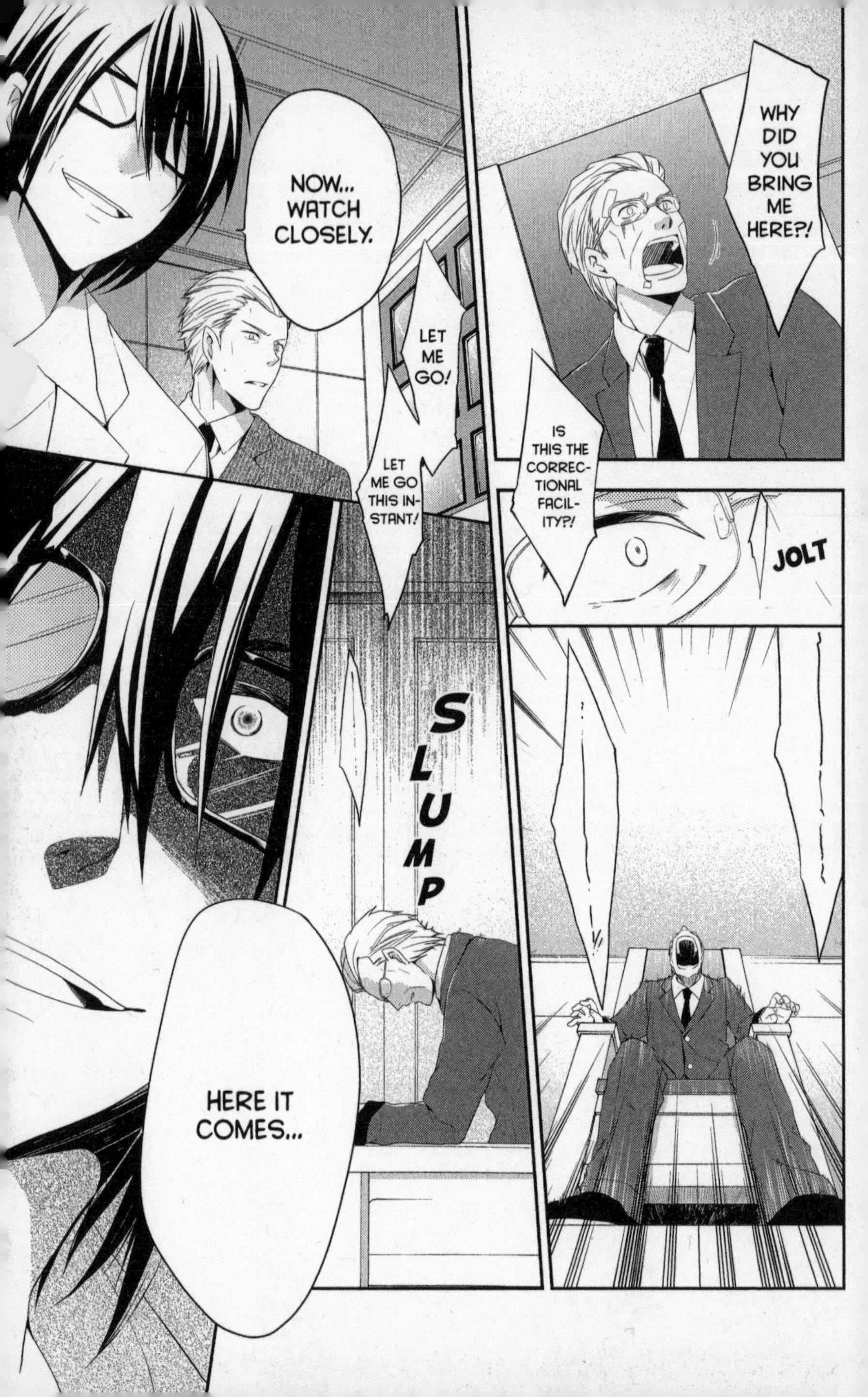
WHY DID YOU BRING ME HERE?!
IS THIS THE CORREC-TIONAL FACIL-ITY?!
JOLT
NOW... WATCH CLOSELY.
LET ME GO!
LET ME GO THIS IN-STANT!
SLUMP
HERE IT COMES...

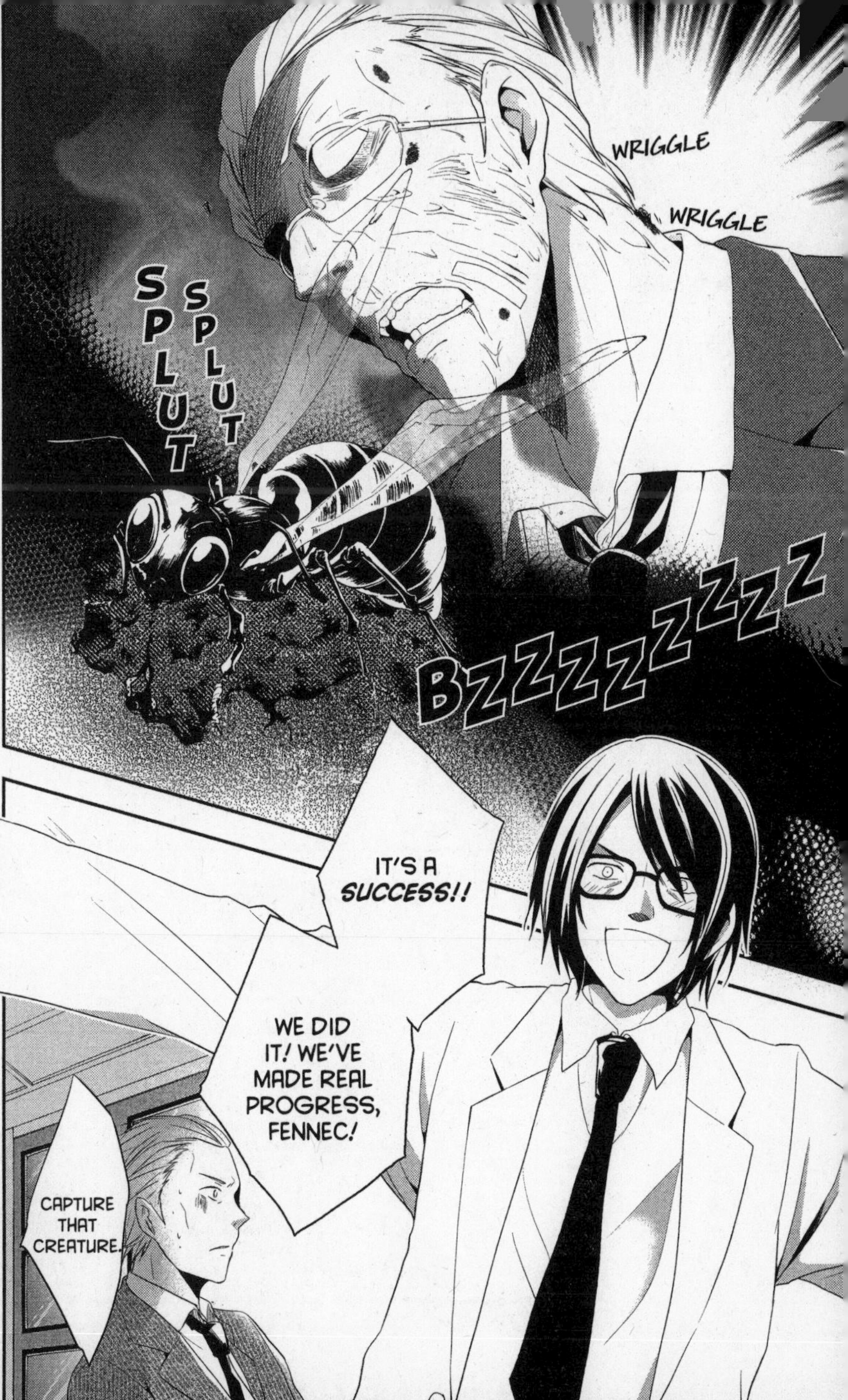
WRIGGLE
WRIGGLE
SPLUT
SPLUT
BZZZZZZZZZ
IT'S A *SUCCESS!!*
WE DID IT! WE'VE MADE REAL PROGRESS, FENNEC!
CAPTURE THAT CREATURE.

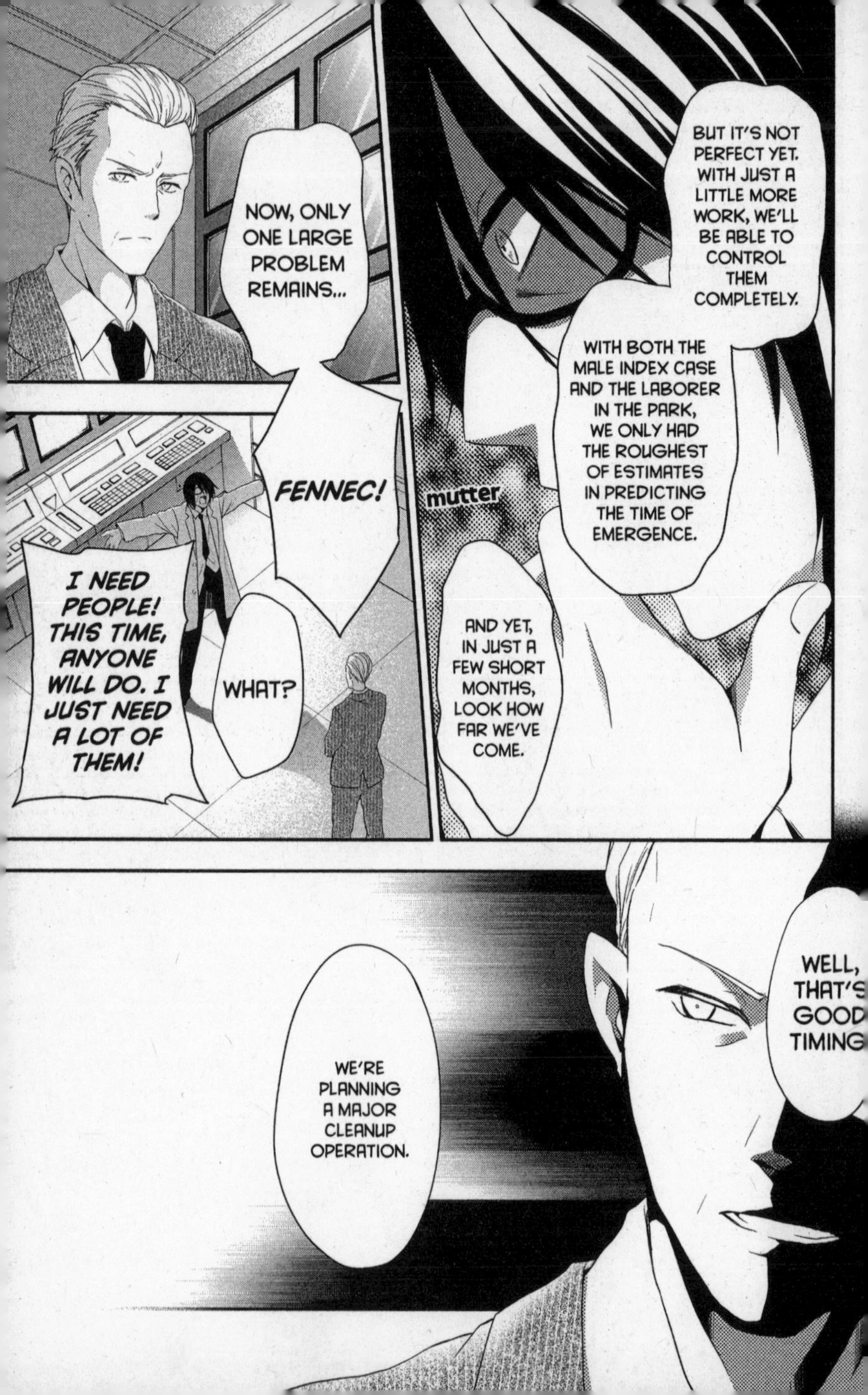
BUT IT'S NOT PERFECT YET. WITH JUST A LITTLE MORE WORK, WE'LL BE ABLE TO CONTROL THEM COMPLETELY.
WITH BOTH THE MALE INDEX CASE AND THE LABORER IN THE PARK, WE ONLY HAD THE ROUGHEST OF ESTIMATES IN PREDICTING THE TIME OF EMERGENCE.
mutter
AND YET, IN JUST A FEW SHORT MONTHS, LOOK HOW FAR WE'VE COME.
NOW, ONLY ONE LARGE PROBLEM REMAINS...
FENNEC!
I NEED PEOPLE! THIS TIME, ANYONE WILL DO. I JUST NEED A LOT OF THEM!
WHAT?
WELL, THAT'S GOOD TIMING
WE'RE PLANNING A MAJOR CLEANUP OPERATION.

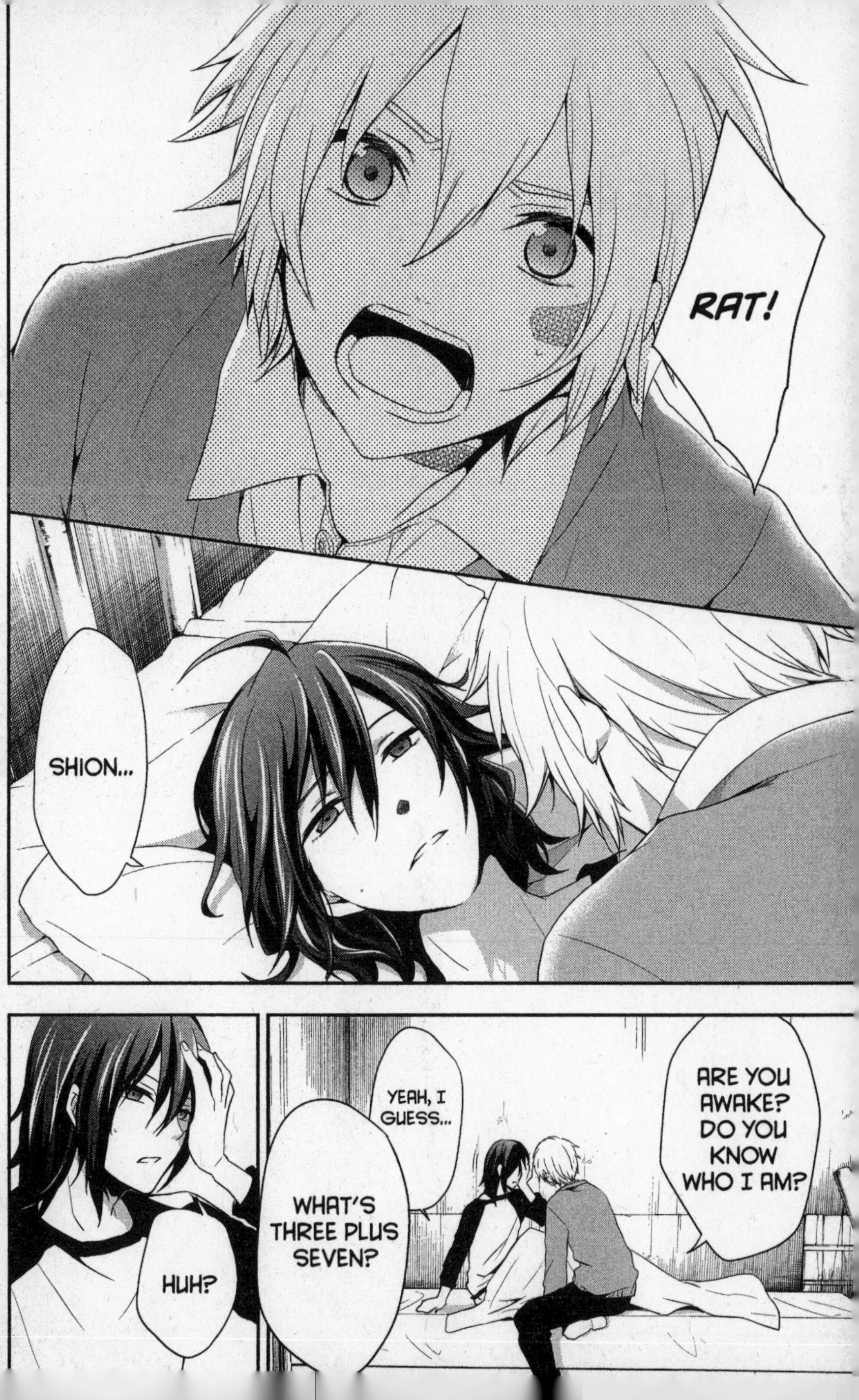
RAT!
SHION...
ARE YOU AWAKE? DO YOU KNOW WHO I AM?
YEAH, I GUESS...
WHAT'S THREE PLUS SEVEN?
HUH?

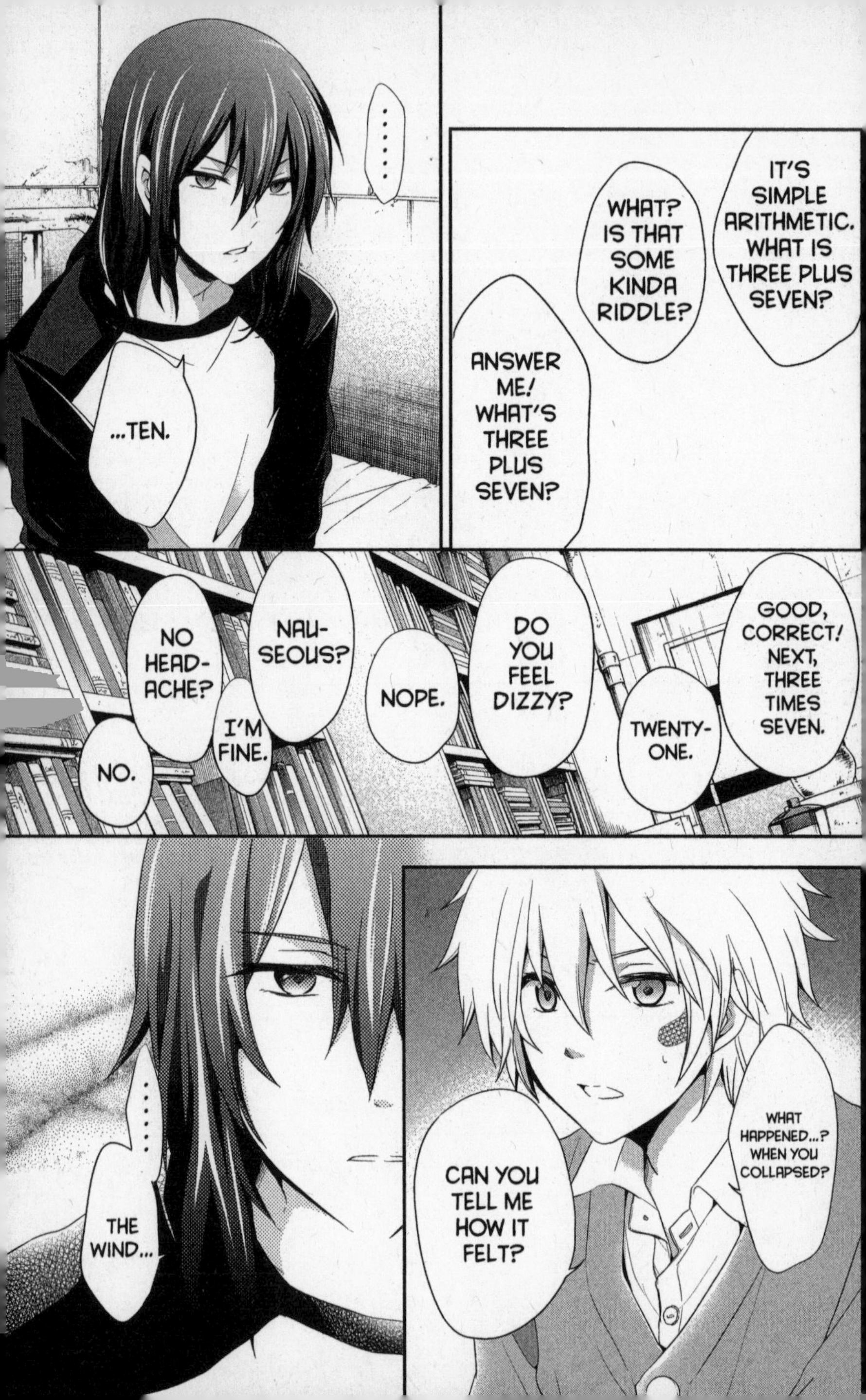
IT'S SIMPLE ARITHMETIC. WHAT IS THREE PLUS SEVEN?
WHAT? IS THAT SOME KINDA RIDDLE?
ANSWER ME! WHAT'S THREE PLUS SEVEN?
......
...TEN.
GOOD, CORRECT! NEXT, THREE TIMES SEVEN.
TWENTY-ONE.
DO YOU FEEL DIZZY?
NOPE.
NAU-SEOUS?
I'M FINE.
NO HEAD-ACHE?
NO.
WHAT HAPPENED...? WHEN YOU COLLAPSED?
CAN YOU TELL ME HOW IT FELT?
......
THE WIND...

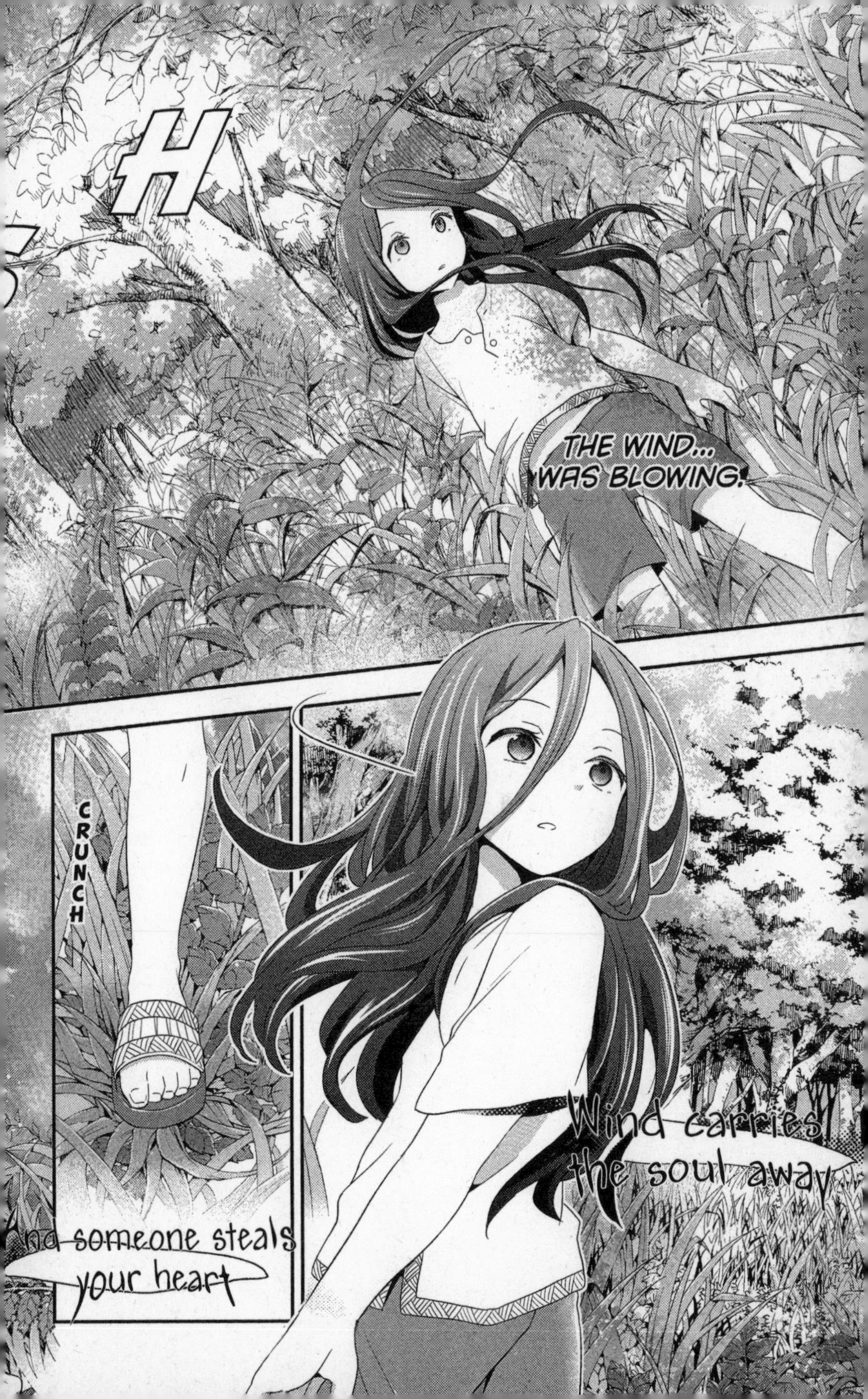
H
THE WIND... WAS BLOWING.
Wind carries the soul away
CRUNCH
And someone steals your heart

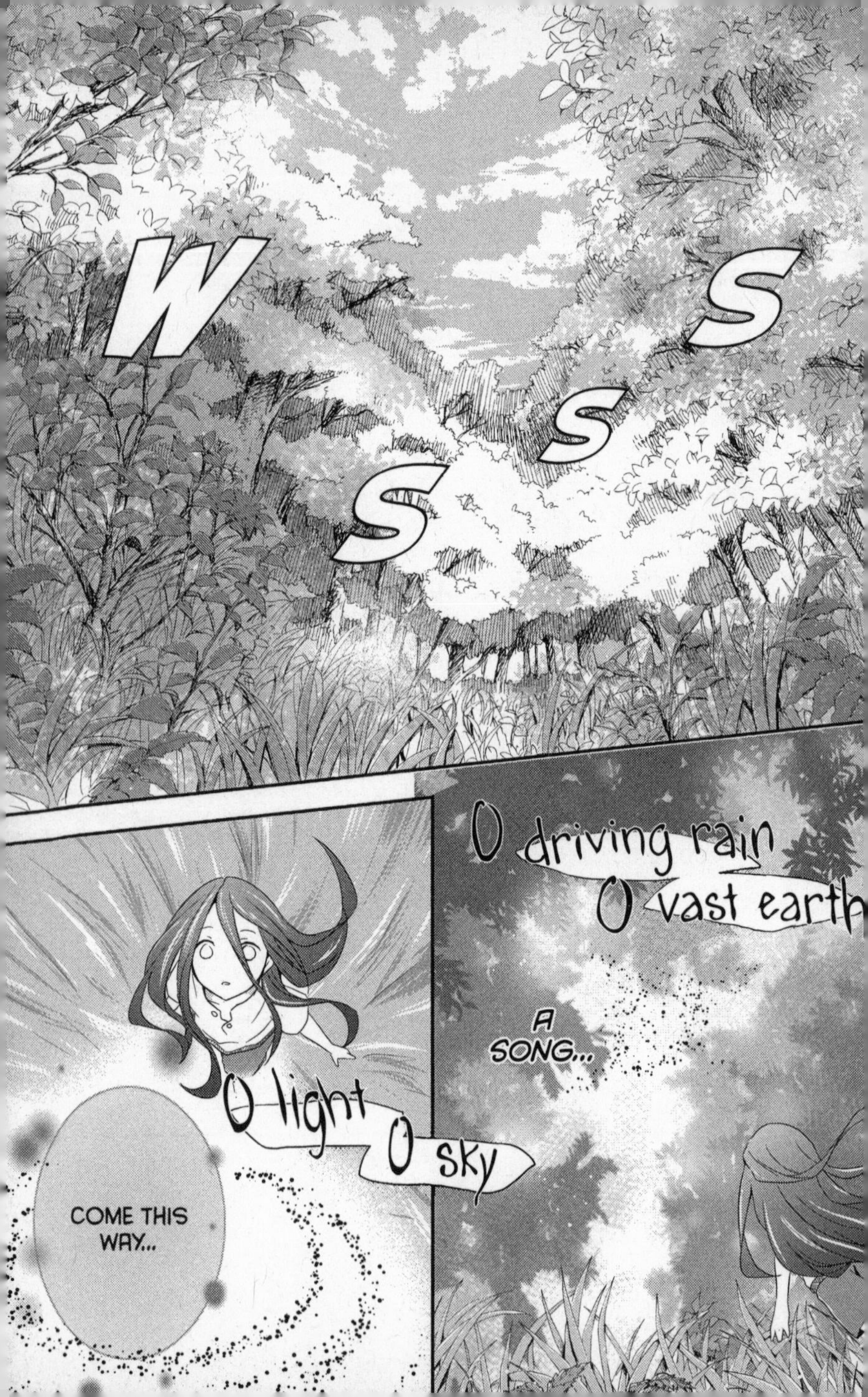
WSSS
O driving rain
O vast earth
A SONG...
O light
O sky
COME THIS WAY...

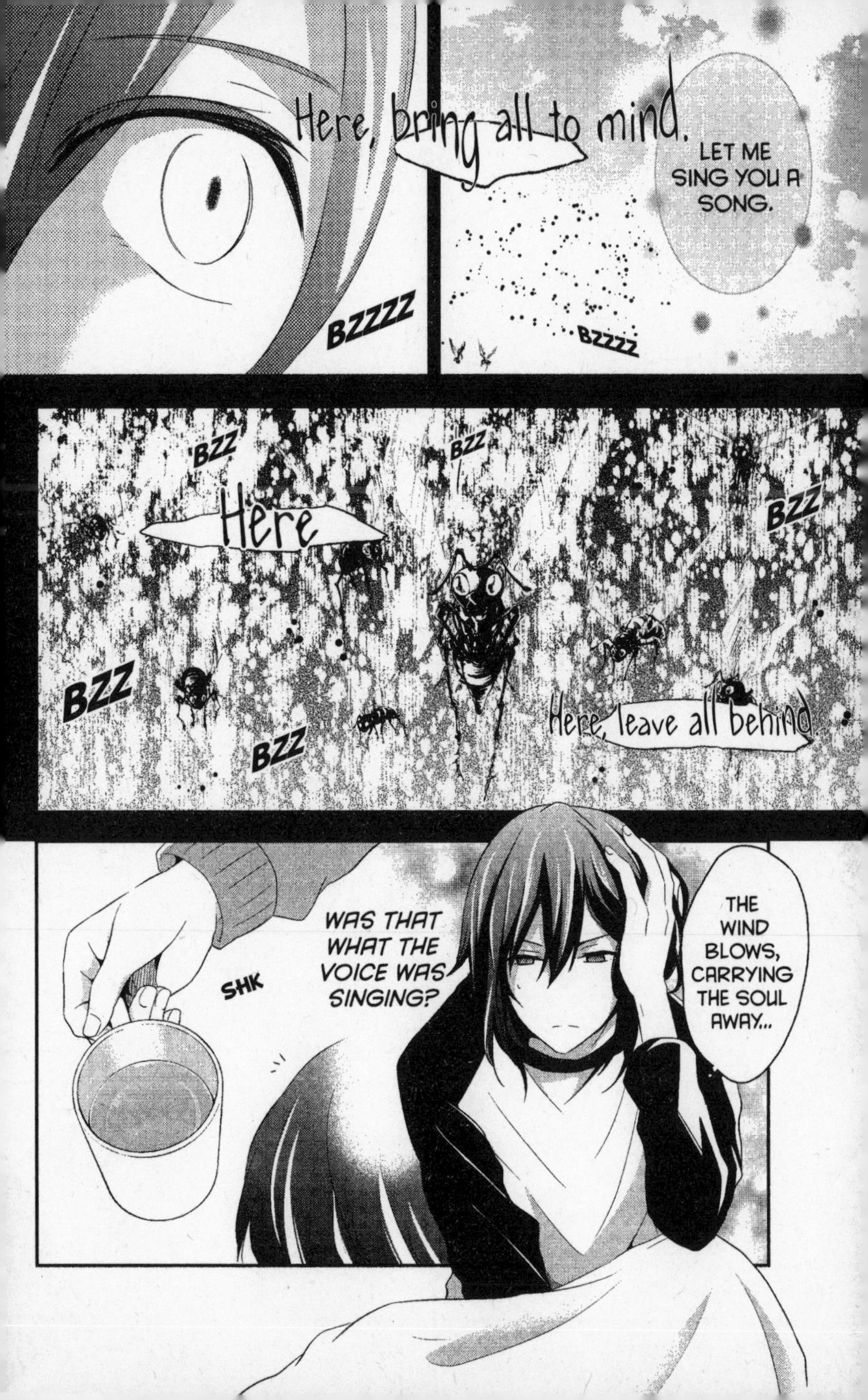
LET ME SING YOU A SONG.
Here, bring all to mind.
BZZZZ
BZZZZ
BZZ
BZZ
BZZ
Here
Here, leave all behind.
BZZ
BZZ
THE WIND BLOWS, CARRYING THE SOUL AWAY...
WAS THAT WHAT THE VOICE WAS SINGING?
SHK

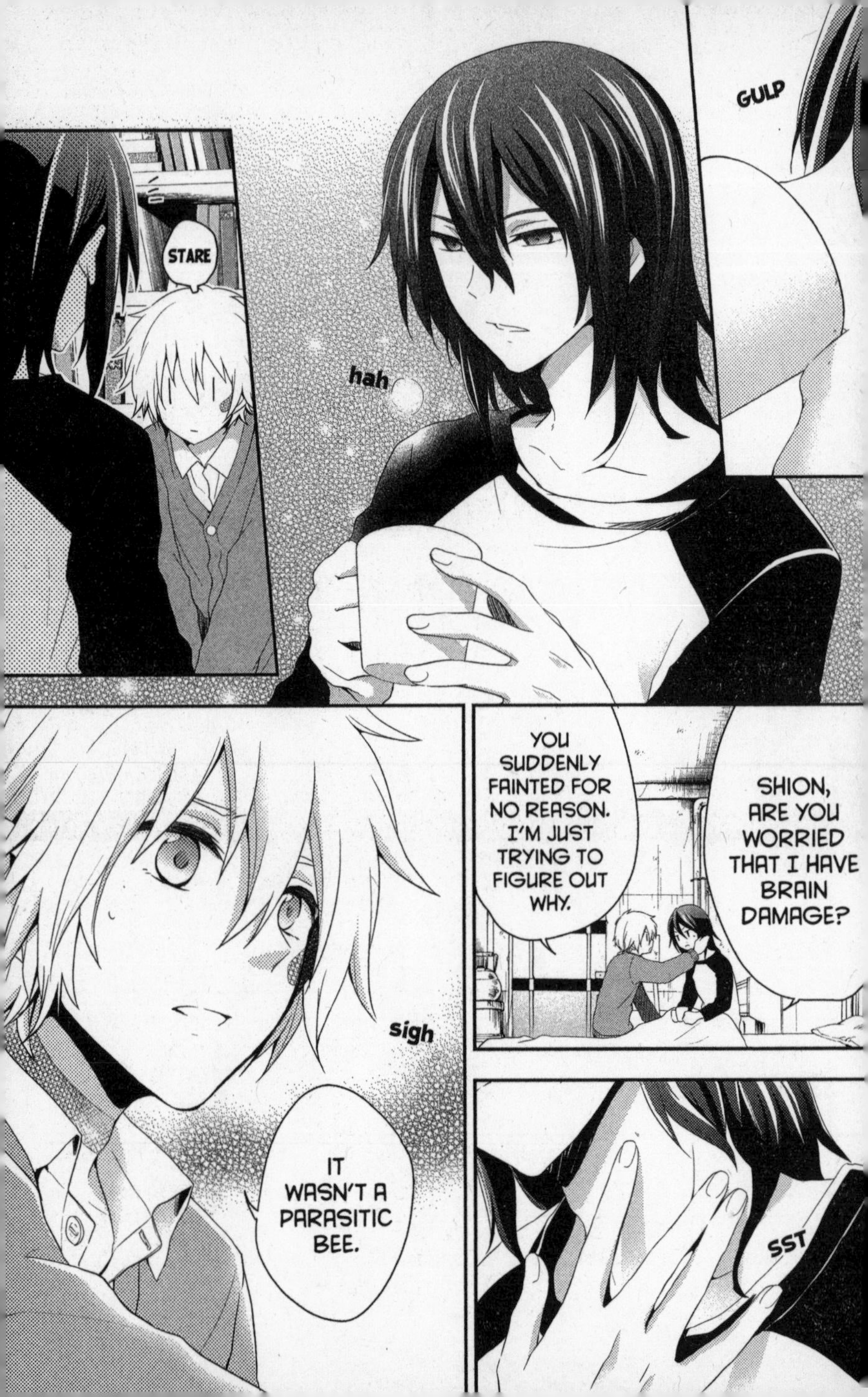
GULP
hah
STARE
SHION, ARE YOU WORRIED THAT I HAVE BRAIN DAMAGE?
YOU SUDDENLY FAINTED FOR NO REASON. I'M JUST TRYING TO FIGURE OUT WHY.
SST
sigh
IT WASN'T A PARASITIC BEE.

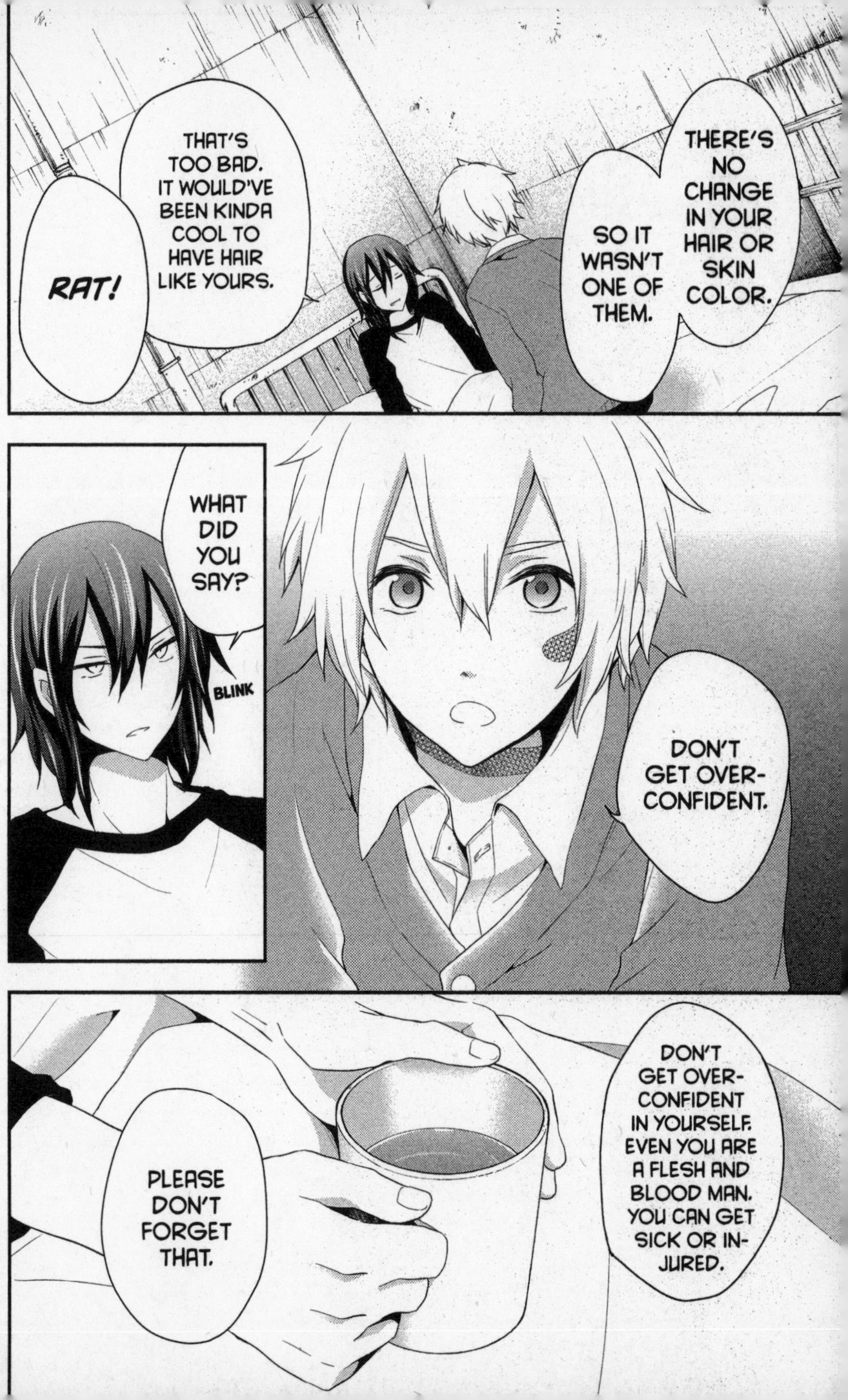
THERE'S NO CHANGE IN YOUR HAIR OR SKIN COLOR.
SO IT WASN'T ONE OF THEM.
THAT'S TOO BAD. IT WOULD'VE BEEN KINDA COOL TO HAVE HAIR LIKE YOURS.
RAT!
DON'T GET OVER-CONFIDENT.
WHAT DID YOU SAY?
BLINK
DON'T GET OVER-CONFIDENT IN YOURSELF. EVEN YOU ARE A FLESH AND BLOOD MAN. YOU CAN GET SICK OR INJURED.
PLEASE DON'T FORGET THAT.

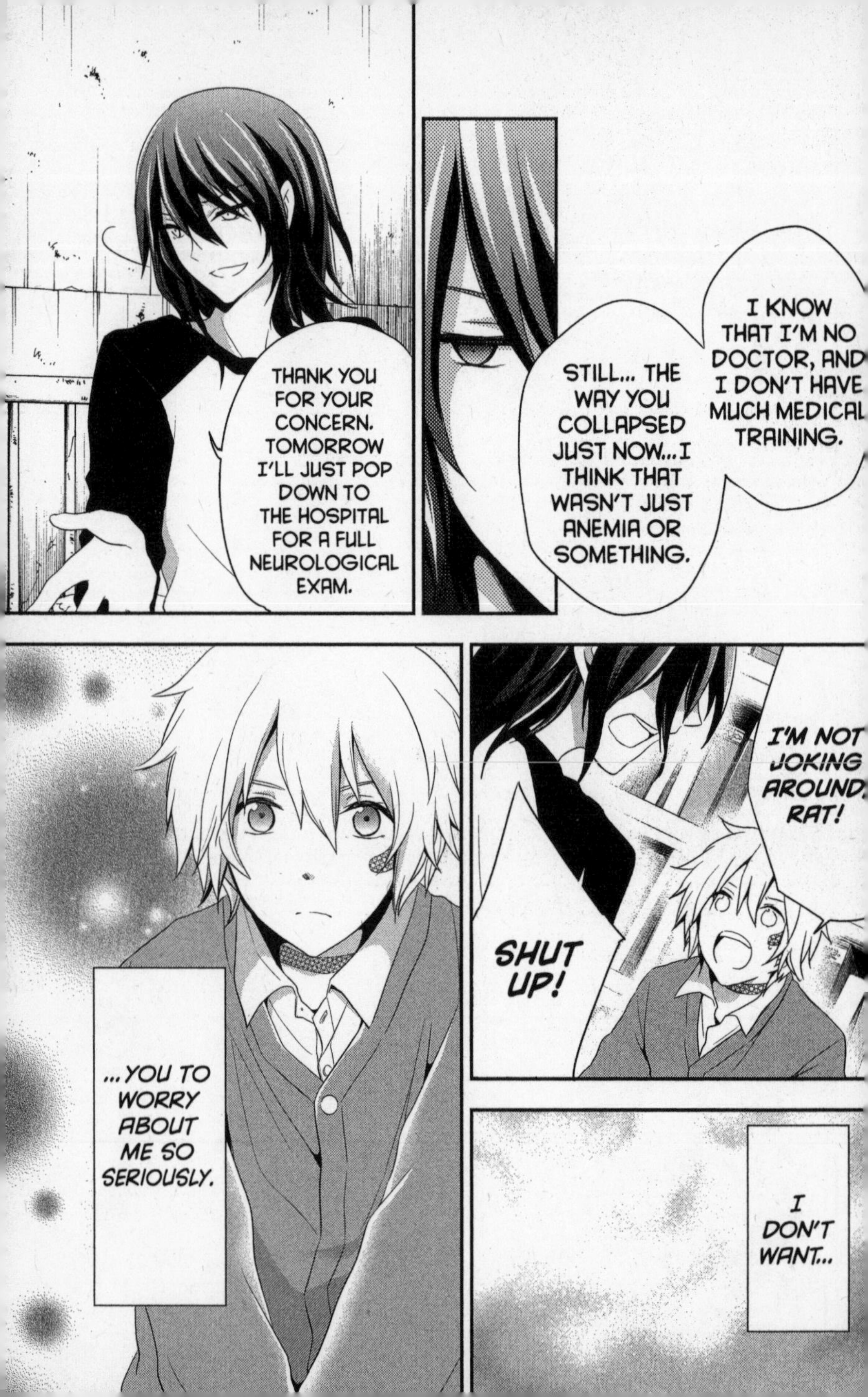
I KNOW THAT I'M NO DOCTOR, AND I DON'T HAVE MUCH MEDICAL TRAINING.
STILL... THE WAY YOU COLLAPSED JUST NOW...I THINK THAT WASN'T JUST ANEMIA OR SOMETHING.
THANK YOU FOR YOUR CONCERN. TOMORROW I'LL JUST POP DOWN TO THE HOSPITAL FOR A FULL NEUROLOGICAL EXAM.
I'M NOT JOKING AROUND, RAT!
SHUT UP!
I DON'T WANT...
...YOU TO WORRY ABOUT ME SO SERIOUSLY.

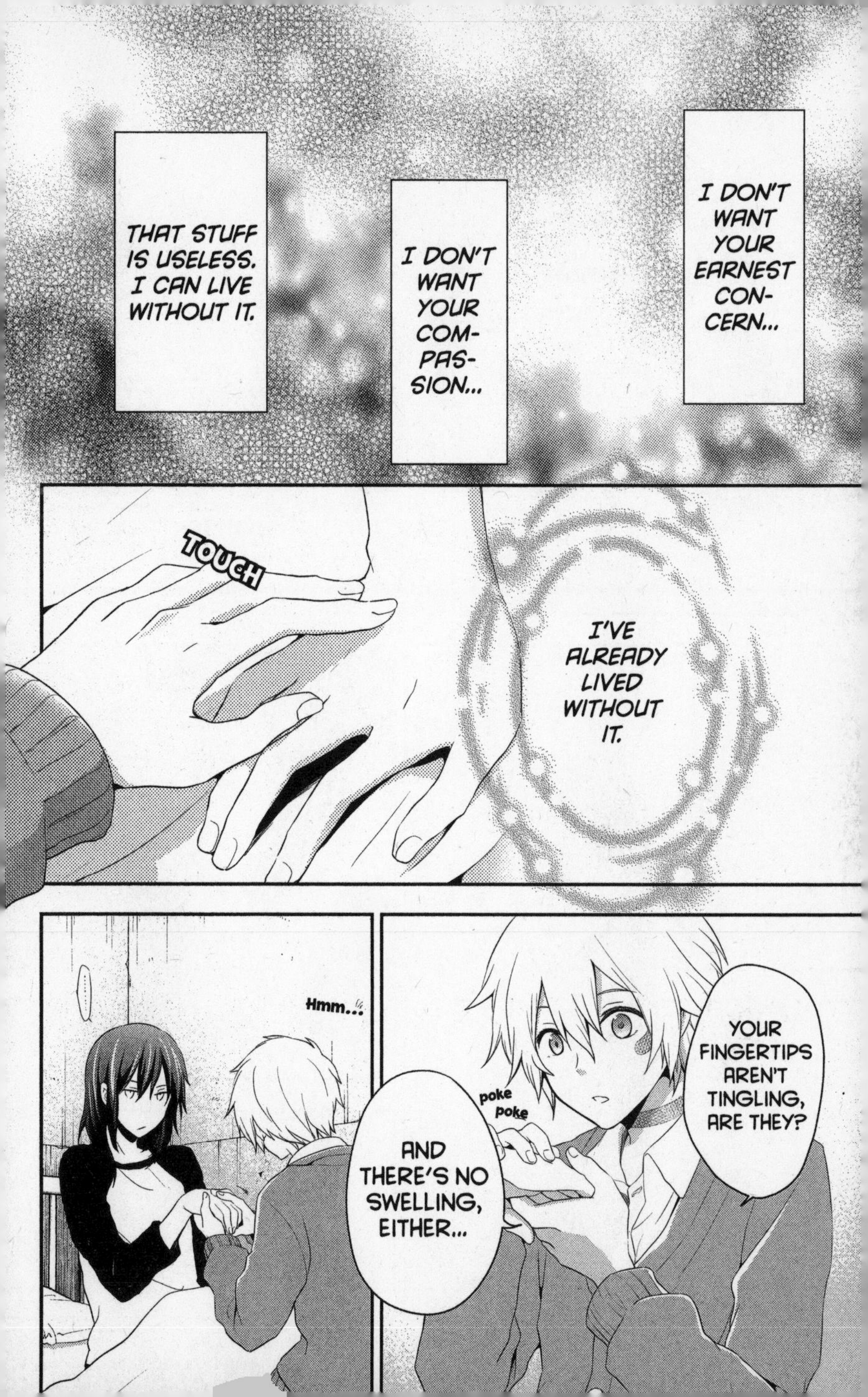
I DON'T WANT YOUR EARNEST CON-CERN...
I DON'T WANT YOUR COM-PAS-SION...
THAT STUFF IS USELESS. I CAN LIVE WITHOUT IT.
TOUCH
I'VE ALREADY LIVED WITHOUT IT.
YOUR FINGERTIPS AREN'T TINGLING, ARE THEY?
poke poke
AND THERE'S NO SWELLING, EITHER...
......
Hmm...

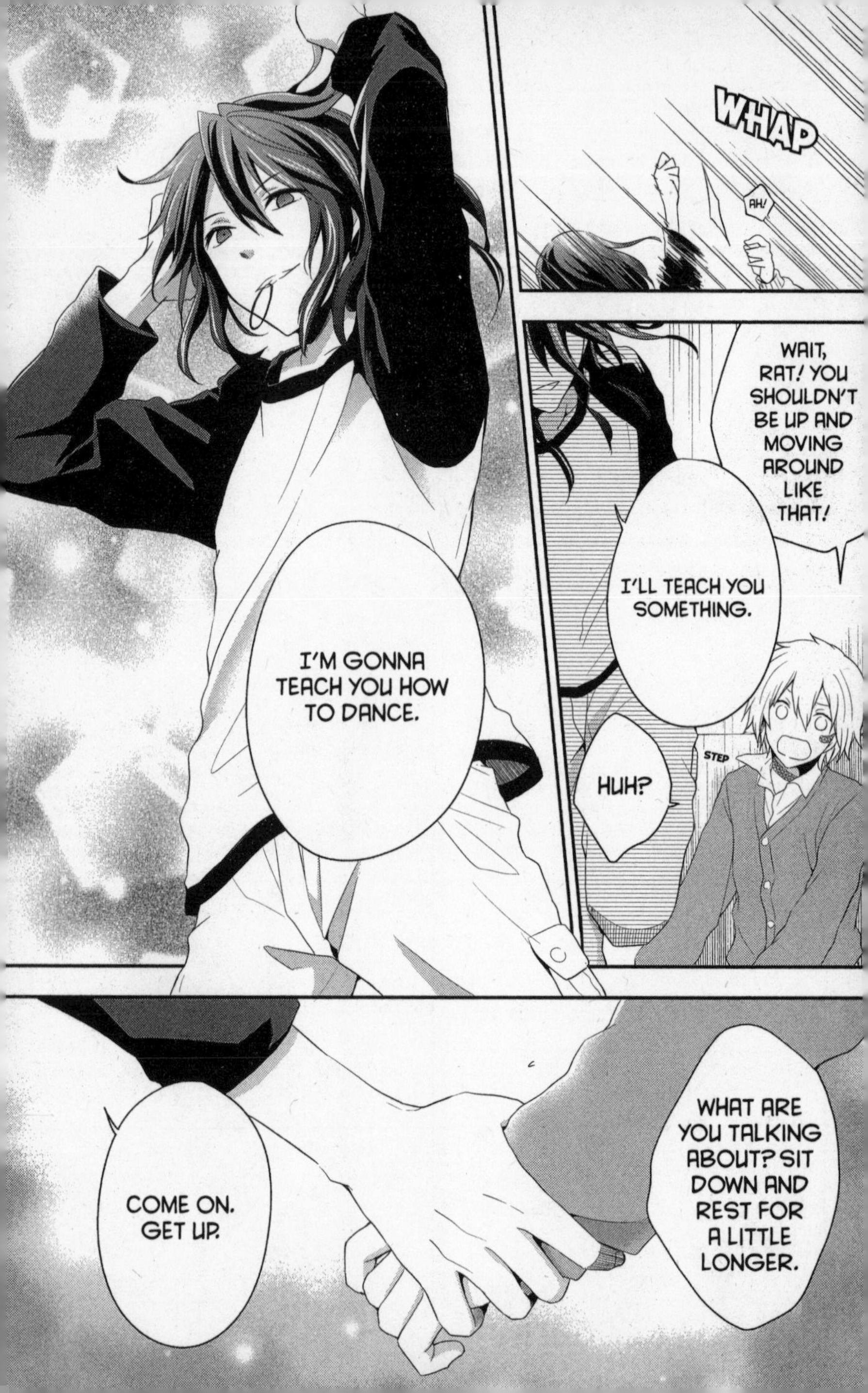
WHAP
AH!
WAIT, RAT! YOU SHOULDN'T BE UP AND MOVING AROUND LIKE THAT!
I'LL TEACH YOU SOMETHING.
STEP
HUH?
I'M GONNA TEACH YOU HOW TO DANCE.
WHAT ARE YOU TALKING ABOUT? SIT DOWN AND REST FOR A LITTLE LONGER.
COME ON. GET UP.

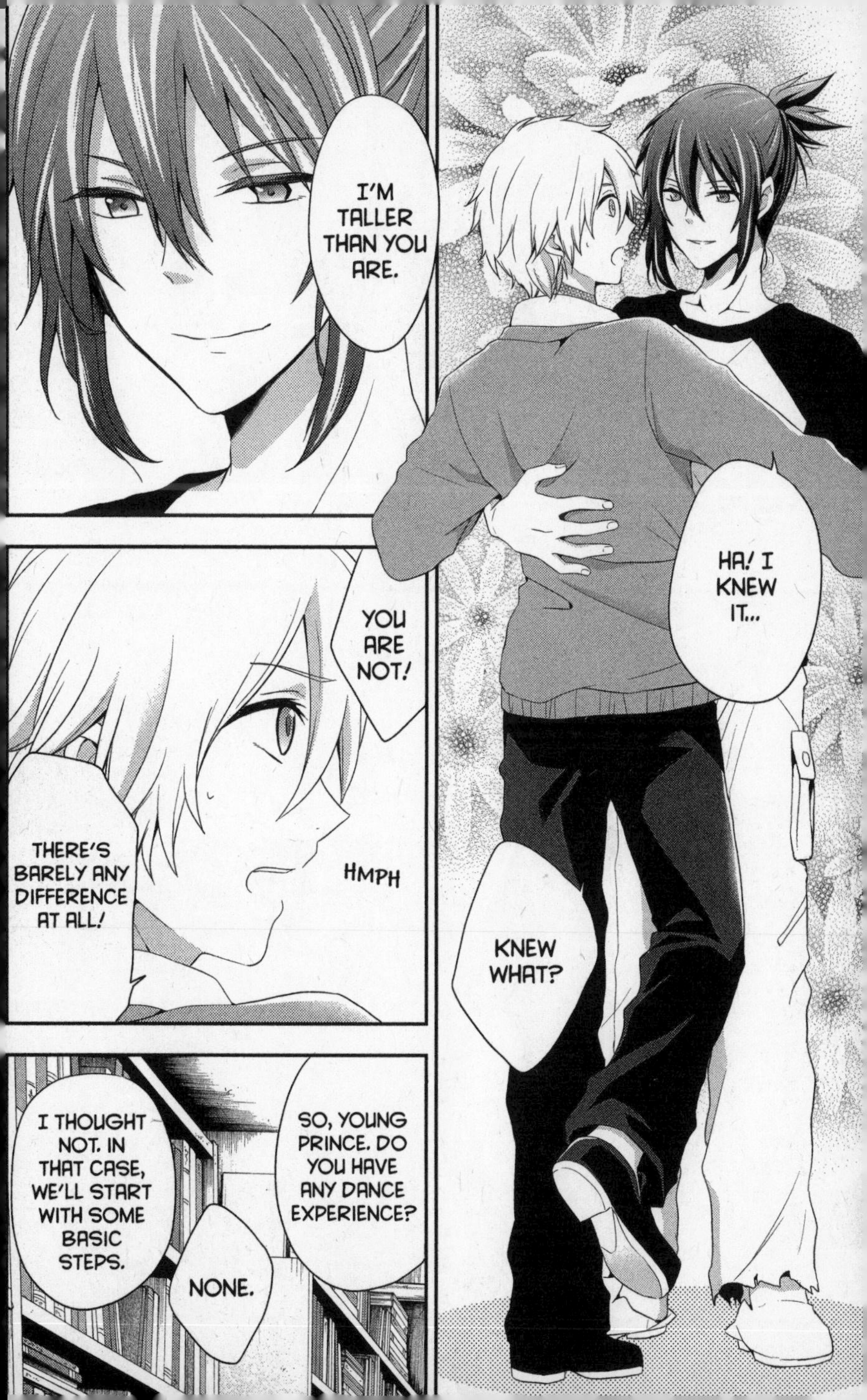
HA! I KNEW IT...
KNEW WHAT?
I'M TALLER THAN YOU ARE.
YOU ARE NOT!
HMPH
THERE'S BARELY ANY DIFFERENCE AT ALL!
SO, YOUNG PRINCE. DO YOU HAVE ANY DANCE EXPERIENCE?
NONE.
I THOUGHT NOT. IN THAT CASE, WE'LL START WITH SOME BASIC STEPS.

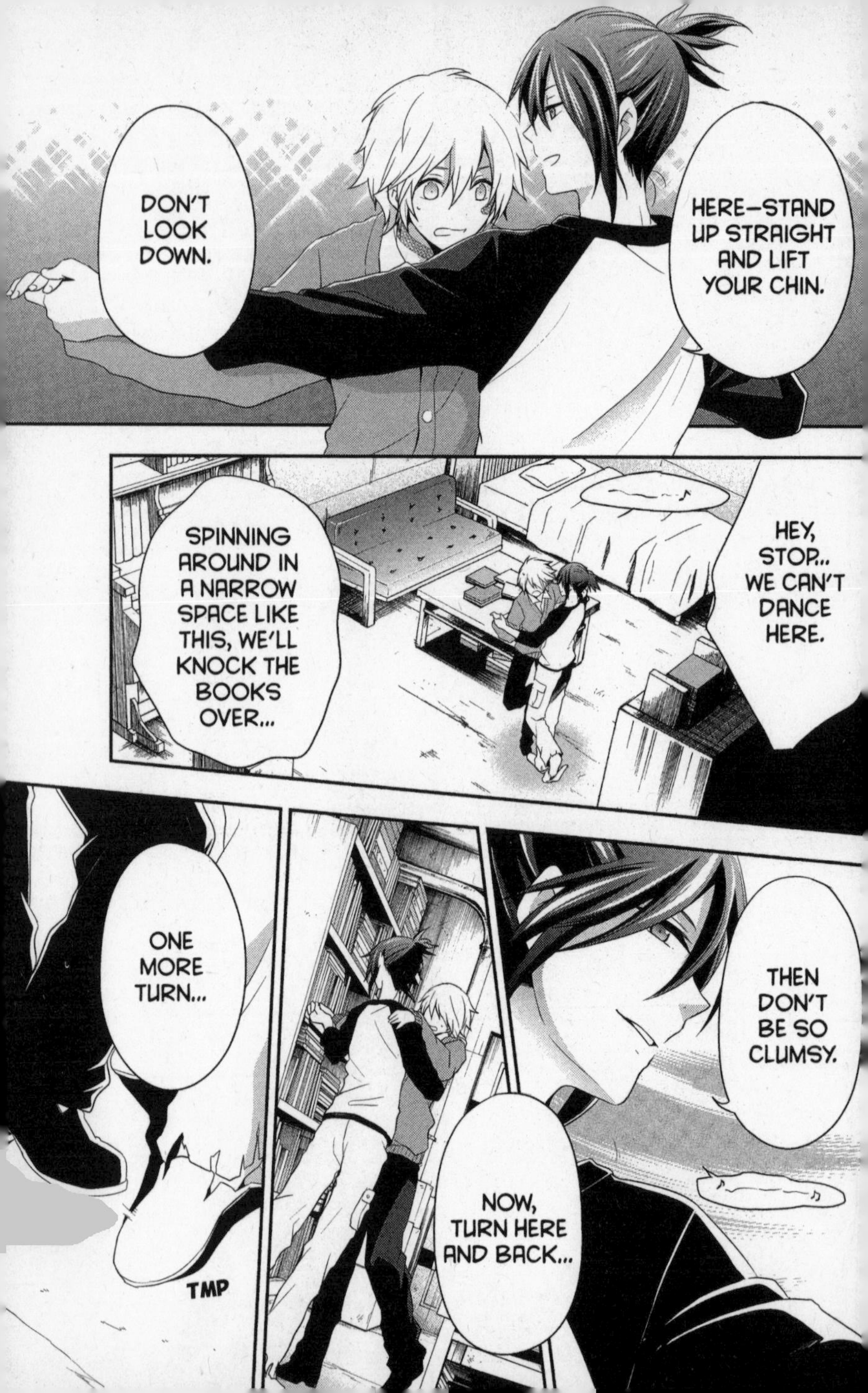
HERE—STAND UP STRAIGHT AND LIFT YOUR CHIN.
DON'T LOOK DOWN.
HEY, STOP... WE CAN'T DANCE HERE.
SPINNING AROUND IN A NARROW SPACE LIKE THIS, WE'LL KNOCK THE BOOKS OVER...
THEN DON'T BE SO CLUMSY.
NOW, TURN HERE AND BACK...
ONE MORE TURN...
TMP

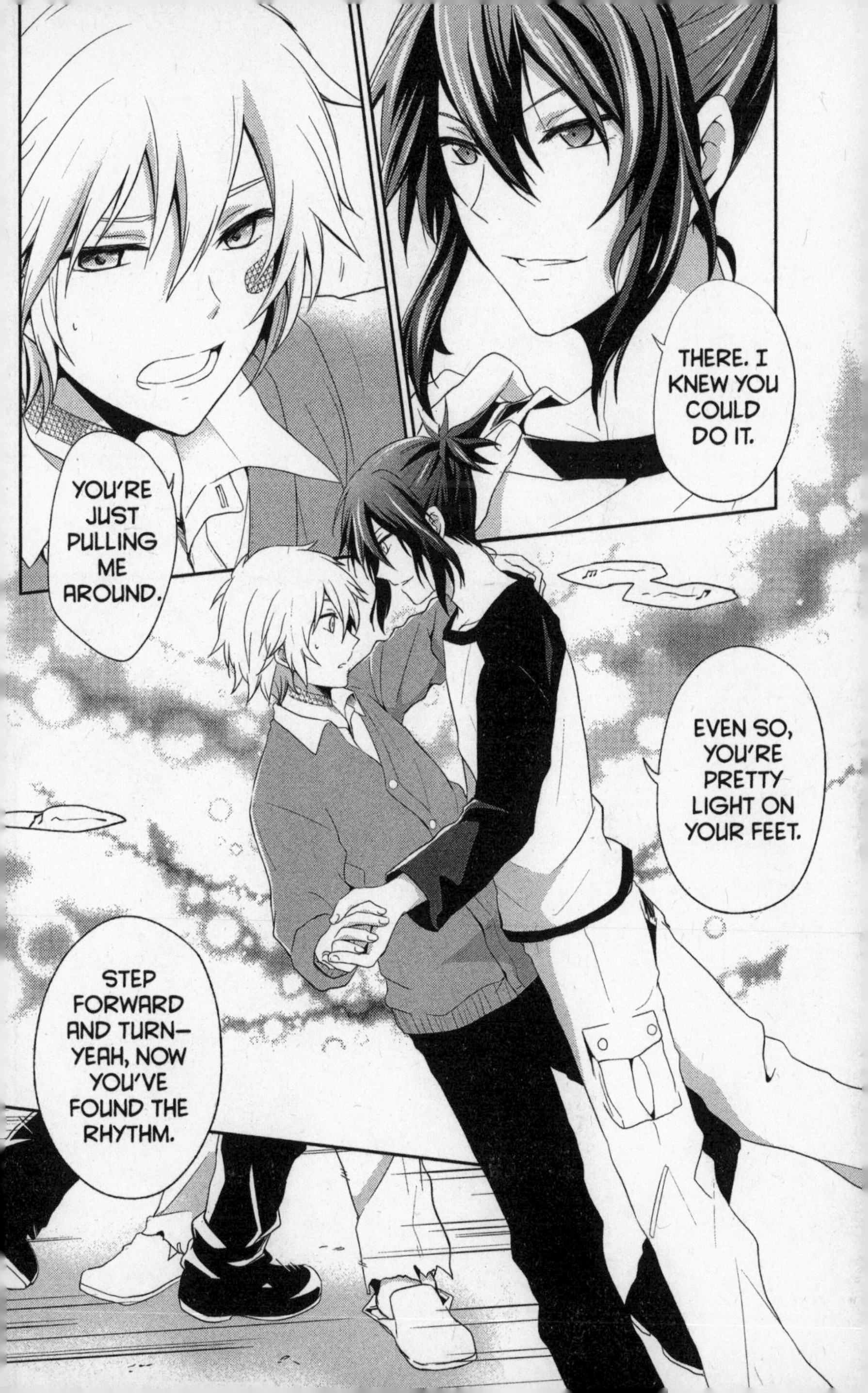
THERE. I KNEW YOU COULD DO IT.
YOU'RE JUST PULLING ME AROUND.
EVEN SO, YOU'RE PRETTY LIGHT ON YOUR FEET.
STEP FORWARD AND TURN—YEAH, NOW YOU'VE FOUND THE RHYTHM.

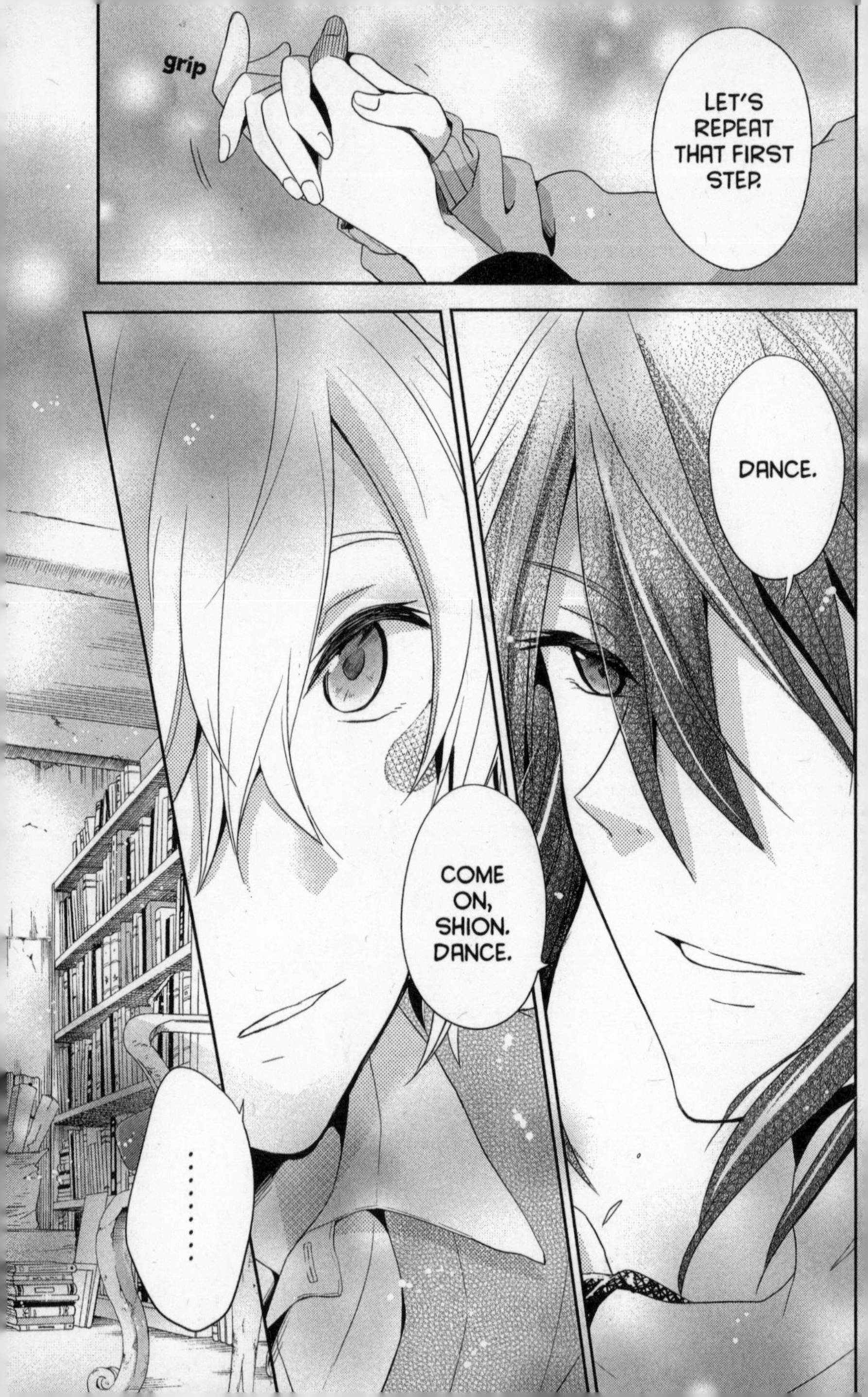
LET'S REPEAT THAT FIRST STEP.
grip
DANCE.
COME ON, SHION. DANCE.
....

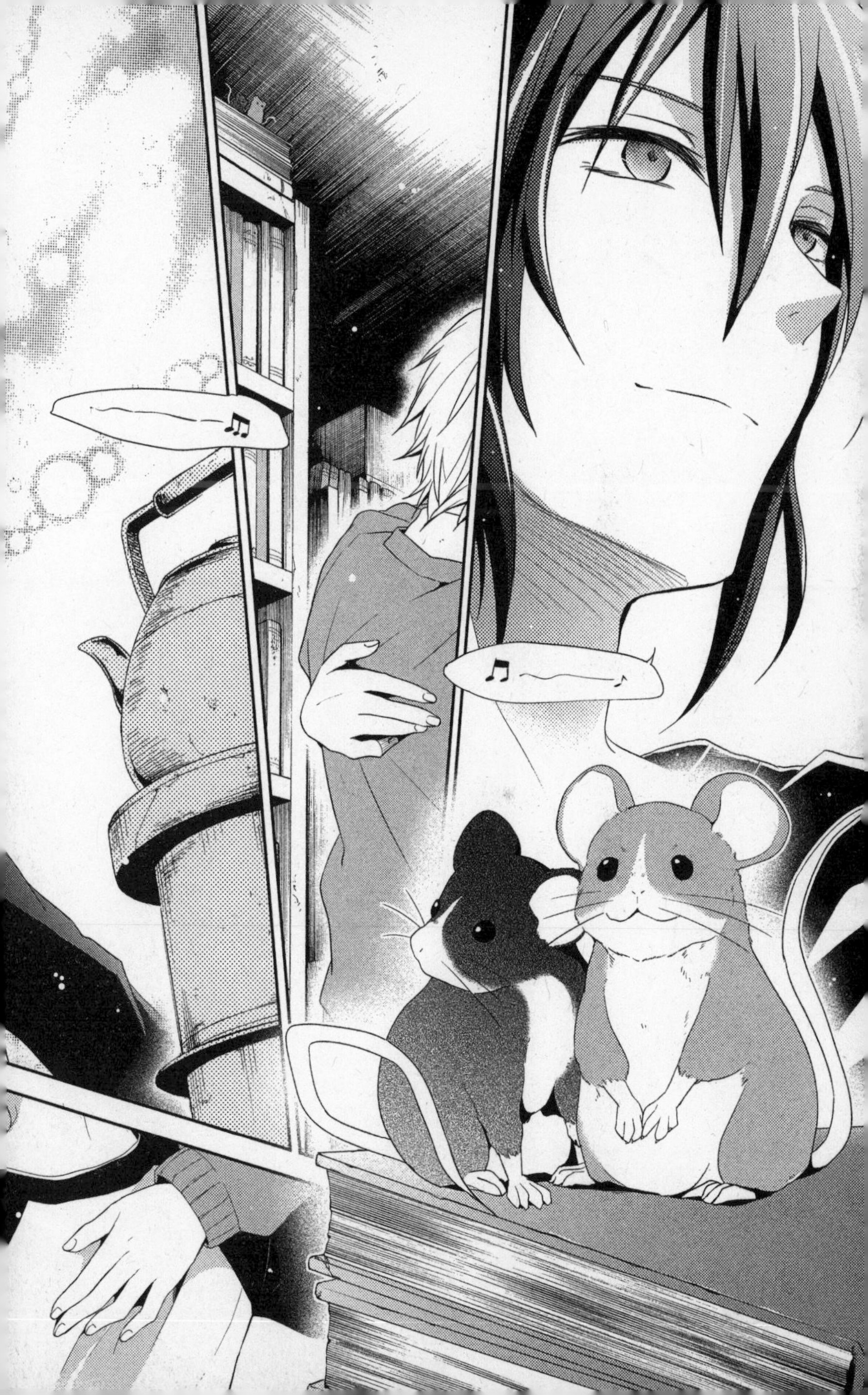

~♫
♫~

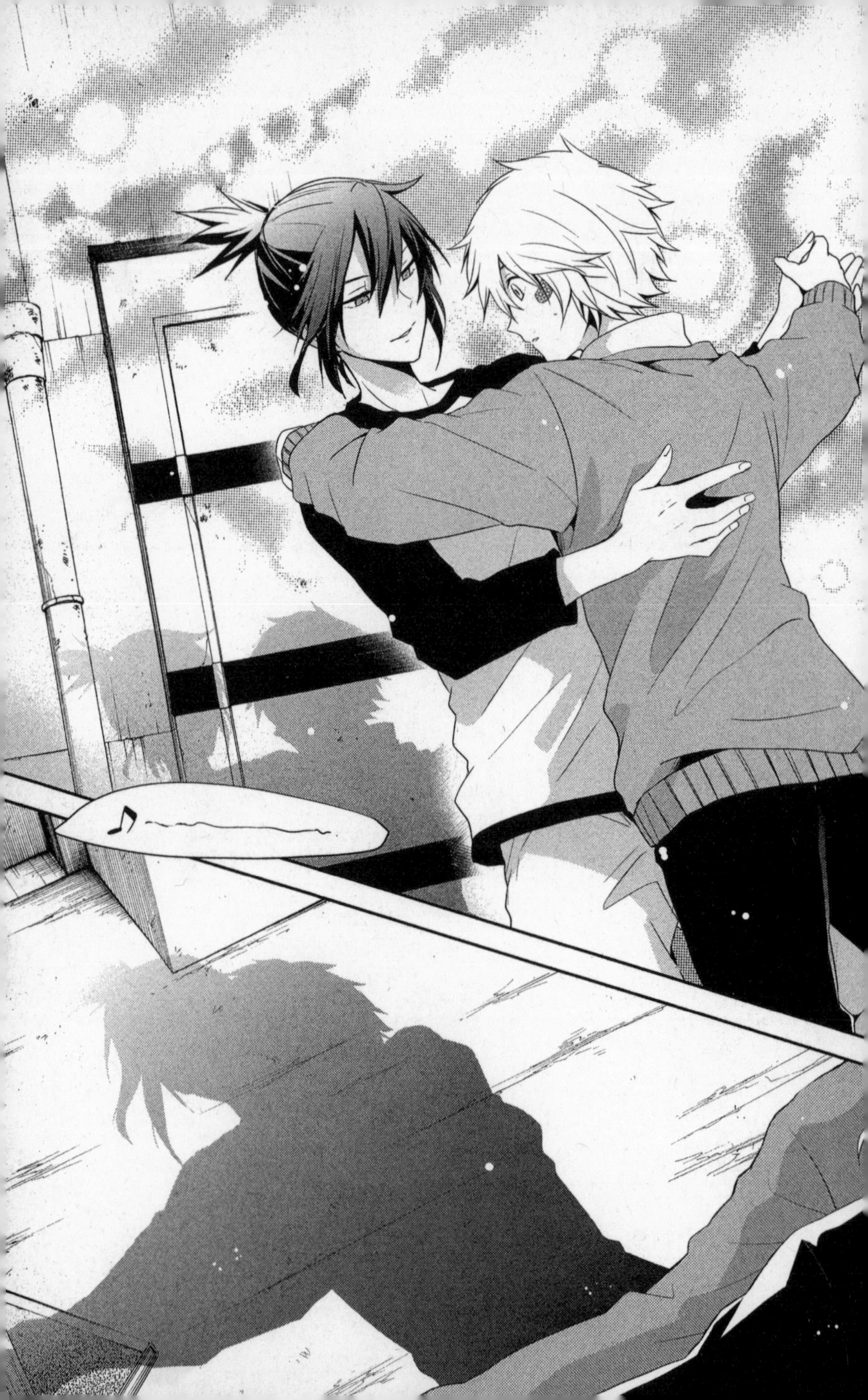

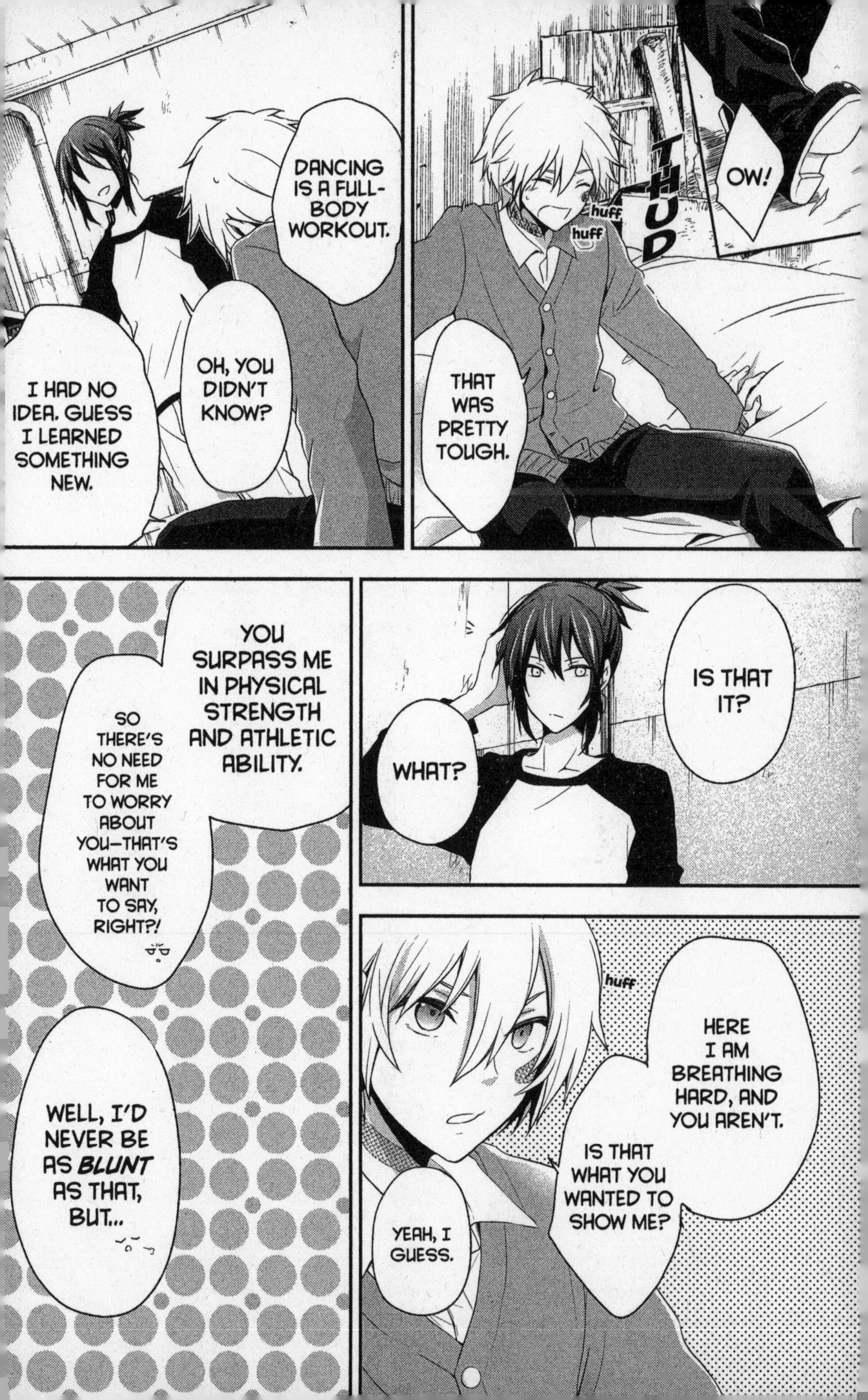
OW!
THUD
huff
huff
THAT WAS PRETTY TOUGH.
DANCING IS A FULL-BODY WORKOUT.
OH, YOU DIDN'T KNOW?
I HAD NO IDEA. GUESS I LEARNED SOMETHING NEW.
IS THAT IT?
WHAT?
huff
HERE I AM BREATHING HARD, AND YOU AREN'T.
IS THAT WHAT YOU WANTED TO SHOW ME?
YEAH, I GUESS.
YOU SURPASS ME IN PHYSICAL STRENGTH AND ATHLETIC ABILITY.
SO THERE'S NO NEED FOR ME TO WORRY ABOUT YOU—THAT'S WHAT YOU WANT TO SAY, RIGHT?!
WELL, I'D NEVER BE AS *BLUNT* AS THAT, BUT...

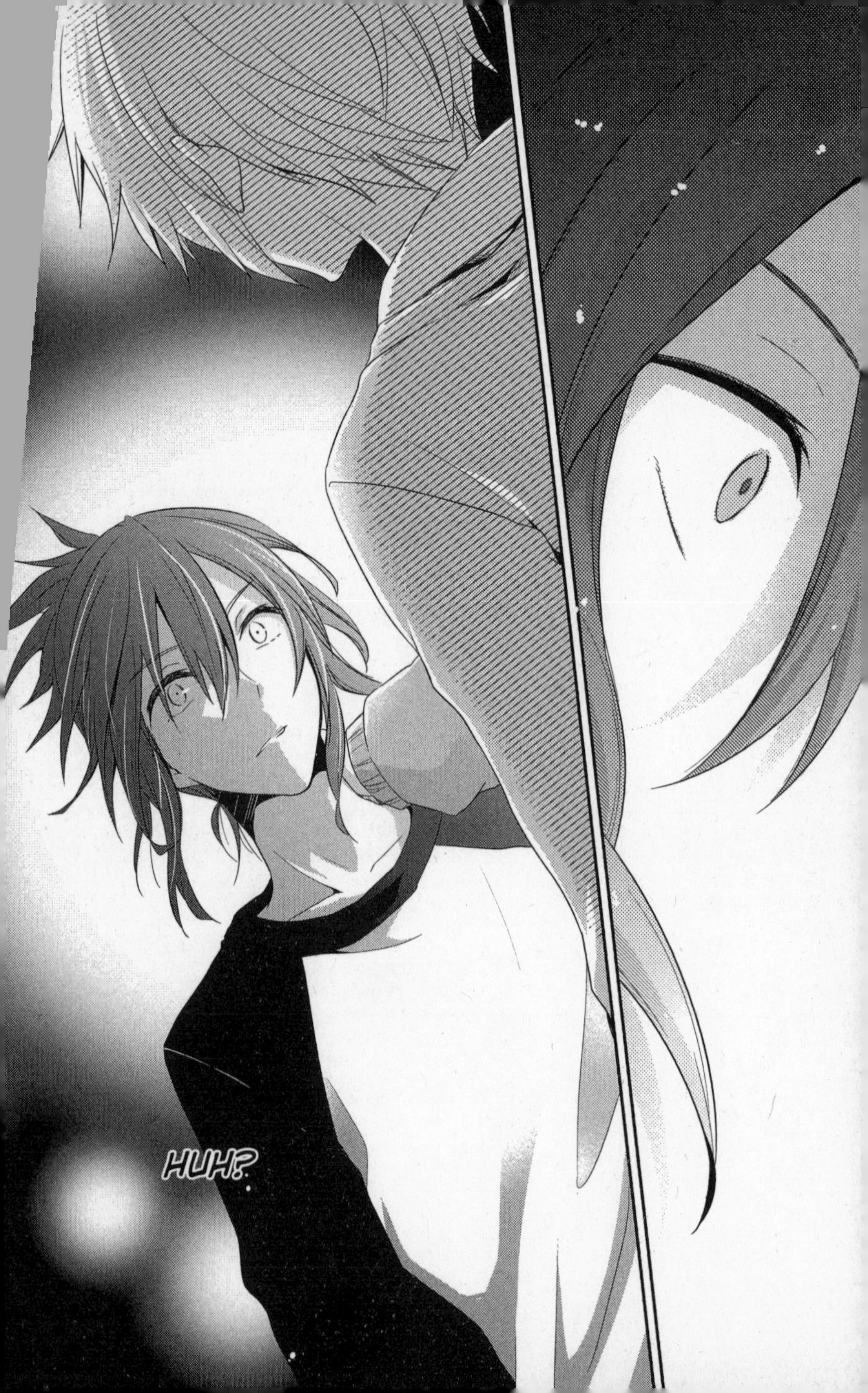
HUH?

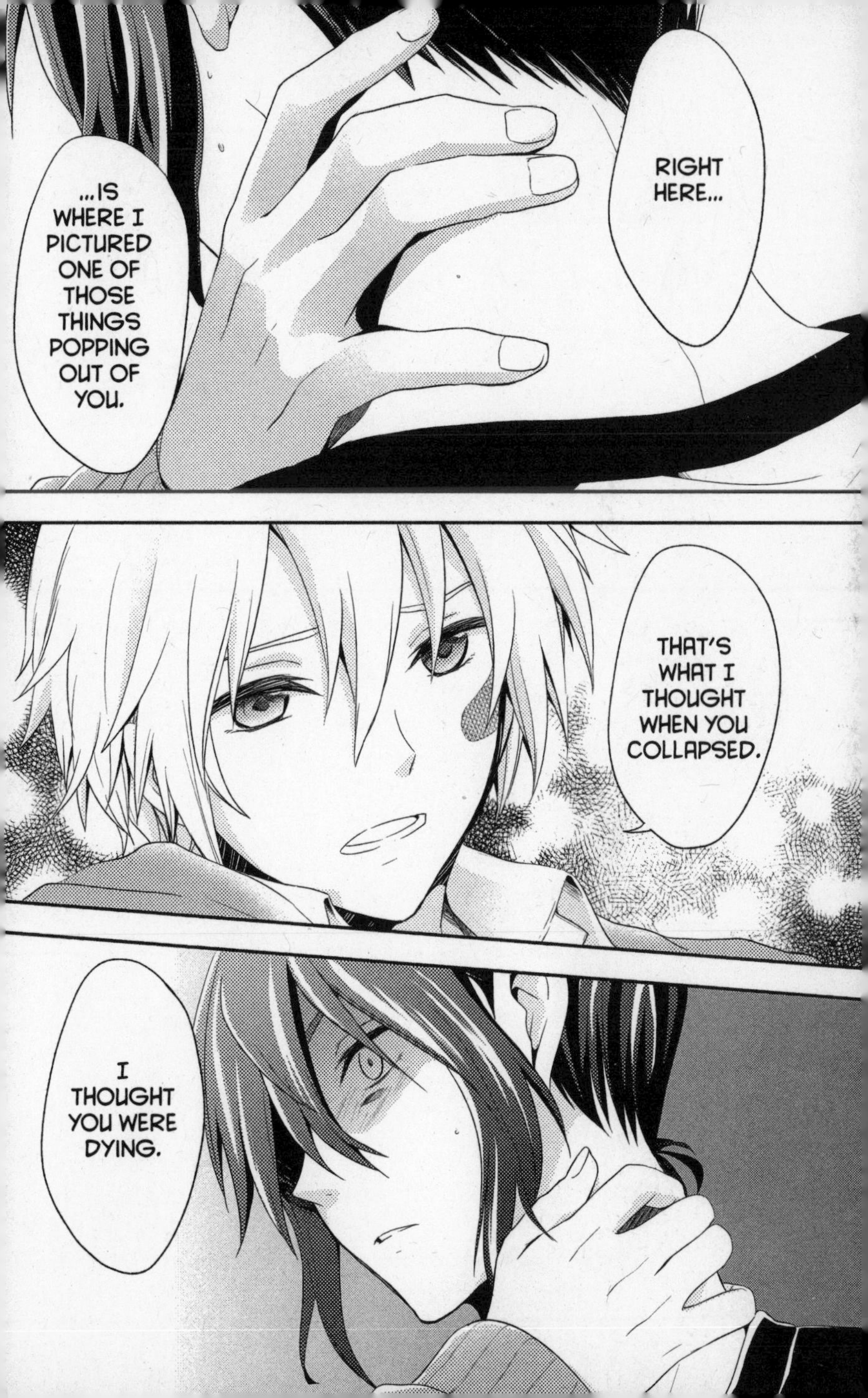
RIGHT HERE...
...IS WHERE I PICTURED ONE OF THOSE THINGS POPPING OUT OF YOU.
THAT'S WHAT I THOUGHT WHEN YOU COLLAPSED.
I THOUGHT YOU WERE DYING.

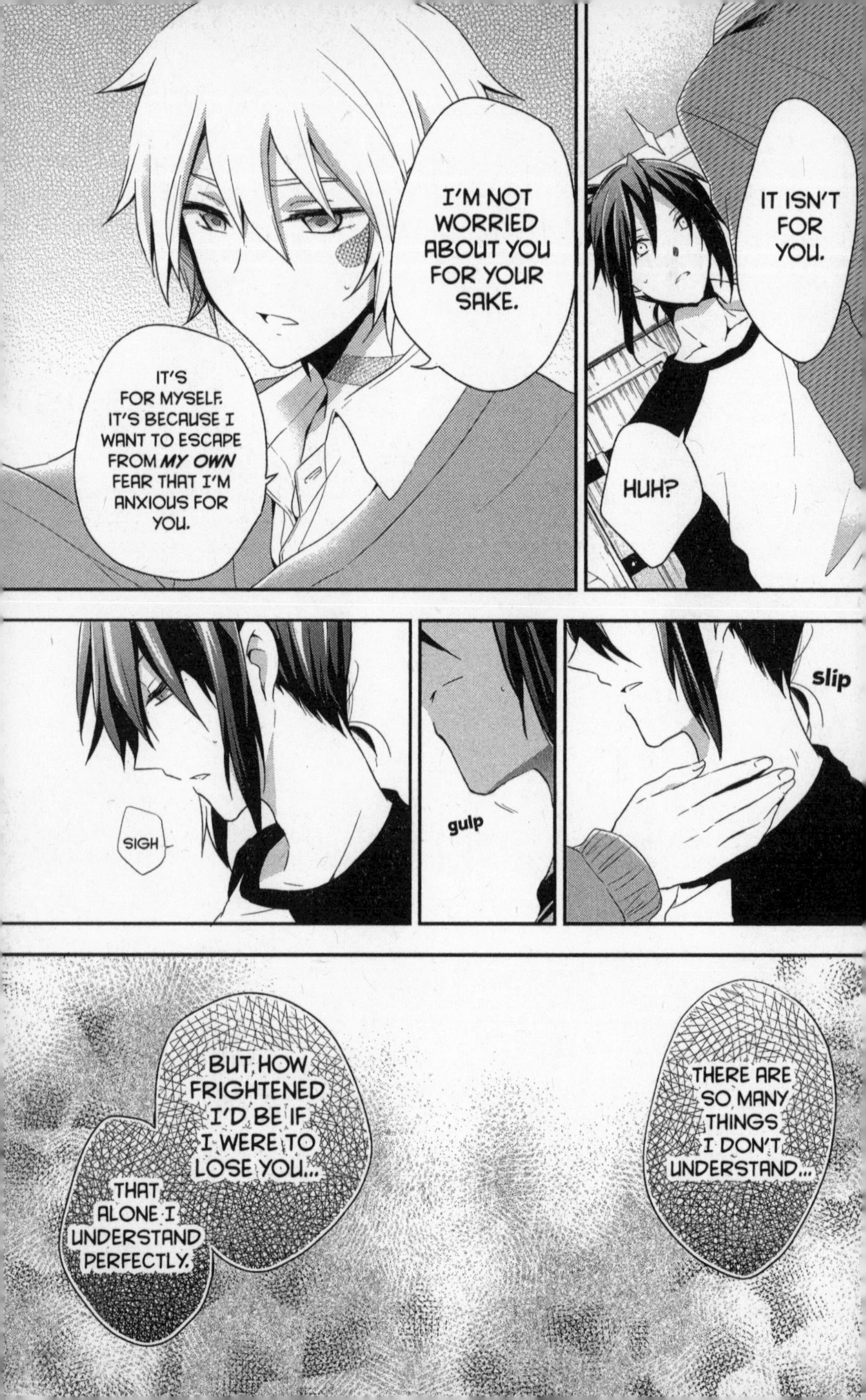
IT ISN'T FOR YOU.
HUH?
I'M NOT WORRIED ABOUT YOU FOR YOUR SAKE.
IT'S FOR MYSELF. IT'S BECAUSE I WANT TO ESCAPE FROM *MY OWN* FEAR THAT I'M ANXIOUS FOR YOU.
slip
gulp
SIGH
THERE ARE SO MANY THINGS I DON'T UNDERSTAND...
BUT, HOW FRIGHTENED I'D BE IF I WERE TO LOSE YOU...
THAT ALONE I UNDERSTAND PERFECTLY.

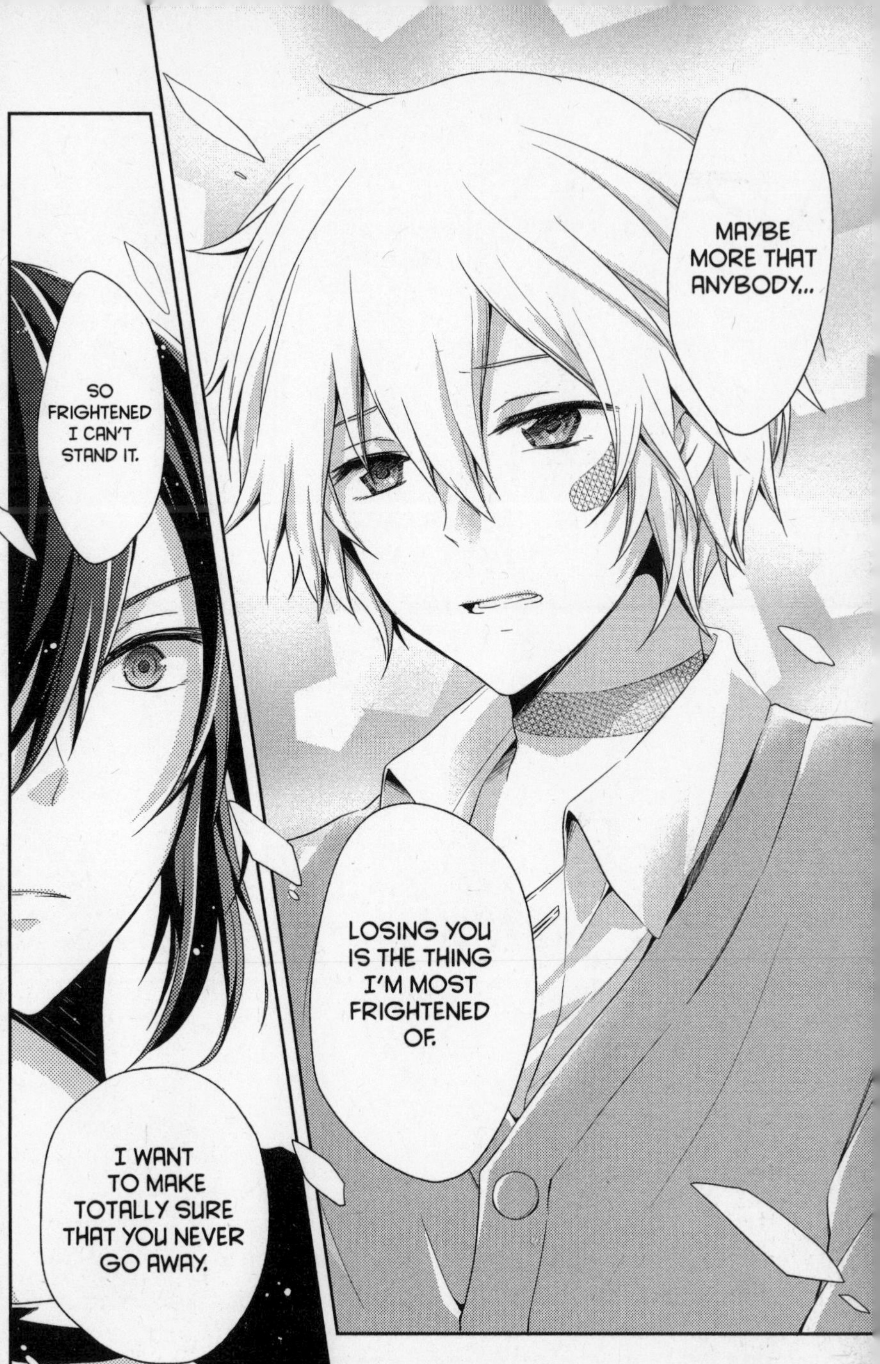
MAYBE MORE THAT ANYBODY...
LOSING YOU IS THE THING I'M MOST FRIGHTENED OF.
SO FRIGHTENED I CAN'T STAND IT.
I WANT TO MAKE TOTALLY SURE THAT YOU NEVER GO AWAY.

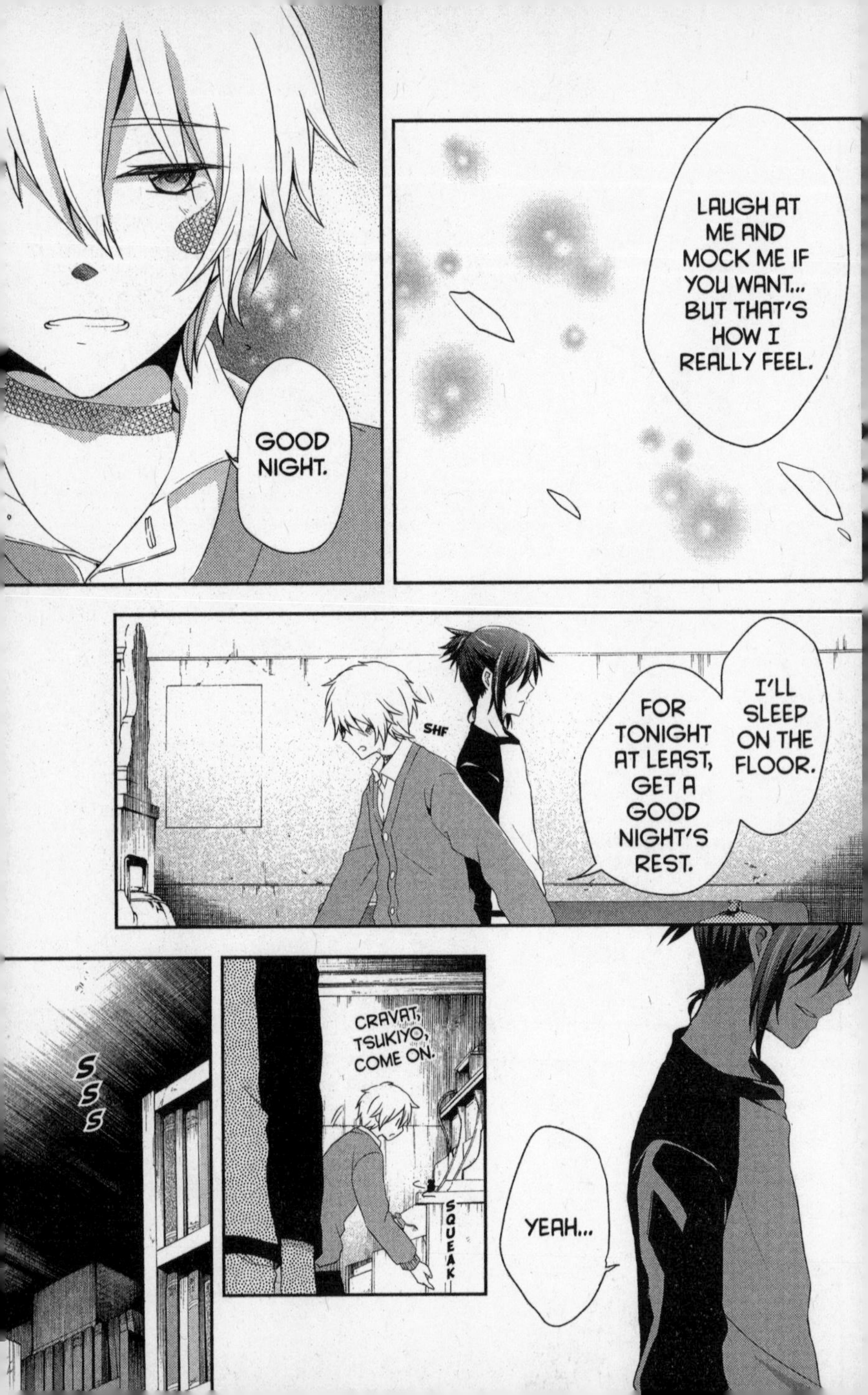
LAUGH AT ME AND MOCK ME IF YOU WANT... BUT THAT'S HOW I REALLY FEEL.
GOOD NIGHT.
I'LL SLEEP ON THE FLOOR.
FOR TONIGHT AT LEAST, GET A GOOD NIGHT'S REST.
SHF
YEAH...
CRAVAT, TSUKIYO, COME ON.
SQUEAK
SSS

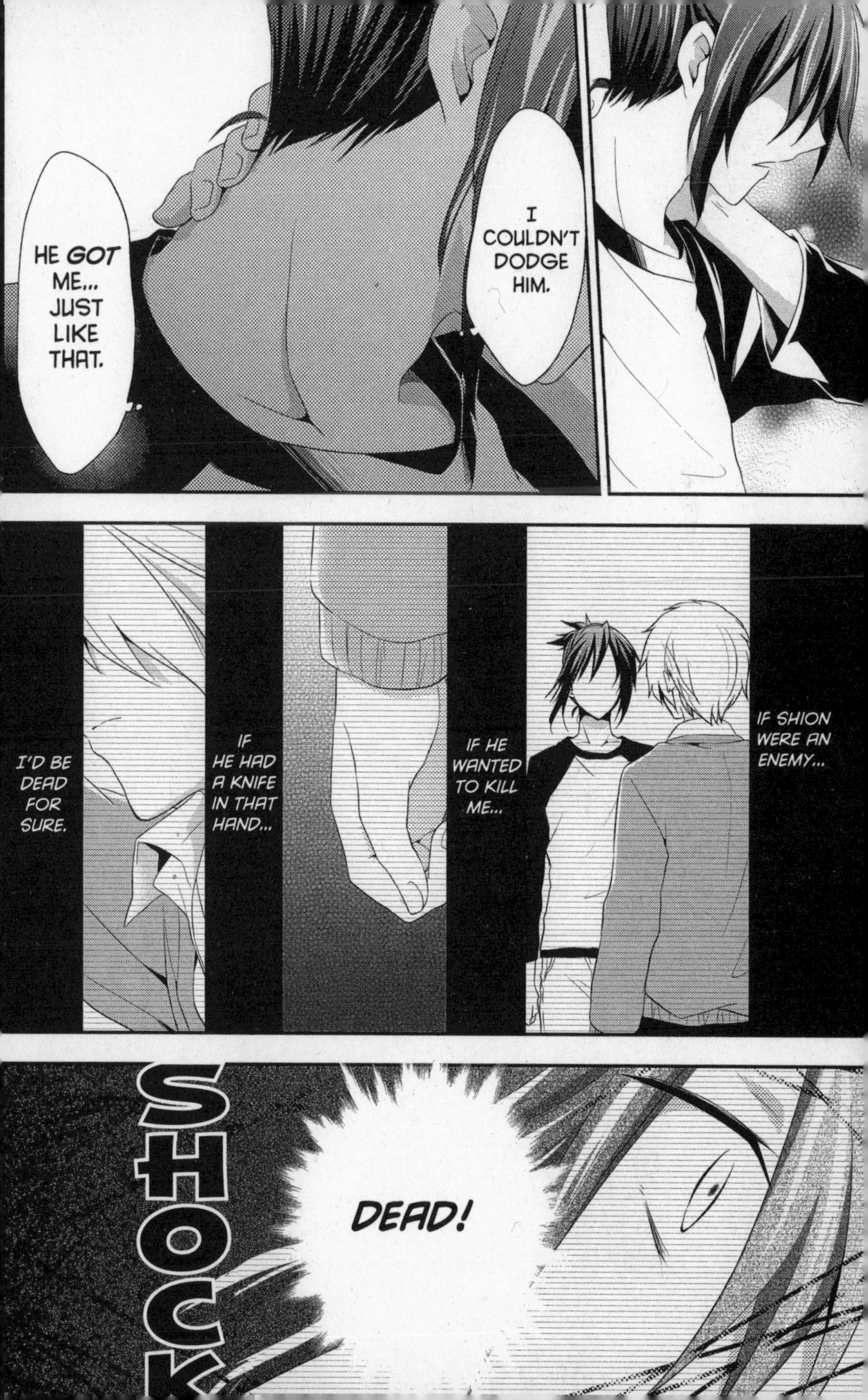
I COULDN'T DODGE HIM.
HE GOT ME... JUST LIKE THAT.
IF SHION WERE AN ENEMY...
IF HE WANTED TO KILL ME...
IF HE HAD A KNIFE IN THAT HAND...
I'D BE DEAD FOR SURE.
DEAD!
SHOCK

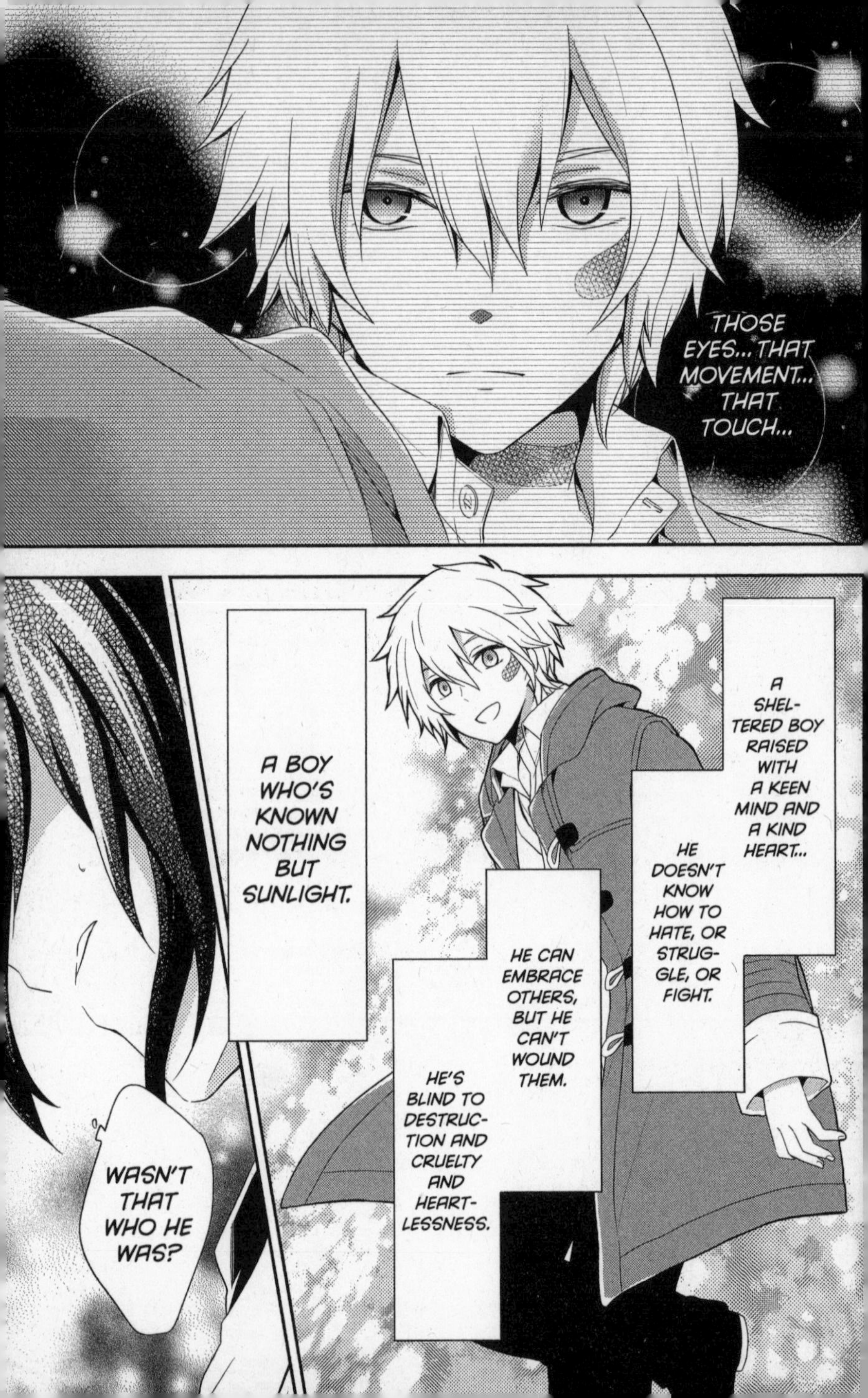
THOSE EYES... THAT MOVEMENT... THAT TOUCH...
A SHELTERED BOY RAISED WITH A KEEN MIND AND A KIND HEART...
HE DOESN'T KNOW HOW TO HATE, OR STRUGGLE, OR FIGHT.
HE CAN EMBRACE OTHERS, BUT HE CAN'T WOUND THEM.
HE'S BLIND TO DESTRUCTION AND CRUELTY AND HEARTLESSNESS.
A BOY WHO'S KNOWN NOTHING BUT SUNLIGHT.
WASN'T THAT WHO HE WAS?

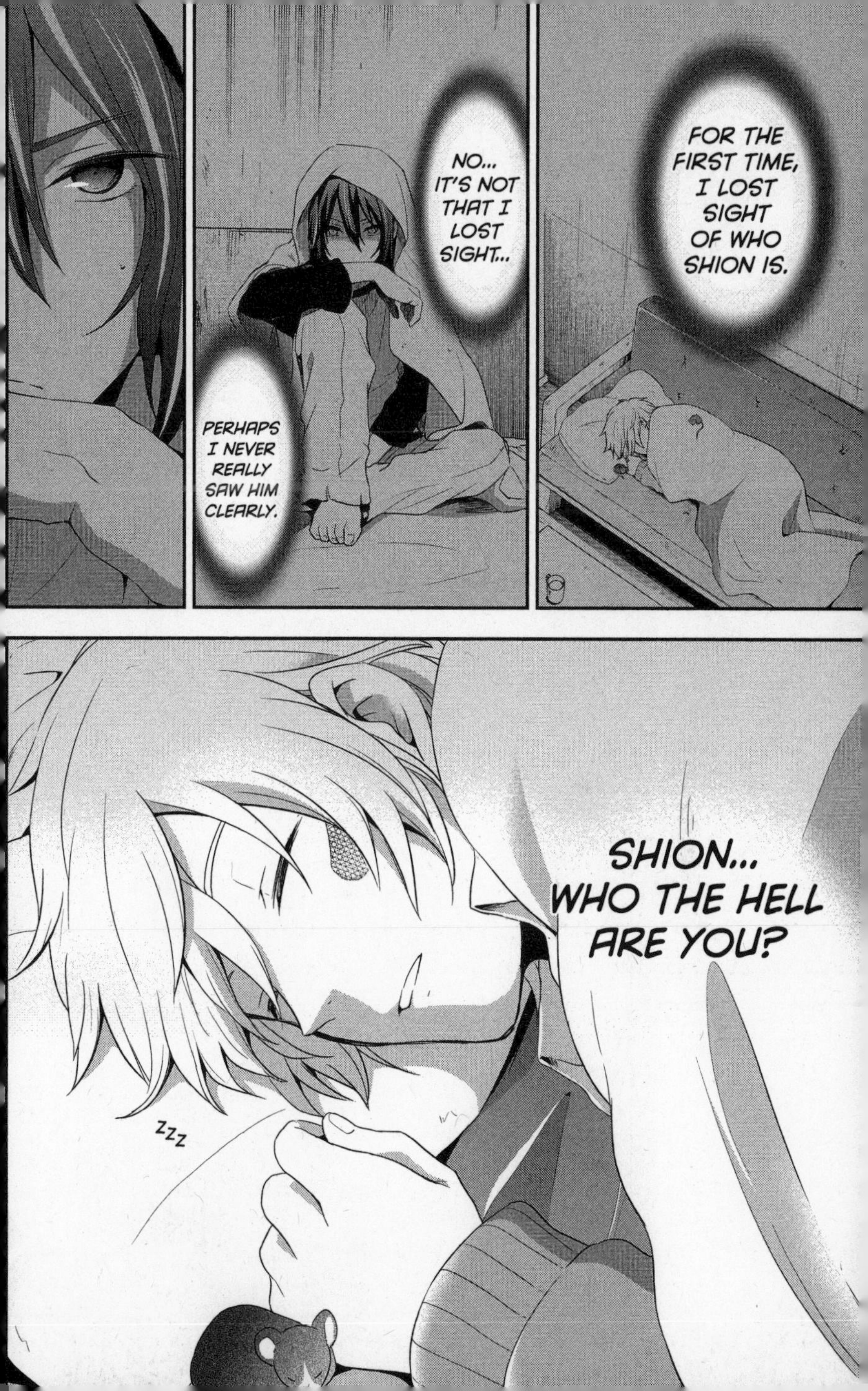
FOR THE FIRST TIME, I LOST SIGHT OF WHO SHION IS.
NO... IT'S NOT THAT I LOST SIGHT...
PERHAPS I NEVER REALLY SAW HIM CLEARLY.
SHION... WHO THE HELL ARE YOU?
ZZZ

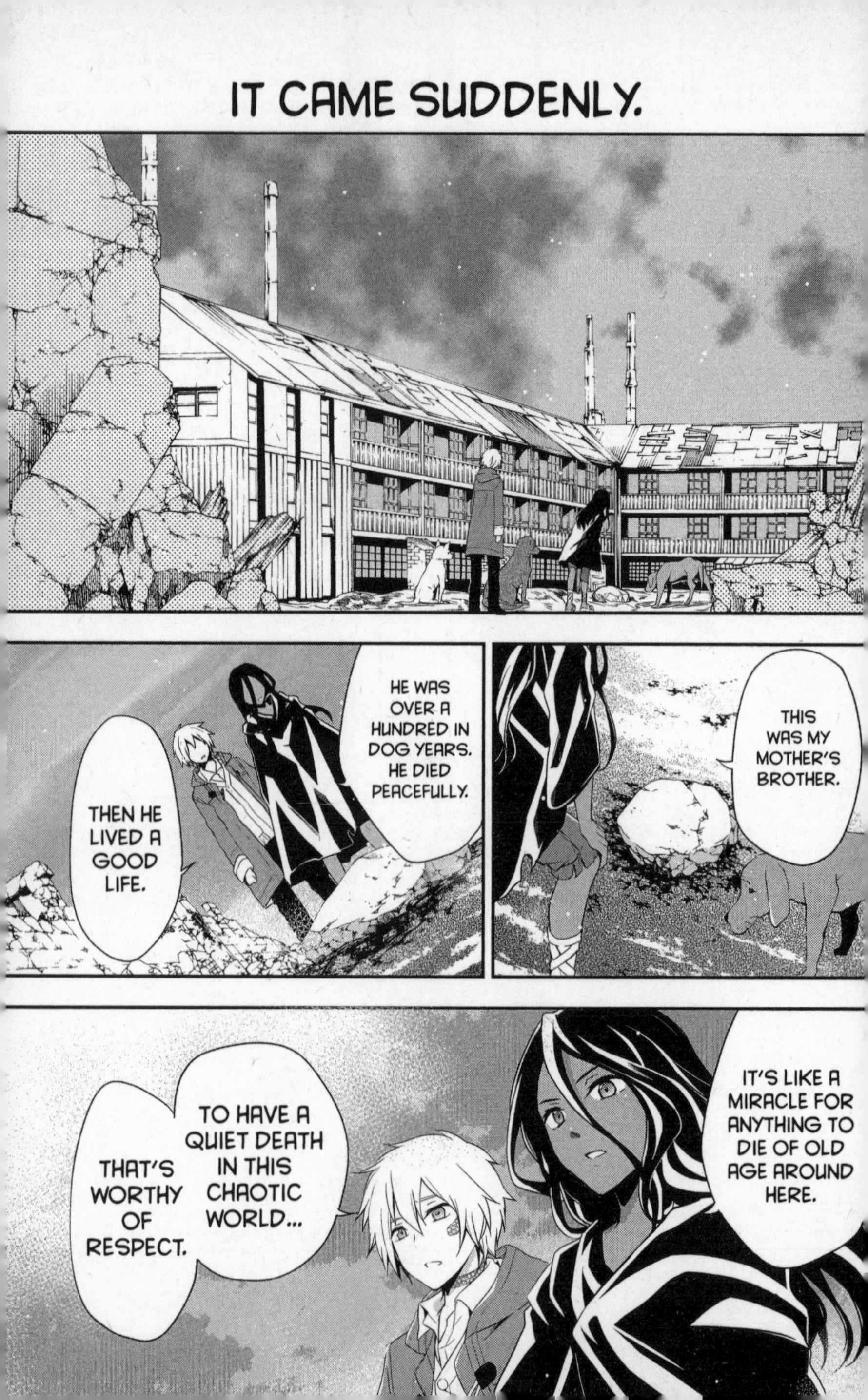
IT CAME SUDDENLY.
THIS WAS MY MOTHER'S BROTHER.
HE WAS OVER A HUNDRED IN DOG YEARS. HE DIED PEACEFULLY.
THEN HE LIVED A GOOD LIFE.
IT'S LIKE A MIRACLE FOR ANYTHING TO DIE OF OLD AGE AROUND HERE.
TO HAVE A QUIET DEATH IN THIS CHAOTIC WORLD...
THAT'S WORTHY OF RESPECT.

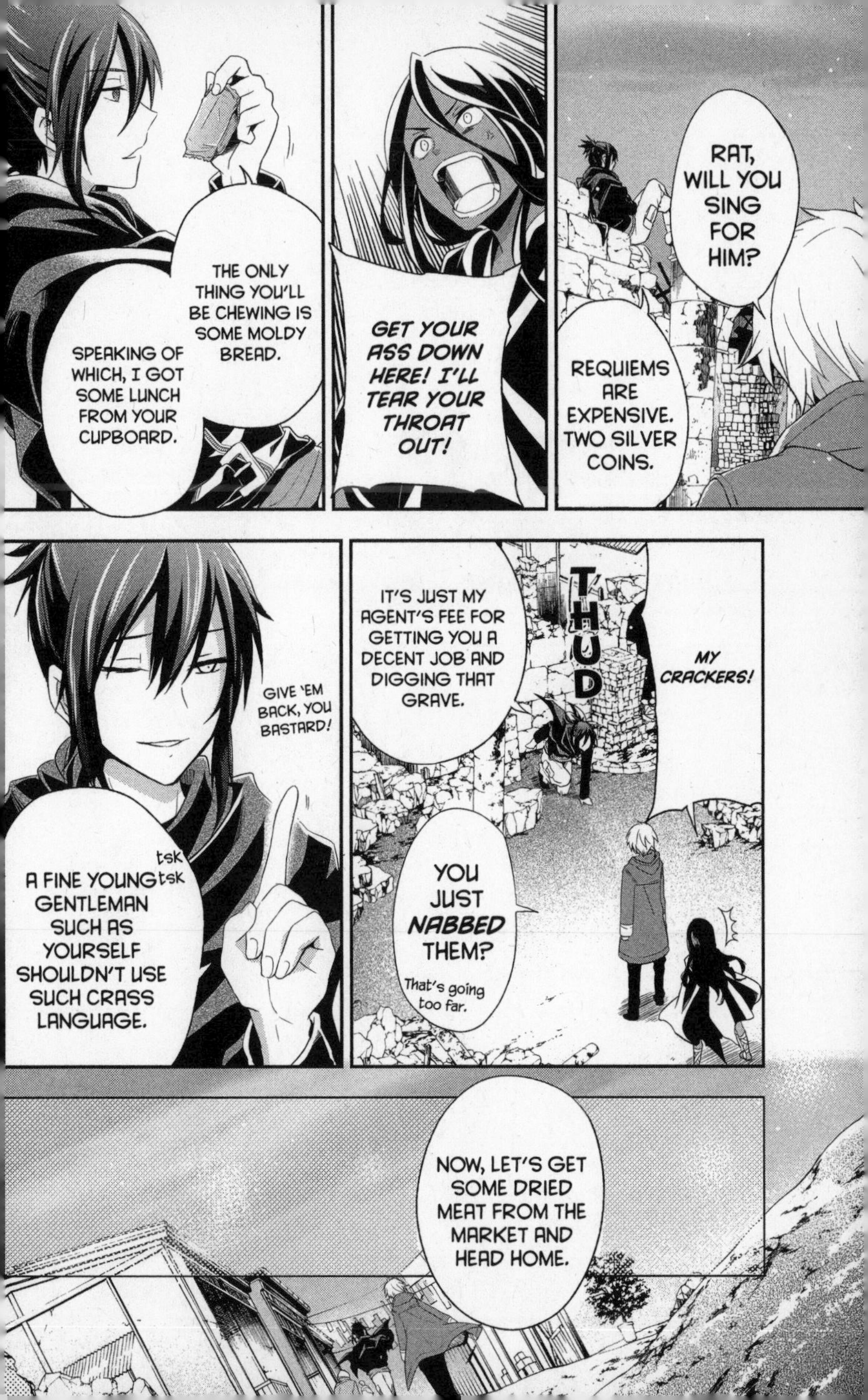
RAT, WILL YOU SING FOR HIM?
REQUIEMS ARE EXPENSIVE. TWO SILVER COINS.
GET YOUR ASS DOWN HERE! I'LL TEAR YOUR THROAT OUT!
THE ONLY THING YOU'LL BE CHEWING IS SOME MOLDY BREAD.
SPEAKING OF WHICH, I GOT SOME LUNCH FROM YOUR CUPBOARD.
MY CRACKERS!
IT'S JUST MY AGENT'S FEE FOR GETTING YOU A DECENT JOB AND DIGGING THAT GRAVE.
THUD
YOU JUST NABBED THEM?
That's going too far.
GIVE 'EM BACK, YOU BASTARD!
tsk tsk
A FINE YOUNG GENTLEMAN SUCH AS YOURSELF SHOULDN'T USE SUCH CRASS LANGUAGE.
NOW, LET'S GET SOME DRIED MEAT FROM THE MARKET AND HEAD HOME.

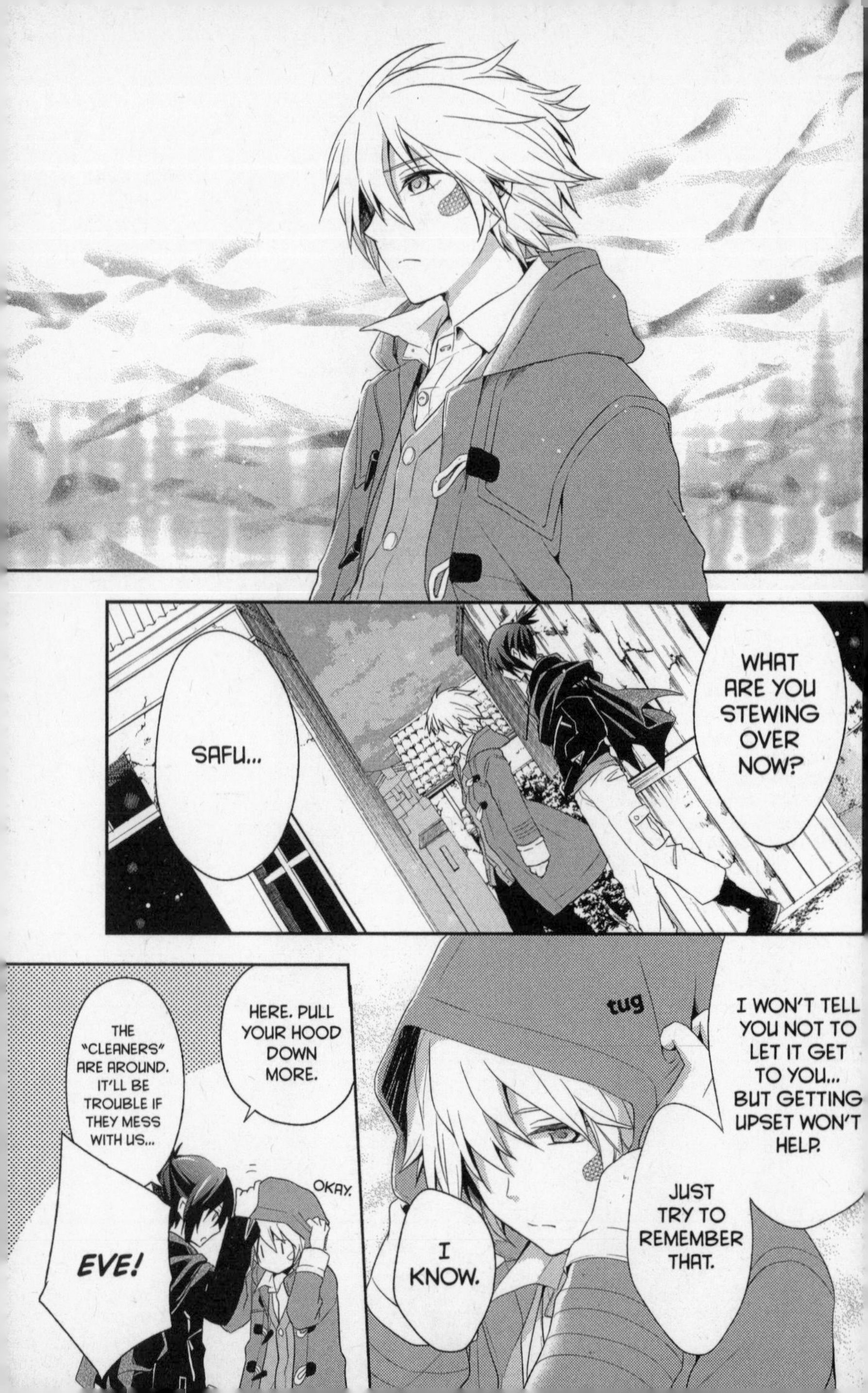
WHAT ARE YOU STEWING OVER NOW?
SAFU...
I WON'T TELL YOU NOT TO LET IT GET TO YOU... BUT GETTING UPSET WON'T HELP.
tug
JUST TRY TO REMEMBER THAT.
I KNOW.
HERE. PULL YOUR HOOD DOWN MORE.
THE "CLEANERS" ARE AROUND. IT'LL BE TROUBLE IF THEY MESS WITH US...
OKAY.
EVE!

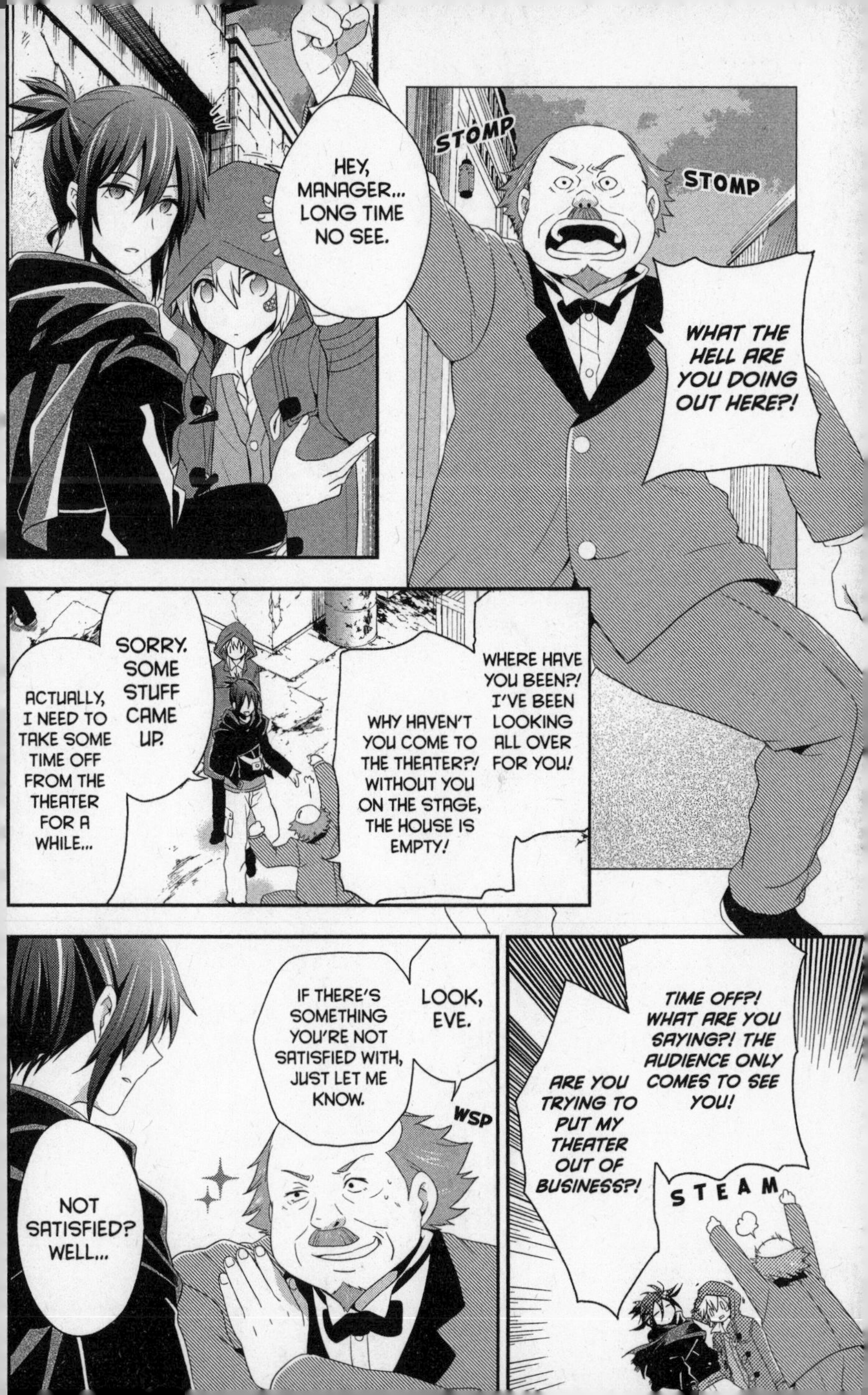
STOMP
STOMP
WHAT THE HELL ARE YOU DOING OUT HERE?!
HEY, MANAGER... LONG TIME NO SEE.
WHERE HAVE YOU BEEN?! I'VE BEEN LOOKING ALL OVER FOR YOU!
WHY HAVEN'T YOU COME TO THE THEATER?! WITHOUT YOU ON THE STAGE, THE HOUSE IS EMPTY!
SORRY. SOME STUFF CAME UP.
ACTUALLY, I NEED TO TAKE SOME TIME OFF FROM THE THEATER FOR A WHILE...
TIME OFF?! WHAT ARE YOU SAYING?! THE AUDIENCE ONLY COMES TO SEE YOU!
ARE YOU TRYING TO PUT MY THEATER OUT OF BUSINESS?!
STEAM
LOOK, EVE.
IF THERE'S SOMETHING YOU'RE NOT SATISFIED WITH, JUST LET ME KNOW.
WSP
NOT SATISFIED? WELL...

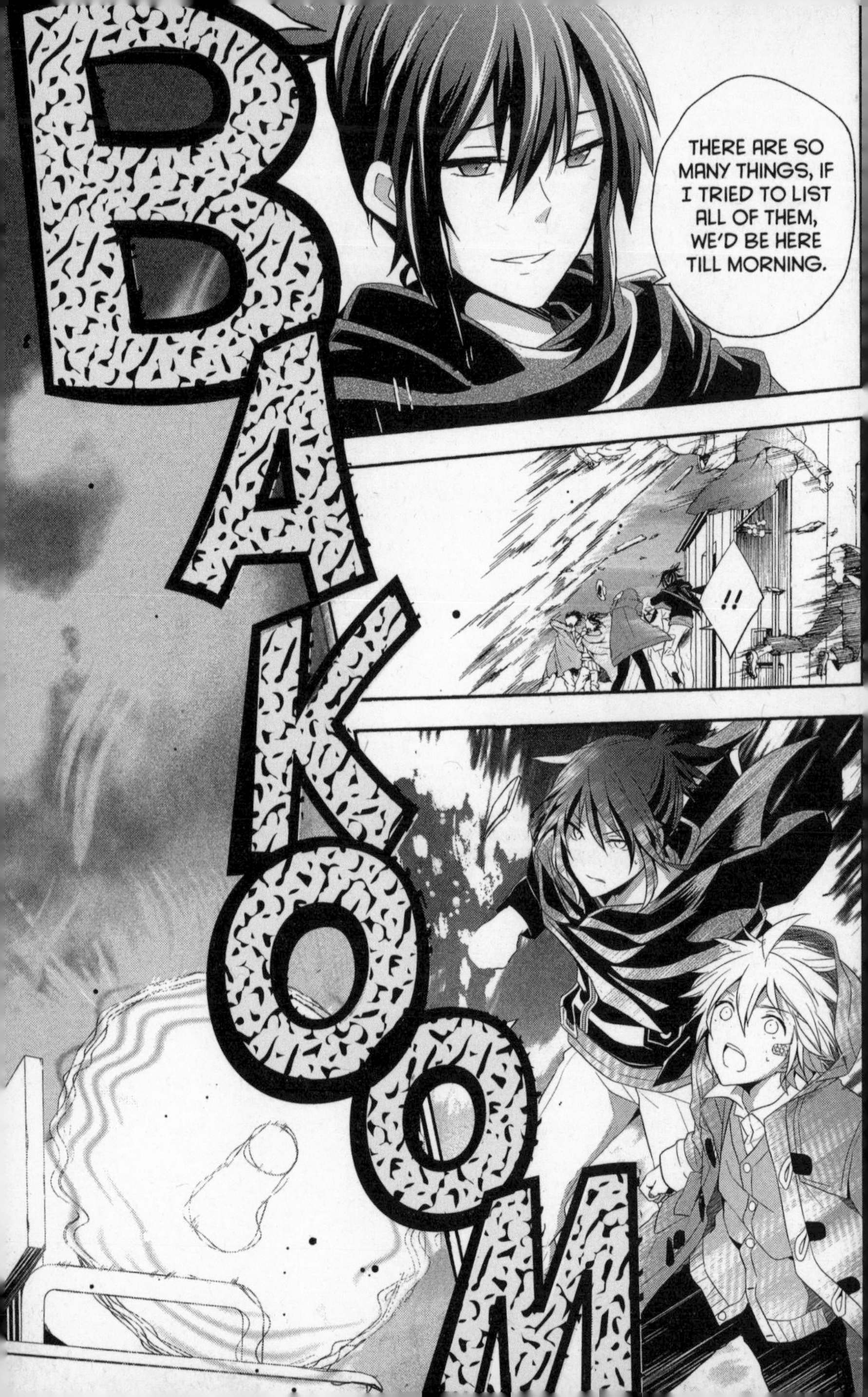
THERE ARE SO MANY THINGS, IF I TRIED TO LIST ALL OF THEM, WE'D BE HERE TILL MORNING.
!!
BAKOOM

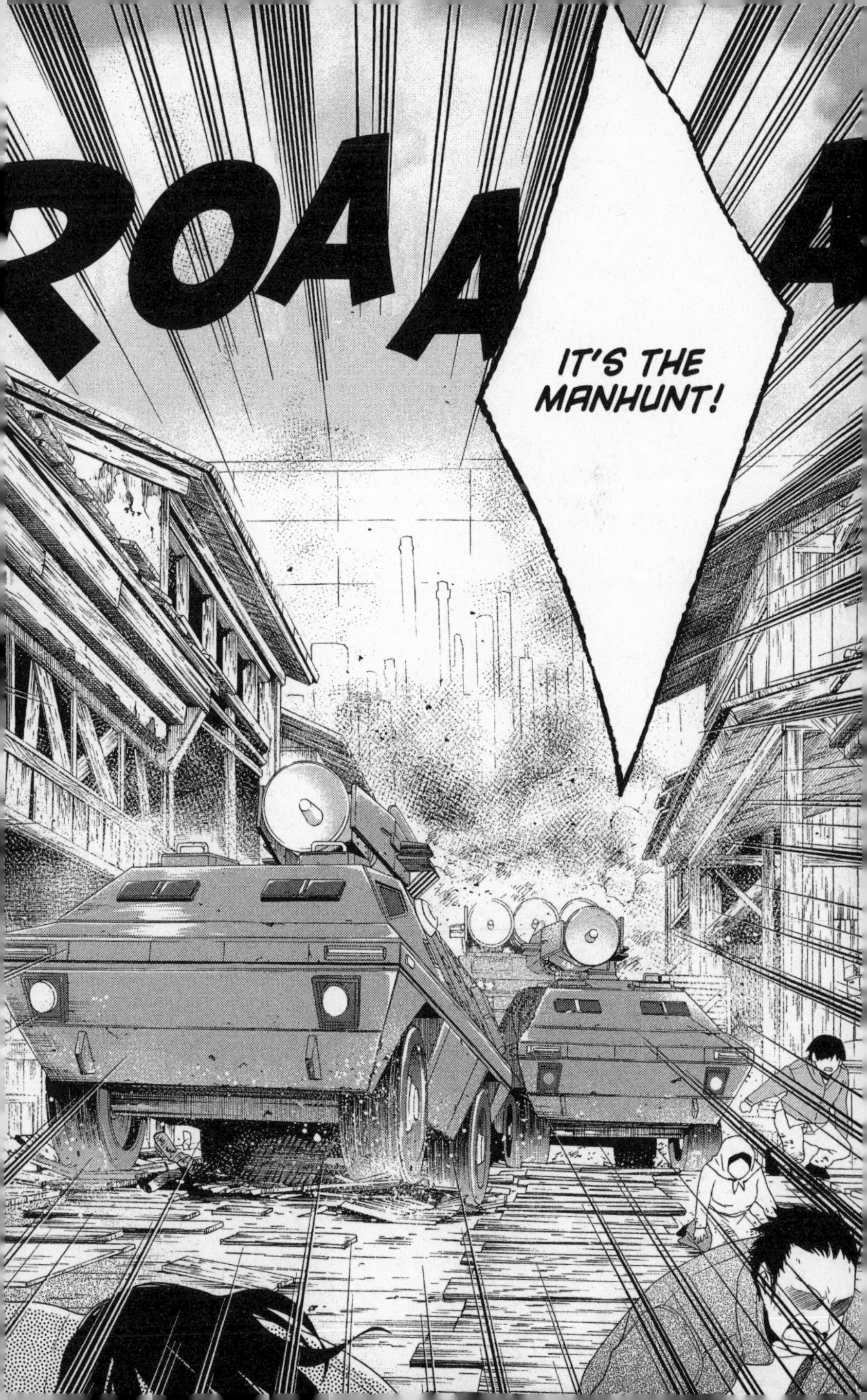
ROAAA
IT'S THE MANHUNT!

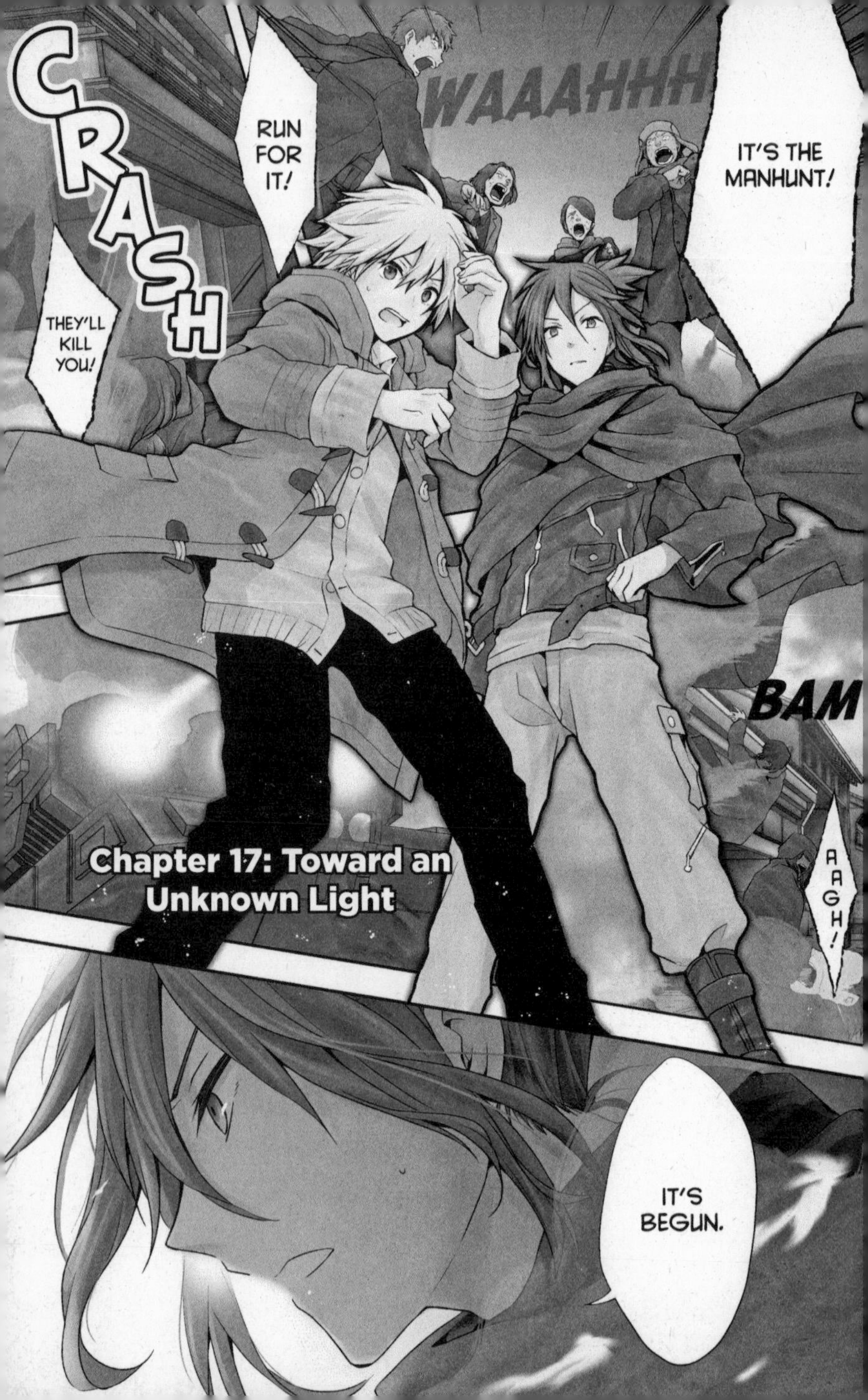
IT'S THE MANHUNT!
WAAAHHH
RUN FOR IT!
CRASH
THEY'LL KILL YOU!
BAM
AAGH!
Chapter 17: Toward an Unknown Light
IT'S BEGUN.

Chapter 17: Toward an Unknown Light

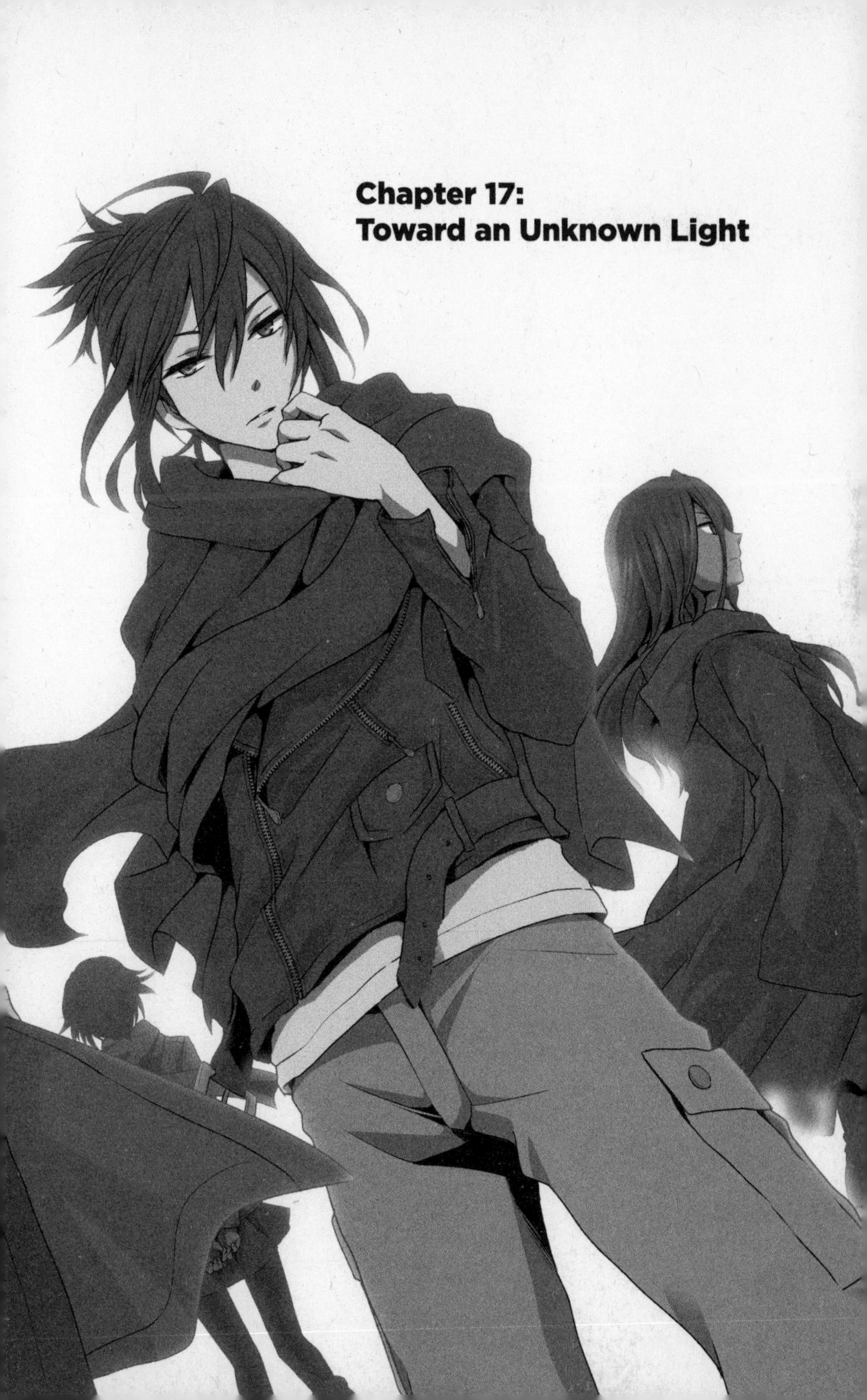

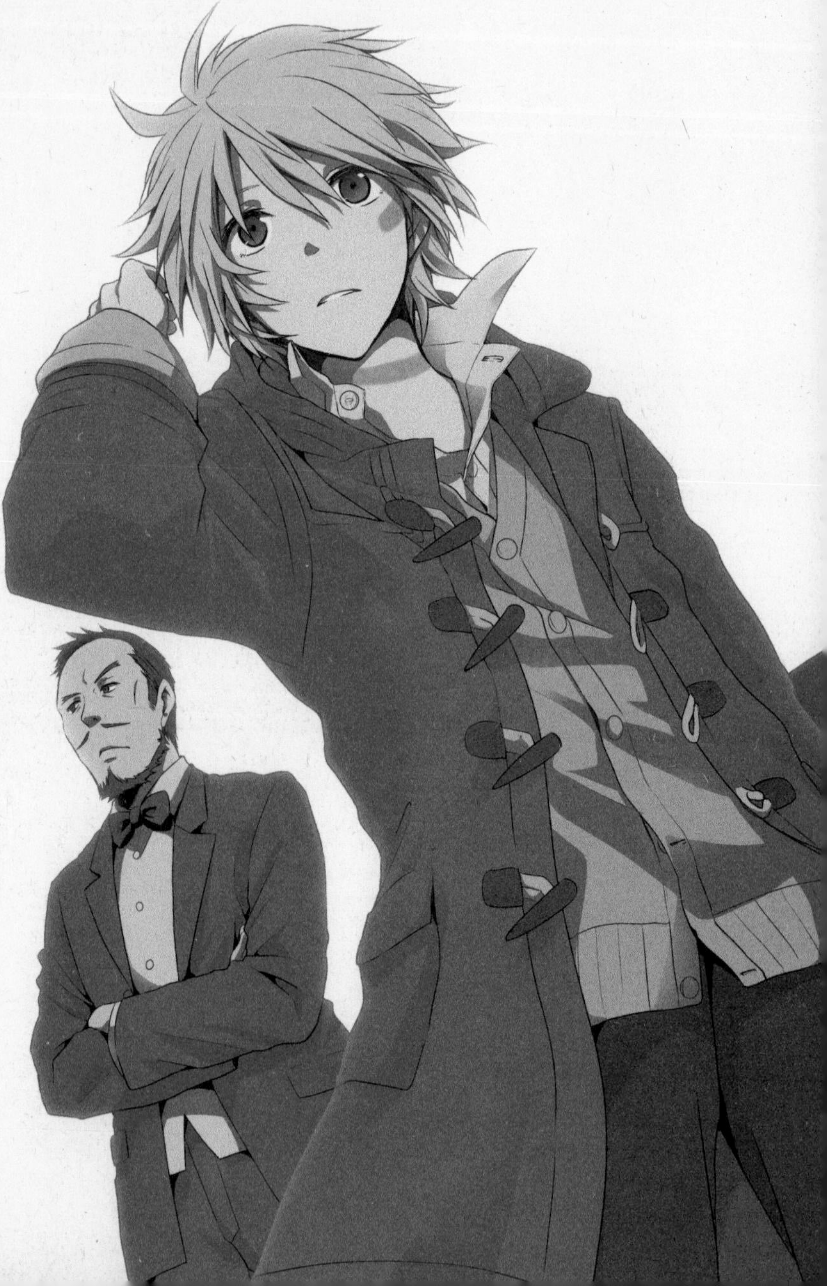

NO.6

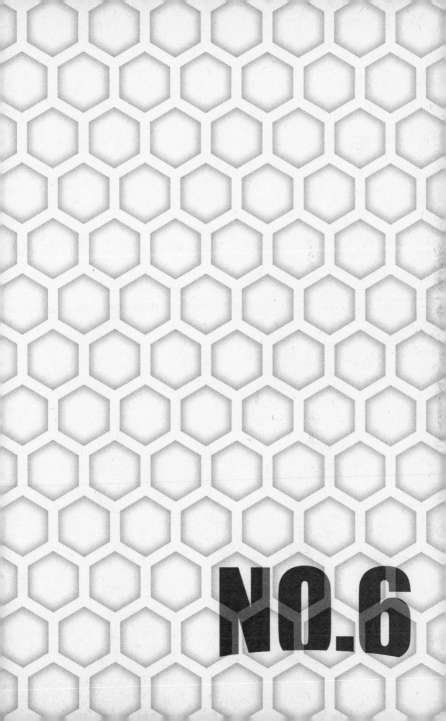

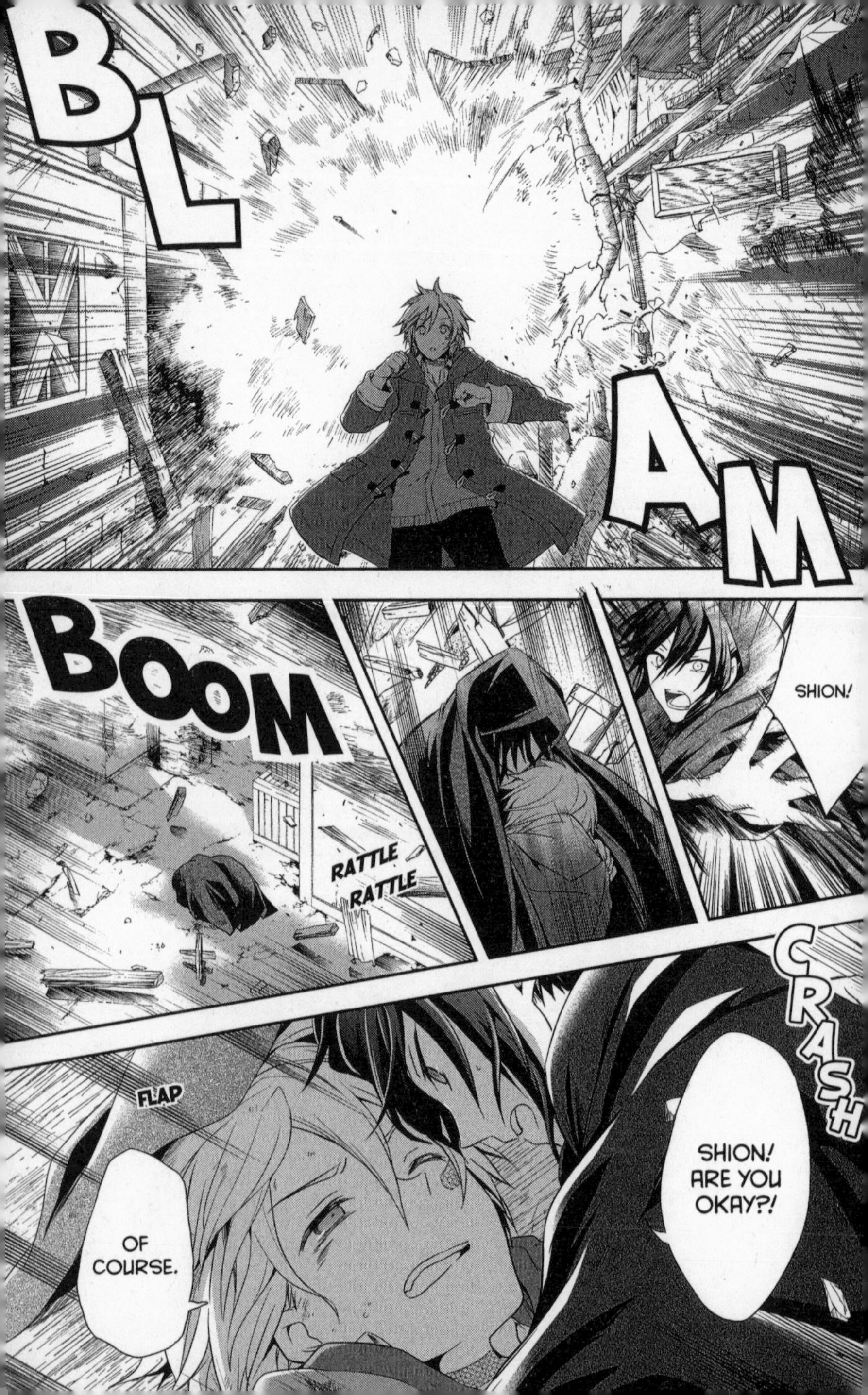
BLAM
SHION!
BOOM
RATTLE RATTLE
CRASH
SHION! ARE YOU OKAY?!
FLAP
OF COURSE.

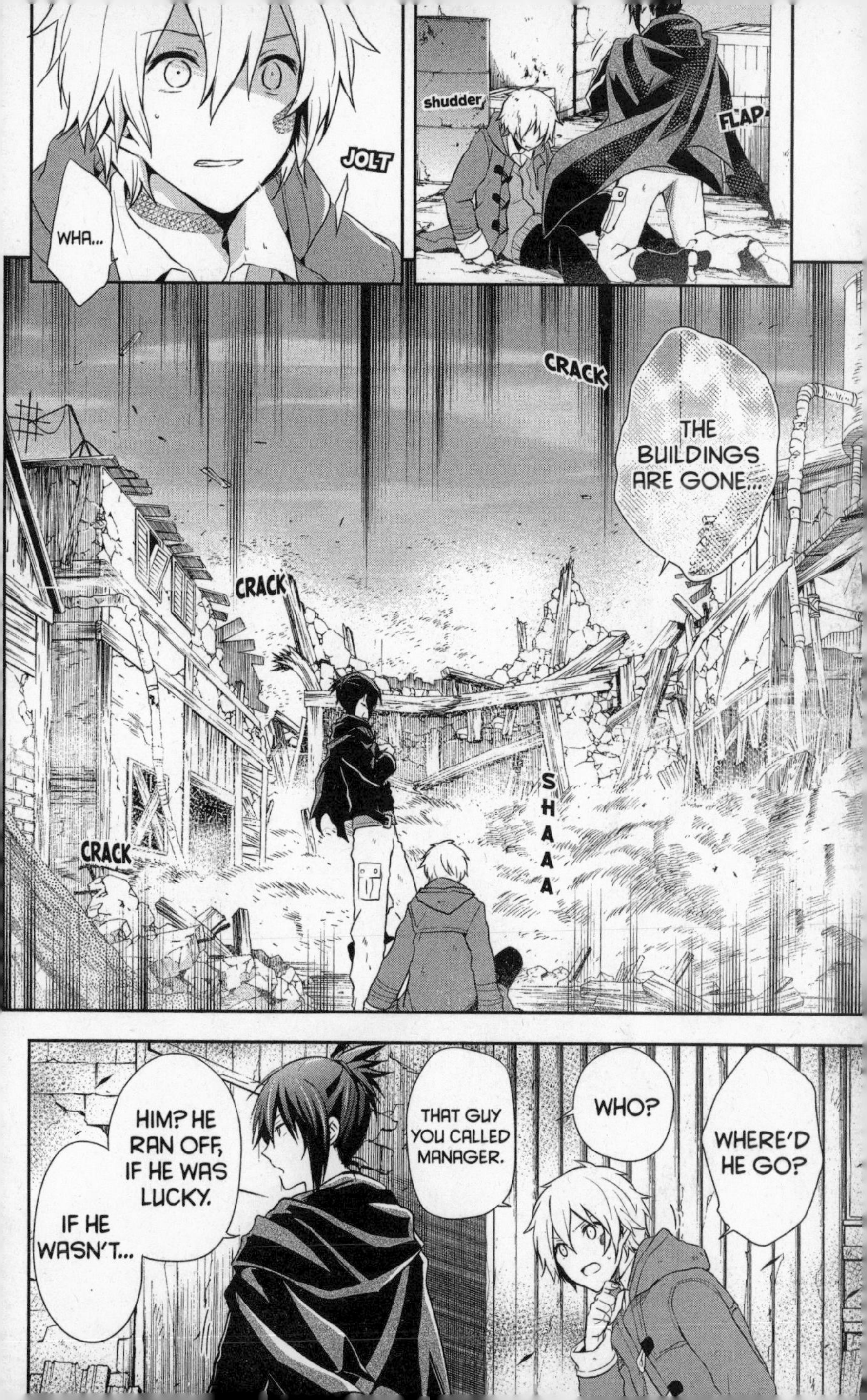
FLAP
shudder
JOLT
WHA...
THE BUILDINGS ARE GONE...
CRACK
CRACK
SHAAA
CRACK
WHERE'D HE GO?
WHO?
THAT GUY YOU CALLED MANAGER.
HIM? HE RAN OFF, IF HE WAS LUCKY.
IF HE WASN'T...

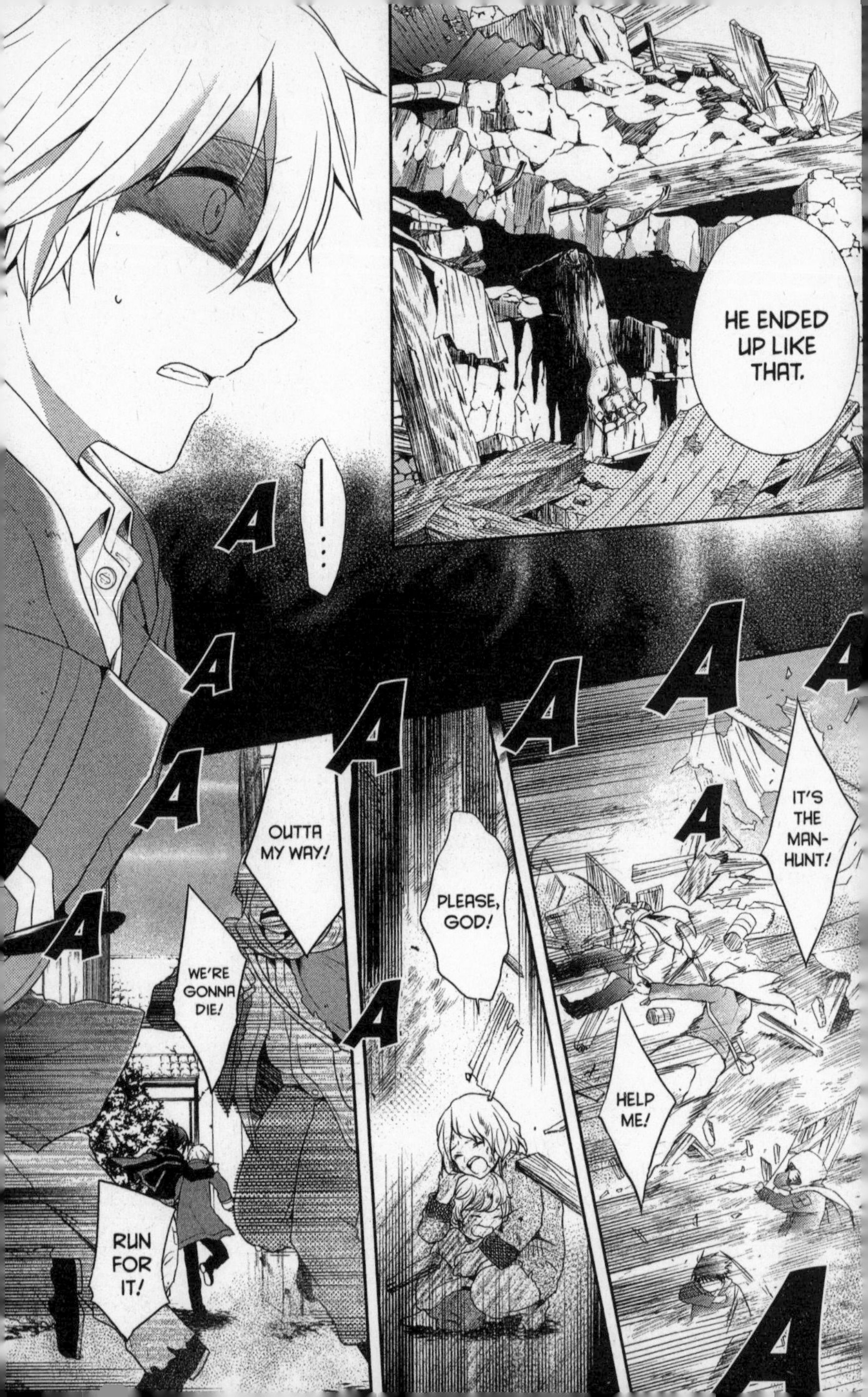
HE ENDED UP LIKE THAT.
—…
AAAAAAAAAAA
IT'S THE MAN-HUNT!
HELP ME!
PLEASE, GOD!
OUTTA MY WAY!
WE'RE GONNA DIE!
RUN FOR IT!

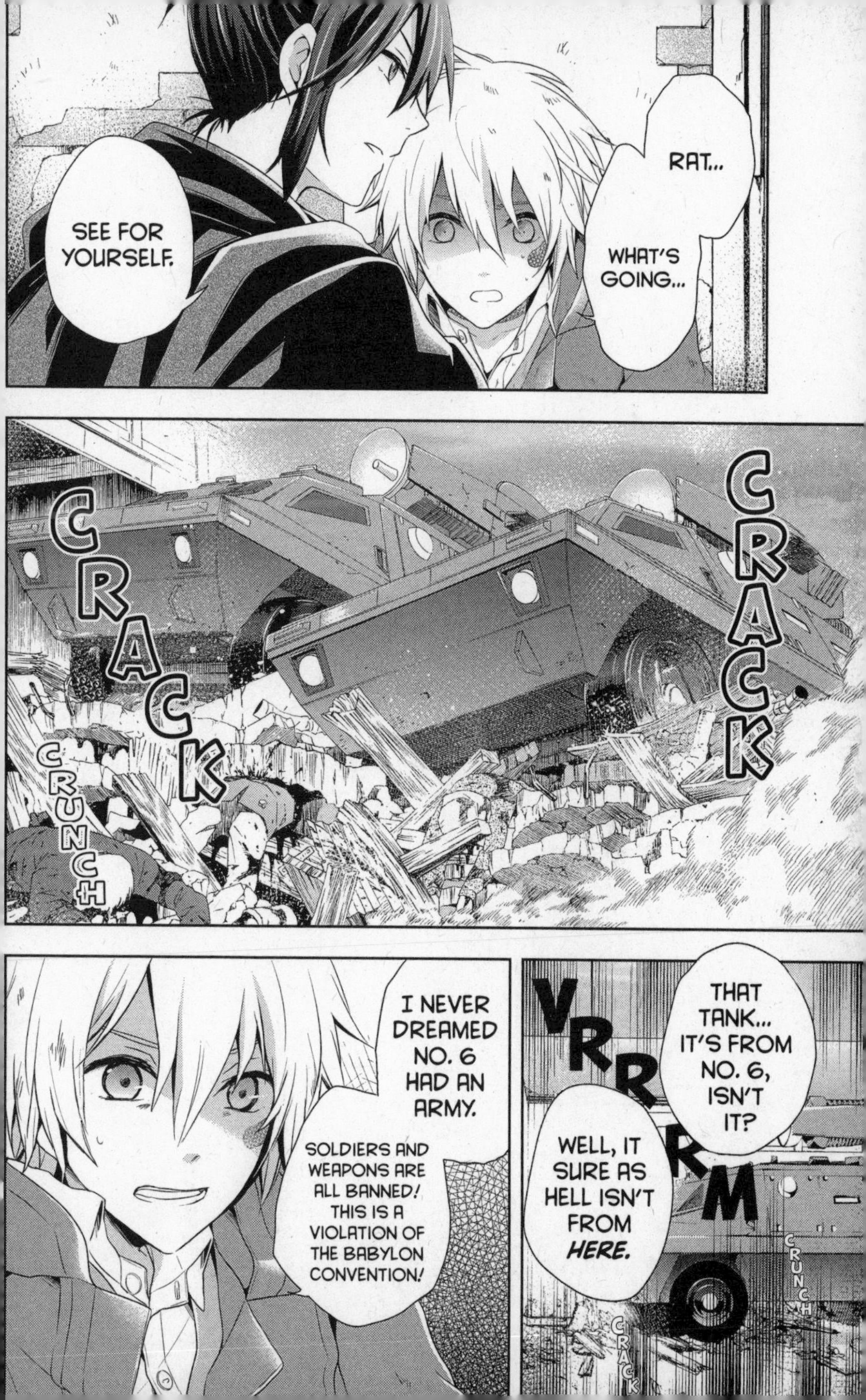
RAT...
WHAT'S GOING...
SEE FOR YOURSELF.
CRACK
CRACK
CRUNCH
THAT TANK... IT'S FROM NO. 6, ISN'T IT?
VRRRM
WELL, IT SURE AS HELL ISN'T FROM *HERE.*
CRUNCH
CRACK
I NEVER DREAMED NO. 6 HAD AN ARMY.
SOLDIERS AND WEAPONS ARE ALL BANNED! THIS IS A VIOLATION OF THE BABYLON CONVENTION!

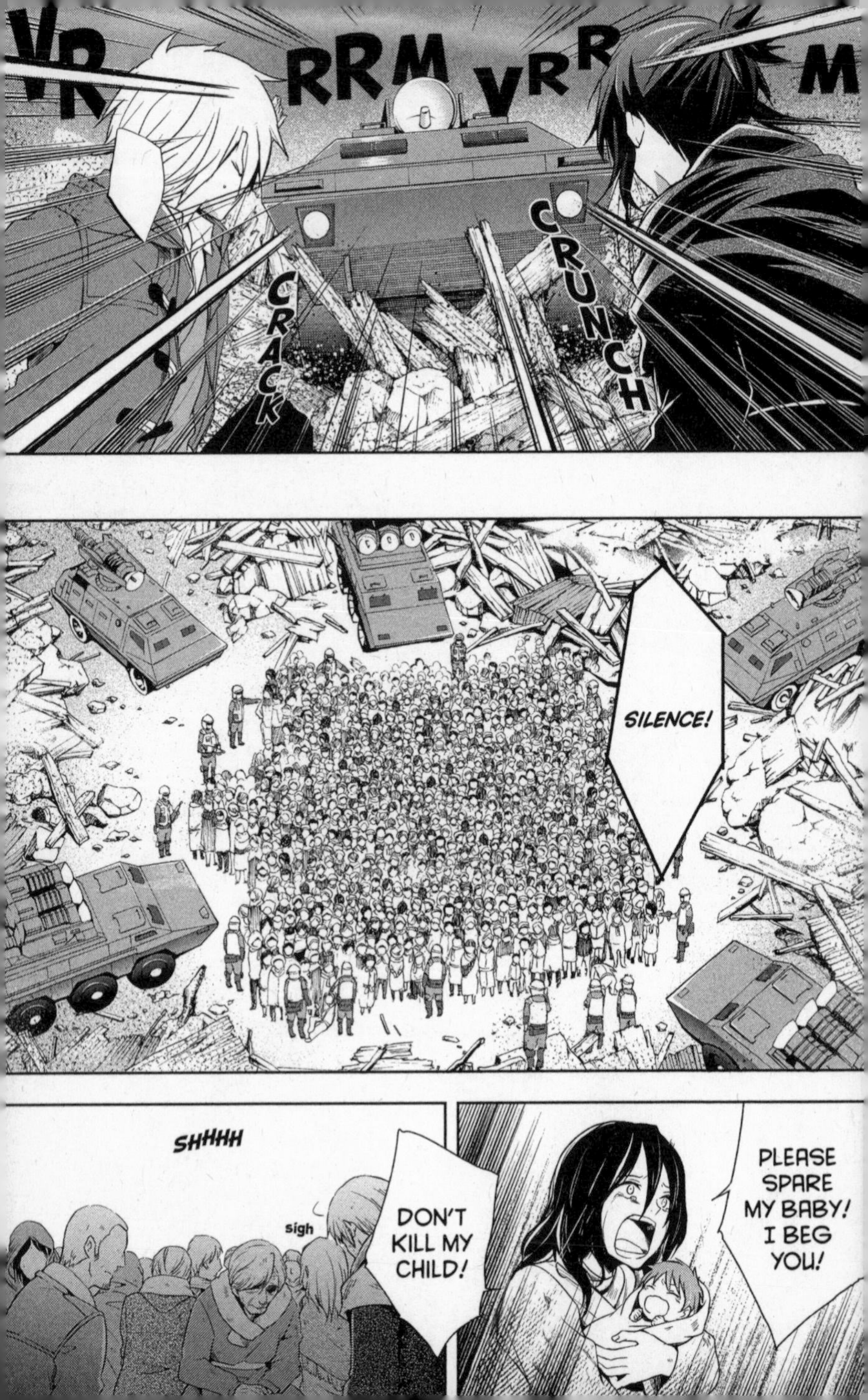
VRRM
CRUNCH
VRRRM
CRACK
SILENCE!
PLEASE SPARE MY BABY! I BEG YOU!
DON'T KILL MY CHILD!
sigh
SHHHH

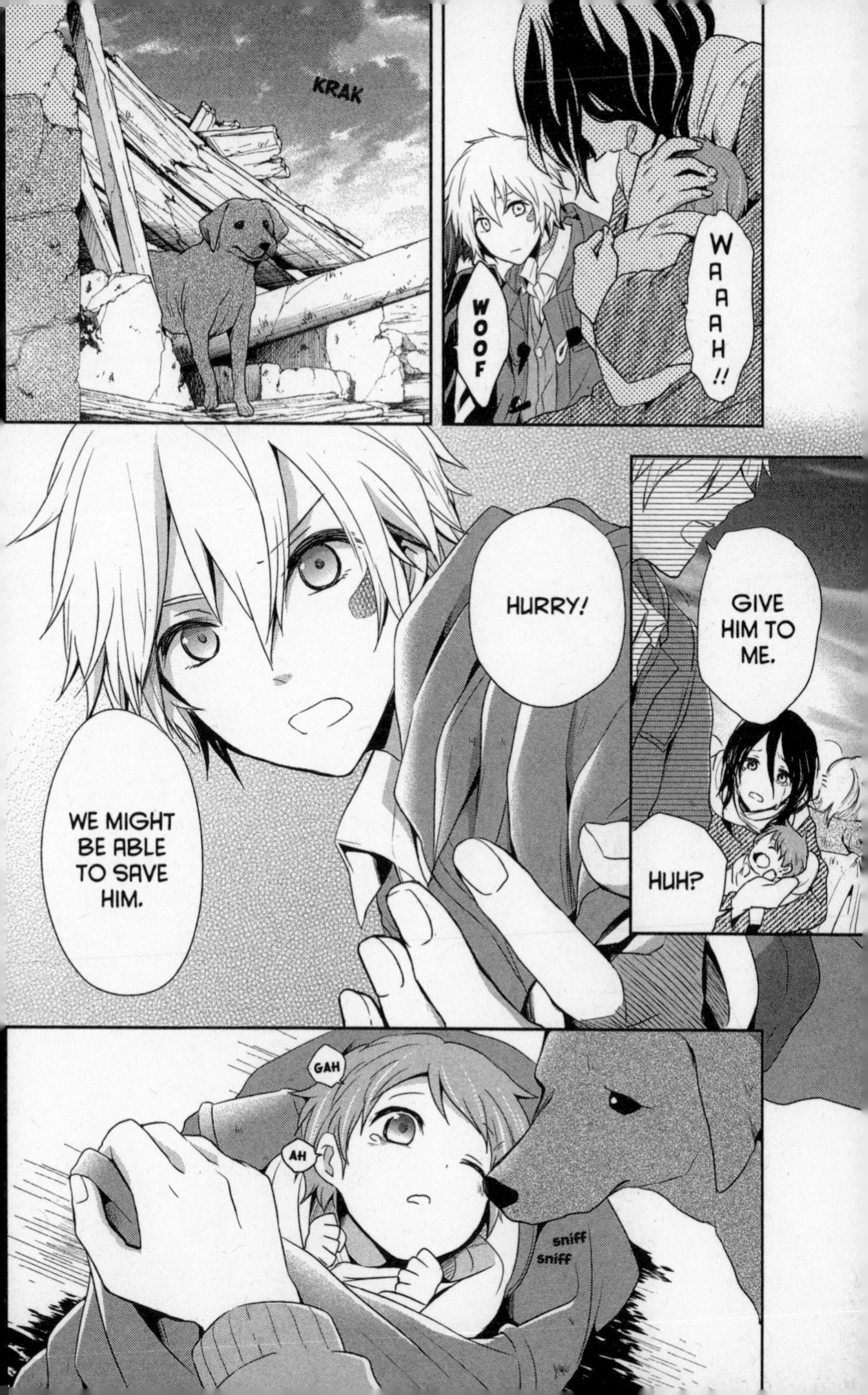
WAAAH!!
WOOF
KRAK
GIVE HIM TO ME.
HUH?
HURRY!
WE MIGHT BE ABLE TO SAVE HIM.
GAH
AH
sniff sniff

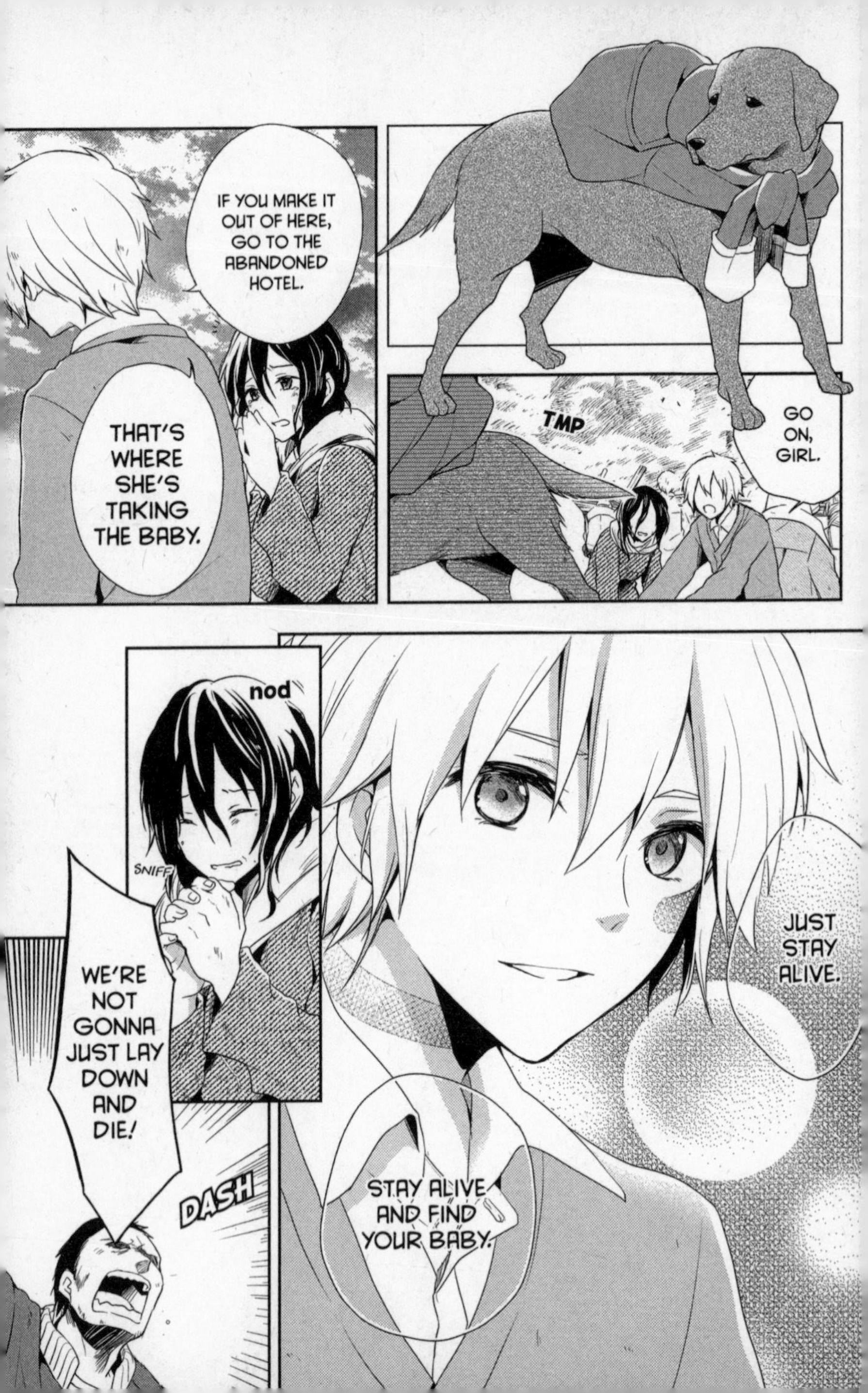
TMP
GO ON, GIRL.
IF YOU MAKE IT OUT OF HERE, GO TO THE ABANDONED HOTEL.
THAT'S WHERE SHE'S TAKING THE BABY.
JUST STAY ALIVE.
STAY ALIVE AND FIND YOUR BABY.
nod
SNIFF
WE'RE NOT GONNA JUST LAY DOWN AND DIE!
DASH

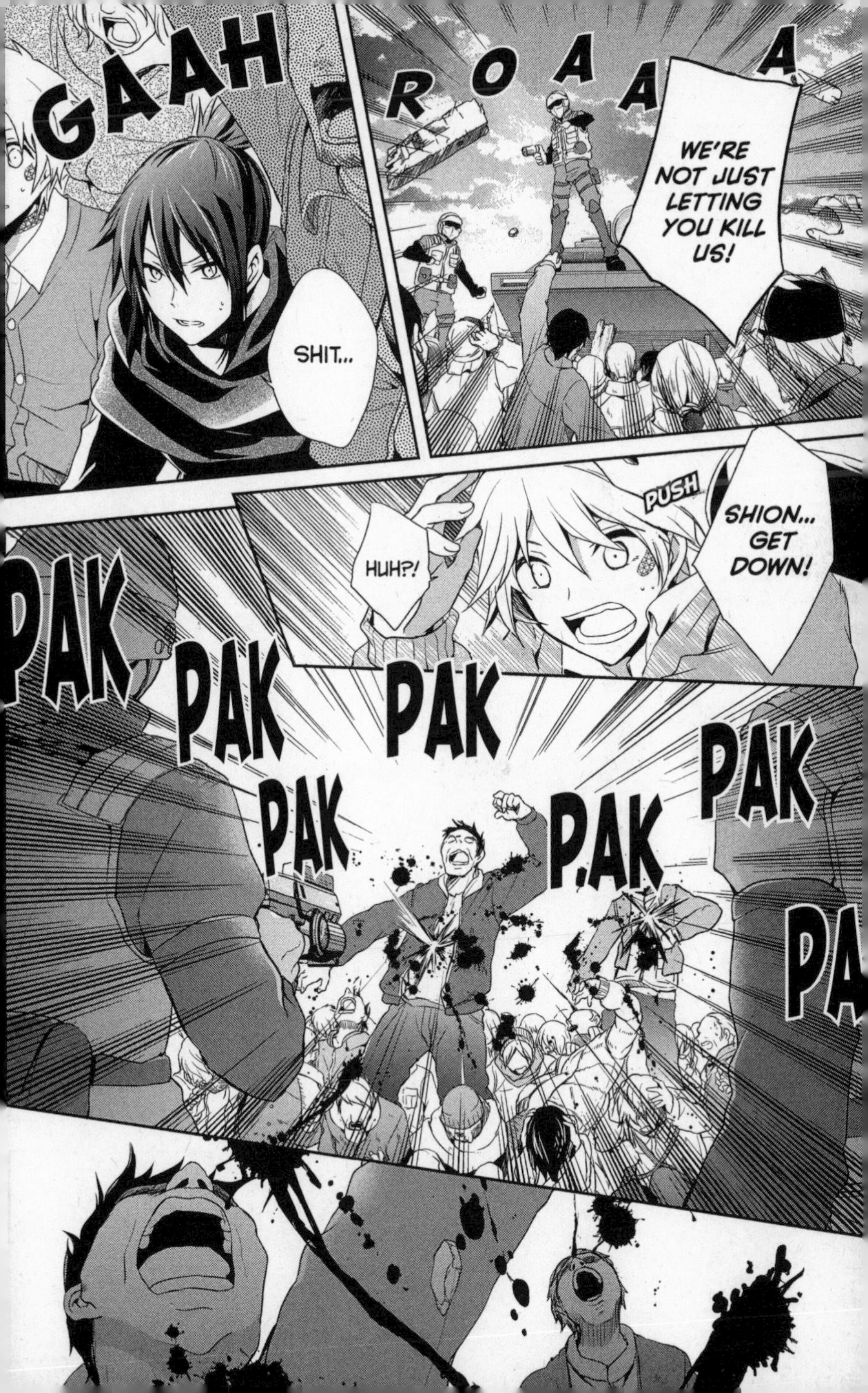

ROAAA
WE'RE NOT JUST LETTING YOU KILL US!
GAAH
SHIT...
PUSH
SHION... GET DOWN!
HUH?!
PAK
PAK
PAK
PAK
PAK
PAK
PA

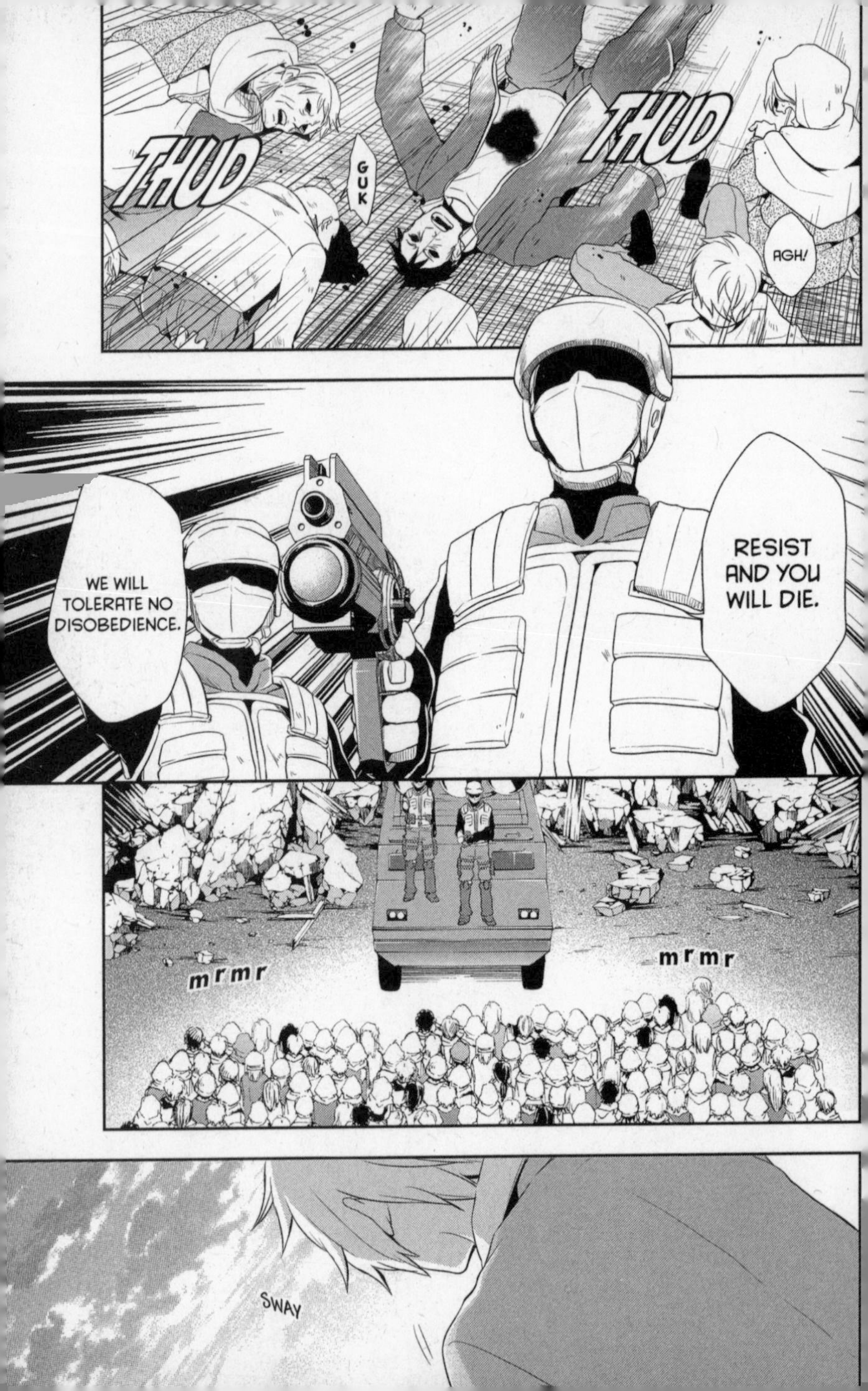
THUD
AGH!
GUK
THUD
RESIST AND YOU WILL DIE.
WE WILL TOLERATE NO DISOBEDIENCE.
mrmr
mrmr
SWAY

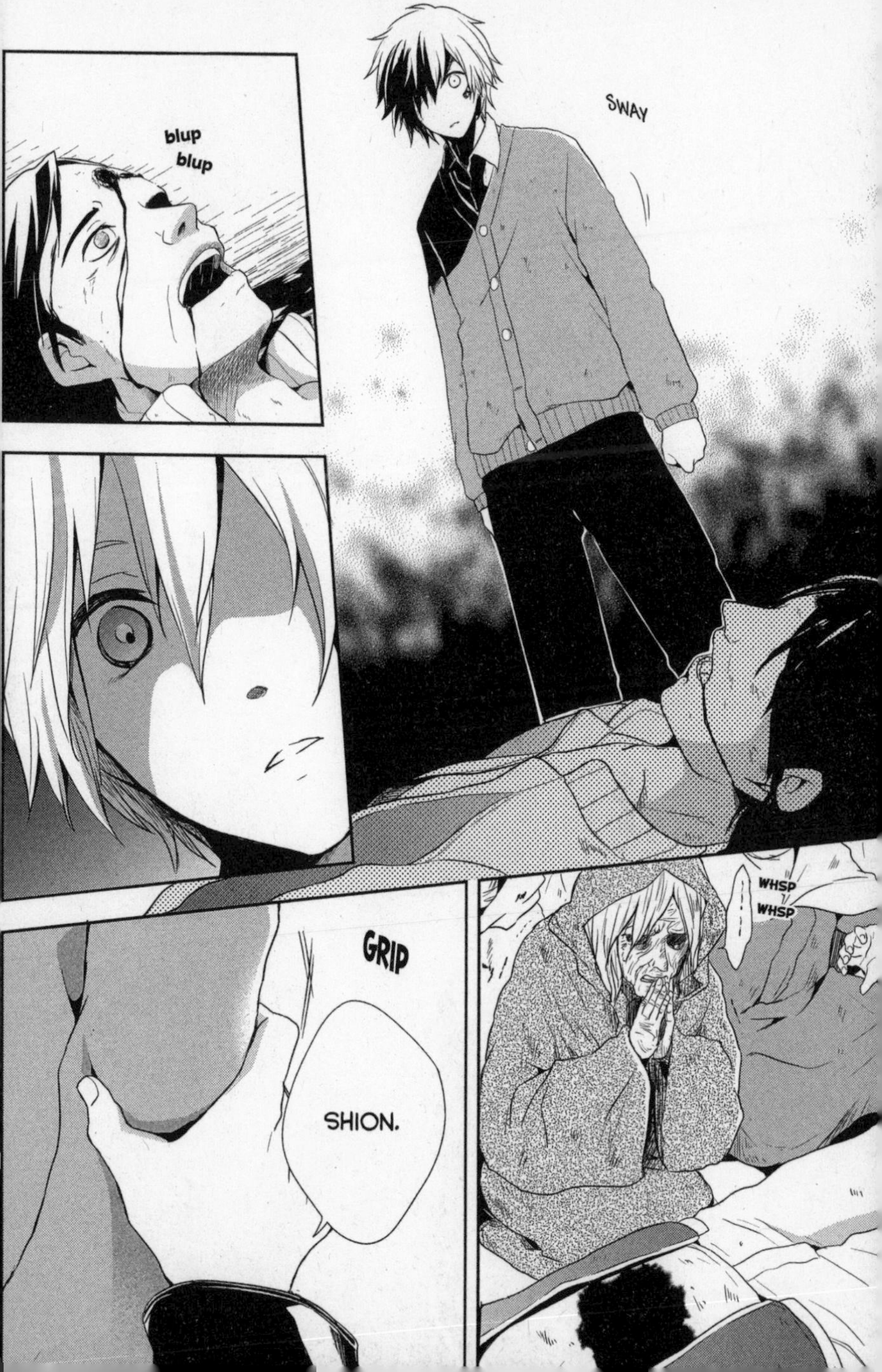
SWAY
blup
blup
WHSP
WHSP
GRIP
SHION.

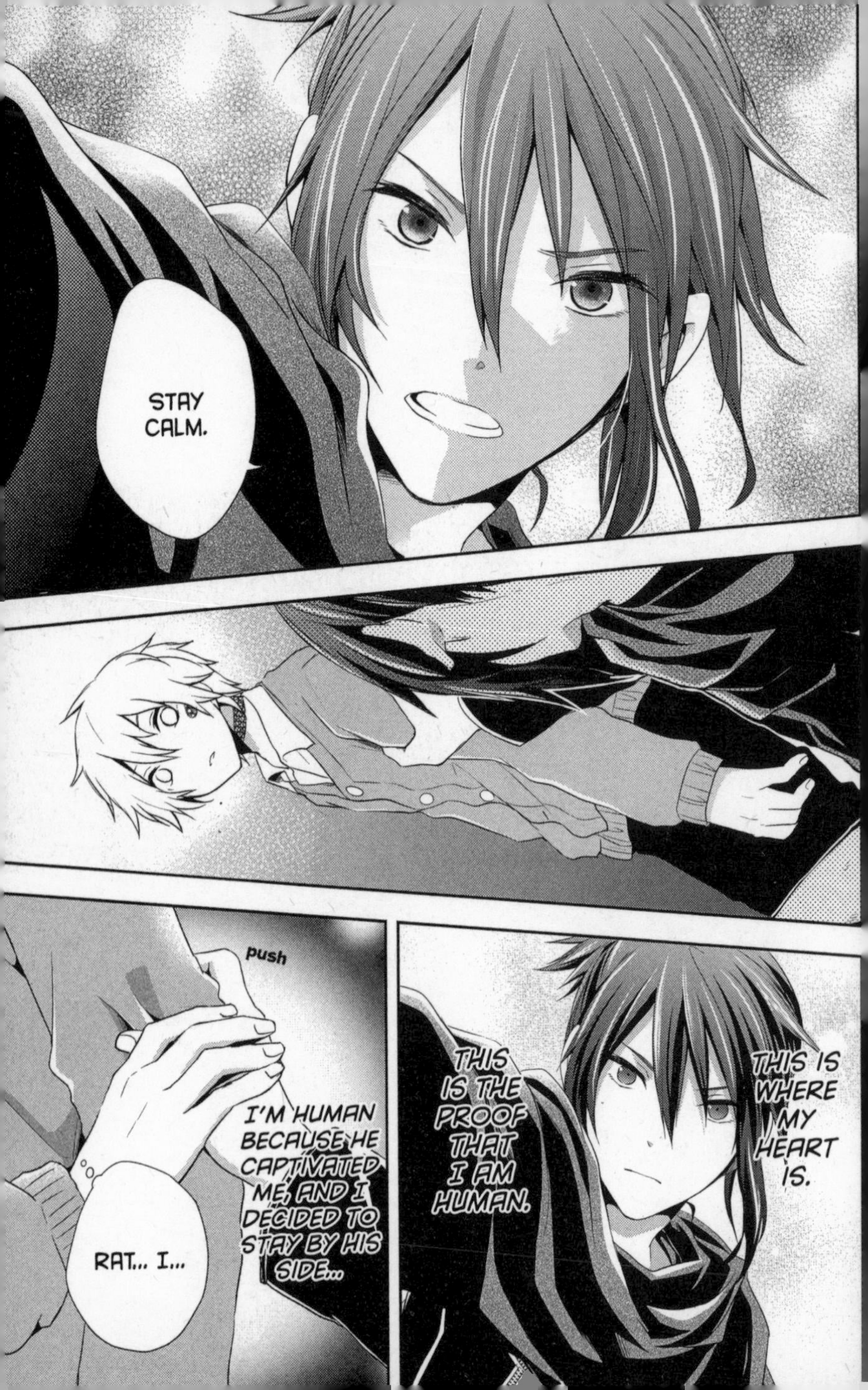
STAY CALM.
THIS IS WHERE MY HEART IS.
THIS IS THE PROOF THAT I AM HUMAN.
push
I'M HUMAN BECAUSE HE CAPTIVATED ME, AND I DECIDED TO STAY BY HIS SIDE...
RAT... I...

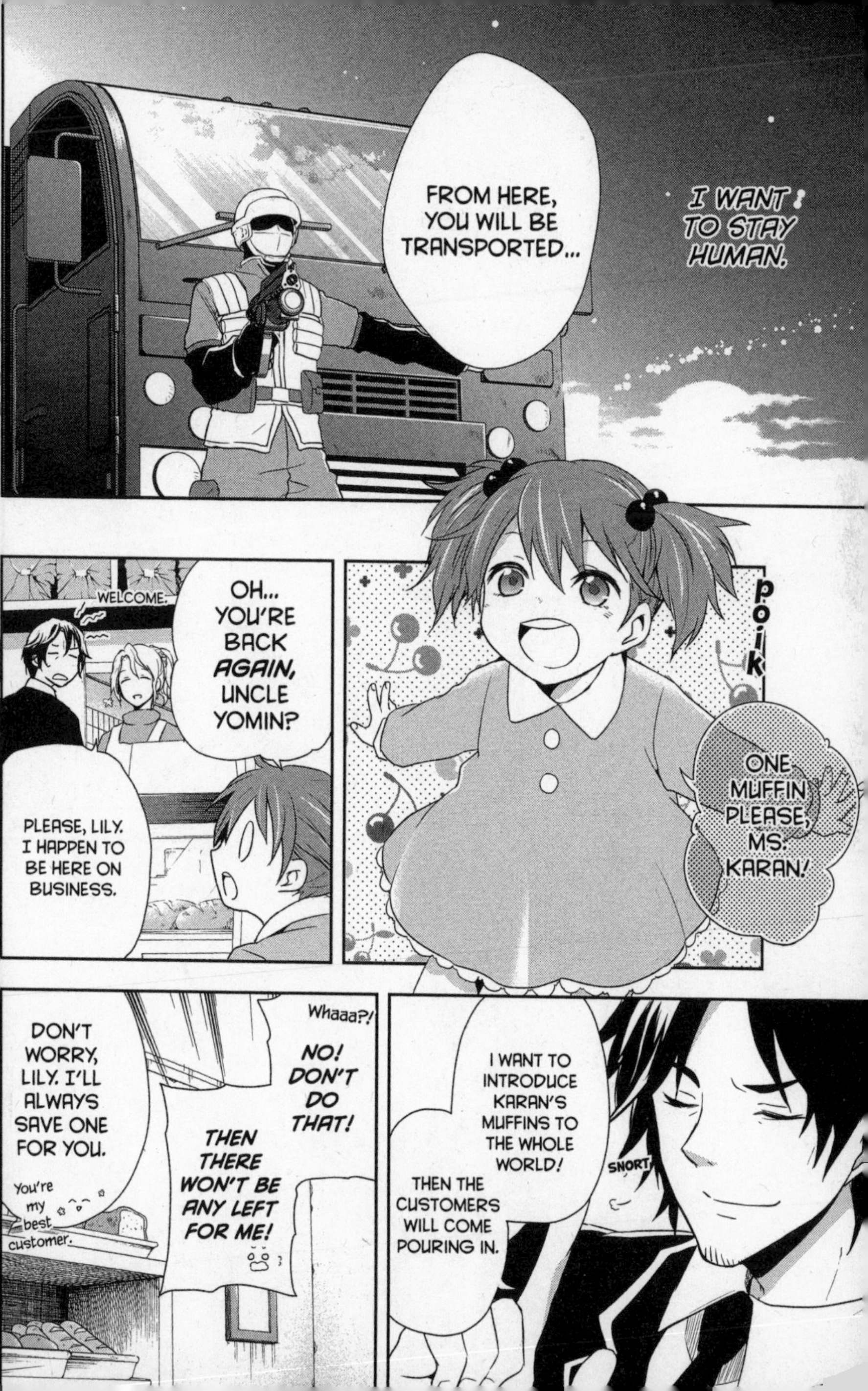
I WANT TO STAY HUMAN.
FROM HERE, YOU WILL BE TRANSPORTED...
poik
ONE MUFFIN PLEASE, MS. KARAN!
WELCOME.
OH... YOU'RE BACK AGAIN, UNCLE YOMIN?
PLEASE, LILY. I HAPPEN TO BE HERE ON BUSINESS.
I WANT TO INTRODUCE KARAN'S MUFFINS TO THE WHOLE WORLD!
SNORT
THEN THE CUSTOMERS WILL COME POURING IN.
Whaaa?!
NO! DON'T DO THAT!
THEN THERE WON'T BE ANY LEFT FOR ME!
DON'T WORRY, LILY. I'LL ALWAYS SAVE ONE FOR YOU.
You're my best customer.

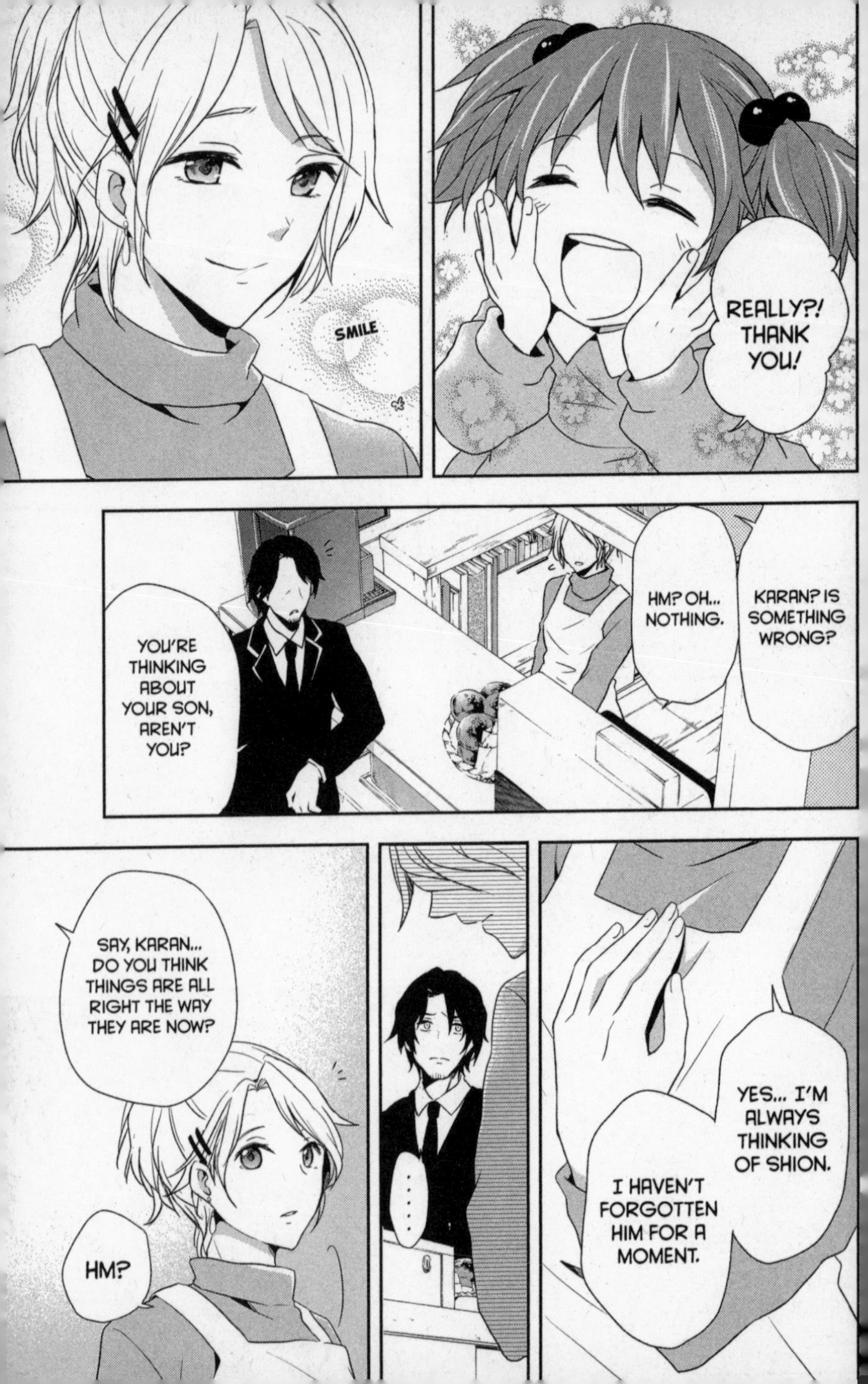
REALLY?! THANK YOU!
SMILE
KARAN? IS SOMETHING WRONG?
HM? OH... NOTHING.
YOU'RE THINKING ABOUT YOUR SON, AREN'T YOU?
YES... I'M ALWAYS THINKING OF SHION.
I HAVEN'T FORGOTTEN HIM FOR A MOMENT.
......
SAY, KARAN... DO YOU THINK THINGS ARE ALL RIGHT THE WAY THEY ARE NOW?
HM?

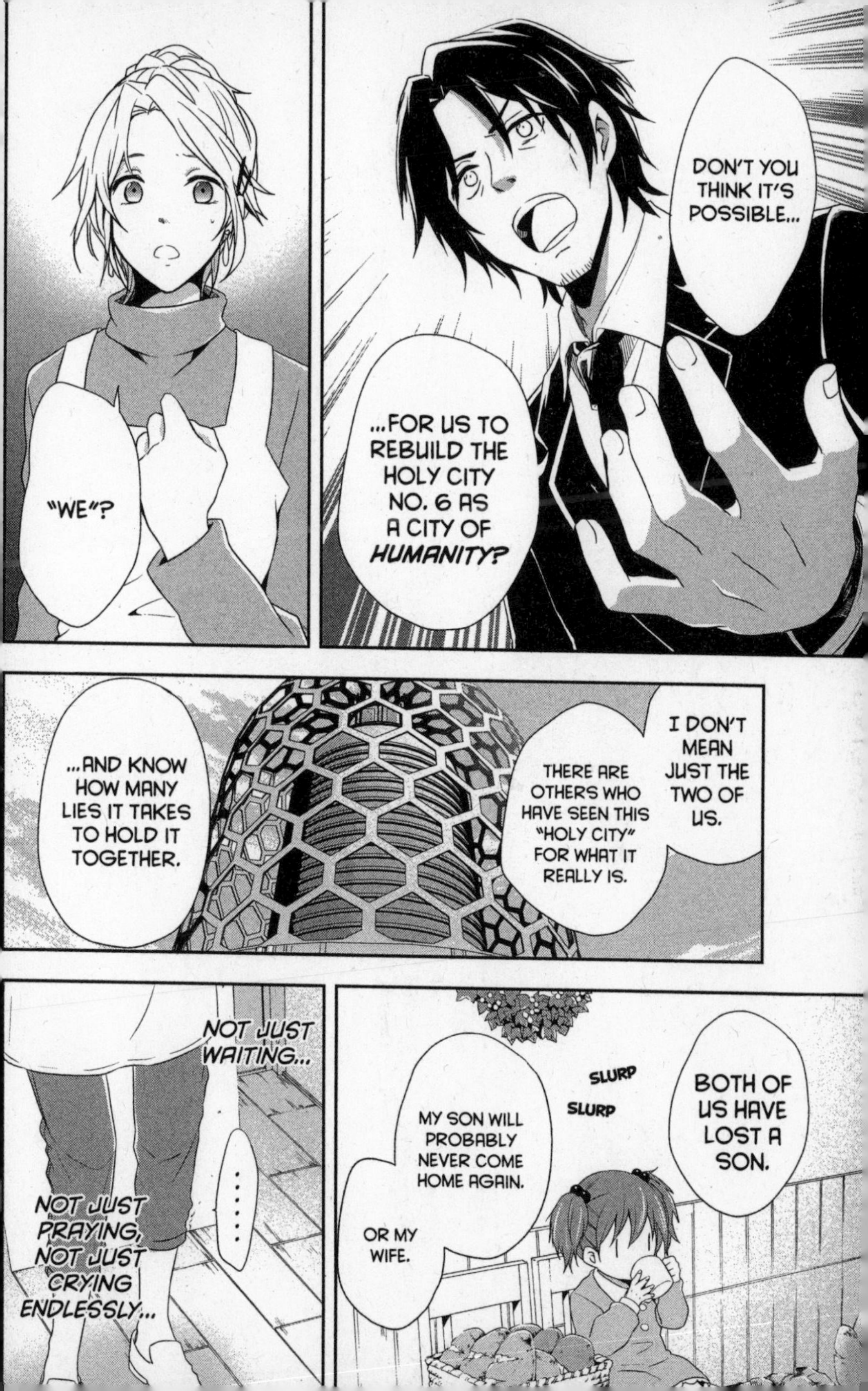
DON'T YOU THINK IT'S POSSIBLE...
...FOR US TO REBUILD THE HOLY CITY NO. 6 AS A CITY OF *HUMANITY?*
"WE"?
I DON'T MEAN JUST THE TWO OF US.
THERE ARE OTHERS WHO HAVE SEEN THIS "HOLY CITY" FOR WHAT IT REALLY IS.
...AND KNOW HOW MANY LIES IT TAKES TO HOLD IT TOGETHER.
BOTH OF US HAVE LOST A SON.
SLURP
SLURP
MY SON WILL PROBABLY NEVER COME HOME AGAIN.
OR MY WIFE.
NOT JUST WAITING...
......
NOT JUST PRAYING, NOT JUST CRYING ENDLESSLY...

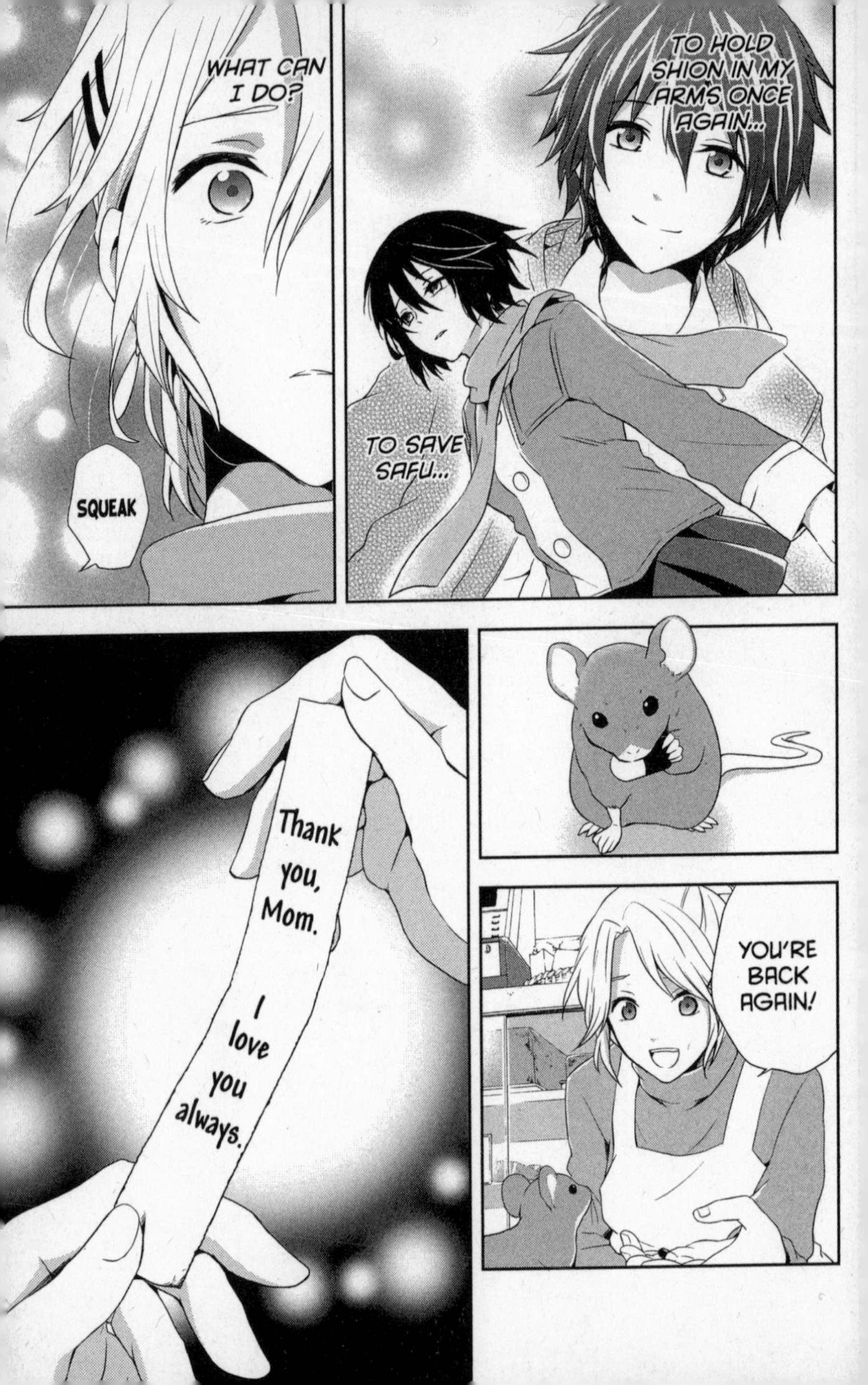
TO HOLD SHION IN MY ARMS ONCE AGAIN...
TO SAVE SAFU...
WHAT CAN I DO?
SQUEAK
YOU'RE BACK AGAIN!
Thank you, Mom.
I love you always.

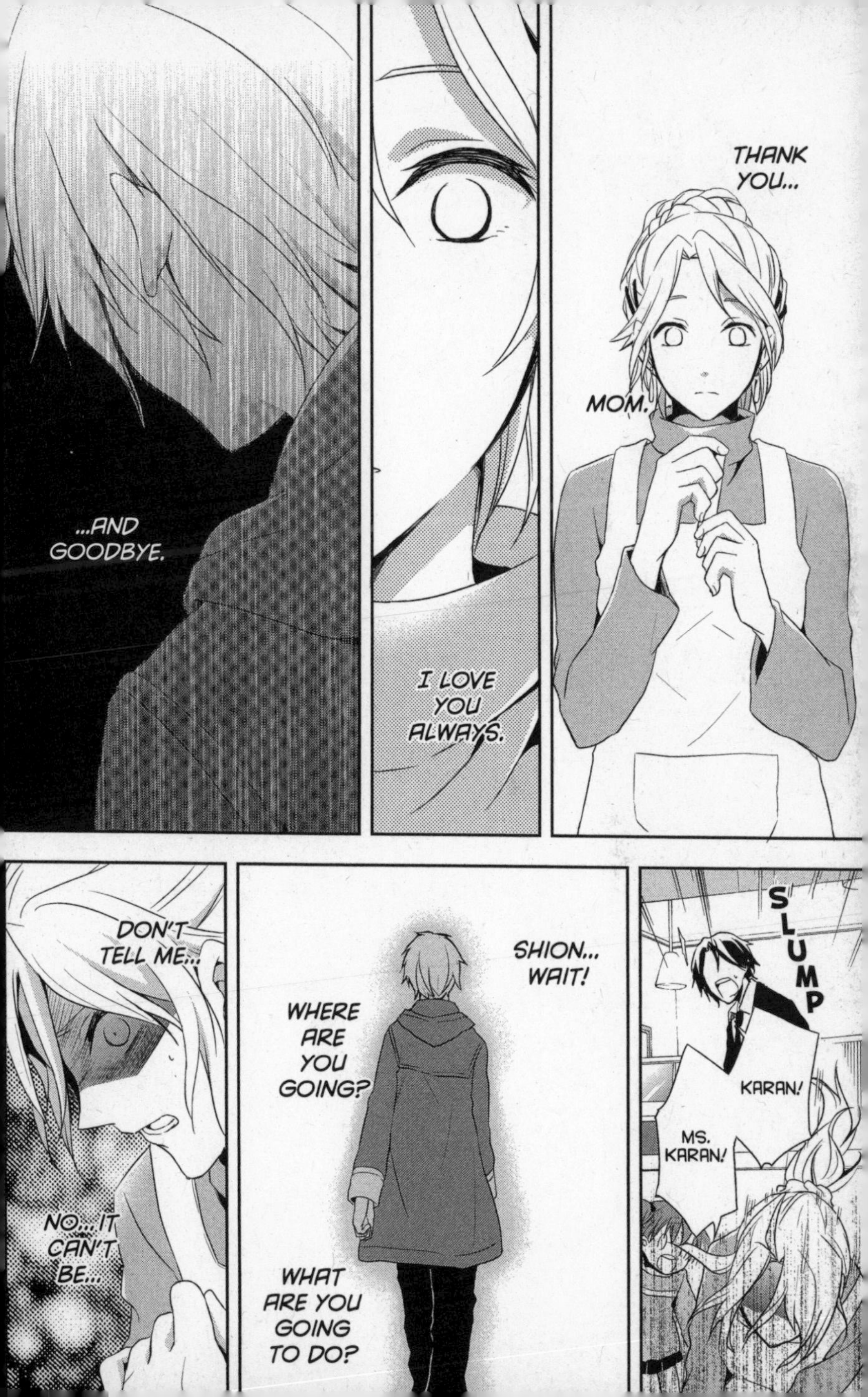
THANK YOU...
MOM.
I LOVE YOU ALWAYS.
...AND GOODBYE.
SLUMP
KARAN!
MS. KARAN!
SHION... WAIT!
WHERE ARE YOU GOING?
WHAT ARE YOU GOING TO DO?
DON'T TELL ME...
NO... IT CAN'T BE...

VRRRRM

THE CORRECTIONAL FACILITY?!

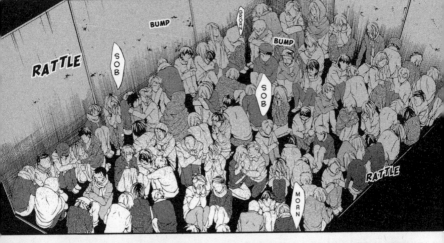

RATTLE

BUMP

GROAN

BUMP

SOB

SOB

RATTLE

MOAN

RATTLE

DEAR GOD...

BUMP

BUMP

AARGH...

UGH...

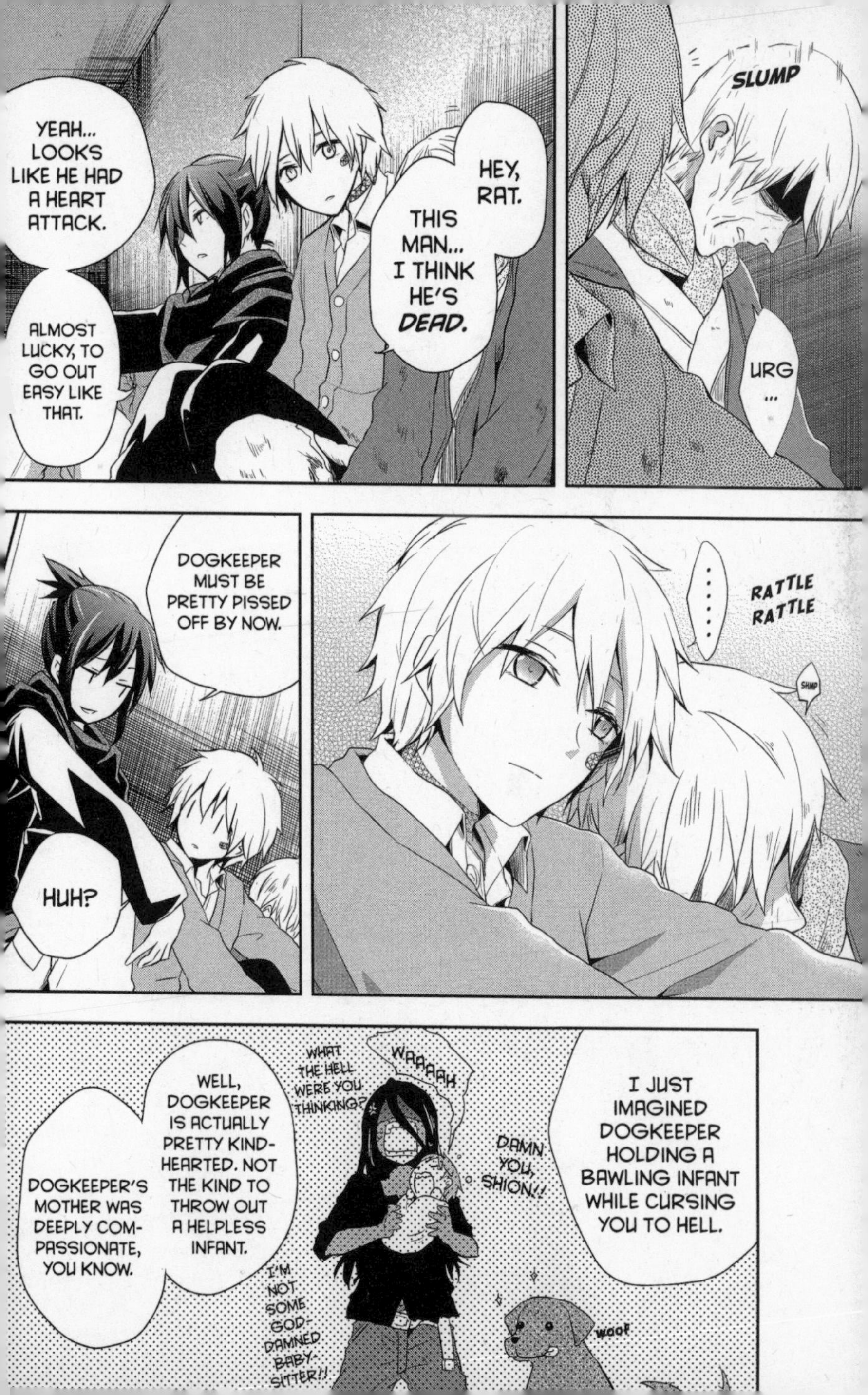
SLUMP
URG...
HEY, RAT.
THIS MAN... I THINK HE'S *DEAD.*
YEAH... LOOKS LIKE HE HAD A HEART ATTACK.
ALMOST LUCKY, TO GO OUT EASY LIKE THAT.
......
RATTLE RATTLE
DOGKEEPER MUST BE PRETTY PISSED OFF BY NOW.
HUH?
I JUST IMAGINED DOGKEEPER HOLDING A BAWLING INFANT WHILE CURSING YOU TO HELL.
WAAAAAH
WHAT THE HELL WERE YOU THINKING?
DAMN YOU, SHION!!
WOOF
I'M NOT SOME GOD-DAMNED BABY-SITTER!!
WELL, DOGKEEPER IS ACTUALLY PRETTY KIND-HEARTED. NOT THE KIND TO THROW OUT A HELPLESS INFANT.
DOGKEEPER'S MOTHER WAS DEEPLY COM-PASSIONATE, YOU KNOW.

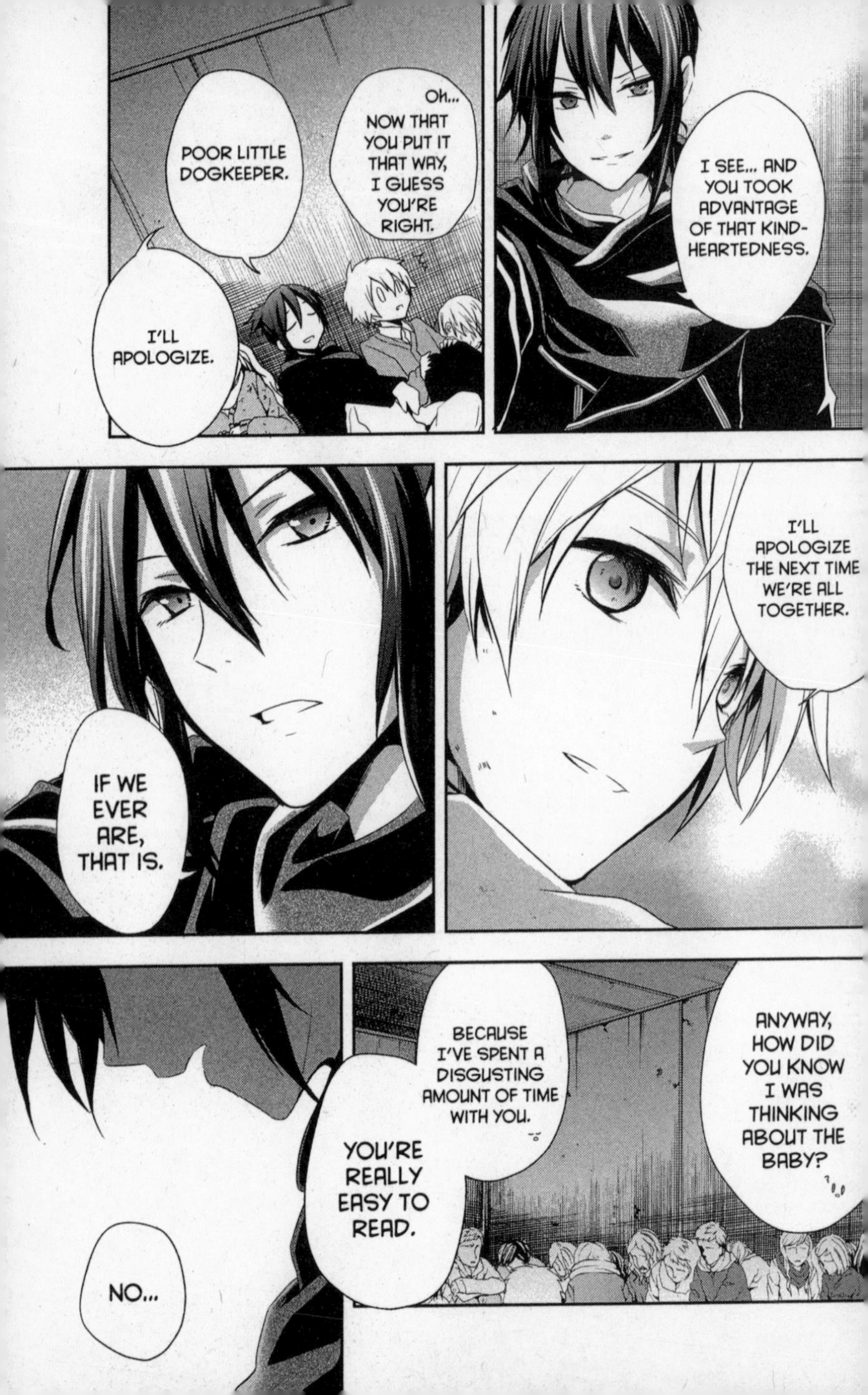
I SEE... AND YOU TOOK ADVANTAGE OF THAT KIND-HEARTEDNESS.
Oh... NOW THAT YOU PUT IT THAT WAY, I GUESS YOU'RE RIGHT.
POOR LITTLE DOGKEEPER.
I'LL APOLOGIZE.
I'LL APOLOGIZE THE NEXT TIME WE'RE ALL TOGETHER.
IF WE EVER ARE, THAT IS.
ANYWAY, HOW DID YOU KNOW I WAS THINKING ABOUT THE BABY?
BECAUSE I'VE SPENT A DISGUSTING AMOUNT OF TIME WITH YOU.
YOU'RE REALLY EASY TO READ.
NO...

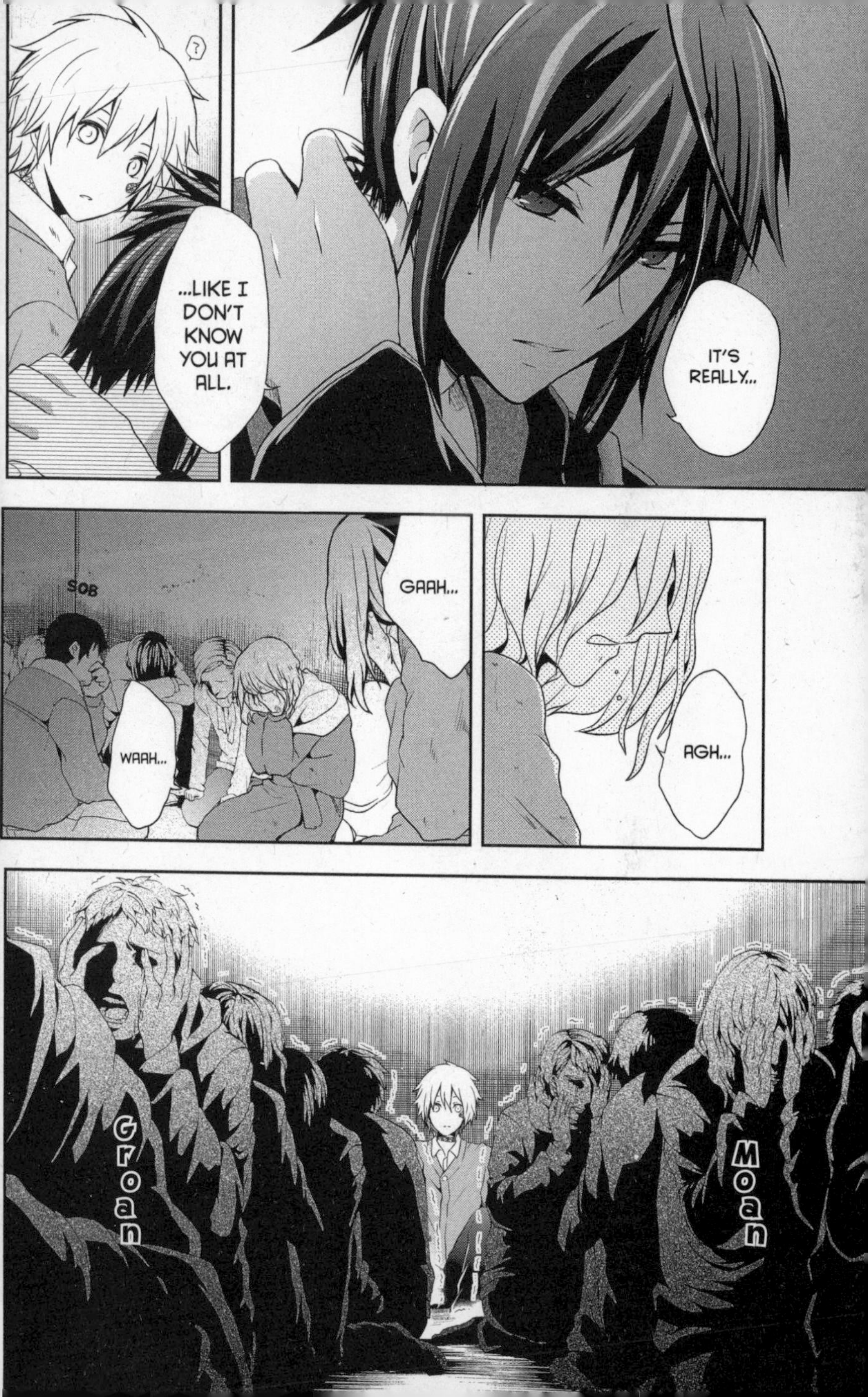
IT'S REALLY...
?
...LIKE I DON'T KNOW YOU AT ALL.
AGH...
GAAH...
SOB
WAAH...
Moan
Groan

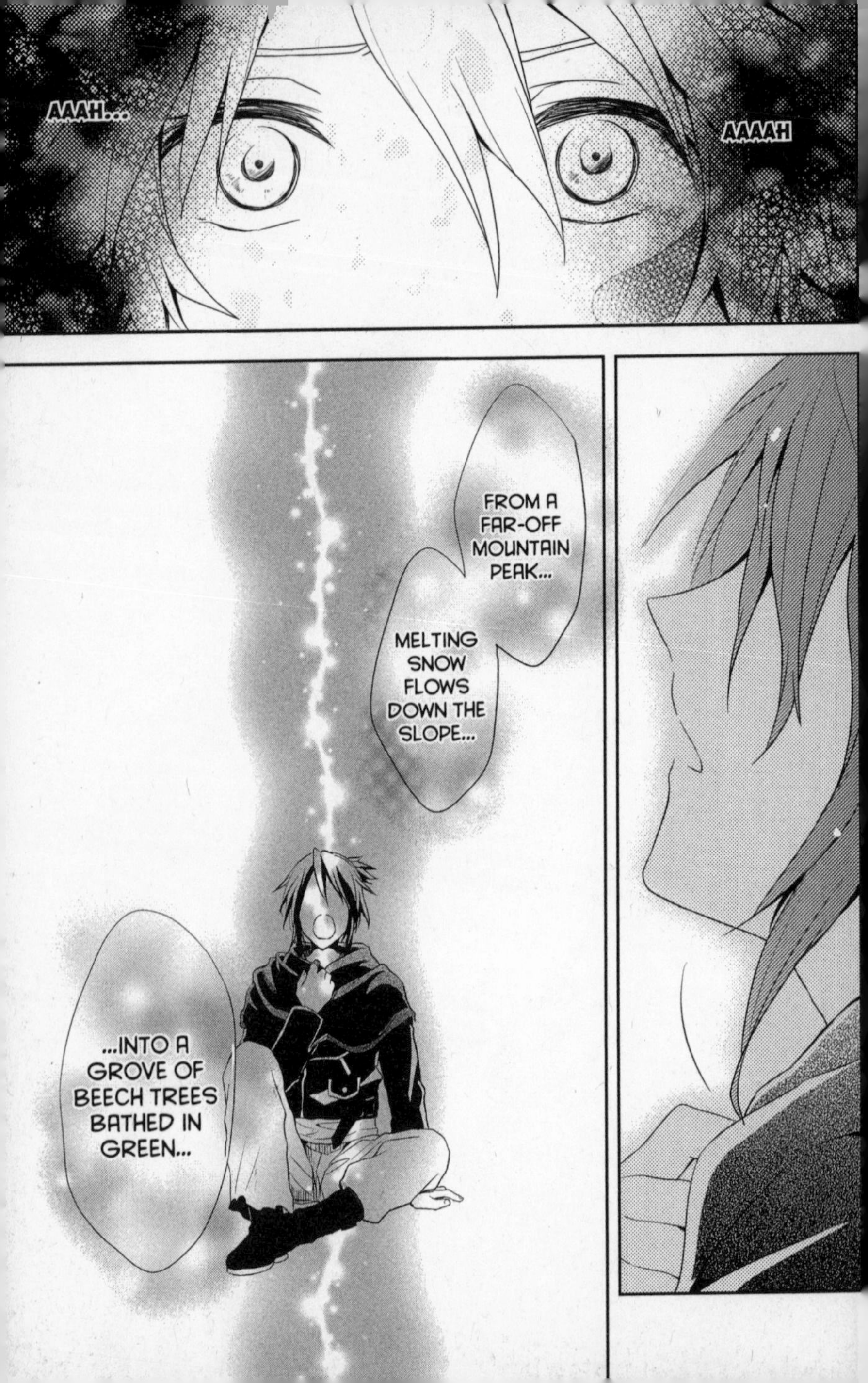
AAAAH
AAAH...
FROM A FAR-OFF MOUNTAIN PEAK...
MELTING SNOW FLOWS DOWN THE SLOPE...
...INTO A GROVE OF BEECH TREES BATHED IN GREEN...

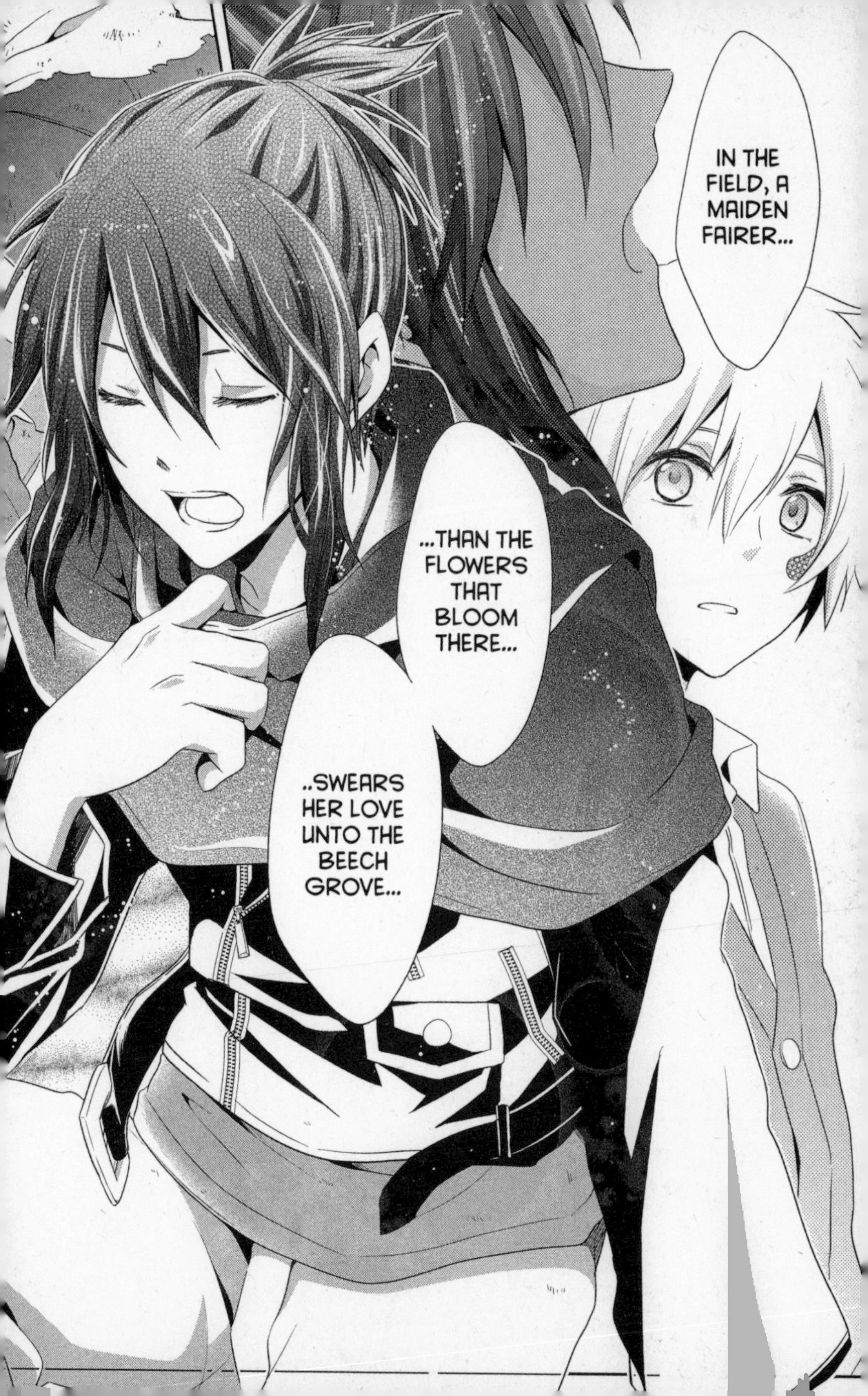
IN THE FIELD, A MAIDEN FAIRER...
...THAN THE FLOWERS THAT BLOOM THERE...
..SWEARS HER LOVE UNTO THE BEECH GROVE...

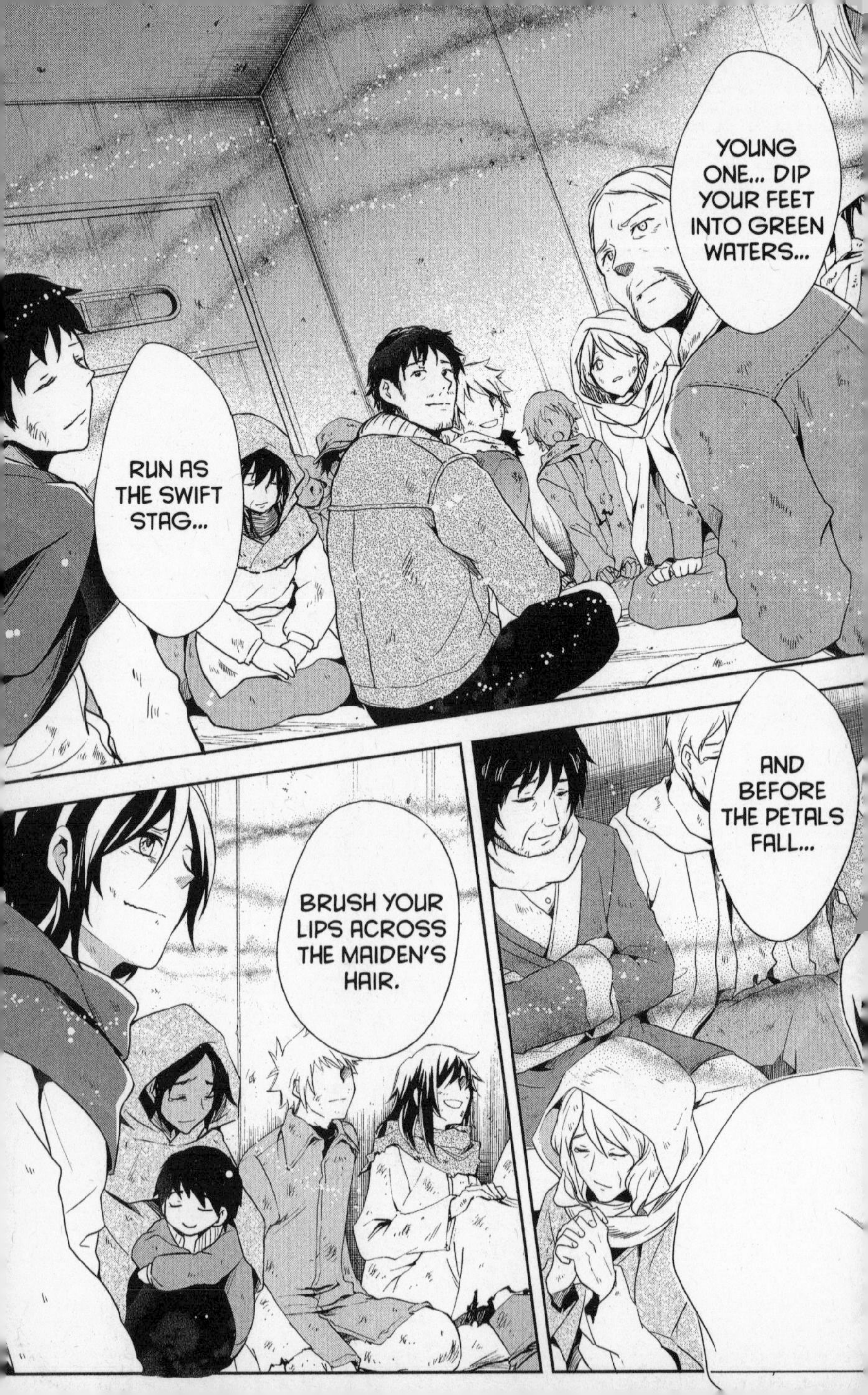
YOUNG ONE... DIP YOUR FEET INTO GREEN WATERS...
RUN AS THE SWIFT STAG...
AND BEFORE THE PETALS FALL...
BRUSH YOUR LIPS ACROSS THE MAIDEN'S HAIR.

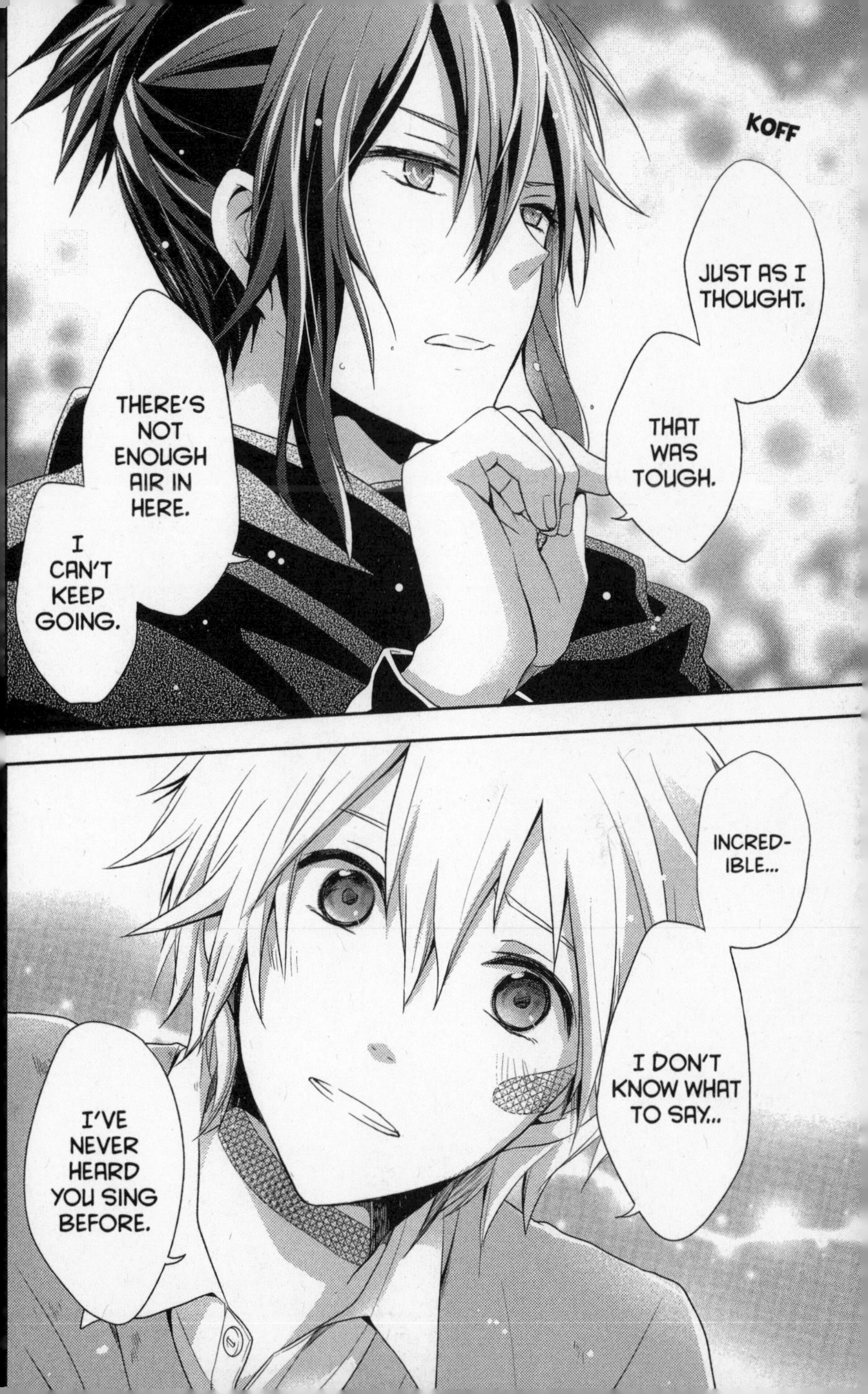
KOFF
JUST AS I THOUGHT.
THAT WAS TOUGH.
THERE'S NOT ENOUGH AIR IN HERE.
I CAN'T KEEP GOING.
INCRED-IBLE...
I DON'T KNOW WHAT TO SAY...
I'VE NEVER HEARD YOU SING BEFORE.

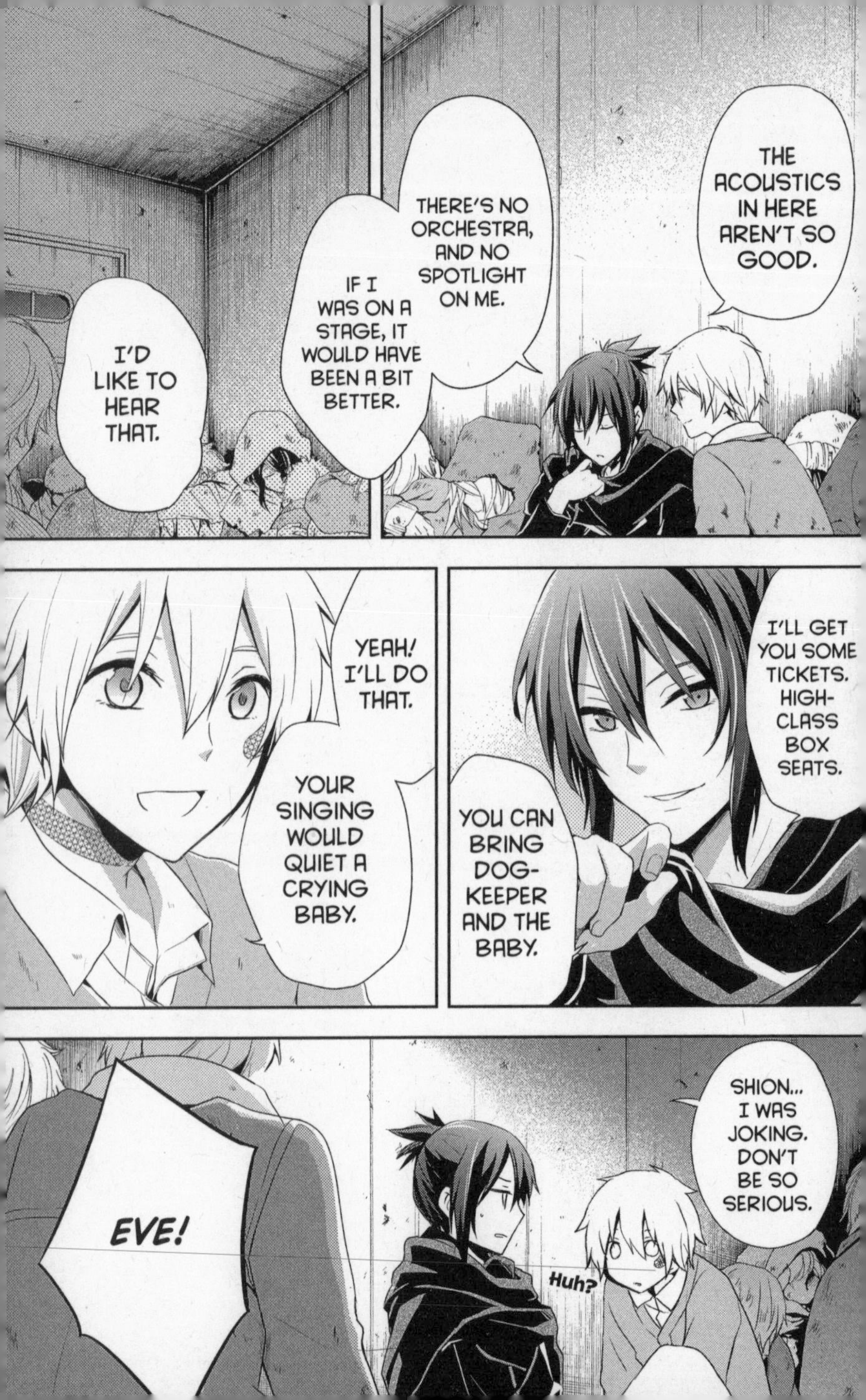
THE ACOUSTICS IN HERE AREN'T SO GOOD.
THERE'S NO ORCHESTRA, AND NO SPOTLIGHT ON ME.
IF I WAS ON A STAGE, IT WOULD HAVE BEEN A BIT BETTER.
I'D LIKE TO HEAR THAT.
I'LL GET YOU SOME TICKETS. HIGH-CLASS BOX SEATS.
YOU CAN BRING DOG-KEEPER AND THE BABY.
YEAH! I'LL DO THAT.
YOUR SINGING WOULD QUIET A CRYING BABY.
SHION... I WAS JOKING. DON'T BE SO SERIOUS.
Huh?
EVE!

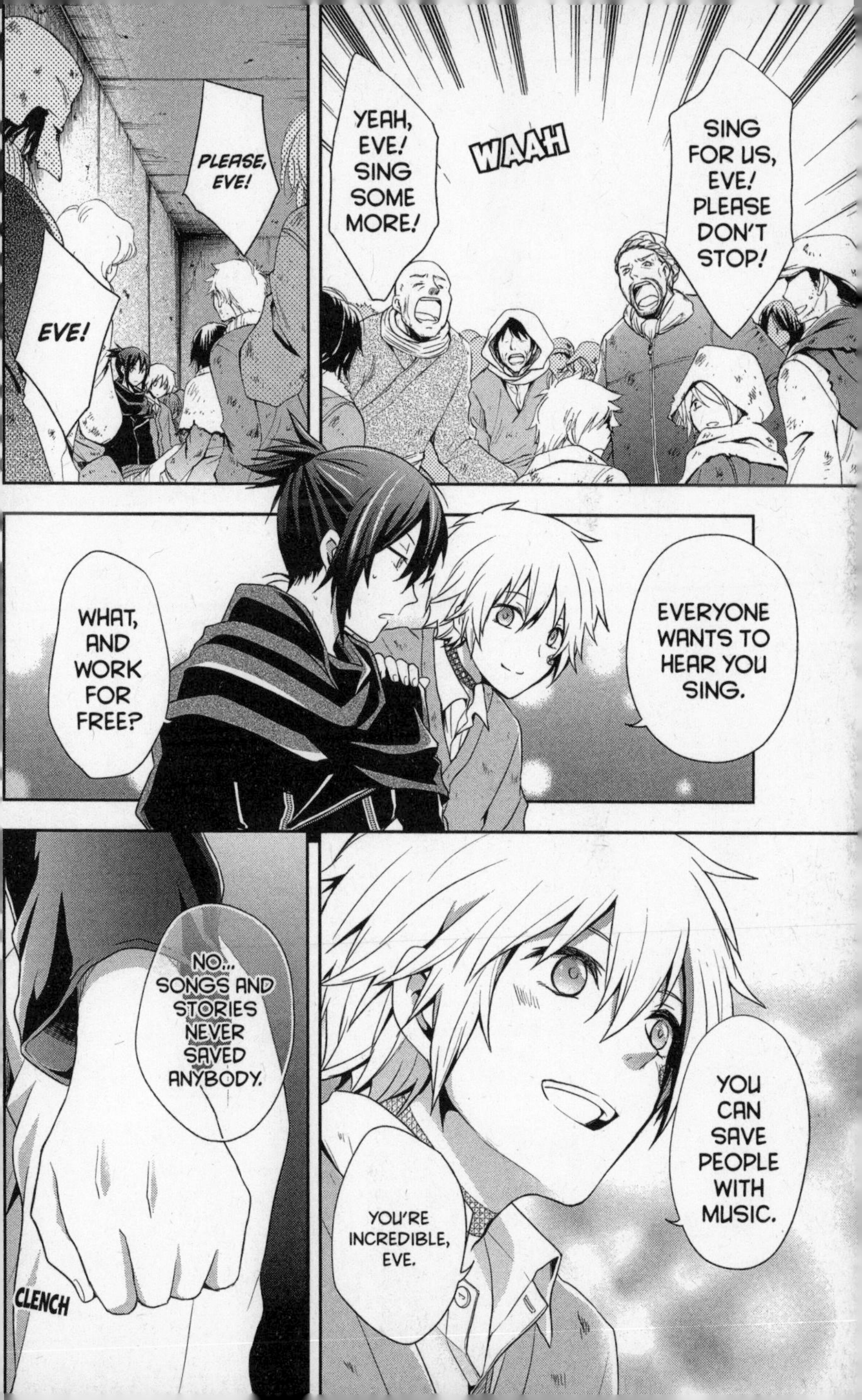
SING FOR US, EVE! PLEASE DON'T STOP!
WAAH
YEAH, EVE! SING SOME MORE!
PLEASE, EVE!
EVE!
EVERYONE WANTS TO HEAR YOU SING.
WHAT, AND WORK FOR FREE?
YOU CAN SAVE PEOPLE WITH MUSIC.
YOU'RE INCREDIBLE, EVE.
NO... SONGS AND STORIES NEVER SAVED ANYBODY.
CLENCH

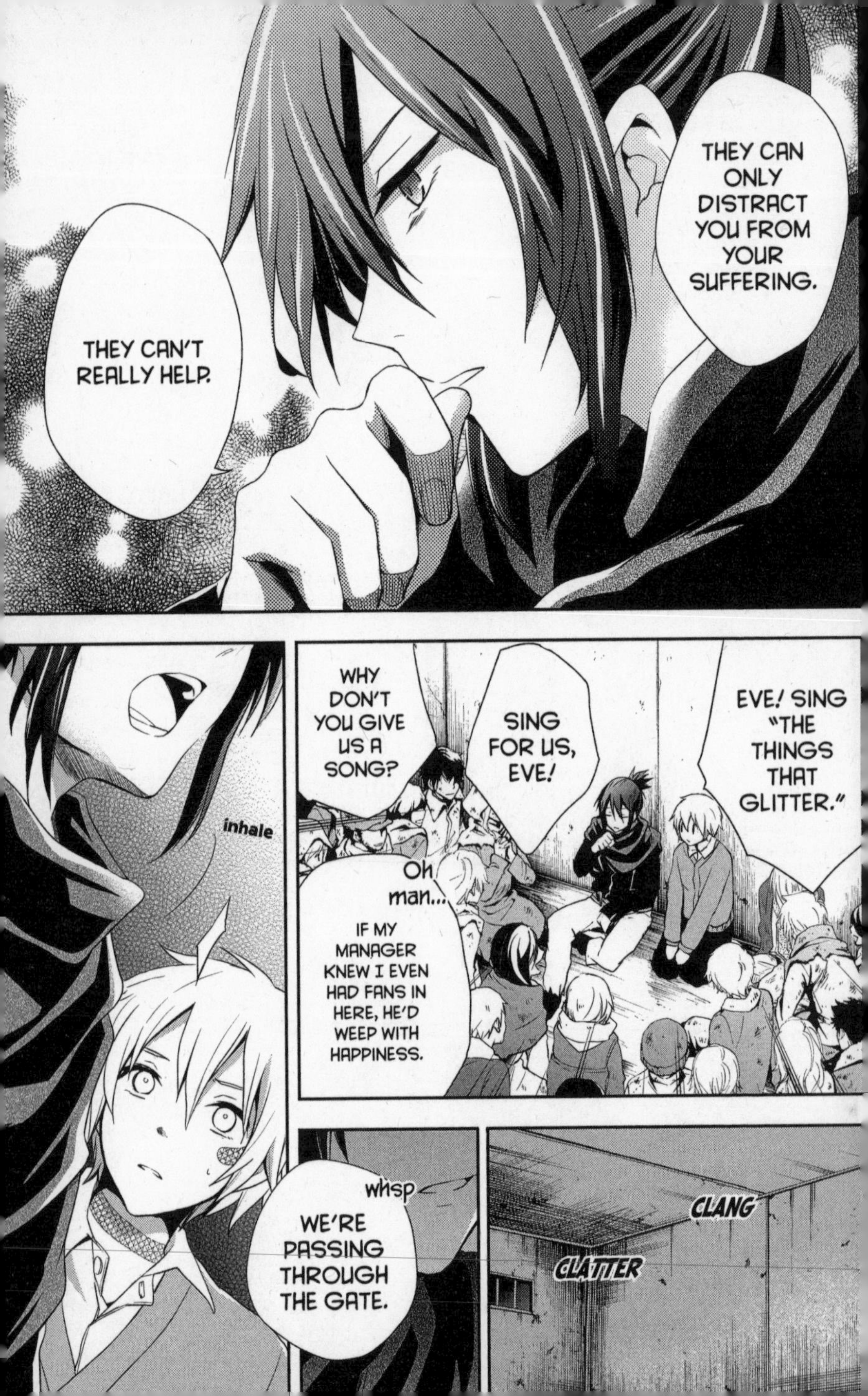
THEY CAN ONLY DISTRACT YOU FROM YOUR SUFFERING.
THEY CAN'T REALLY HELP.
EVE! SING "THE THINGS THAT GLITTER."
SING FOR US, EVE!
WHY DON'T YOU GIVE US A SONG?
Oh man...
IF MY MANAGER KNEW I EVEN HAD FANS IN HERE, HE'D WEEP WITH HAPPINESS.
CLANG
CLATTER
whsp
WE'RE PASSING THROUGH THE GATE.
inhale

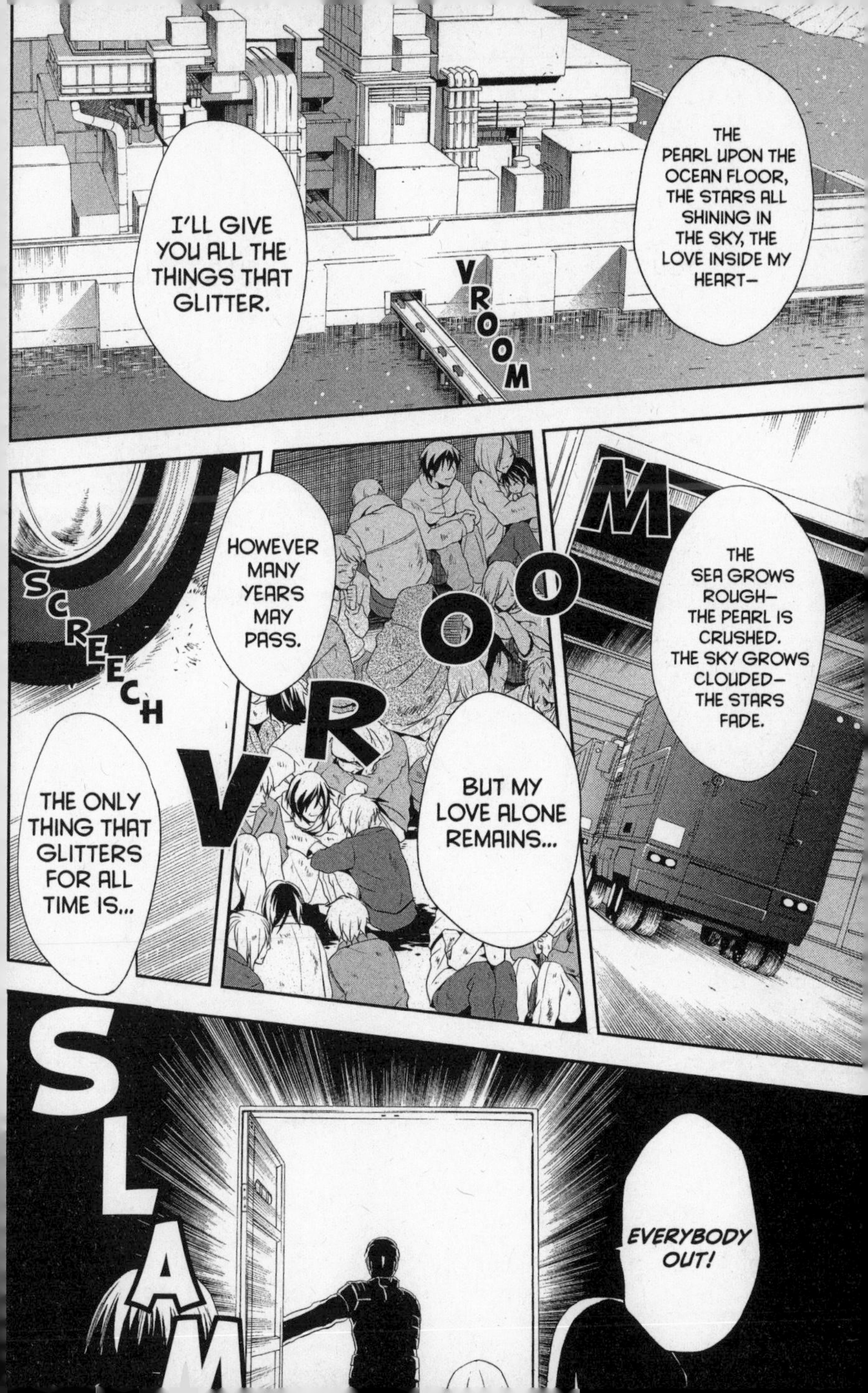
THE PEARL UPON THE OCEAN FLOOR, THE STARS ALL SHINING IN THE SKY, THE LOVE INSIDE MY HEART—
VROOM
I'LL GIVE YOU ALL THE THINGS THAT GLITTER.
THE SEA GROWS ROUGH— THE PEARL IS CRUSHED. THE SKY GROWS CLOUDED— THE STARS FADE.
VROOM
HOWEVER MANY YEARS MAY PASS.
BUT MY LOVE ALONE REMAINS...
SCREECH
THE ONLY THING THAT GLITTERS FOR ALL TIME IS...
EVERYBODY OUT!
SLAM

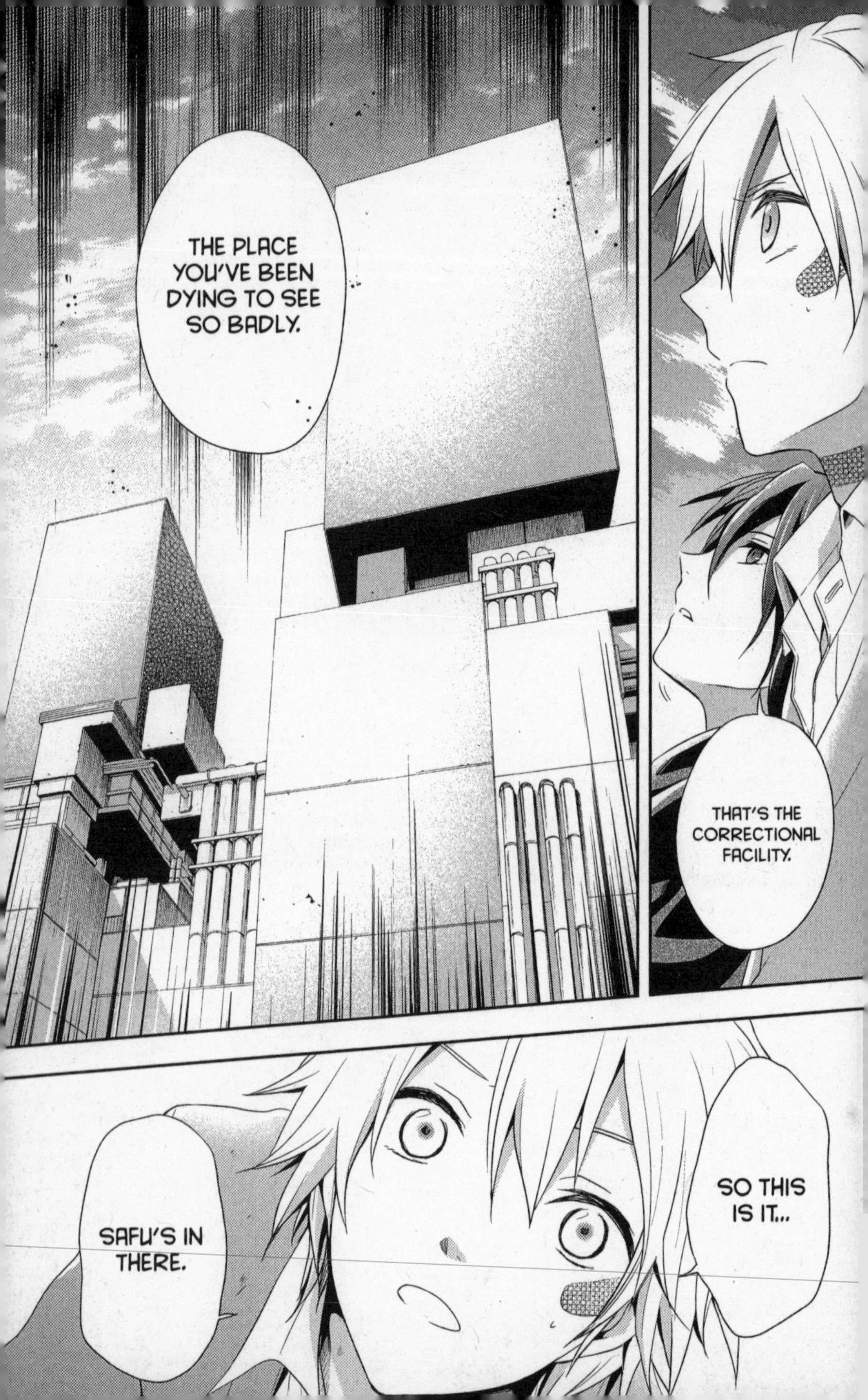
THAT'S THE CORRECTIONAL FACILITY.
THE PLACE YOU'VE BEEN DYING TO SEE SO BADLY.
SO THIS IS IT...
SAFU'S IN THERE.

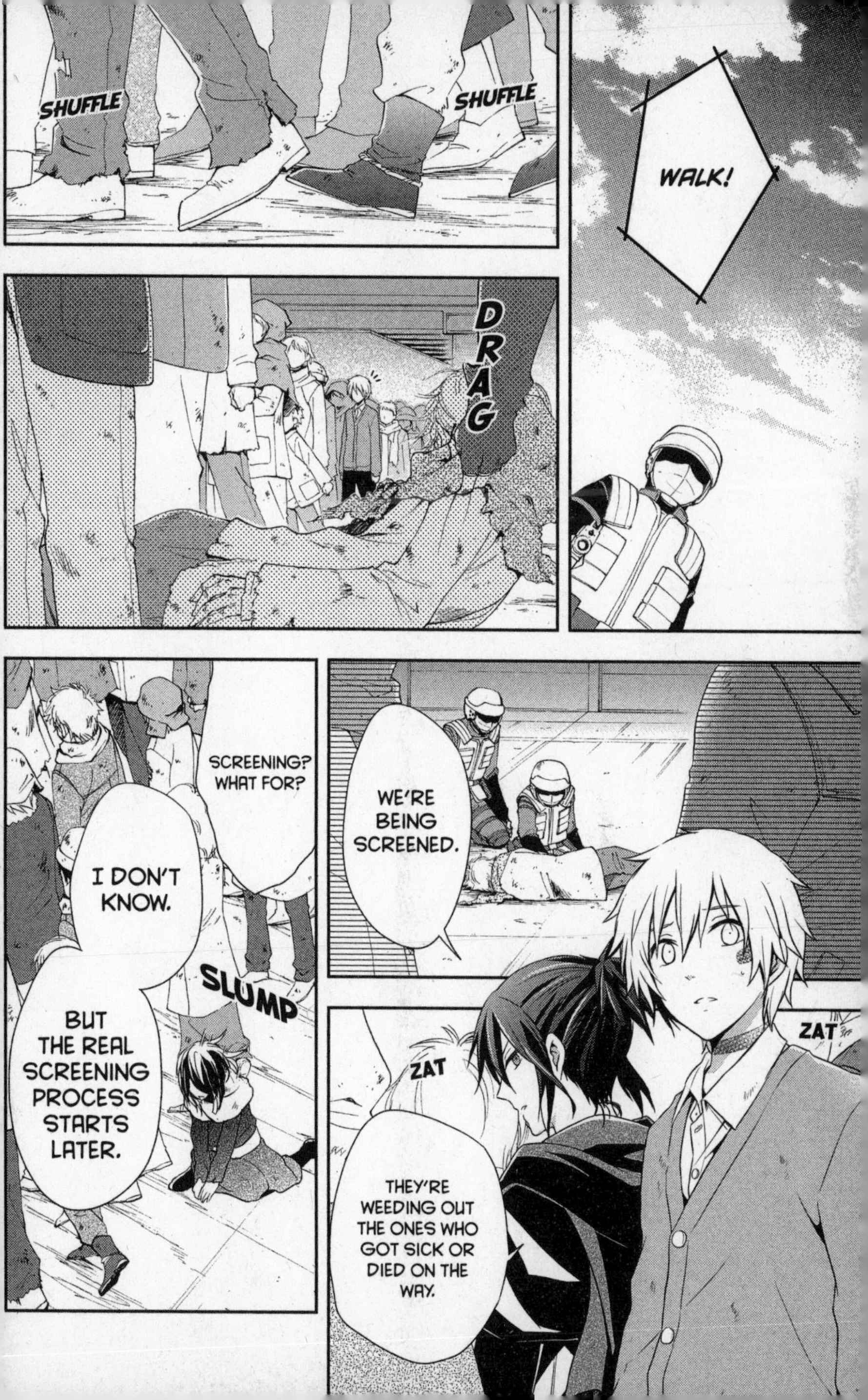
WALK!
SHUFFLE
SHUFFLE
DRAG
WE'RE BEING SCREENED.
ZAT
ZAT
THEY'RE WEEDING OUT THE ONES WHO GOT SICK OR DIED ON THE WAY.
SCREENING? WHAT FOR?
I DON'T KNOW.
SLUMP
BUT THE REAL SCREENING PROCESS STARTS LATER.

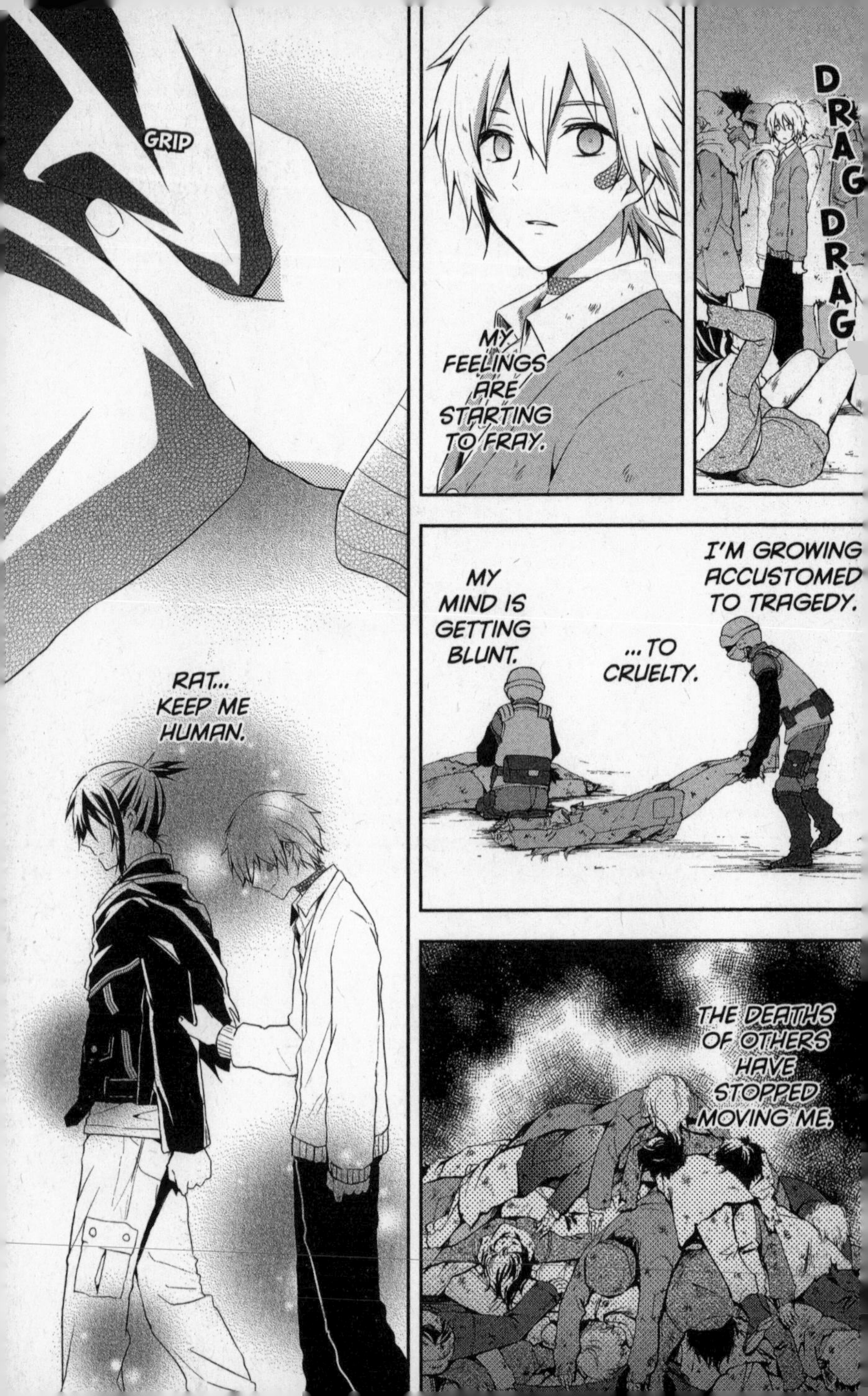
DRAG DRAG
MY FEELINGS ARE STARTING TO FRAY.
I'M GROWING ACCUSTOMED TO TRAGEDY.
...TO CRUELTY.
MY MIND IS GETTING BLUNT.
THE DEATHS OF OTHERS HAVE STOPPED MOVING ME.
GRIP
RAT... KEEP ME HUMAN.

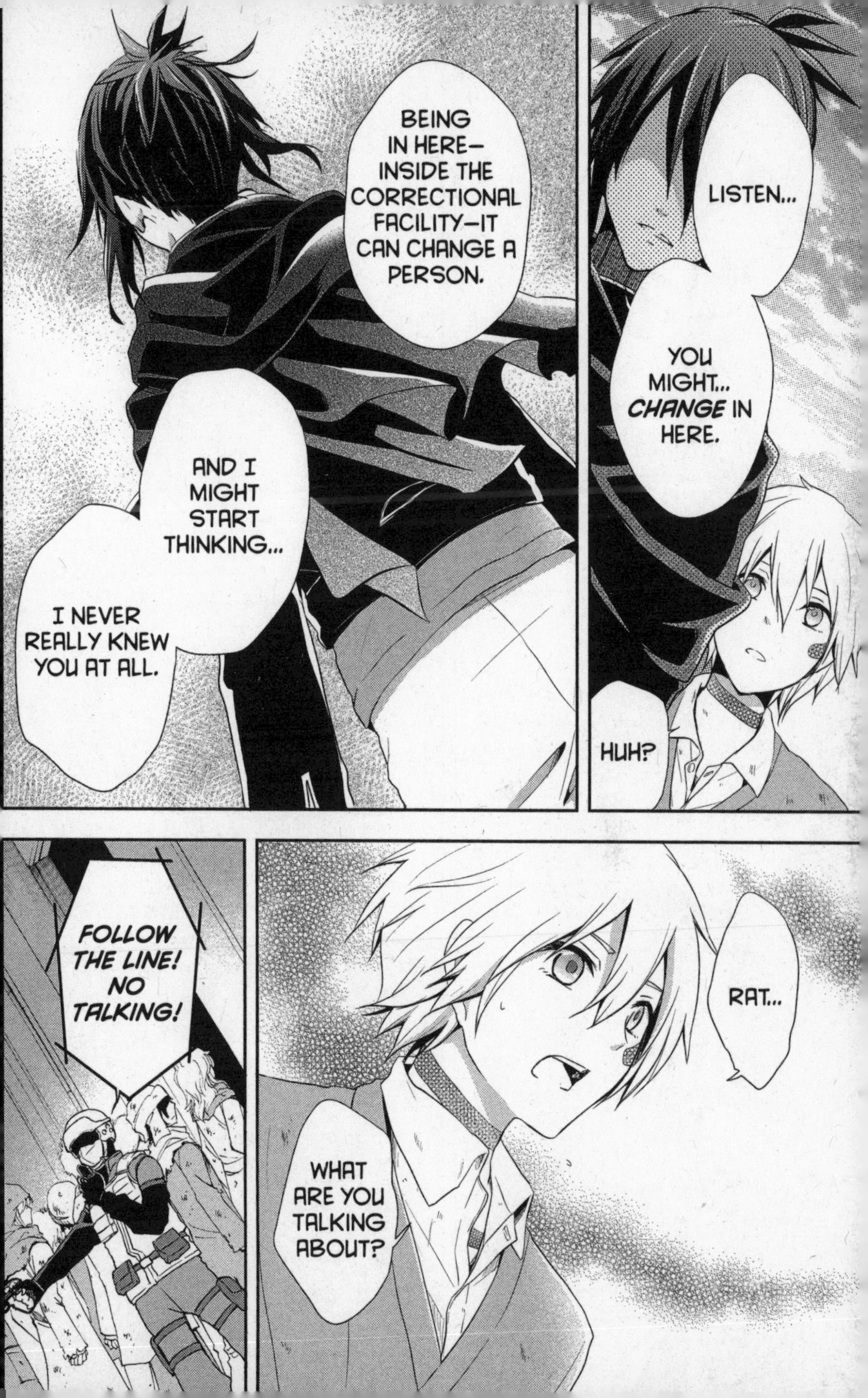
LISTEN...
YOU MIGHT... *CHANGE* IN HERE.
HUH?
BEING IN HERE— INSIDE THE CORRECTIONAL FACILITY—IT CAN CHANGE A PERSON.
AND I MIGHT START THINKING...
I NEVER REALLY KNEW YOU AT ALL.
RAT...
WHAT ARE YOU TALKING ABOUT?
FOLLOW THE LINE! NO TALKING!

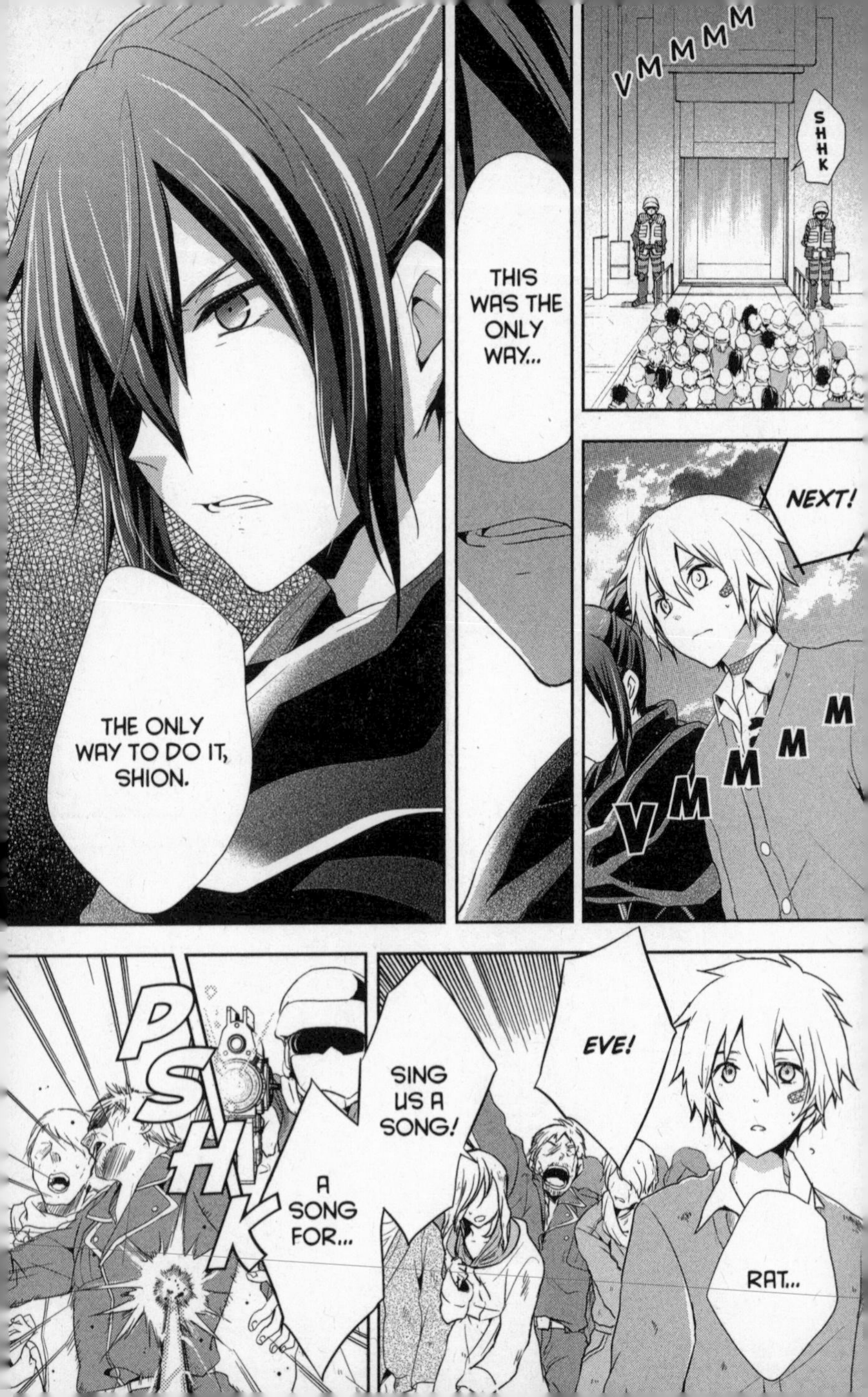
VMMMMM
SHHK
NEXT!
VMMMMM
THIS WAS THE ONLY WAY...
THE ONLY WAY TO DO IT, SHION.
EVE!
SING US A SONG!
A SONG FOR...
RAT...
PSHK

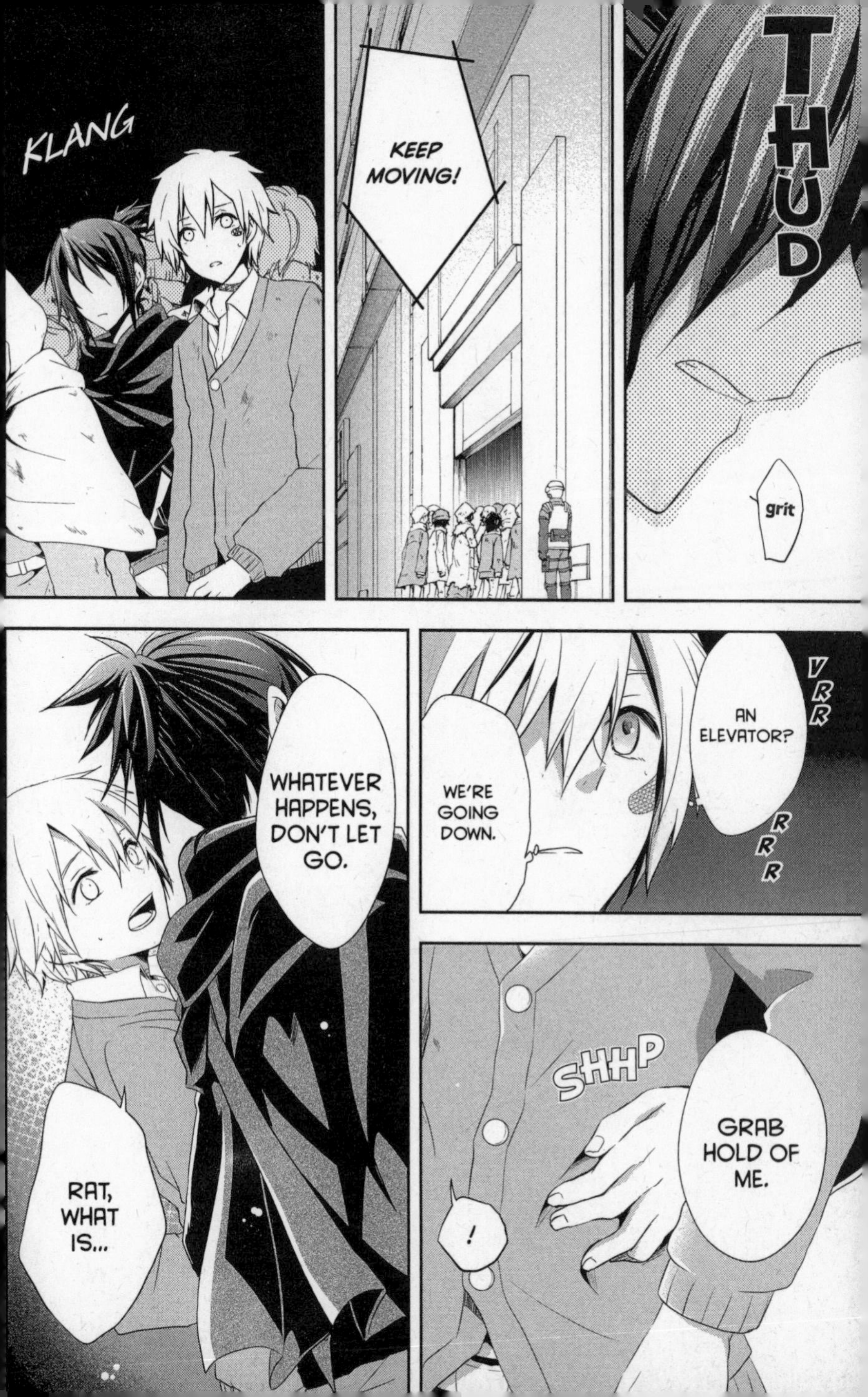
THUD
grit
KEEP MOVING!
KLANG
VRR
AN ELEVATOR?
RRR
WE'RE GOING DOWN.
GRAB HOLD OF ME.
SHHP
!
WHATEVER HAPPENS, DON'T LET GO.
RAT, WHAT IS...

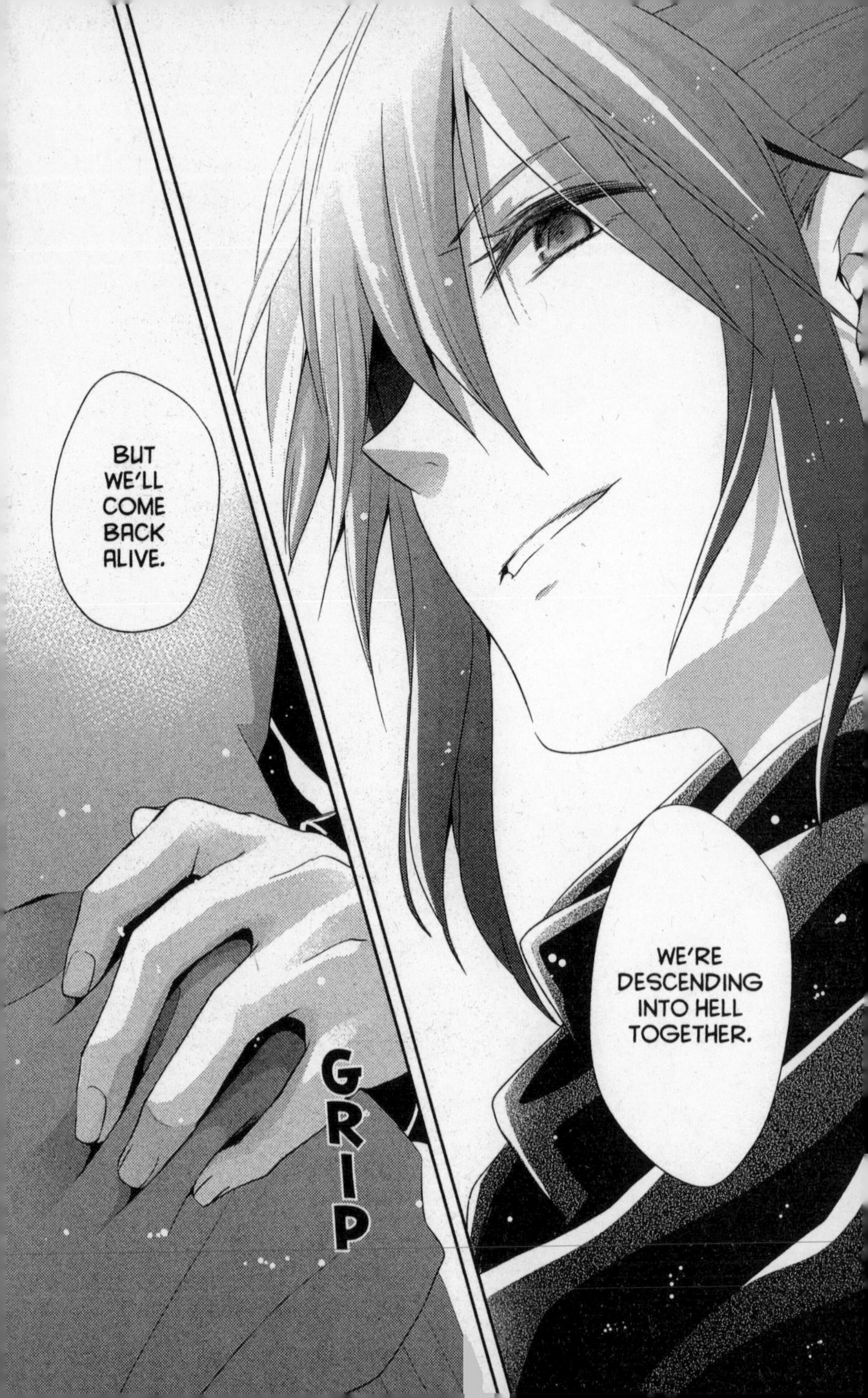
WE'RE DESCENDING INTO HELL TOGETHER.
BUT WE'LL COME BACK ALIVE.
GRIP

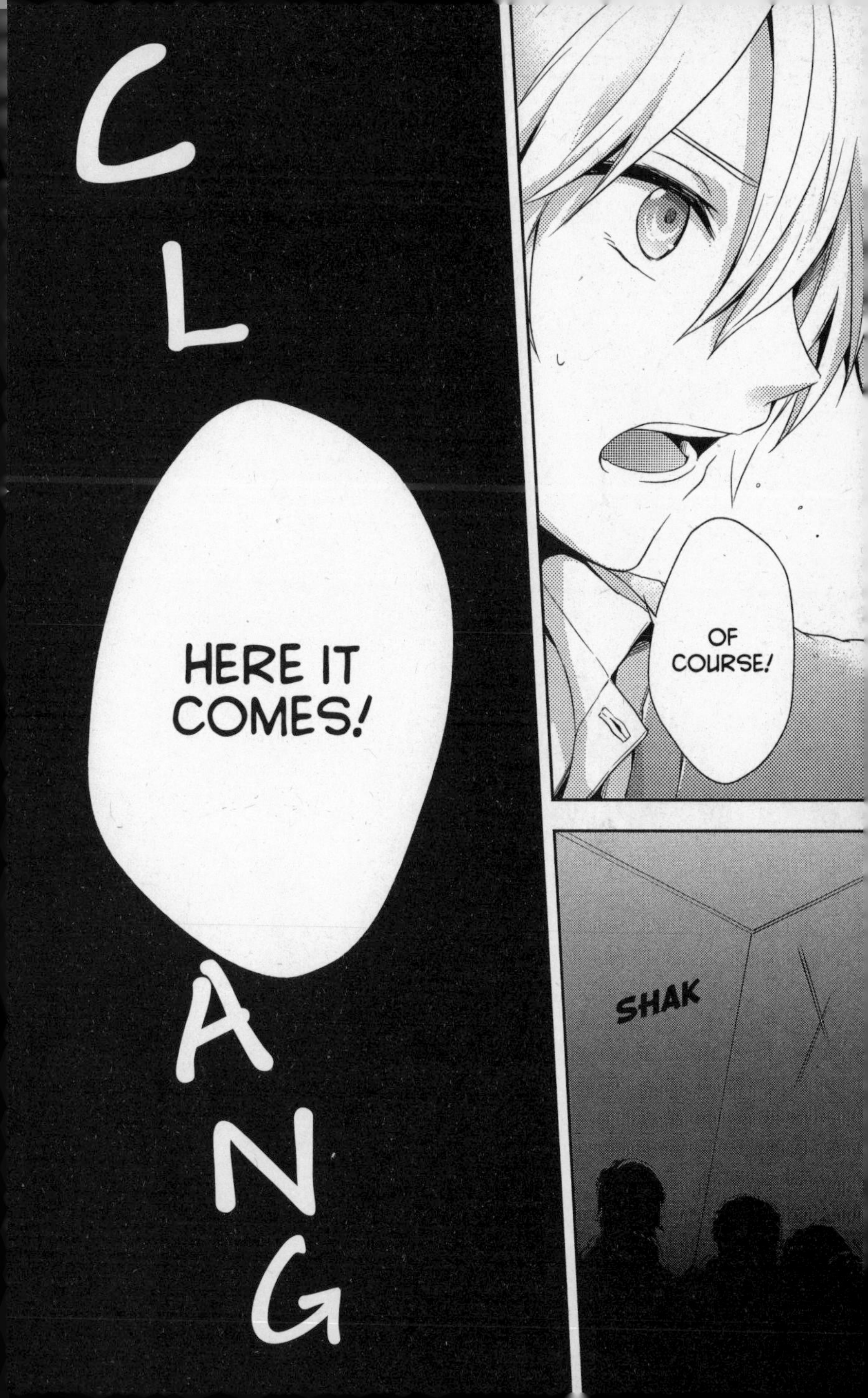
OF COURSE!
SHAK
HERE IT COMES!
CLANG

Chapter 18: That Which Is in the Abyss

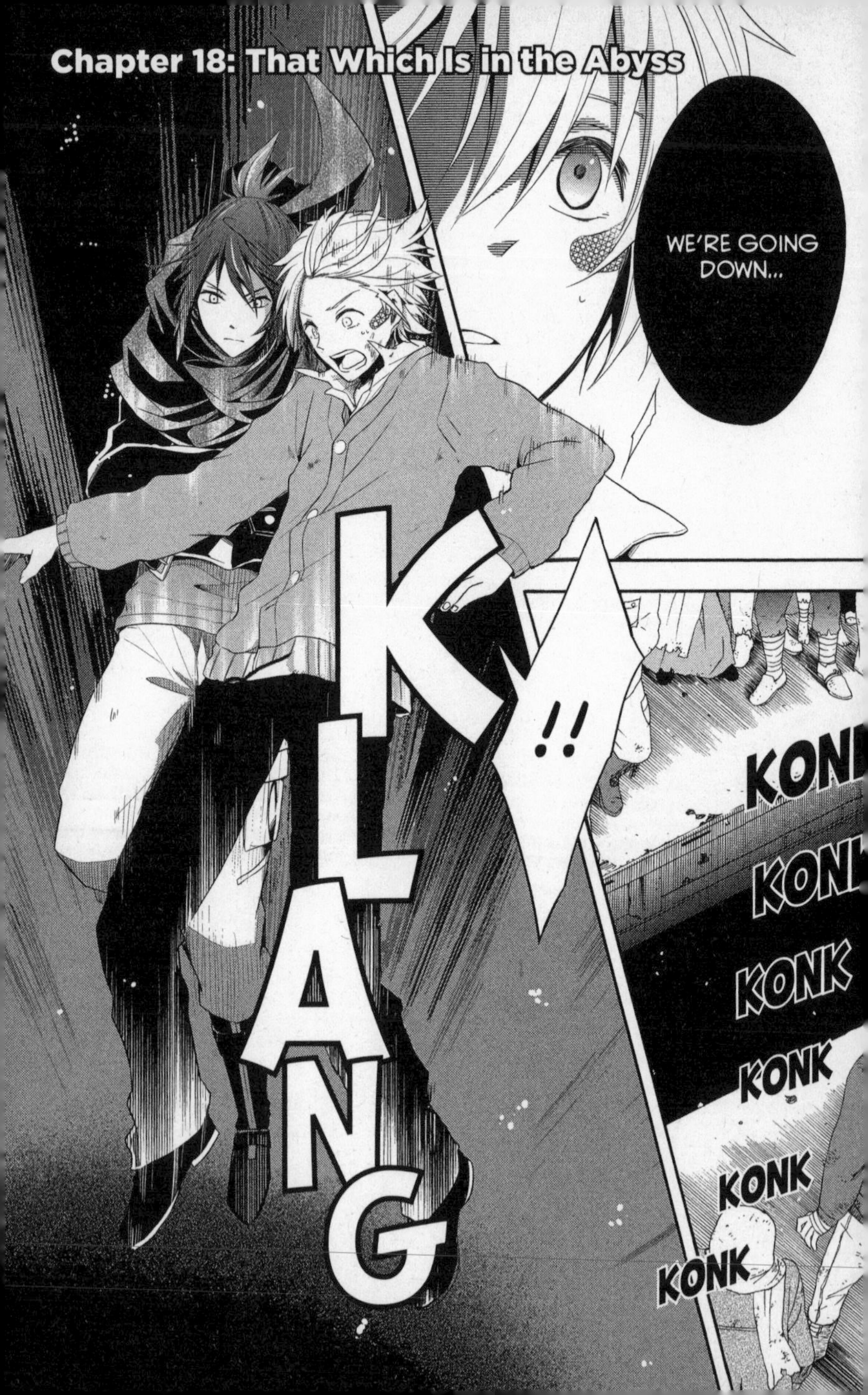

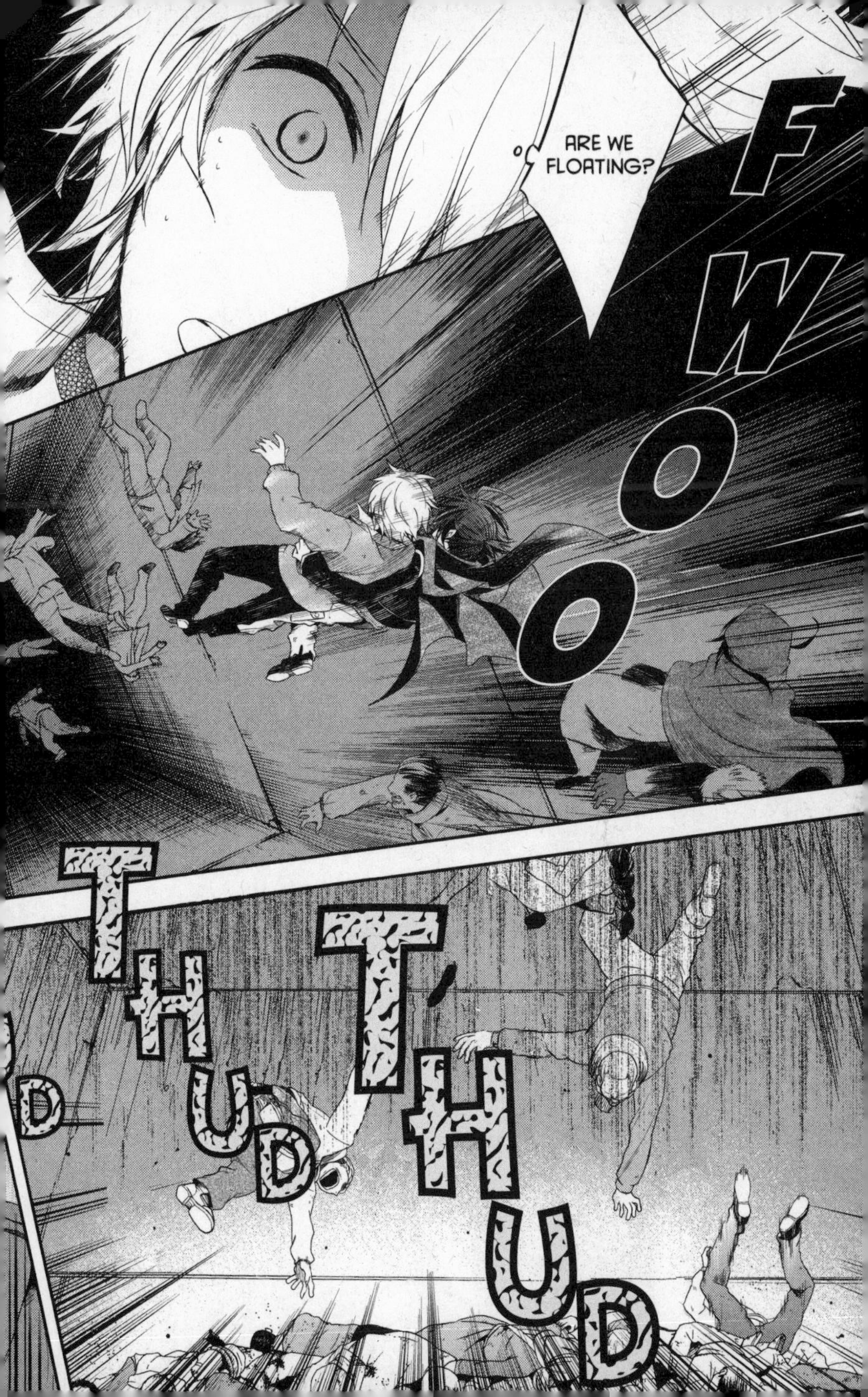
FWOOO
ARE WE FLOATING?
THUD
THUD
THUD

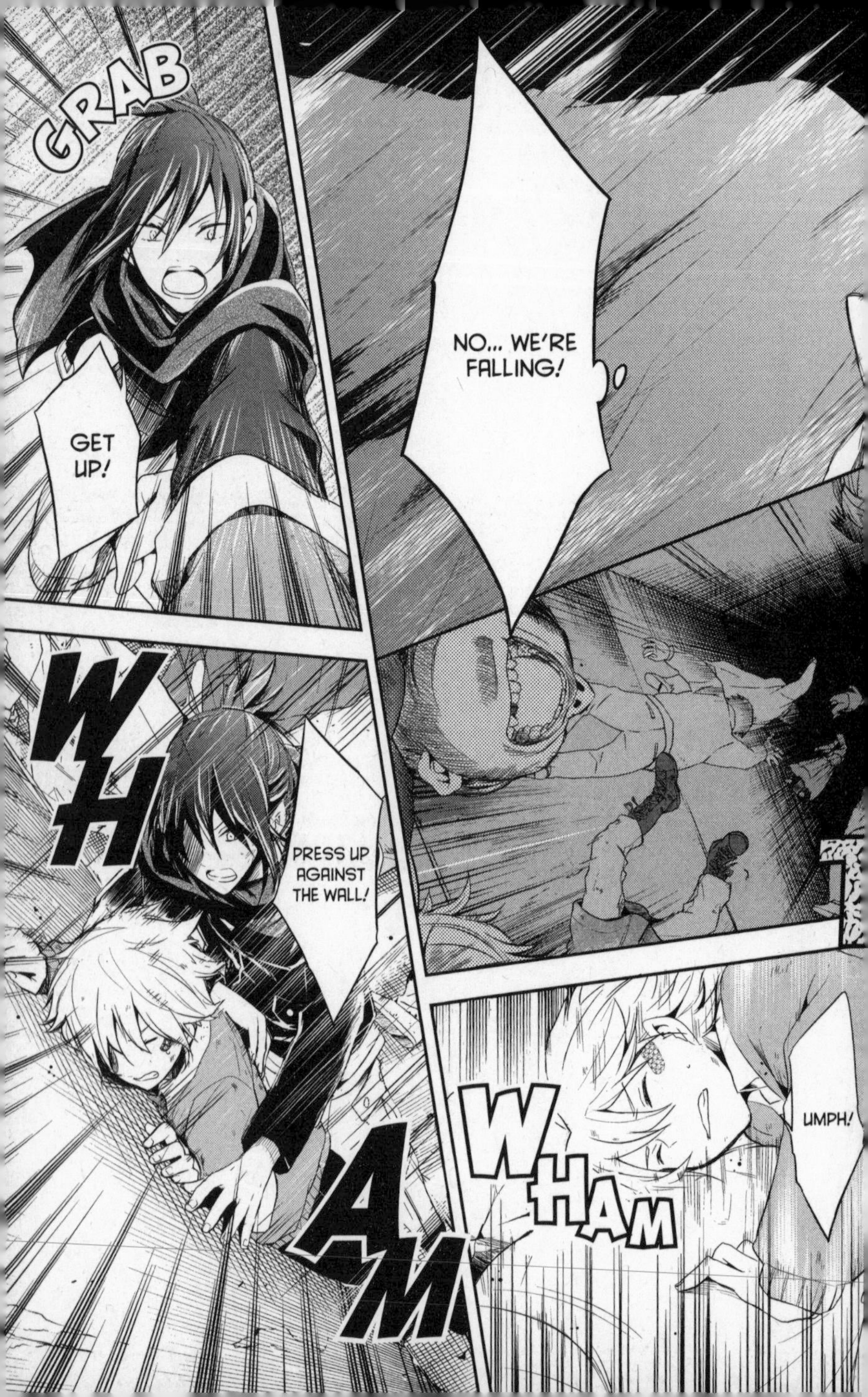
NO... WE'RE FALLING!
GRAB
GET UP!
WHAM
PRESS UP AGAINST THE WALL!
WHAM
UMPH!

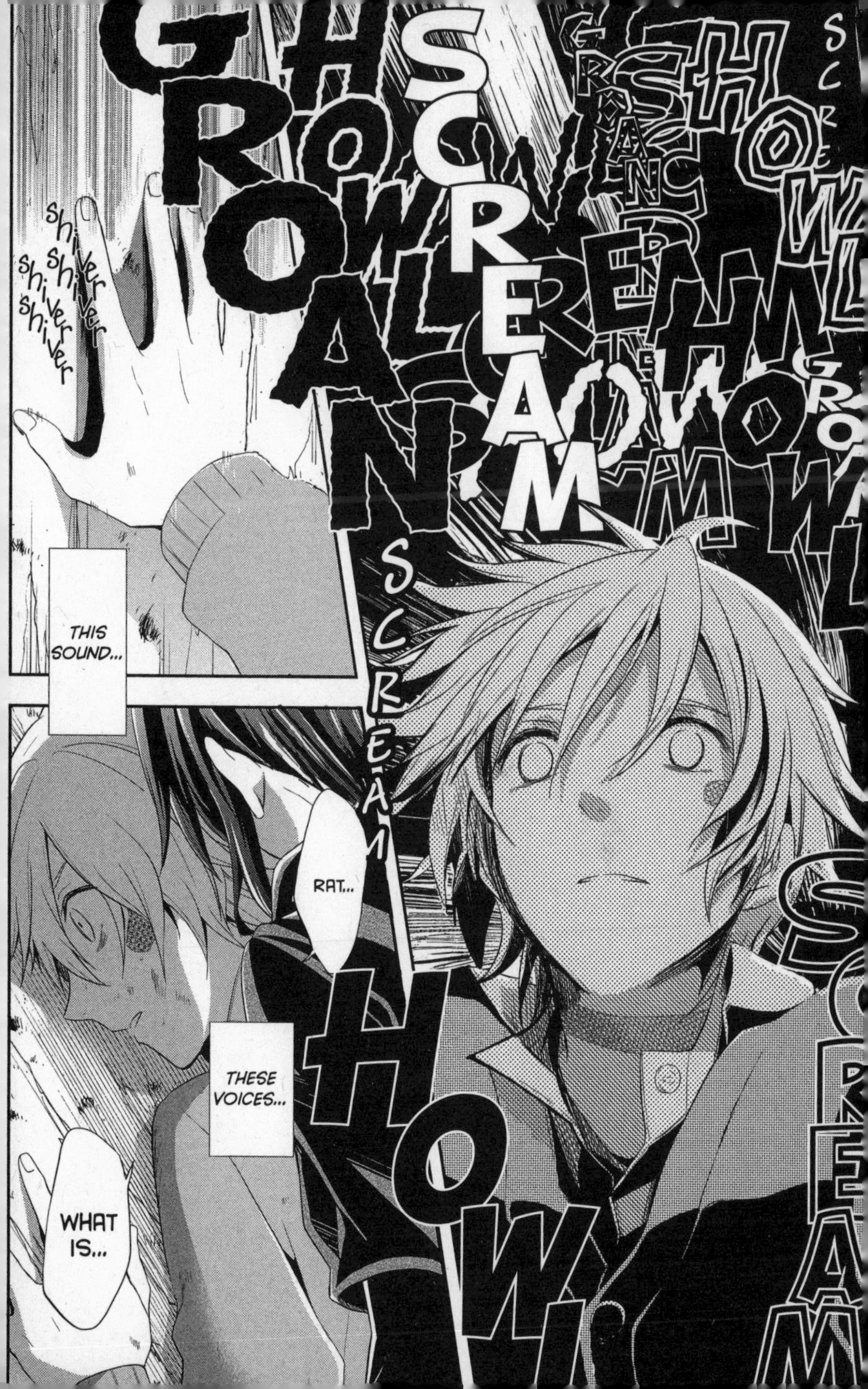
SCREAM
SCREAM
SCREAM
HOWL
RAT...
shiver shiver shiver shiver
THIS SOUND...
THESE VOICES...
WHAT IS...

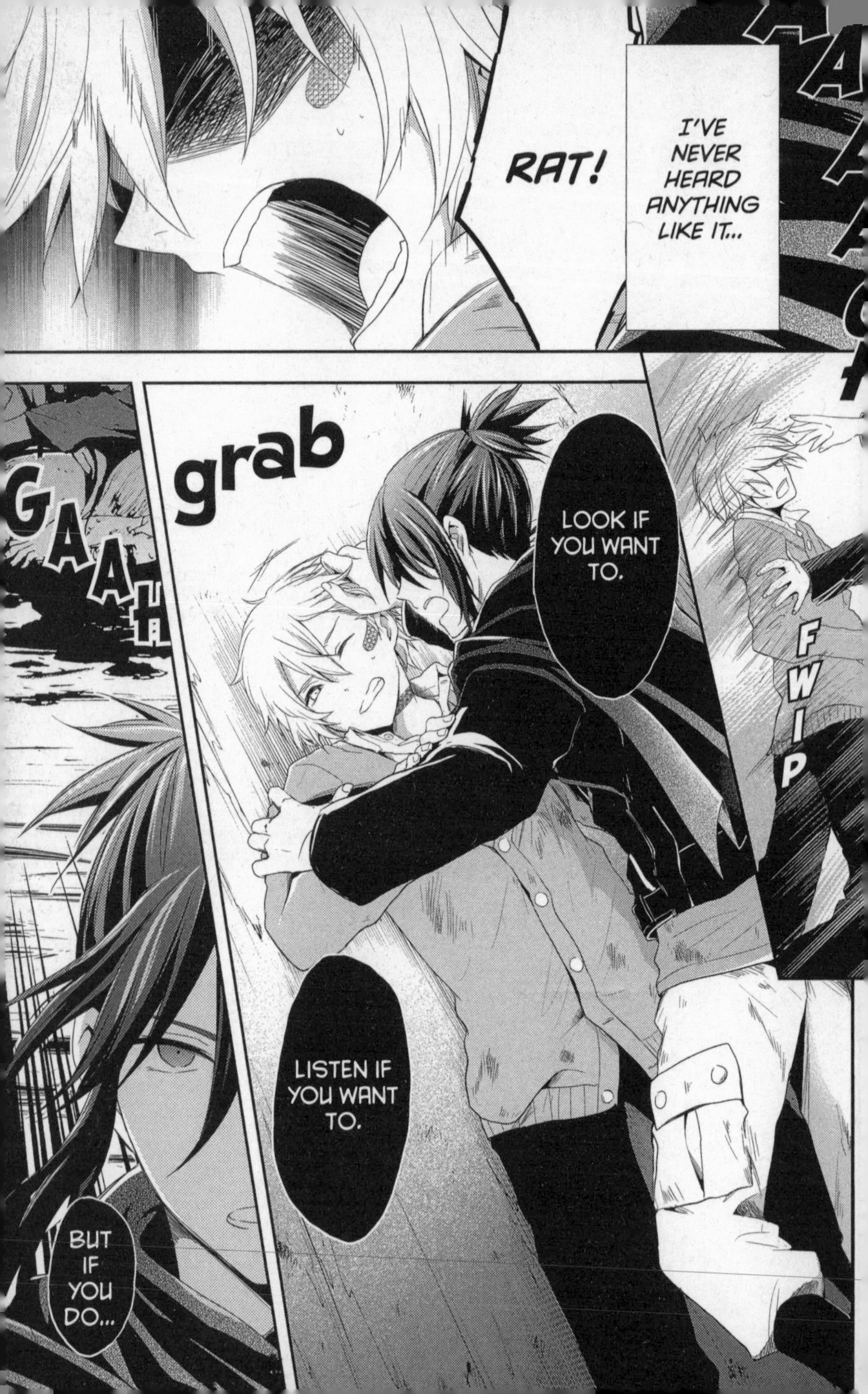
I'VE NEVER HEARD ANYTHING LIKE IT...
RAT!
FWIP
grab
LOOK IF YOU WANT TO.
LISTEN IF YOU WANT TO.
GAAh
BUT IF YOU DO...

GAAAAAH
YOU'LL HAVE NIGHTMARES ABOUT THIS FOR THE REST OF YOUR LIFE.

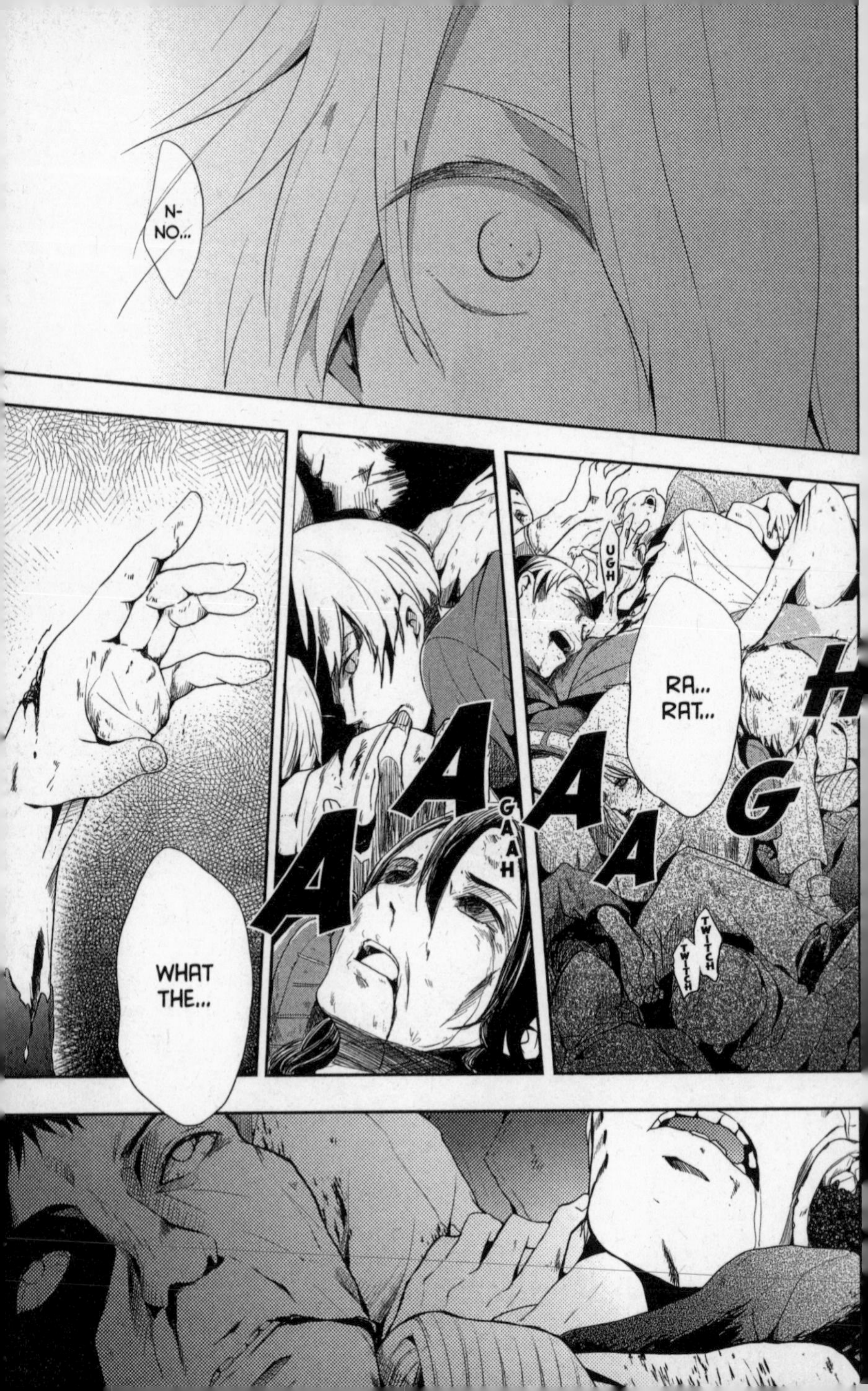
N-NO...
UGH
RA... RAT...
AAAAGH
TWITCH TWITCH
GAAH
WHAT THE...

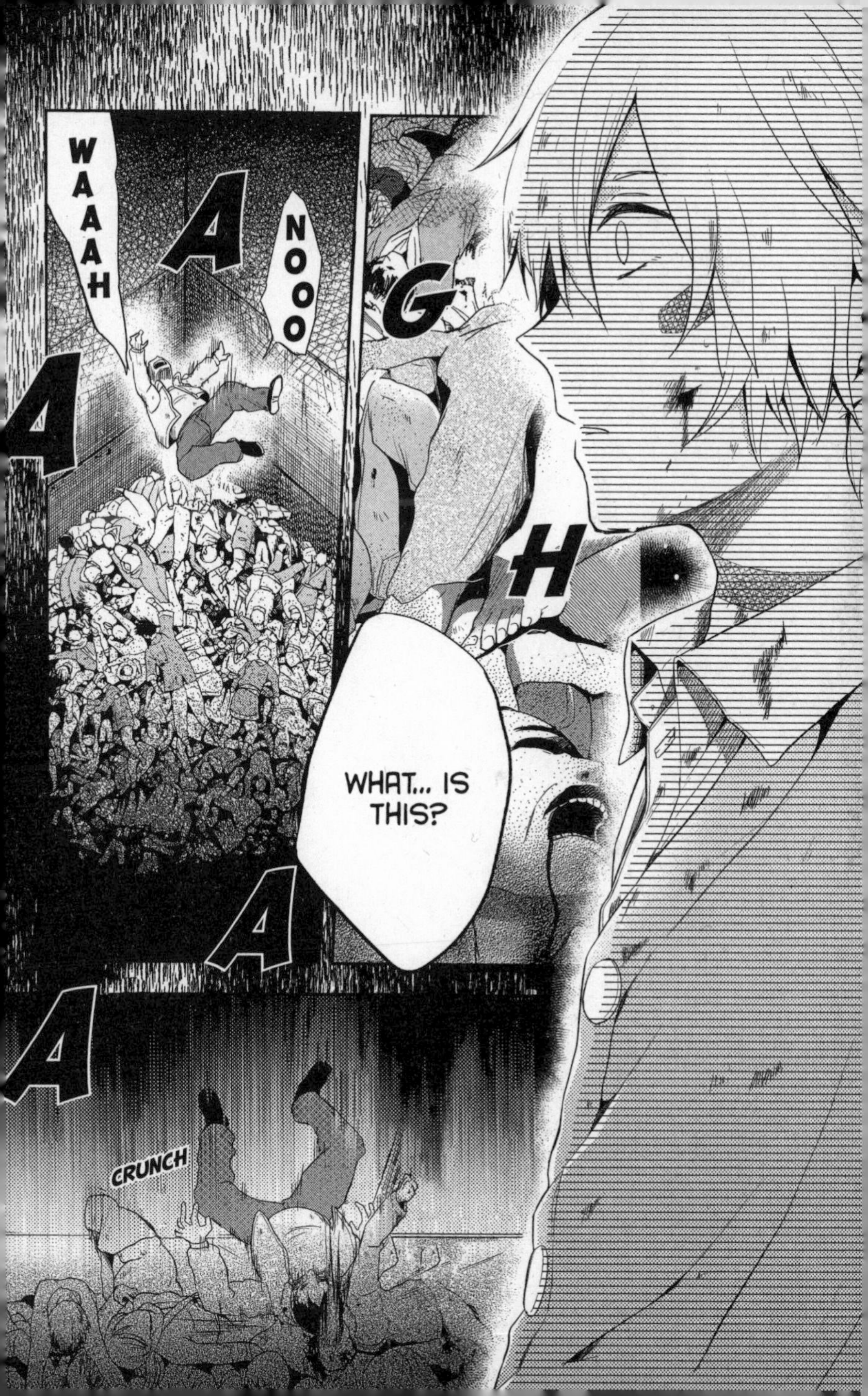
G
H
WHAT... IS THIS?
NOOO
A
WAAAH
A
A
A
CRUNCH

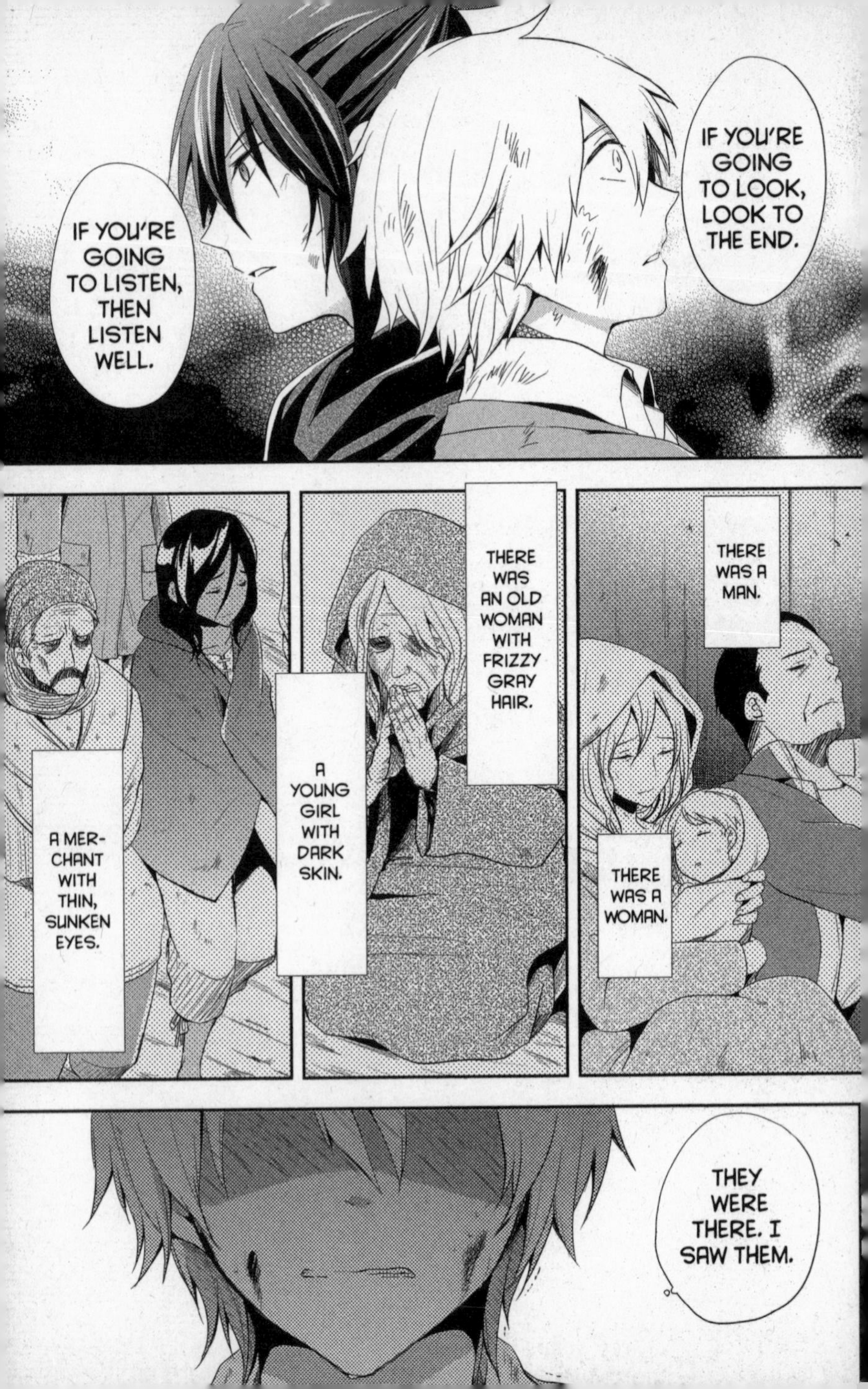
IF YOU'RE GOING TO LOOK, LOOK TO THE END.
IF YOU'RE GOING TO LISTEN, THEN LISTEN WELL.
THERE WAS A MAN.
THERE WAS A WOMAN.
THERE WAS AN OLD WOMAN WITH FRIZZY GRAY HAIR.
A YOUNG GIRL WITH DARK SKIN.
A MER-CHANT WITH THIN, SUNKEN EYES.
THEY WERE THERE. I SAW THEM.

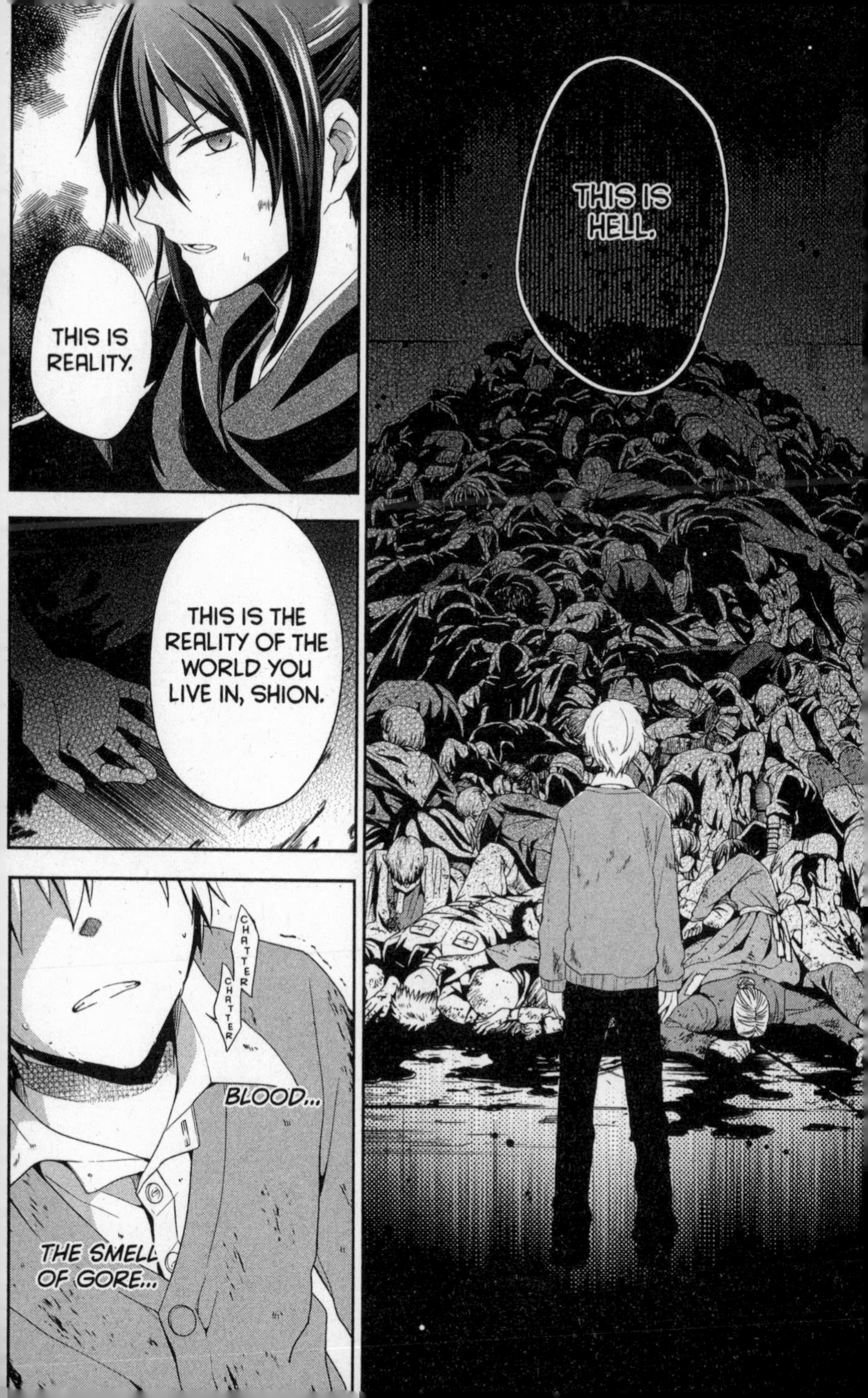
THIS IS HELL.
THIS IS REALITY.
THIS IS THE REALITY OF THE WORLD YOU LIVE IN, SHION.
CHATTER CHATTER
BLOOD...
THE SMELL OF GORE...

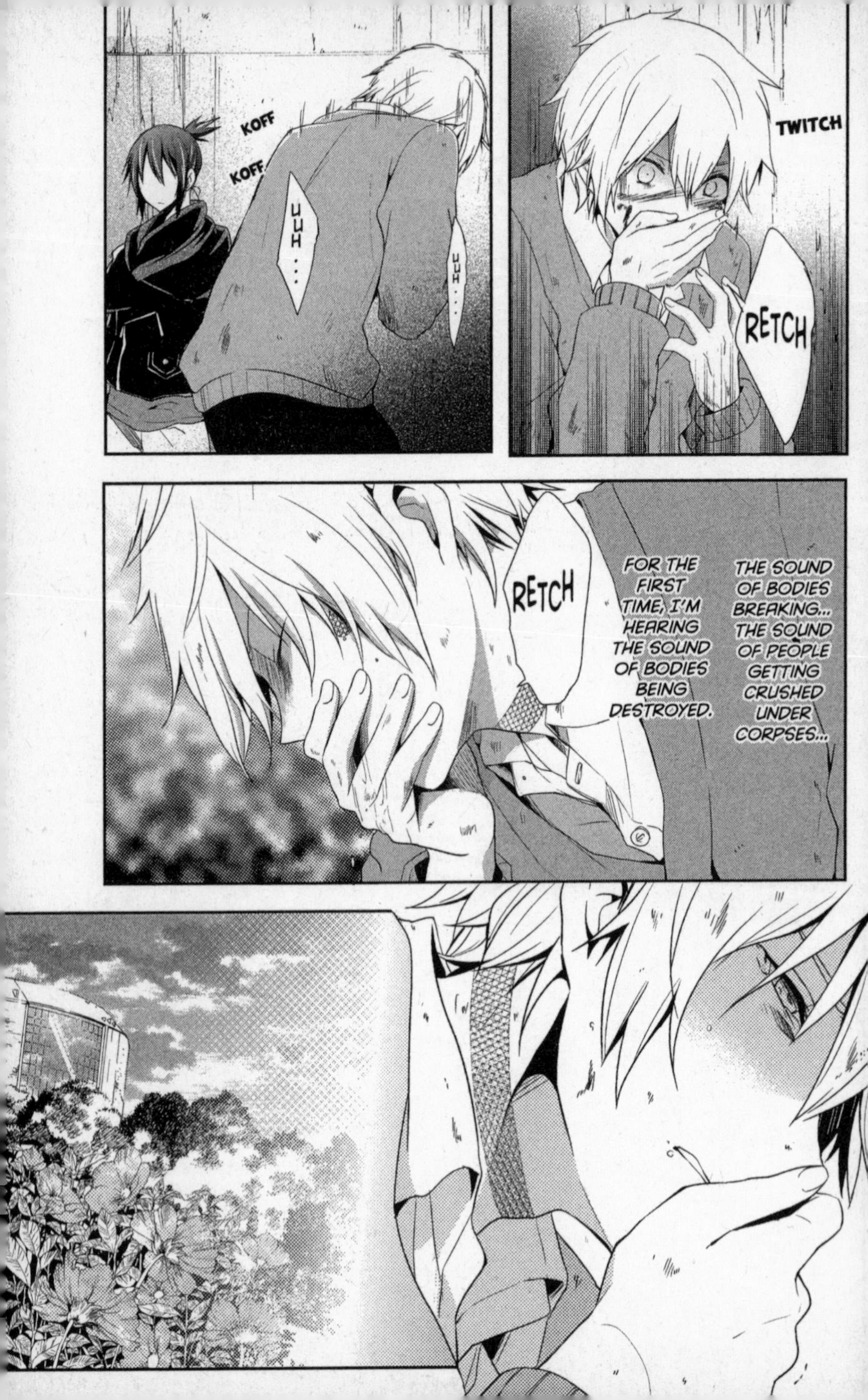
TWITCH
RETCH
KOFF
KOFF
UUH...
UUH...
THE SOUND OF BODIES BREAKING... THE SOUND OF PEOPLE GETTING CRUSHED UNDER CORPSES...
FOR THE FIRST TIME, I'M HEARING THE SOUND OF BODIES BEING DESTROYED.
RETCH

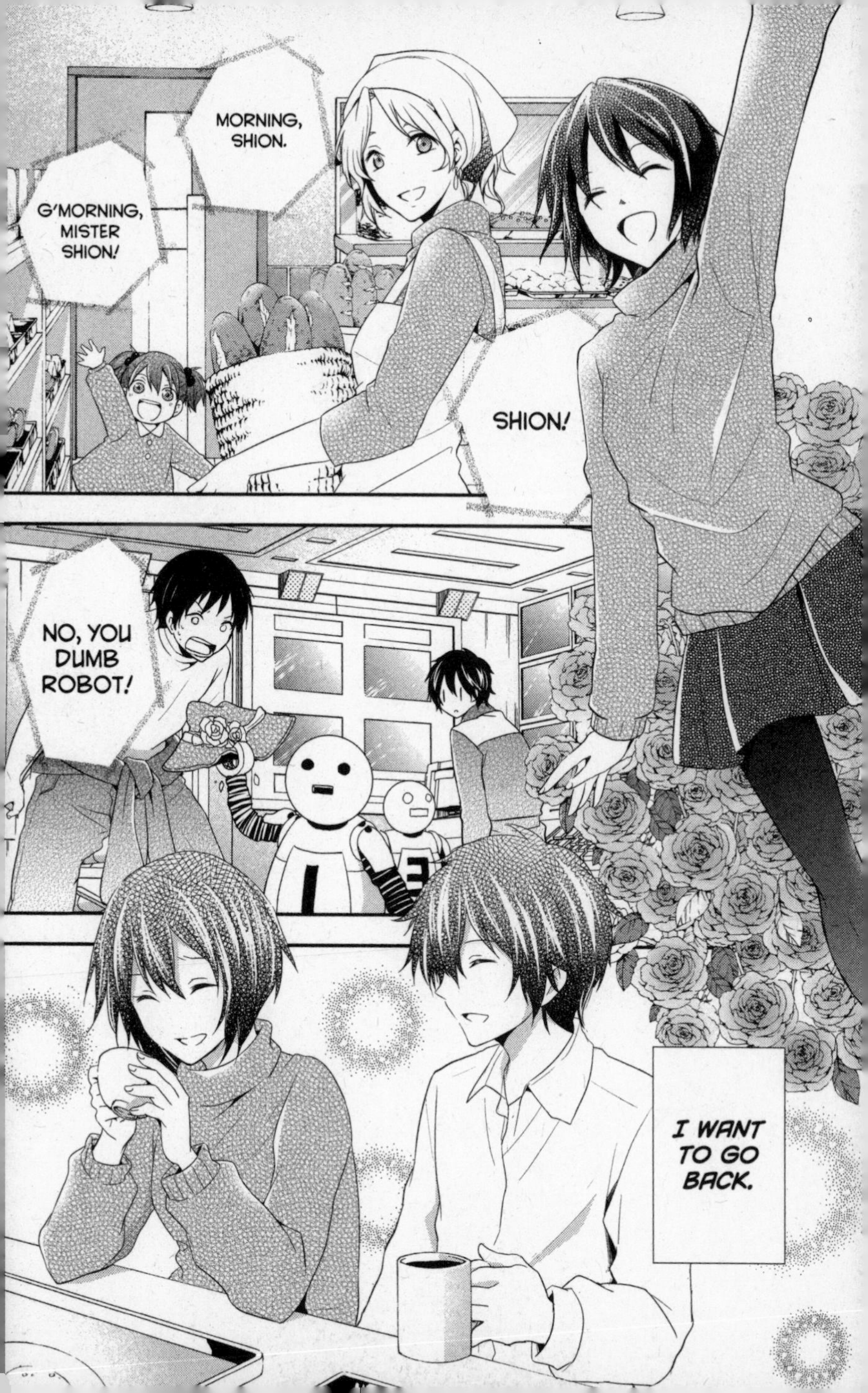
SHION!
MORNING, SHION.
G'MORNING, MISTER SHION!
NO, YOU DUMB ROBOT!
I WANT TO GO BACK.

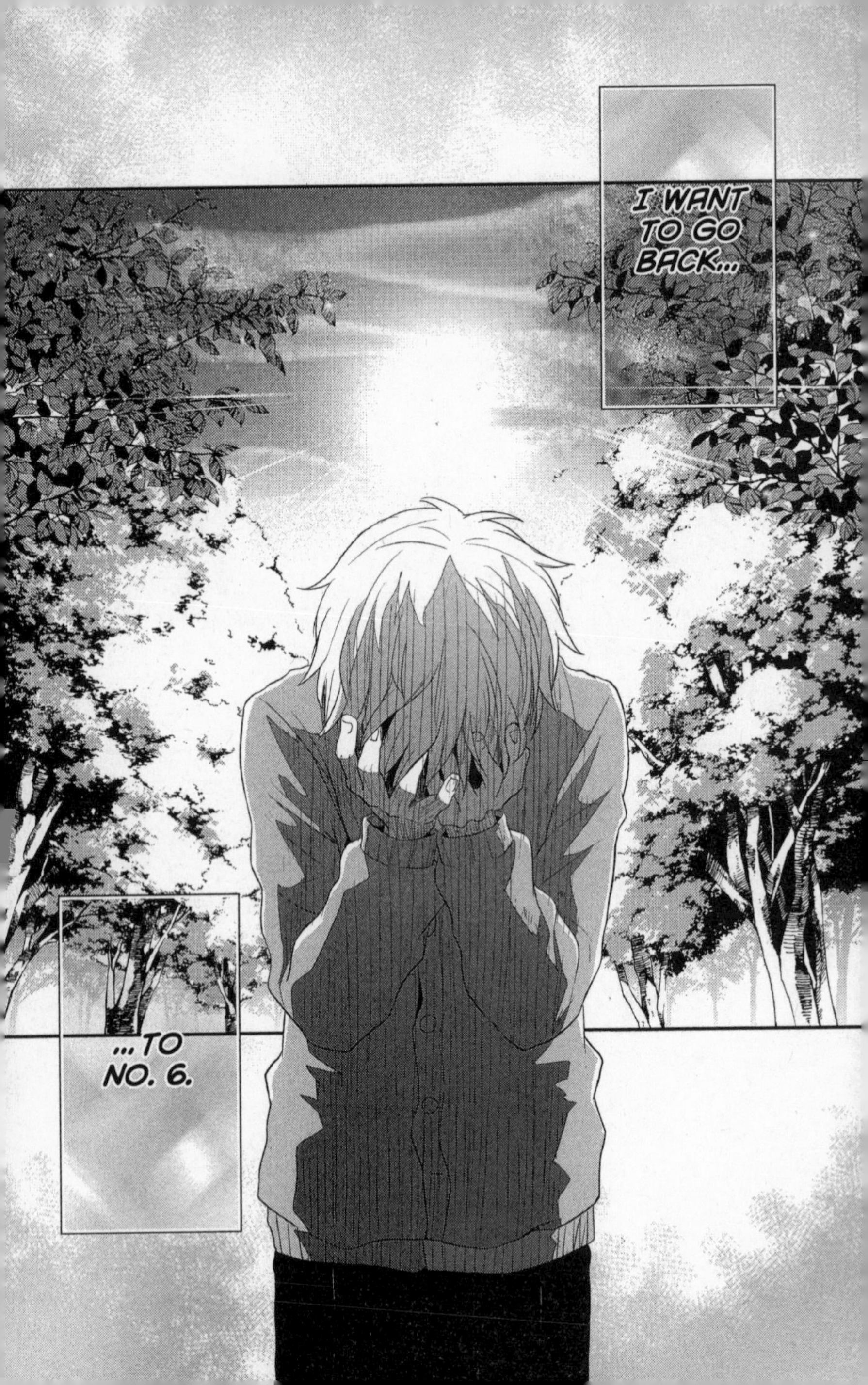
I WANT TO GO BACK...
...TO NO. 6.

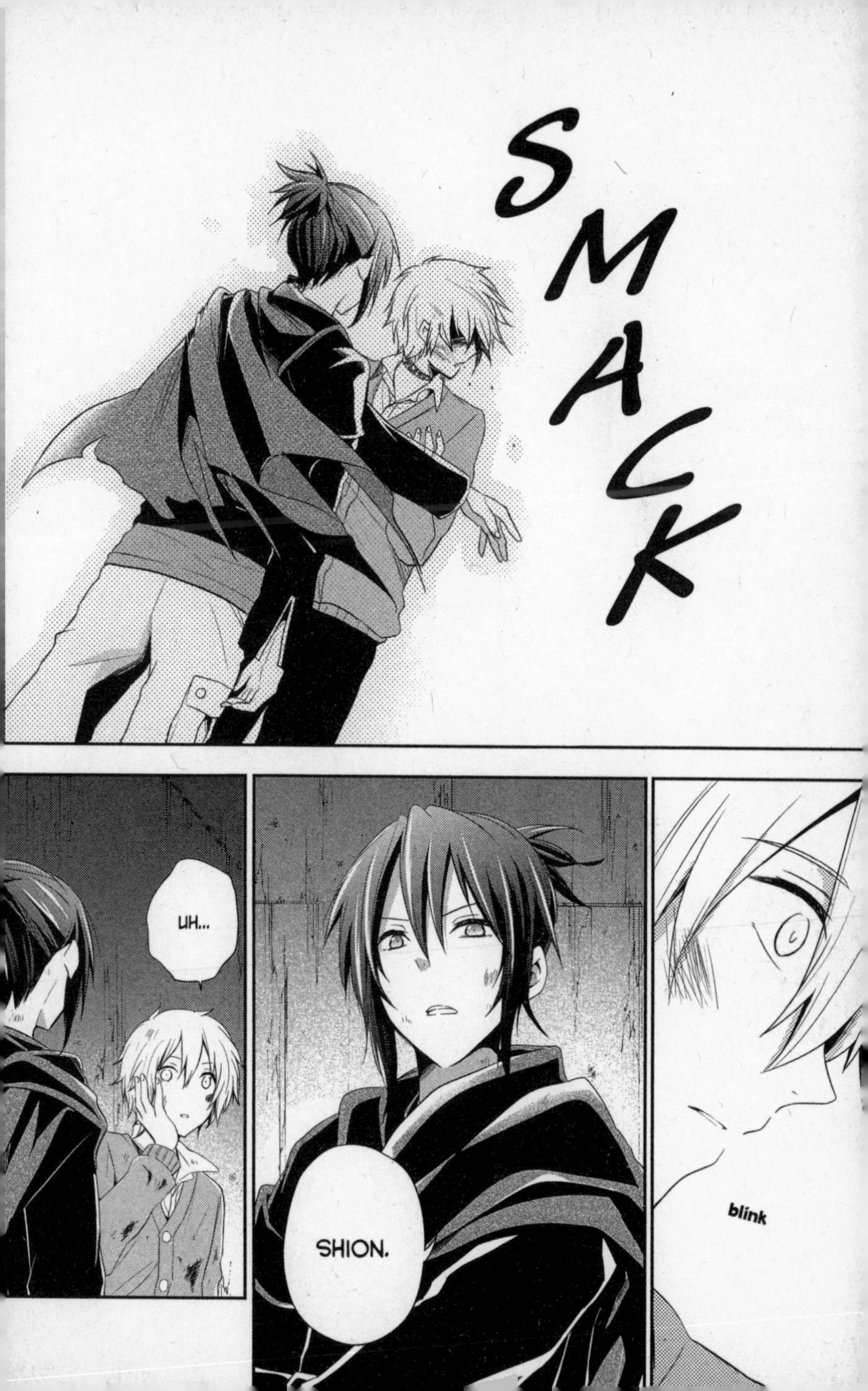
SMACK
blink
SHION.
UH...

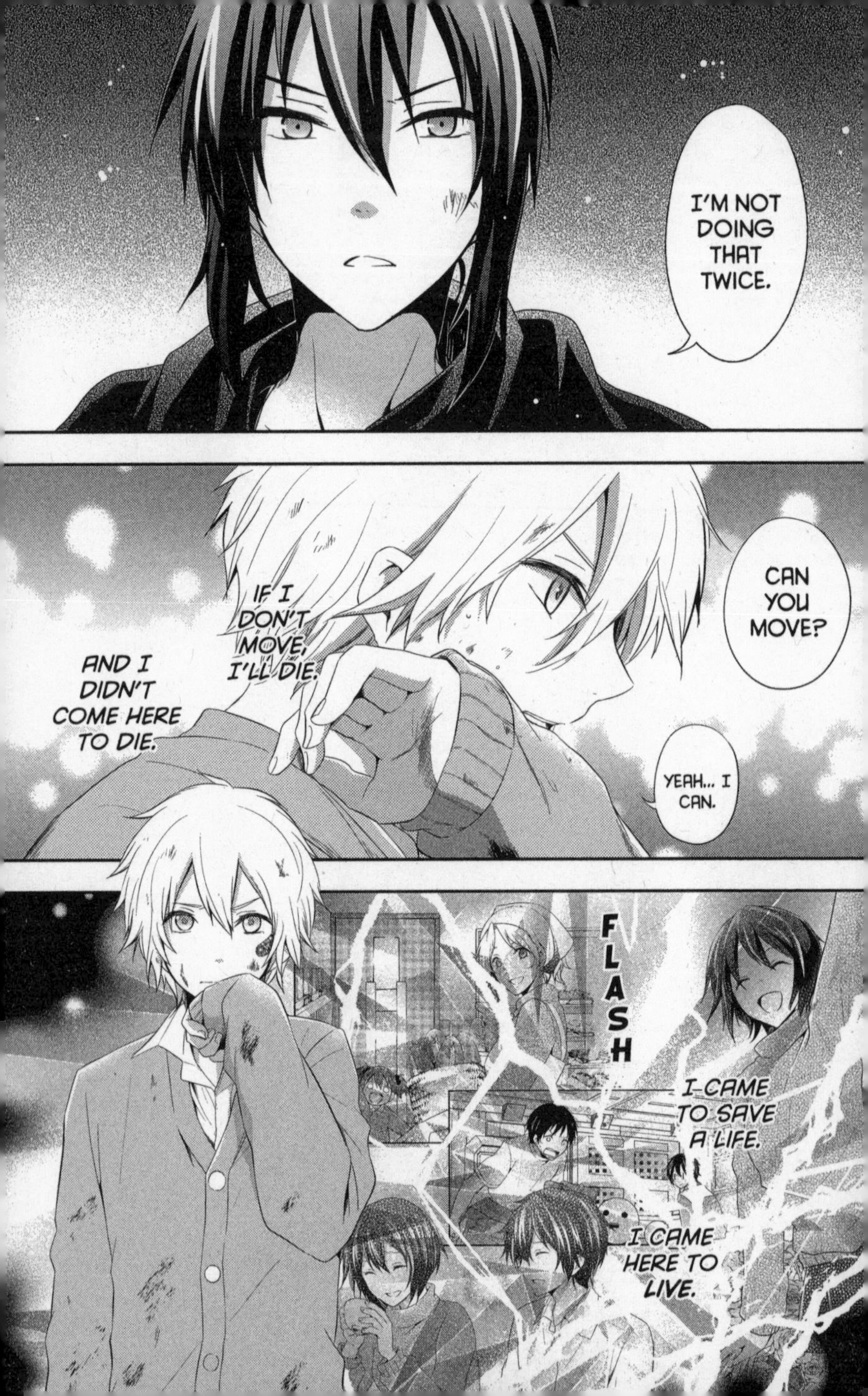
I'M NOT DOING THAT TWICE.
CAN YOU MOVE?
IF I DON'T MOVE, I'LL DIE.
AND I DIDN'T COME HERE TO DIE.
YEAH... I CAN.
FLASH
I CAME TO SAVE A LIFE.
I CAME HERE TO LIVE.

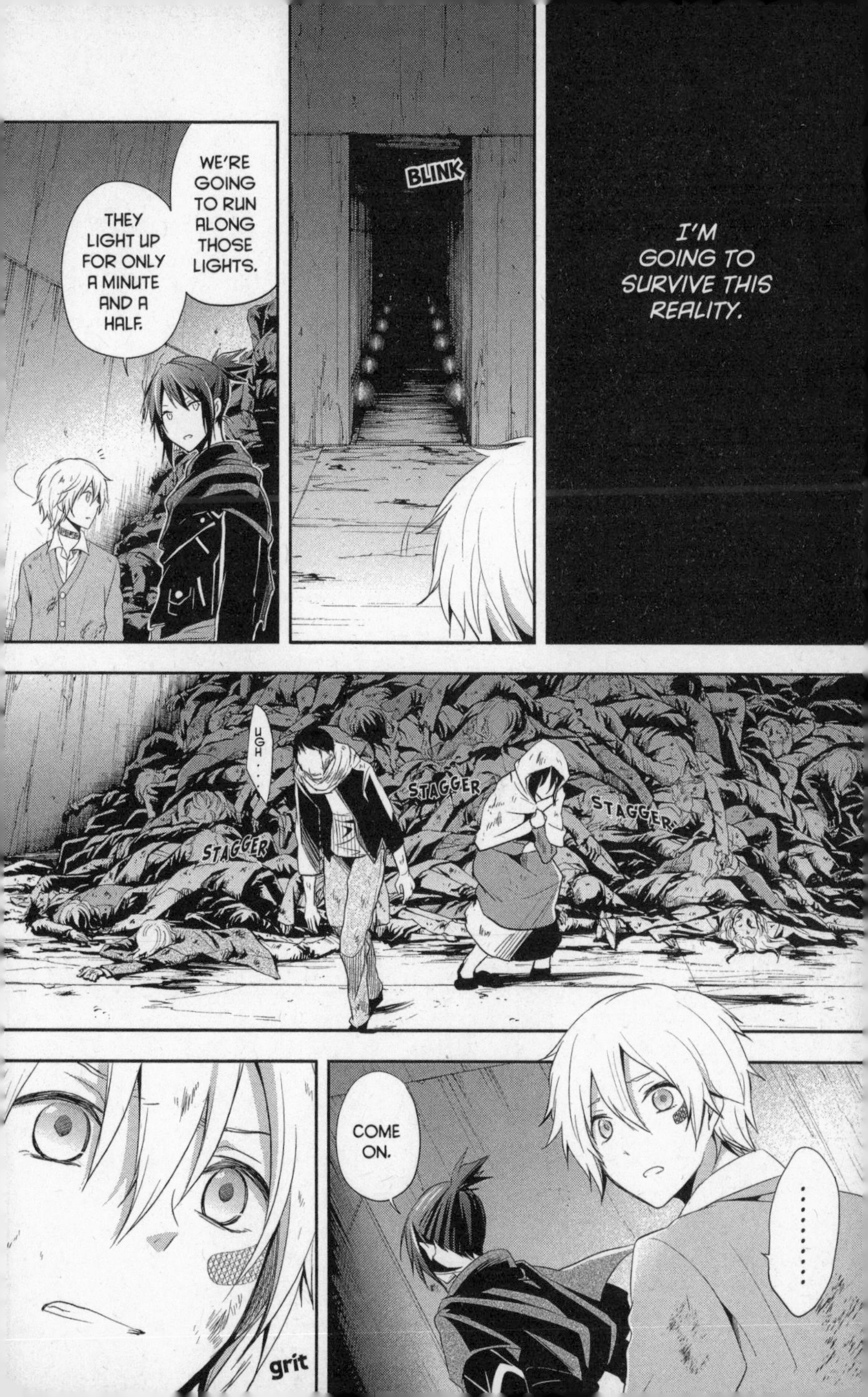
I'M GOING TO SURVIVE THIS REALITY.
BLINK
WE'RE GOING TO RUN ALONG THOSE LIGHTS.
THEY LIGHT UP FOR ONLY A MINUTE AND A HALF.
STAGGER
STAGGER
UGH...
STAGGER
......
COME ON.
grit

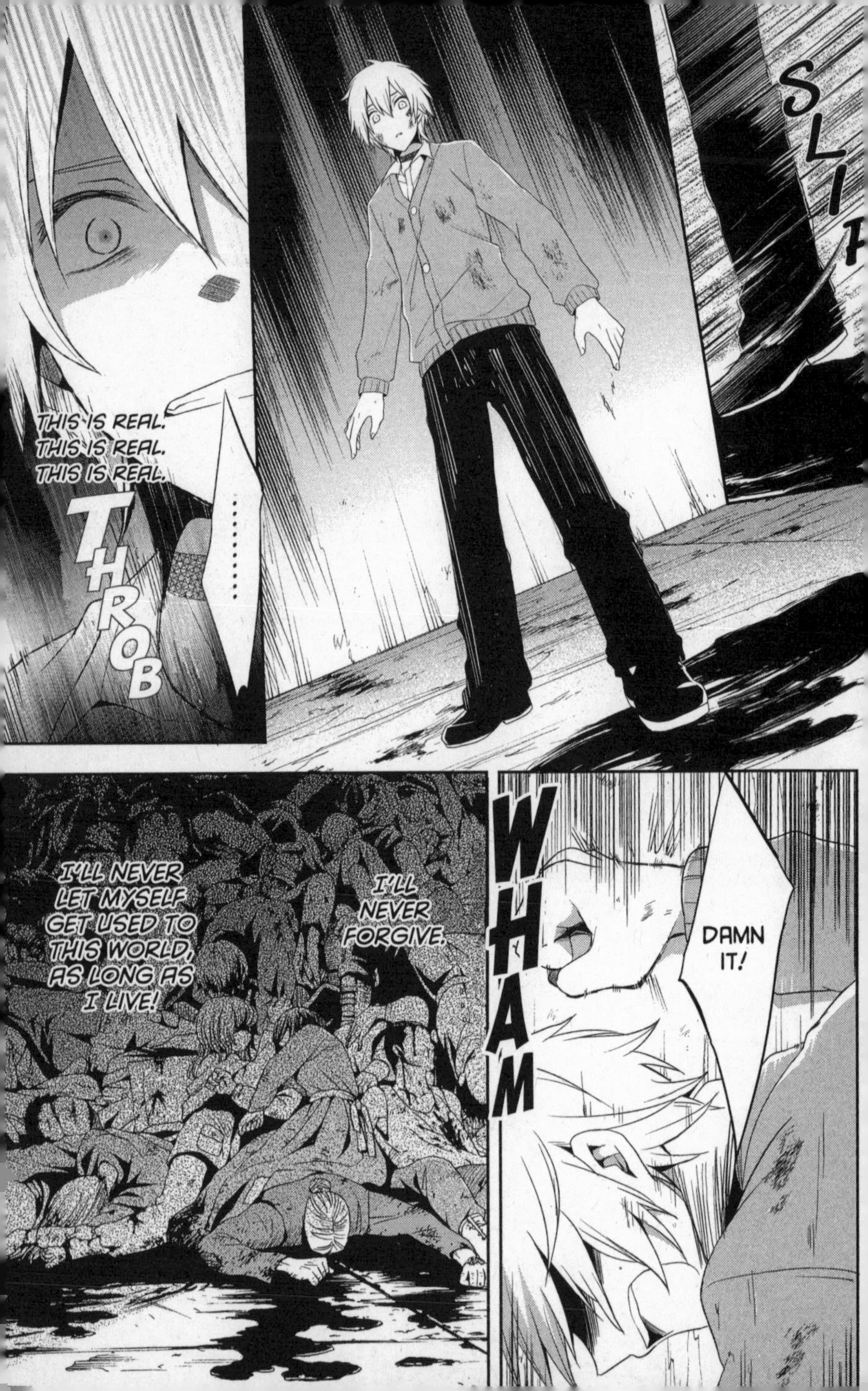
SLI
THIS IS REAL. THIS IS REAL. THIS IS REAL.
THROB
......
WHAM
DAMN IT!
I'LL NEVER FORGIVE.
I'LL NEVER LET MYSELF GET USED TO THIS WORLD, AS LONG AS I LIVE!

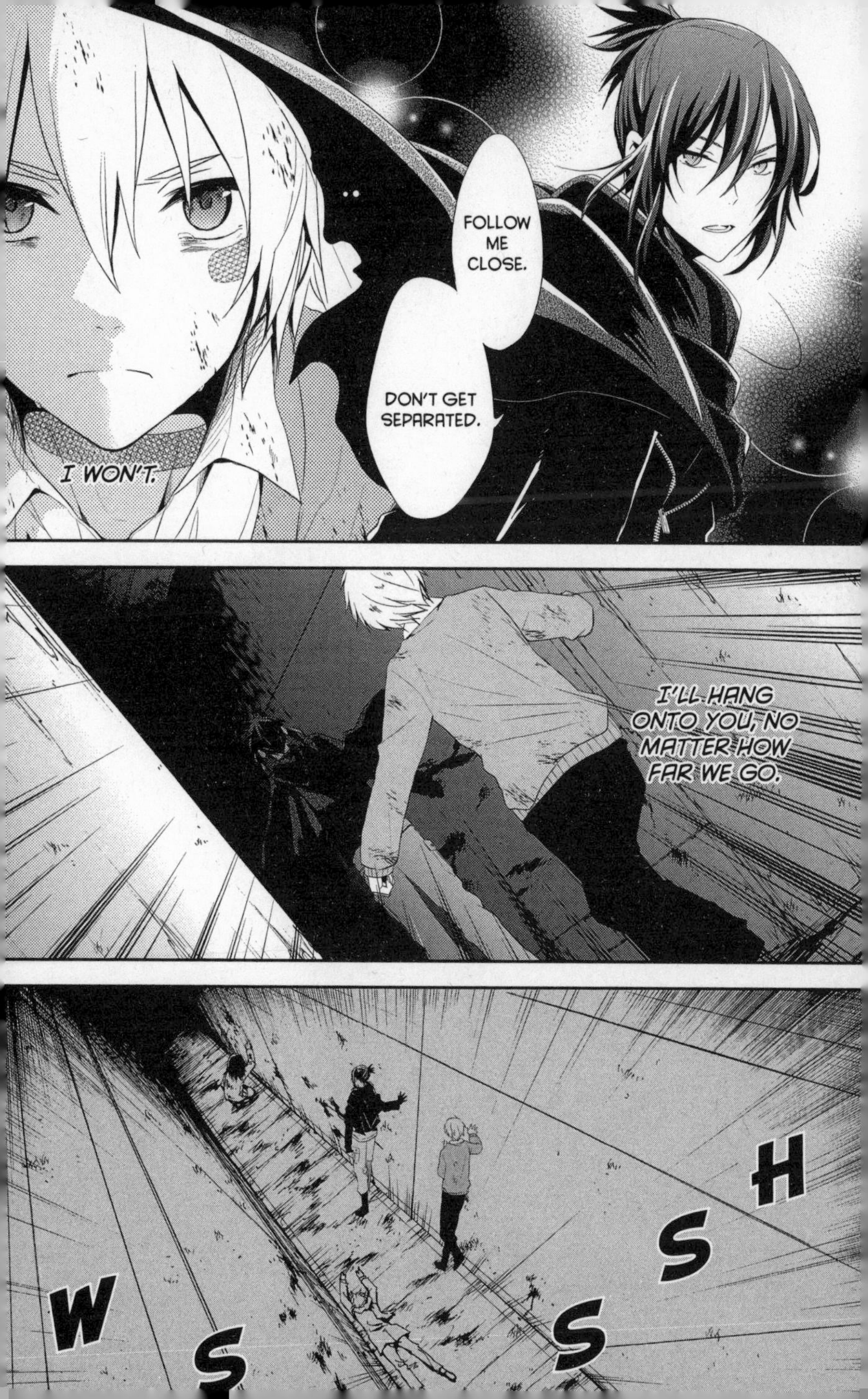
FOLLOW ME CLOSE.
DON'T GET SEPARATED.
I WON'T.
I'LL HANG ONTO YOU, NO MATTER HOW FAR WE GO.
WSSSH

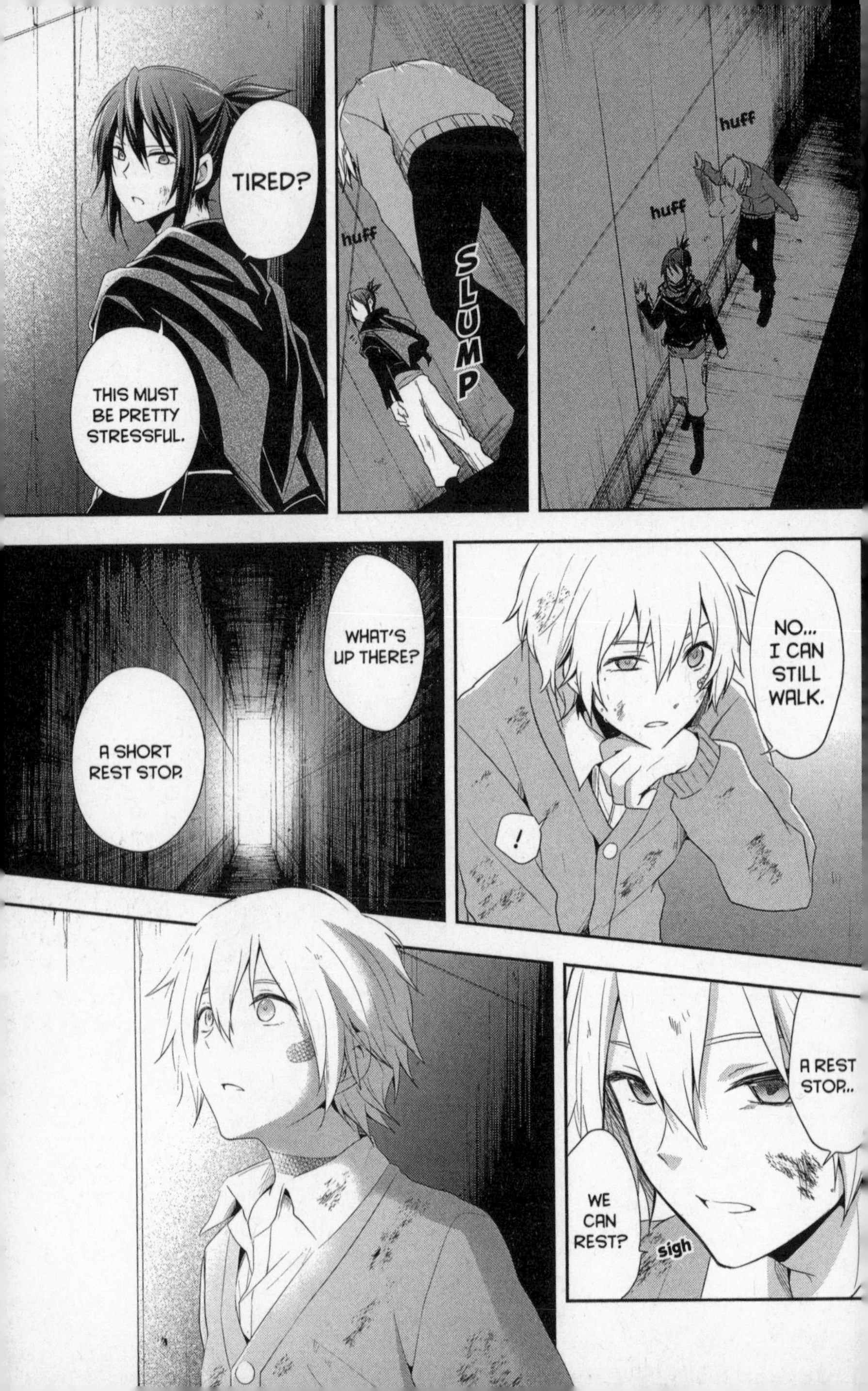
huff
huff
SLUMP
huff
TIRED?
THIS MUST BE PRETTY STRESSFUL.
NO... I CAN STILL WALK.
!
WHAT'S UP THERE?
A SHORT REST STOP.
A REST STOP...
WE CAN REST?
sigh

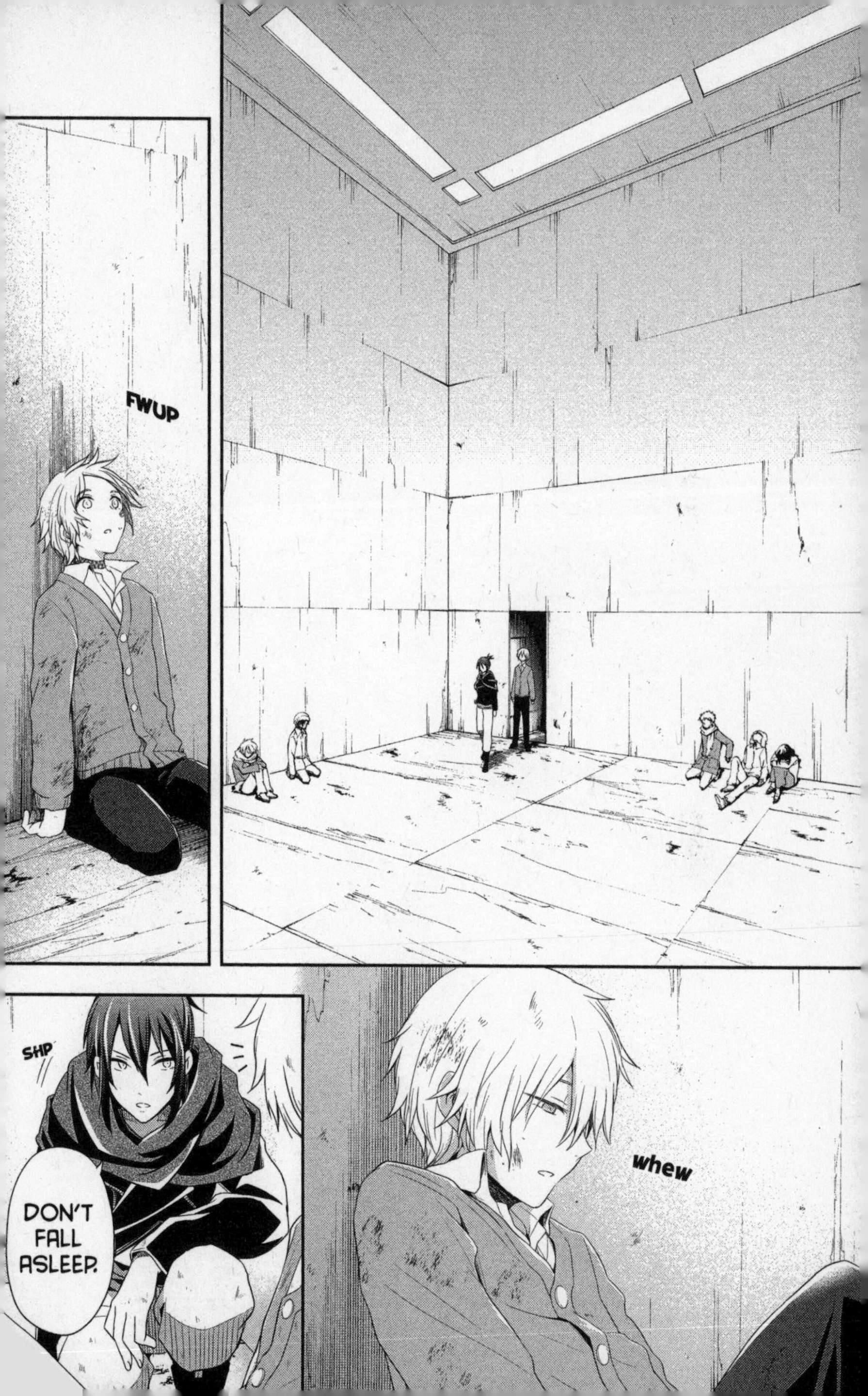
FWUP
whew
SHP
DON'T FALL ASLEEP.

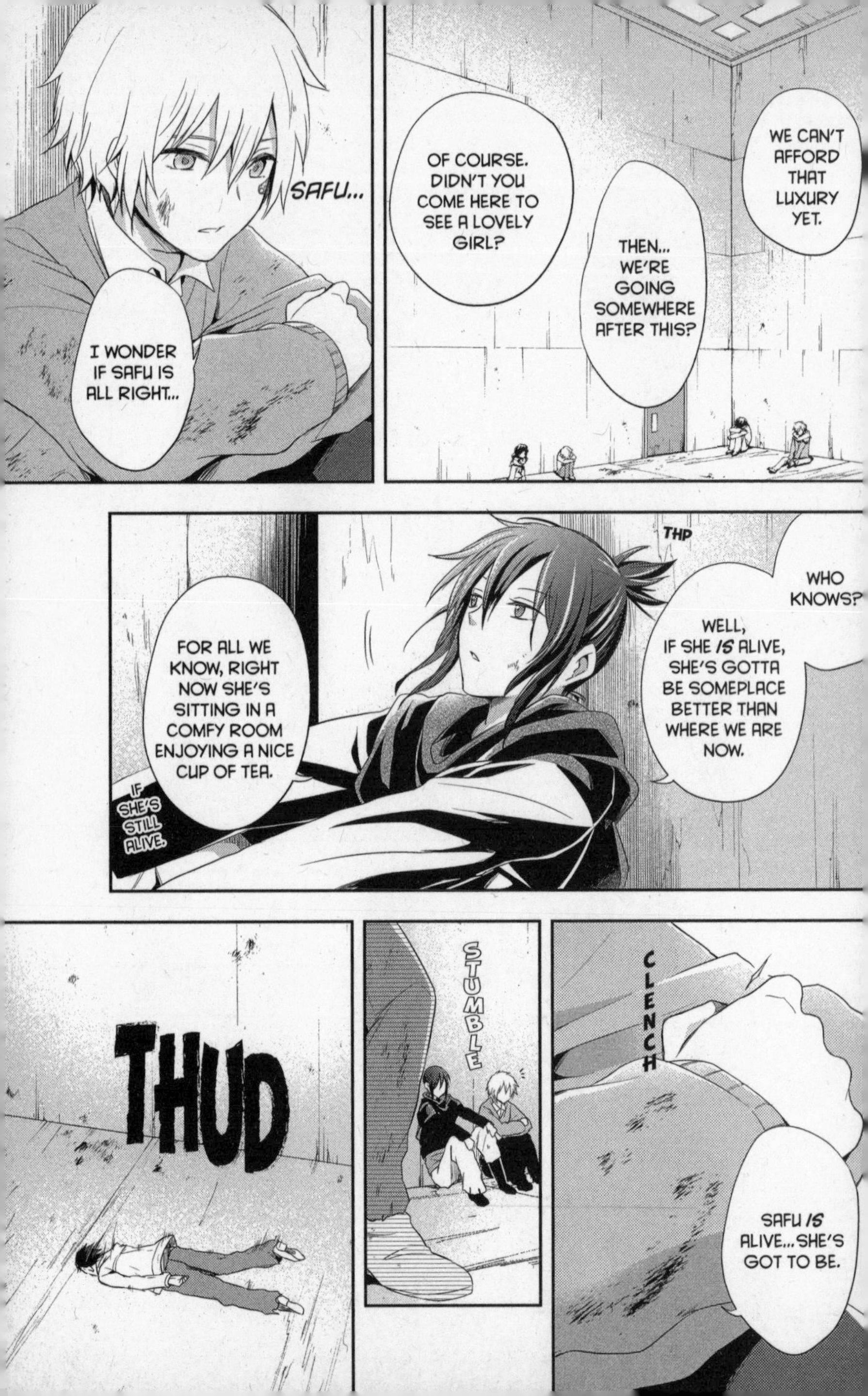
WE CAN'T AFFORD THAT LUXURY YET.
THEN... WE'RE GOING SOMEWHERE AFTER THIS?
OF COURSE. DIDN'T YOU COME HERE TO SEE A LOVELY GIRL?
SAFU...
I WONDER IF SAFU IS ALL RIGHT...
WHO KNOWS?
THP
WELL, IF SHE *IS* ALIVE, SHE'S GOTTA BE SOMEPLACE BETTER THAN WHERE WE ARE NOW.
FOR ALL WE KNOW, RIGHT NOW SHE'S SITTING IN A COMFY ROOM ENJOYING A NICE CUP OF TEA.
IF SHE'S STILL ALIVE.
CLENCH
SAFU *IS* ALIVE... SHE'S GOT TO BE.
STUMBLE
THUD

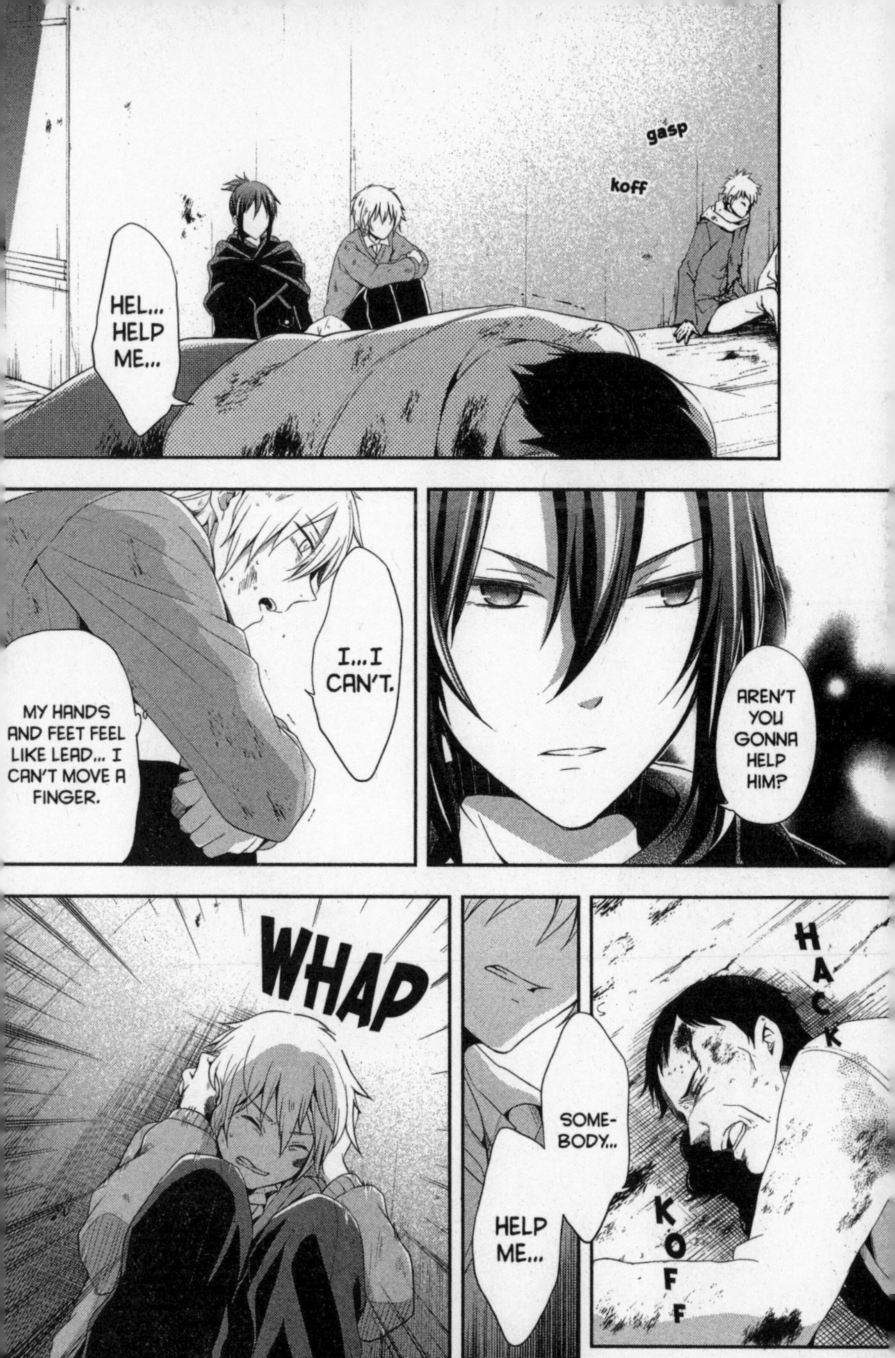
gasp
koff
HEL... HELP ME...
AREN'T YOU GONNA HELP HIM?
I...I CAN'T.
MY HANDS AND FEET FEEL LIKE LEAD... I CAN'T MOVE A FINGER.
HACK
KOFF
SOME-BODY...
HELP ME...
WHAP

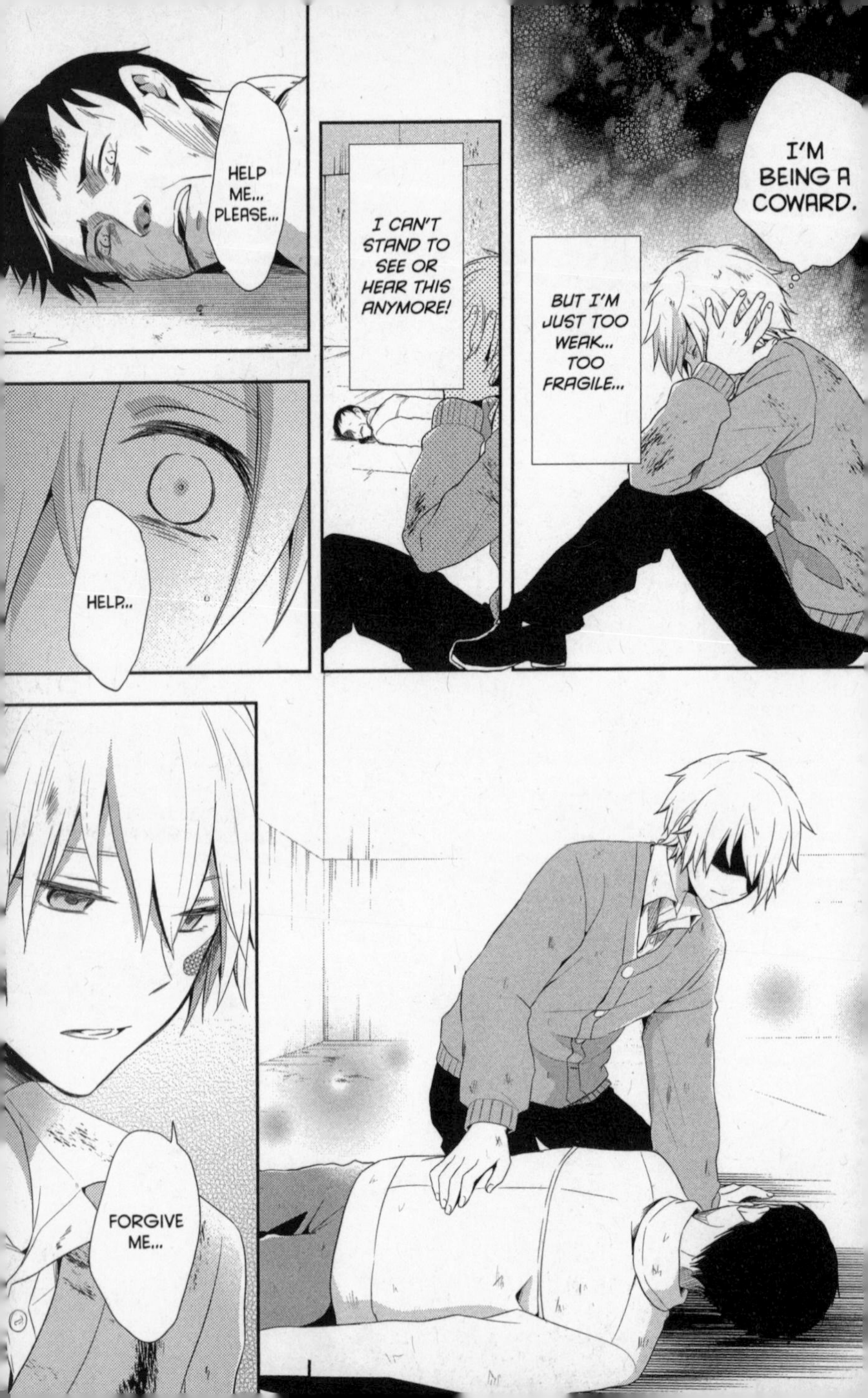
I'M BEING A COWARD.
BUT I'M JUST TOO WEAK... TOO FRAGILE...
I CAN'T STAND TO SEE OR HEAR THIS ANYMORE!
HELP ME... PLEASE...
HELP...
FORGIVE ME...

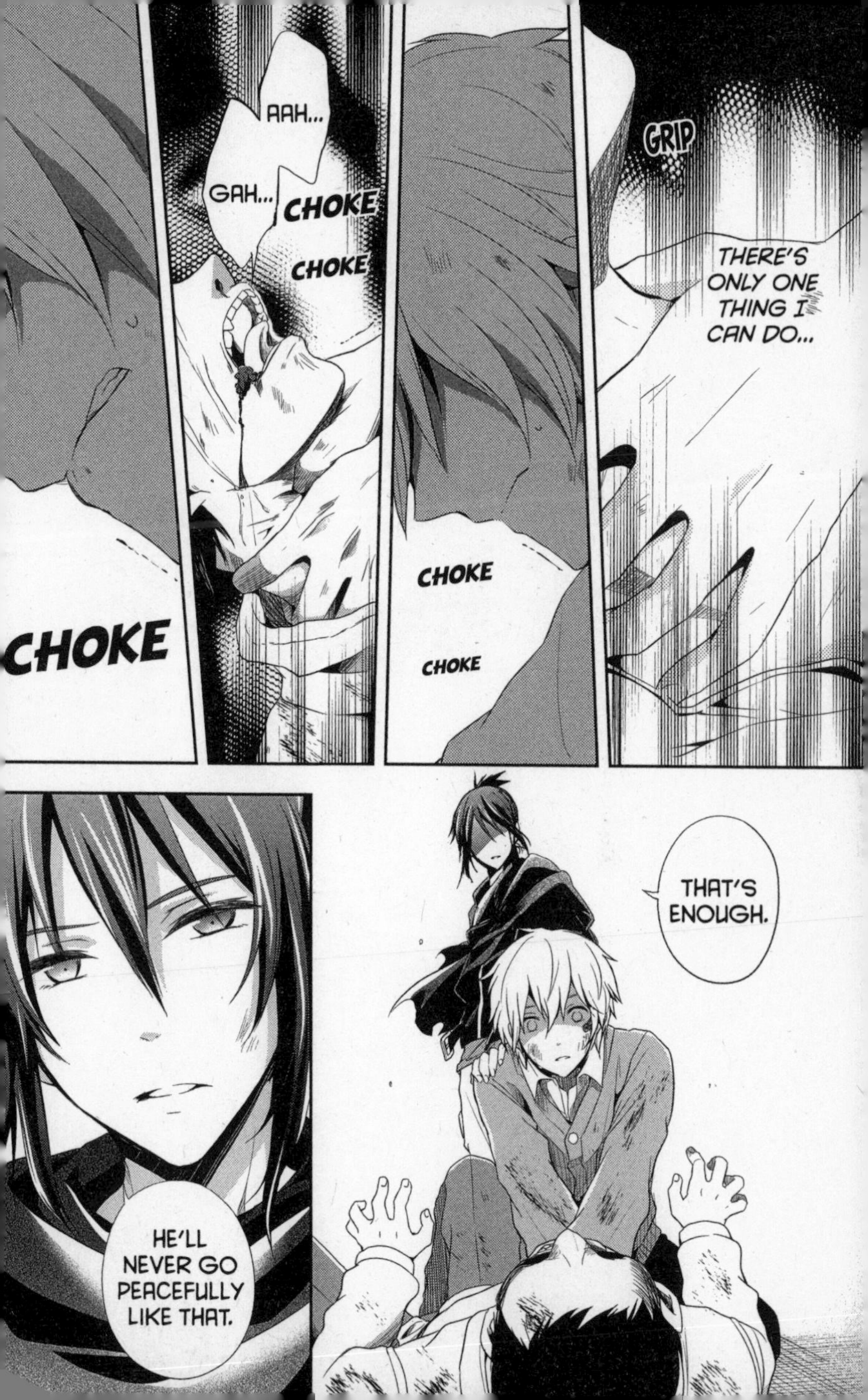
GRIP
THERE'S ONLY ONE THING I CAN DO...
CHOKE
CHOKE
AAH...
GAH...
CHOKE
CHOKE
CHOKE
THAT'S ENOUGH.
HE'LL NEVER GO PEACEFULLY LIKE THAT.

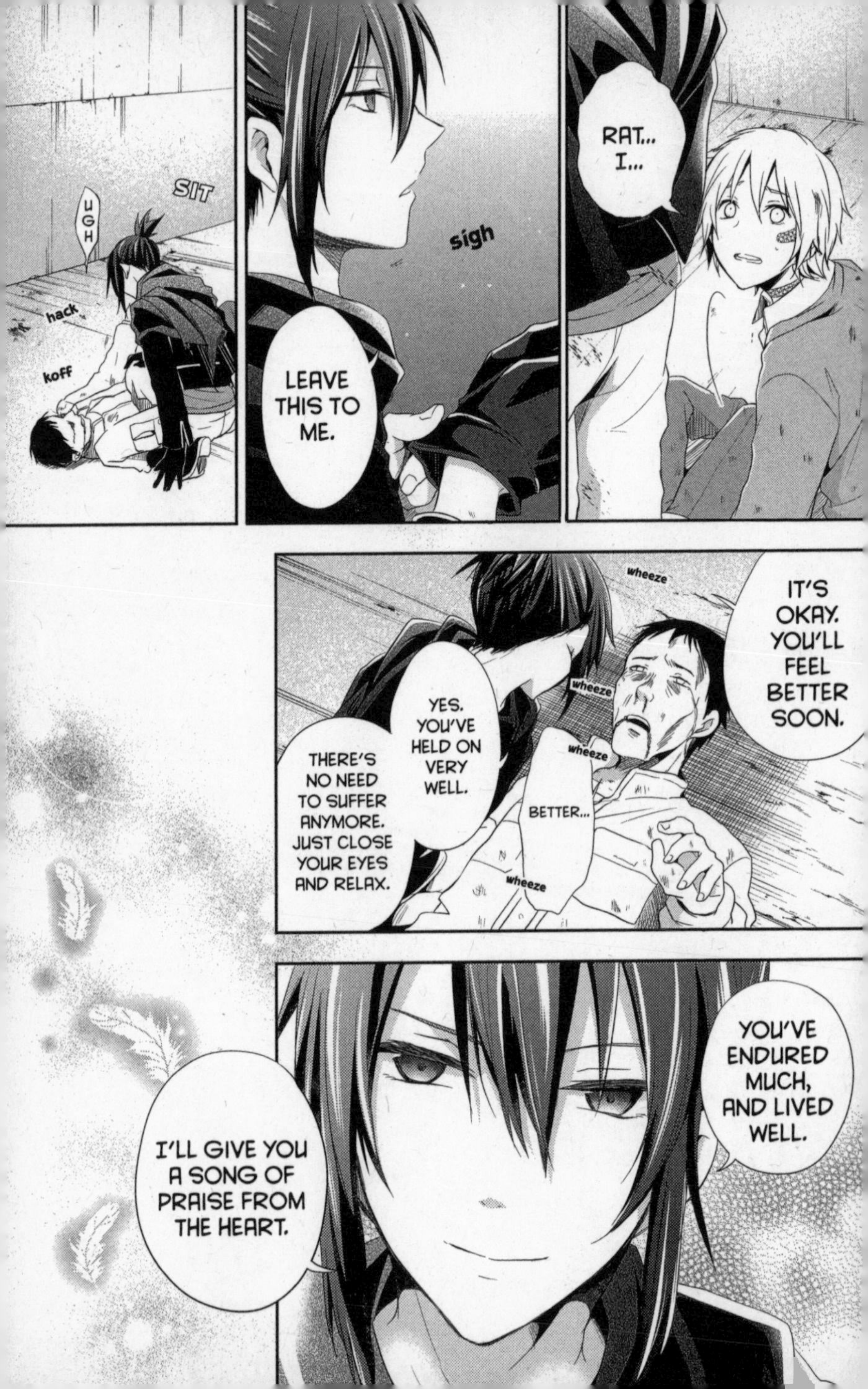
RAT... I...
sigh
LEAVE THIS TO ME.
SIT
UGH
hack
koff
wheeze
IT'S OKAY. YOU'LL FEEL BETTER SOON.
wheeze
YES. YOU'VE HELD ON VERY WELL.
wheeze
BETTER...
THERE'S NO NEED TO SUFFER ANYMORE. JUST CLOSE YOUR EYES AND RELAX.
wheeze
YOU'VE ENDURED MUCH, AND LIVED WELL.
I'LL GIVE YOU A SONG OF PRAISE FROM THE HEART.

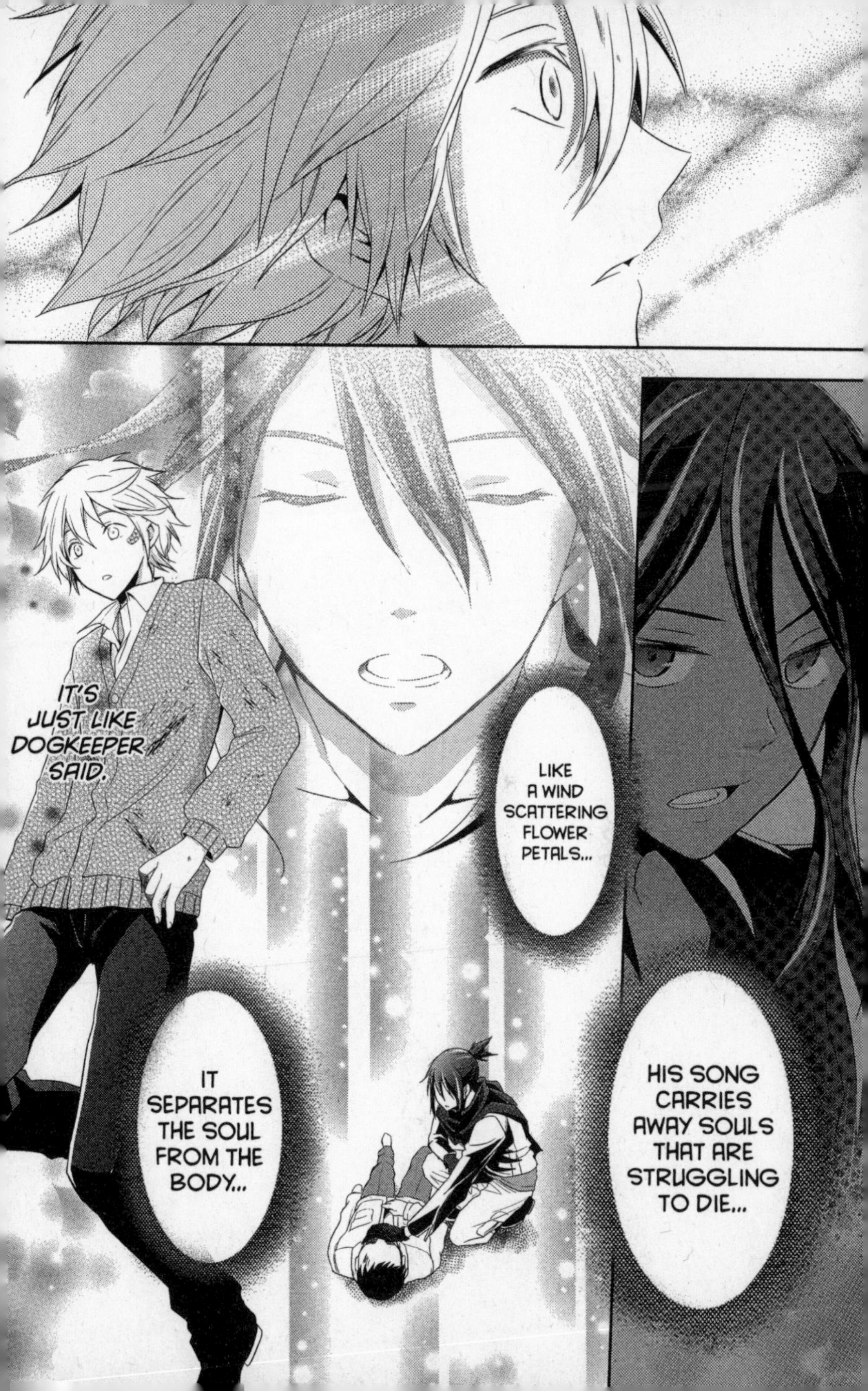
IT'S JUST LIKE DOGKEEPER SAID.
LIKE A WIND SCATTERING FLOWER PETALS...
HIS SONG CARRIES AWAY SOULS THAT ARE STRUGGLING TO DIE...
IT SEPARATES THE SOUL FROM THE BODY...

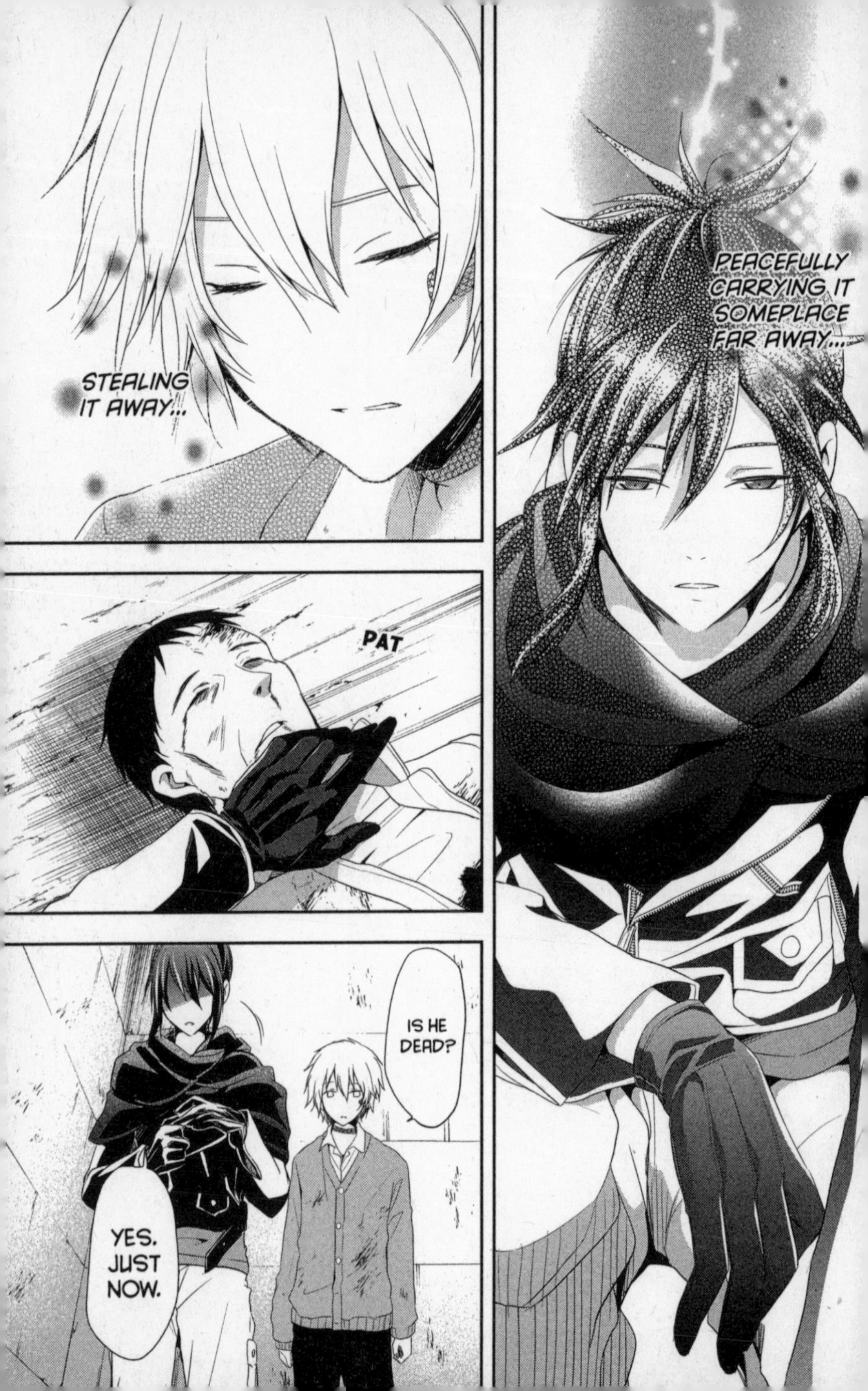
PEACEFULLY CARRYING IT SOMEPLACE FAR AWAY...
STEALING IT AWAY...
PAT
IS HE DEAD?
YES. JUST NOW.

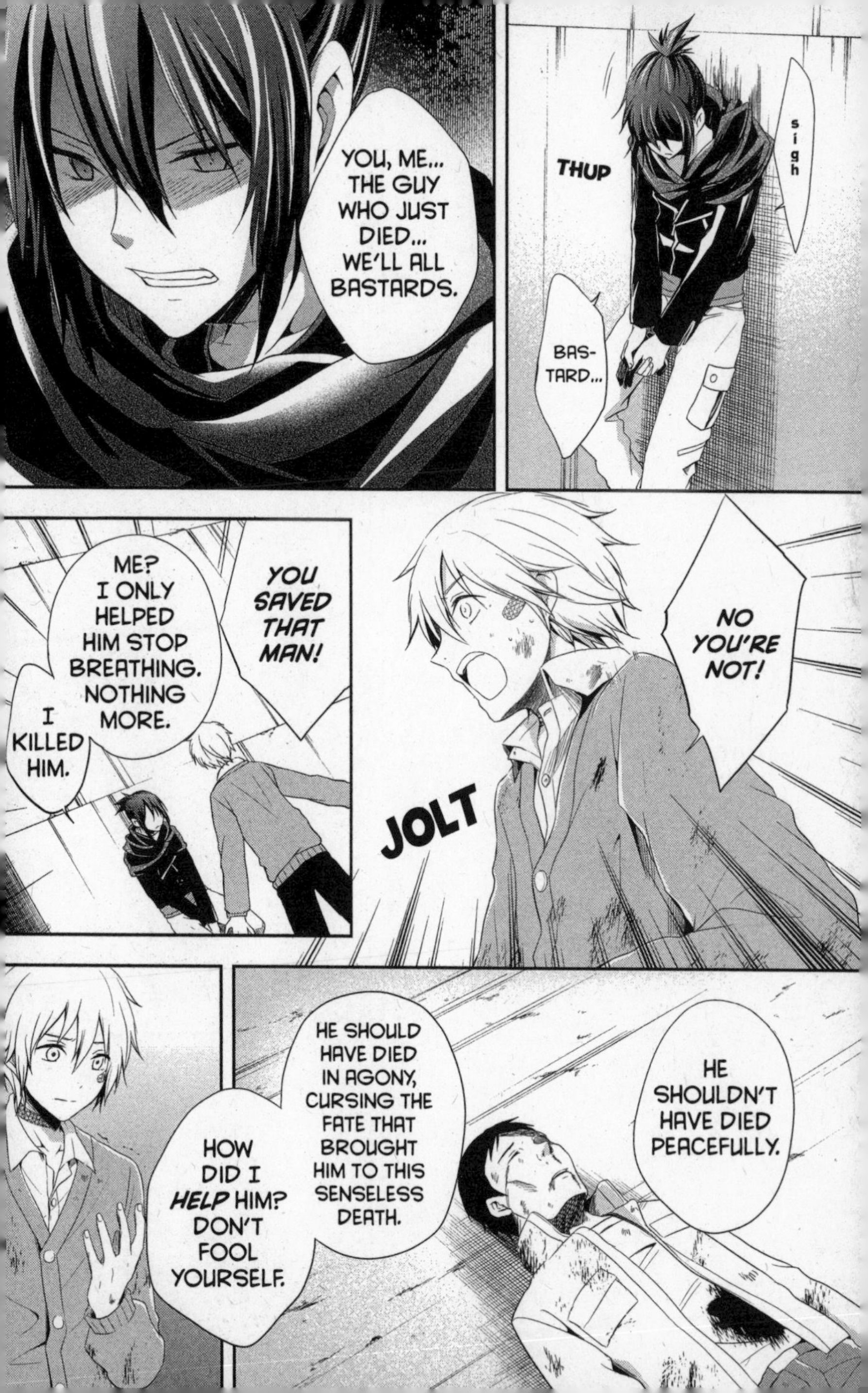
sigh
THUP
BASTARD...
YOU, ME... THE GUY WHO JUST DIED... WE'LL ALL BASTARDS.
NO YOU'RE NOT!
JOLT
YOU SAVED THAT MAN!
ME? I ONLY HELPED HIM STOP BREATHING. NOTHING MORE.
I KILLED HIM.
HE SHOULDN'T HAVE DIED PEACEFULLY.
HE SHOULD HAVE DIED IN AGONY, CURSING THE FATE THAT BROUGHT HIM TO THIS SENSELESS DEATH.
HOW DID I HELP HIM? DON'T FOOL YOURSELF.

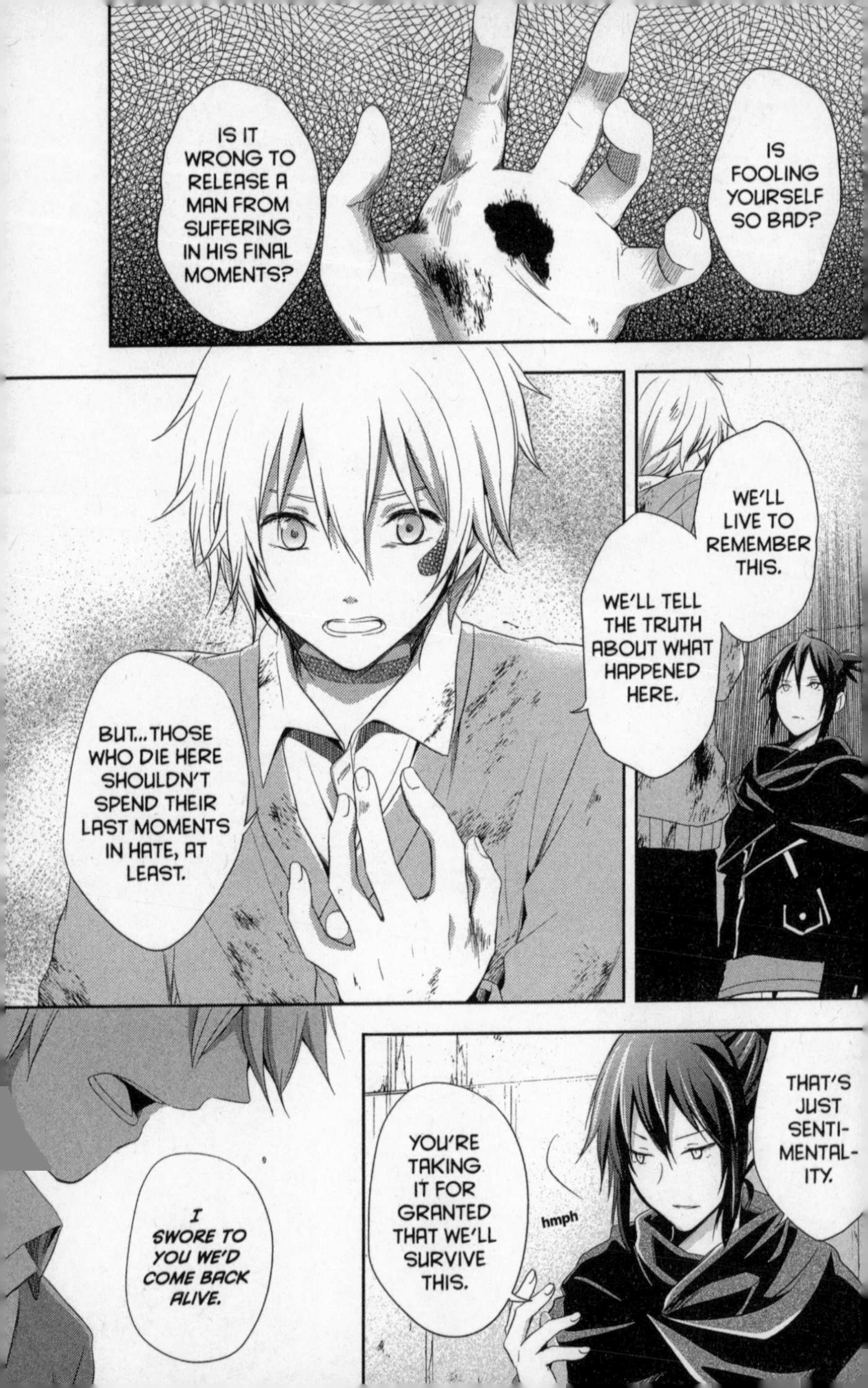
IS FOOLING YOURSELF SO BAD?
IS IT WRONG TO RELEASE A MAN FROM SUFFERING IN HIS FINAL MOMENTS?
WE'LL LIVE TO REMEMBER THIS.
WE'LL TELL THE TRUTH ABOUT WHAT HAPPENED HERE.
BUT... THOSE WHO DIE HERE SHOULDN'T SPEND THEIR LAST MOMENTS IN HATE, AT LEAST.
THAT'S JUST SENTI-MENTAL-ITY.
hmph
YOU'RE TAKING IT FOR GRANTED THAT WE'LL SURVIVE THIS.
I SWORE TO YOU WE'D COME BACK ALIVE.

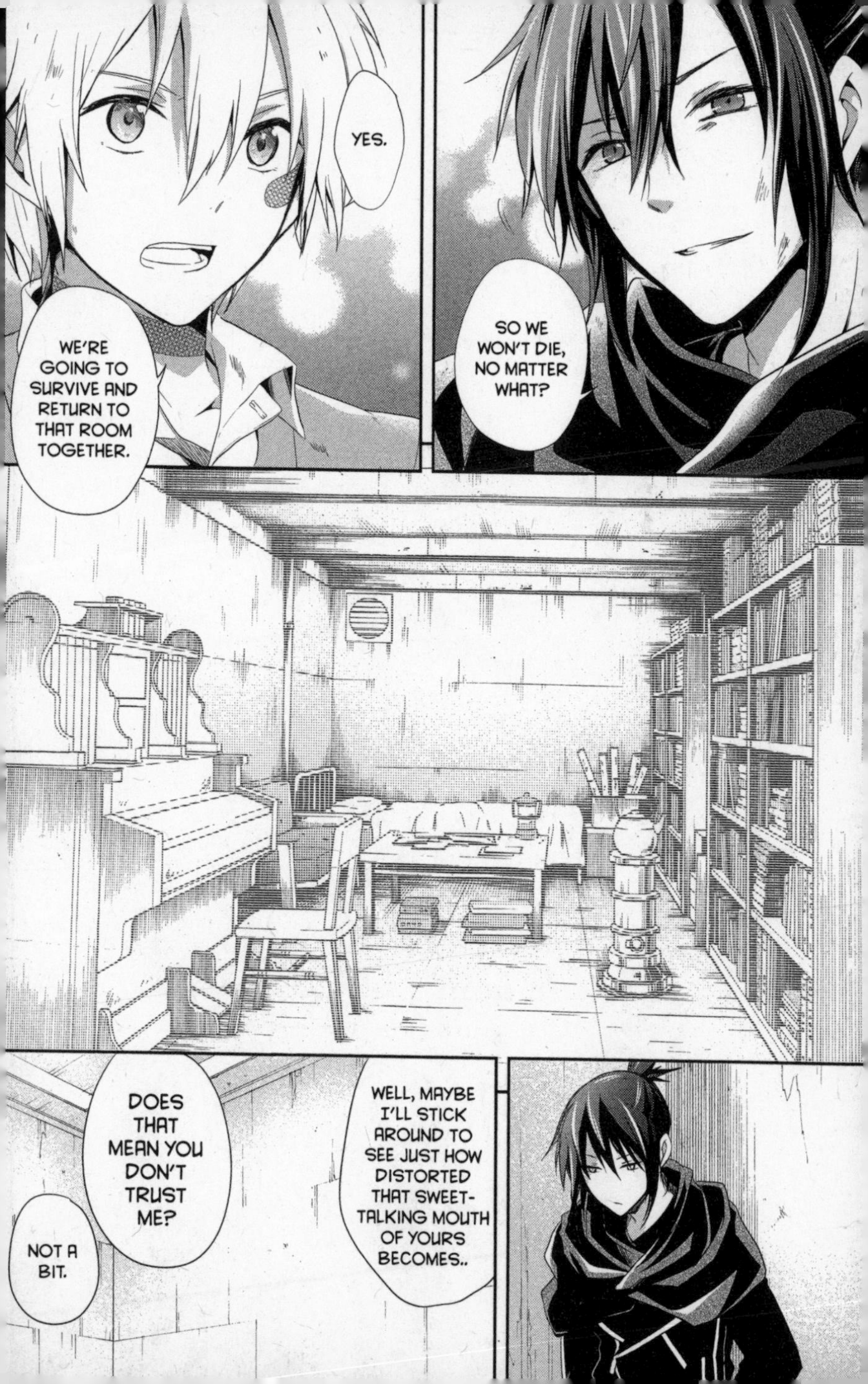
SO WE WON'T DIE, NO MATTER WHAT?
YES.
WE'RE GOING TO SURVIVE AND RETURN TO THAT ROOM TOGETHER.
WELL, MAYBE I'LL STICK AROUND TO SEE JUST HOW DISTORTED THAT SWEET-TALKING MOUTH OF YOURS BECOMES..
DOES THAT MEAN YOU DON'T TRUST ME?
NOT A BIT.

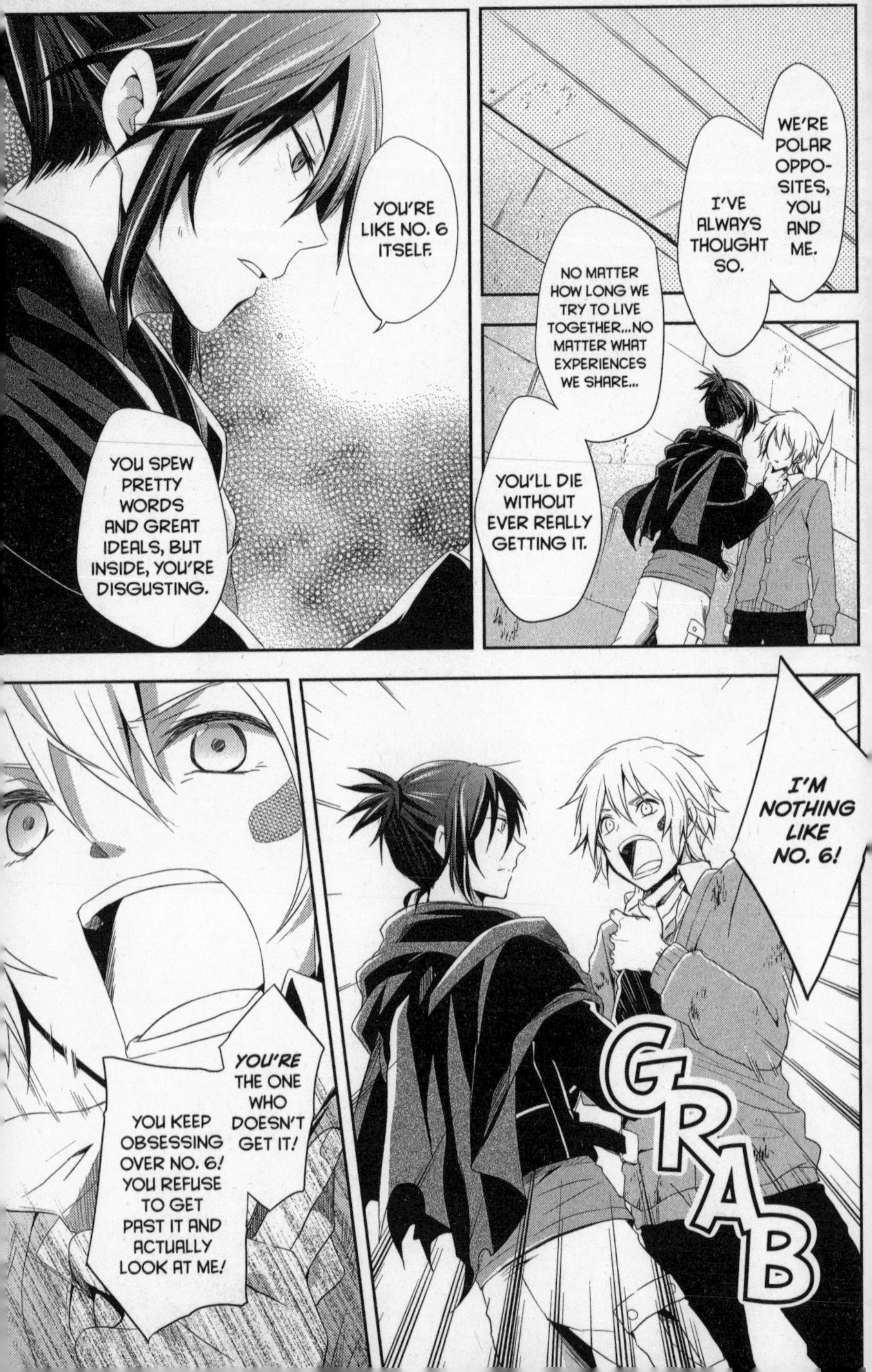
WE'RE POLAR OPPOSITES, YOU AND ME.
I'VE ALWAYS THOUGHT SO.
NO MATTER HOW LONG WE TRY TO LIVE TOGETHER...NO MATTER WHAT EXPERIENCES WE SHARE...
YOU'LL DIE WITHOUT EVER REALLY GETTING IT.
YOU'RE LIKE NO. 6 ITSELF.
YOU SPEW PRETTY WORDS AND GREAT IDEALS, BUT INSIDE, YOU'RE DISGUSTING.
I'M NOTHING LIKE NO. 6!
GRAB
YOU'RE THE ONE WHO DOESN'T GET IT!
YOU KEEP OBSESSING OVER NO. 6! YOU REFUSE TO GET PAST IT AND ACTUALLY LOOK AT ME!

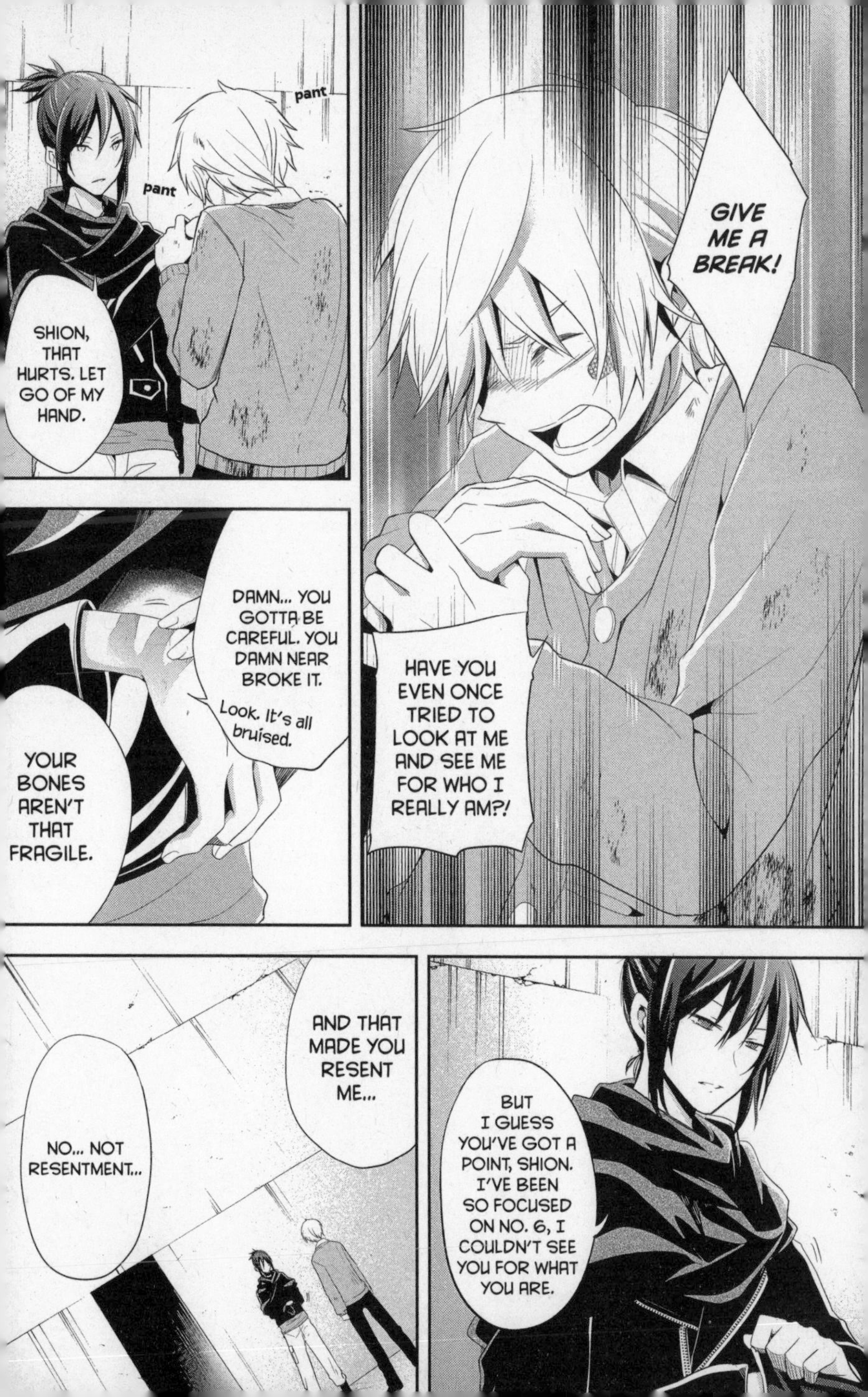
GIVE ME A BREAK!
HAVE YOU EVEN ONCE TRIED TO LOOK AT ME AND SEE ME FOR WHO I REALLY AM?!
pant
pant
SHION, THAT HURTS. LET GO OF MY HAND.
DAMN... YOU GOTTA BE CAREFUL. YOU DAMN NEAR BROKE IT.
Look. It's all bruised.
YOUR BONES AREN'T THAT FRAGILE.
BUT I GUESS YOU'VE GOT A POINT, SHION. I'VE BEEN SO FOCUSED ON NO. 6, I COULDN'T SEE YOU FOR WHAT YOU ARE.
AND THAT MADE YOU RESENT ME...
NO... NOT RESENTMENT...

IT'S MORE LIKE... FEAR.

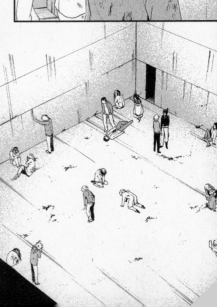

FEAR? WHAT DO YOU MEAN?

LOOKS LIKE IT'S ALL OVER.

C'MON, LET'S GO.

HUH?

WE'RE GOING BACK UP THAT TUNNEL.

GOING BACK?! WHAT FOR?!

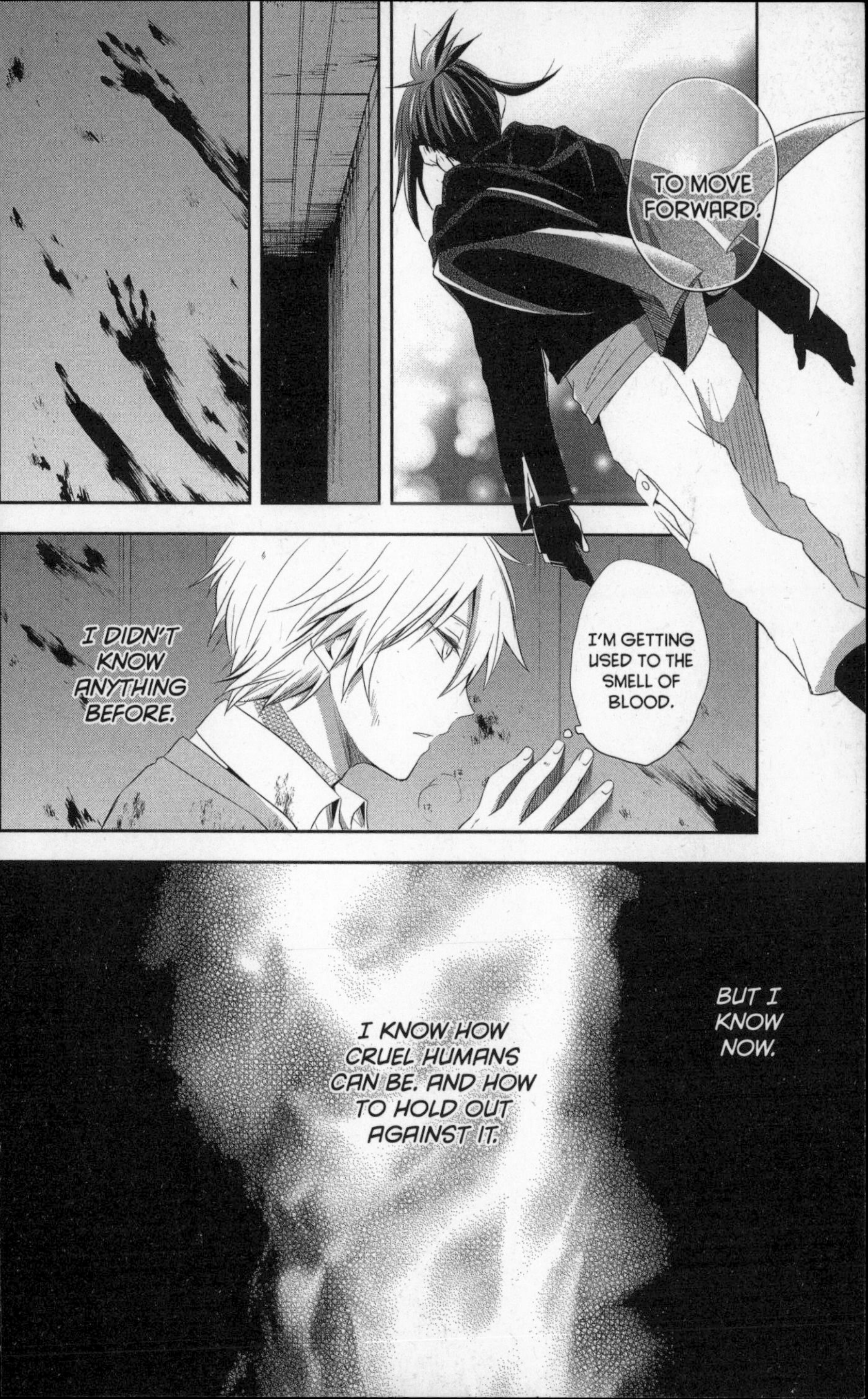
TO MOVE FORWARD.
I'M GETTING USED TO THE SMELL OF BLOOD.
I DIDN'T KNOW ANYTHING BEFORE.
BUT I KNOW NOW.
I KNOW HOW CRUEL HUMANS CAN BE. AND HOW TO HOLD OUT AGAINST IT.

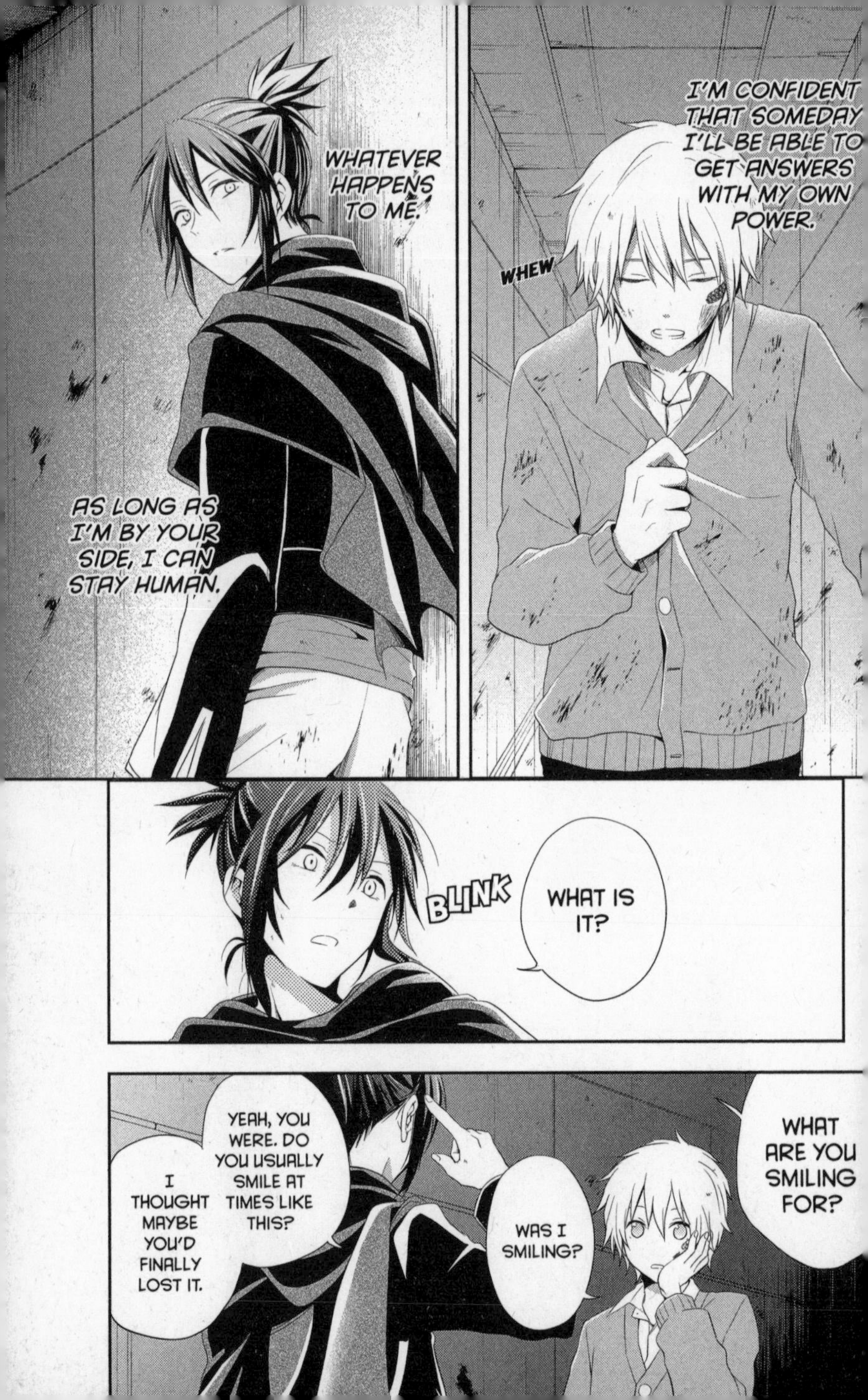
I'M CONFIDENT THAT SOMEDAY I'LL BE ABLE TO GET ANSWERS WITH MY OWN POWER.
WHEW
WHATEVER HAPPENS TO ME.
AS LONG AS I'M BY YOUR SIDE, I CAN STAY HUMAN.
BLINK
WHAT IS IT?
WHAT ARE YOU SMILING FOR?
WAS I SMILING?
YEAH, YOU WERE. DO YOU USUALLY SMILE AT TIMES LIKE THIS?
I THOUGHT MAYBE YOU'D FINALLY LOST IT.

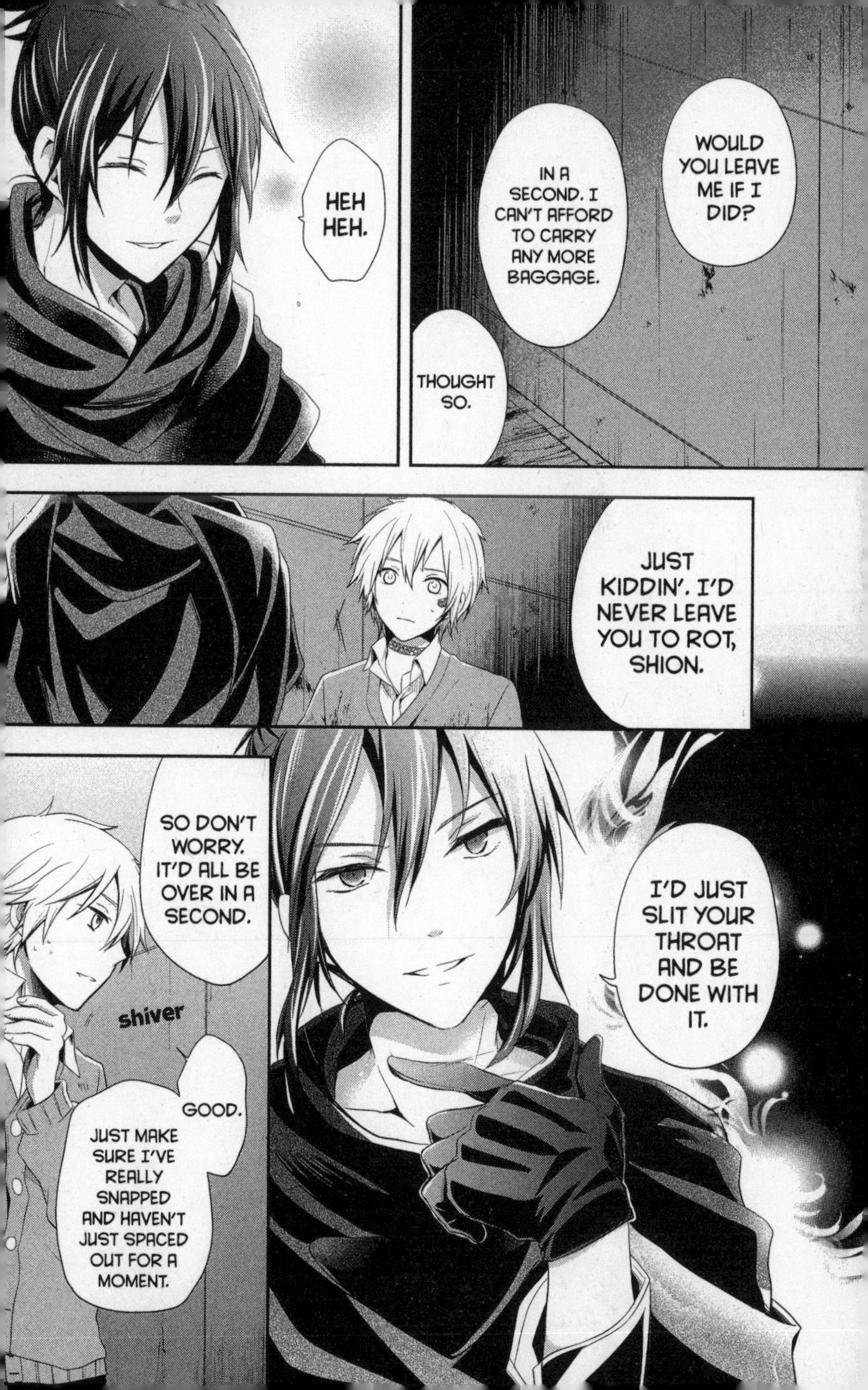
WOULD YOU LEAVE ME IF I DID?
IN A SECOND. I CAN'T AFFORD TO CARRY ANY MORE BAGGAGE.
THOUGHT SO.
HEH HEH.
JUST KIDDIN'. I'D NEVER LEAVE YOU TO ROT, SHION.
I'D JUST SLIT YOUR THROAT AND BE DONE WITH IT.
SO DON'T WORRY. IT'D ALL BE OVER IN A SECOND.
shiver
GOOD.
JUST MAKE SURE I'VE REALLY SNAPPED AND HAVEN'T JUST SPACED OUT FOR A MOMENT.

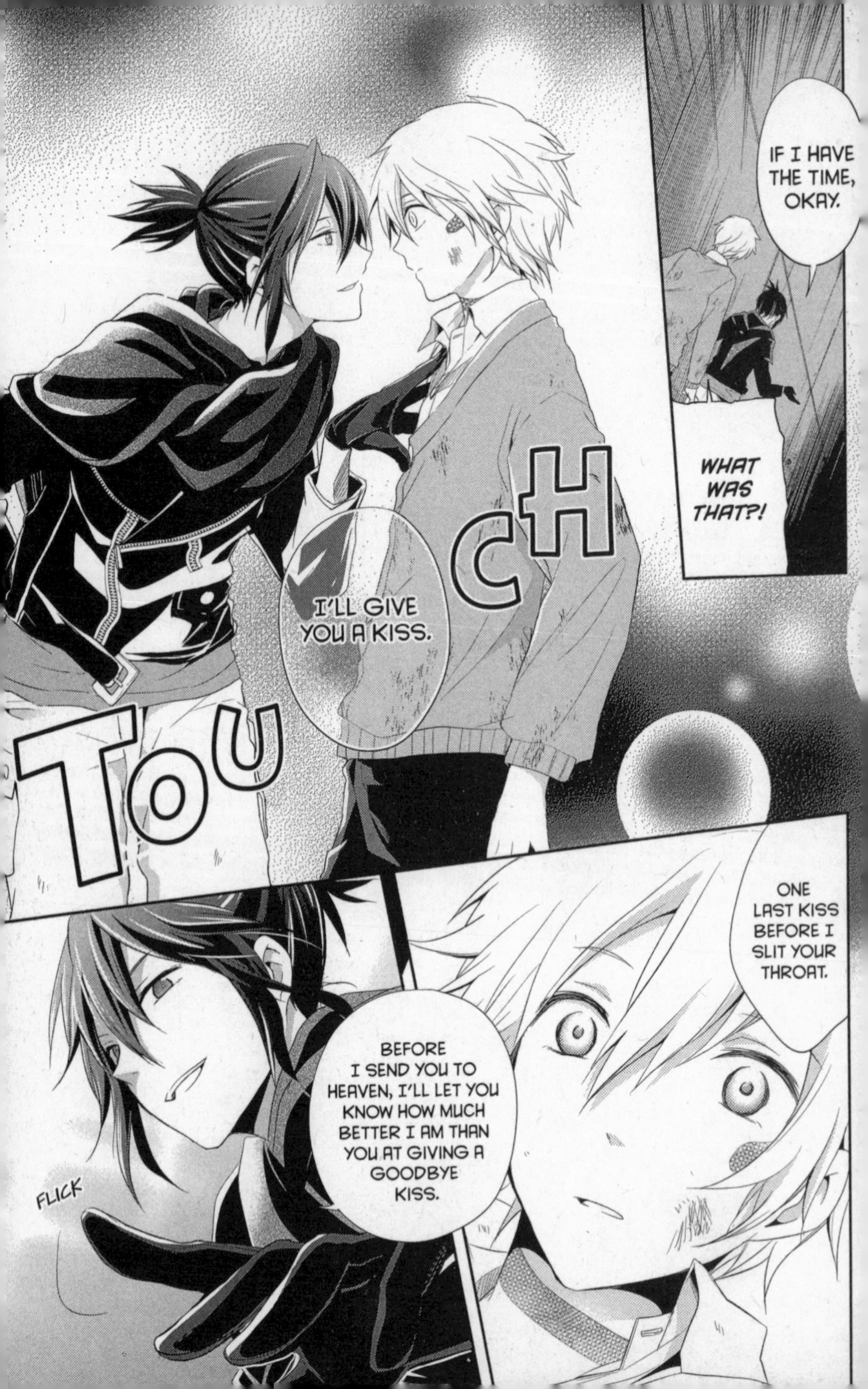
IF I HAVE THE TIME, OKAY.
WHAT WAS THAT?!
TOUCH
I'LL GIVE YOU A KISS.
ONE LAST KISS BEFORE I SLIT YOUR THROAT.
BEFORE I SEND YOU TO HEAVEN, I'LL LET YOU KNOW HOW MUCH BETTER I AM THAN YOU AT GIVING A GOODBYE KISS.
FLICK

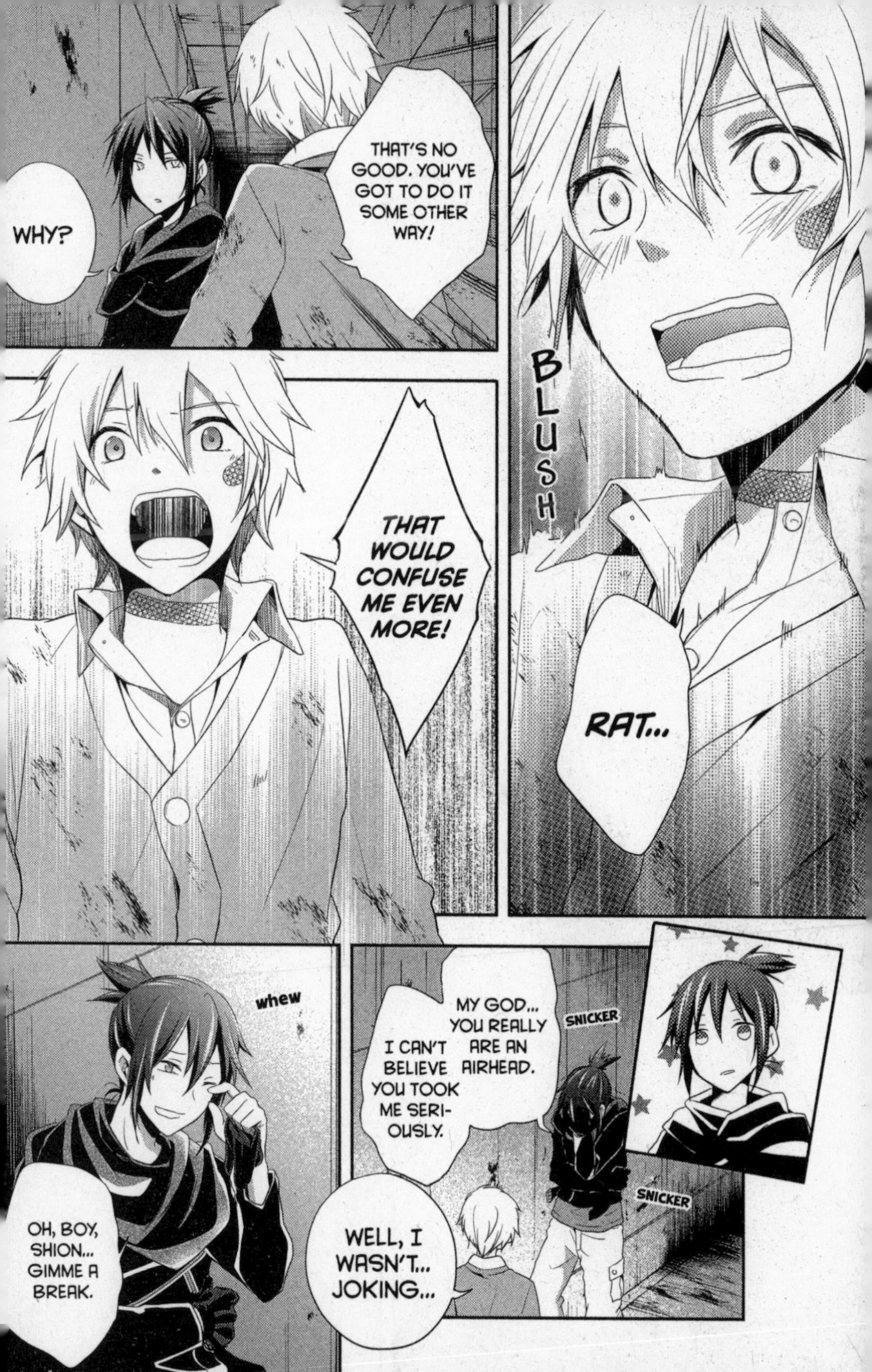
BLUSH
RAT...
THAT'S NO GOOD. YOU'VE GOT TO DO IT SOME OTHER WAY!
WHY?
THAT WOULD CONFUSE ME EVEN MORE!
SNICKER
MY GOD... YOU REALLY ARE AN AIRHEAD.
I CAN'T BELIEVE YOU TOOK ME SERIOUSLY.
SNICKER
WELL, I WASN'T... JOKING...
whew
OH, BOY, SHION... GIMME A BREAK.

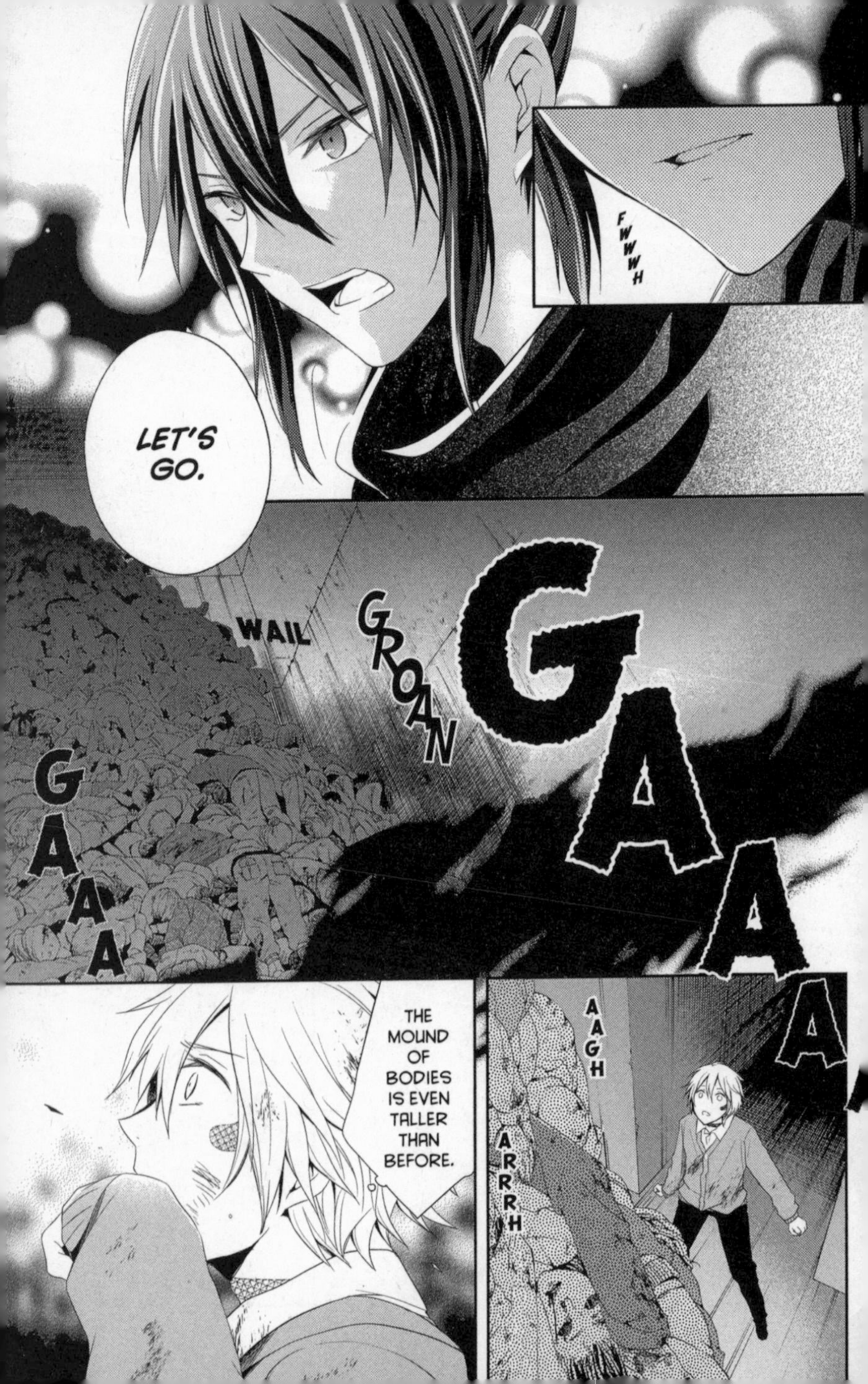
FWWWH
LET'S GO.
GAAAA
GROAN
WAIL
GAAA
AAGH
ARRRH
THE MOUND OF BODIES IS EVEN TALLER THAN BEFORE.

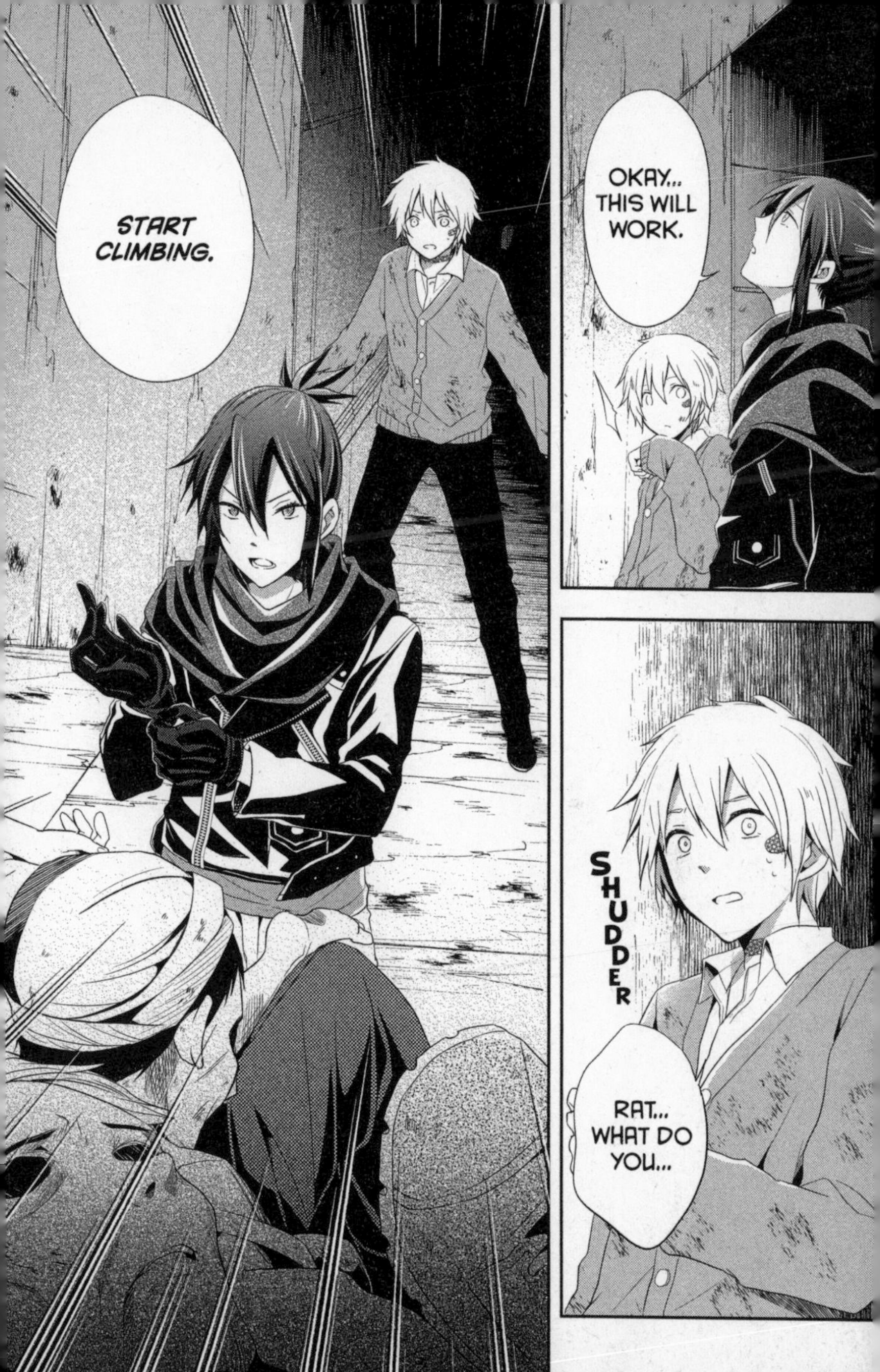
OKAY... THIS WILL WORK.
SHUDDER
RAT... WHAT DO YOU...
START CLIMBING.

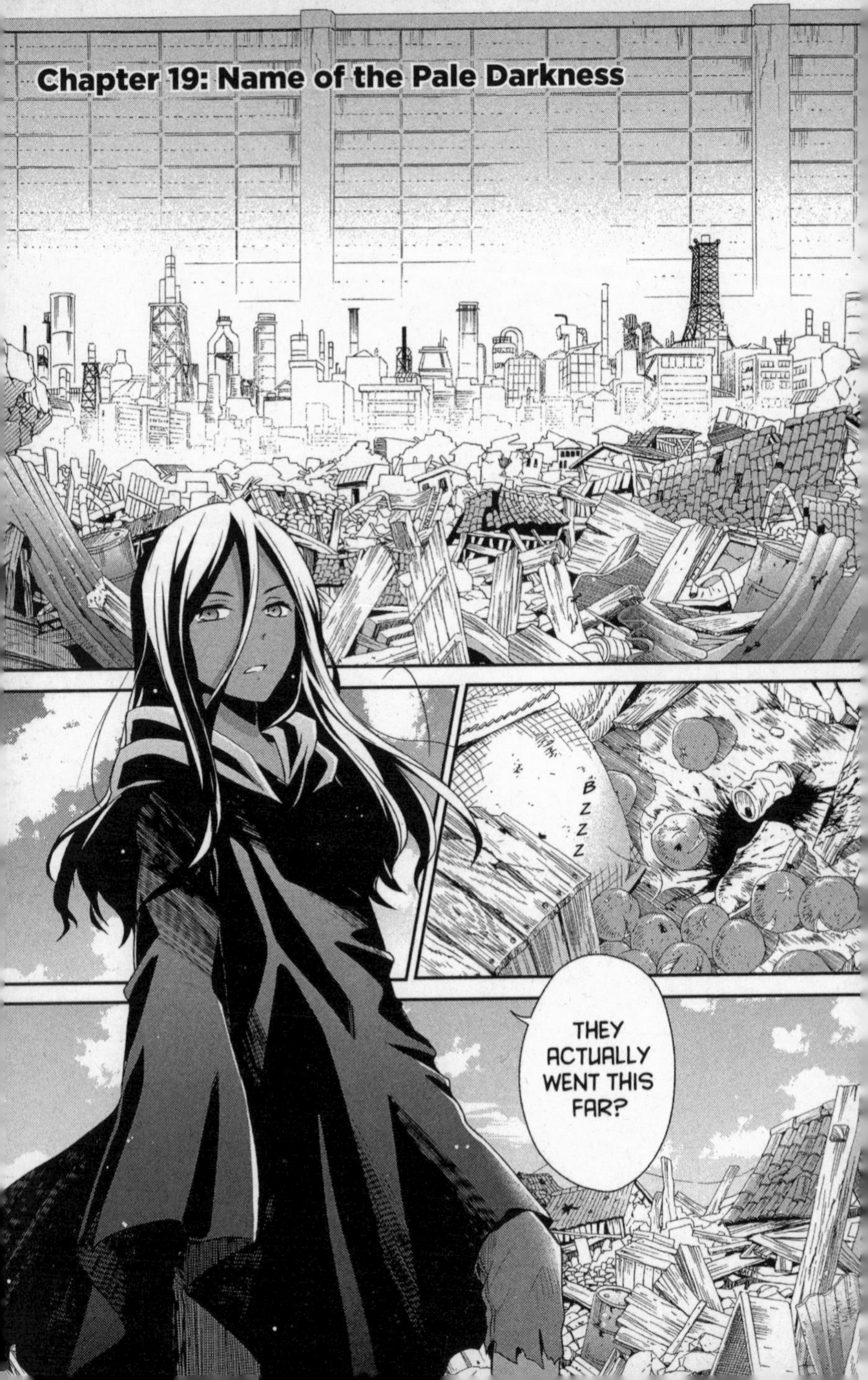
Chapter 19: Name of the Pale Darkness
BZZZ
THEY ACTUALLY WENT THIS FAR?

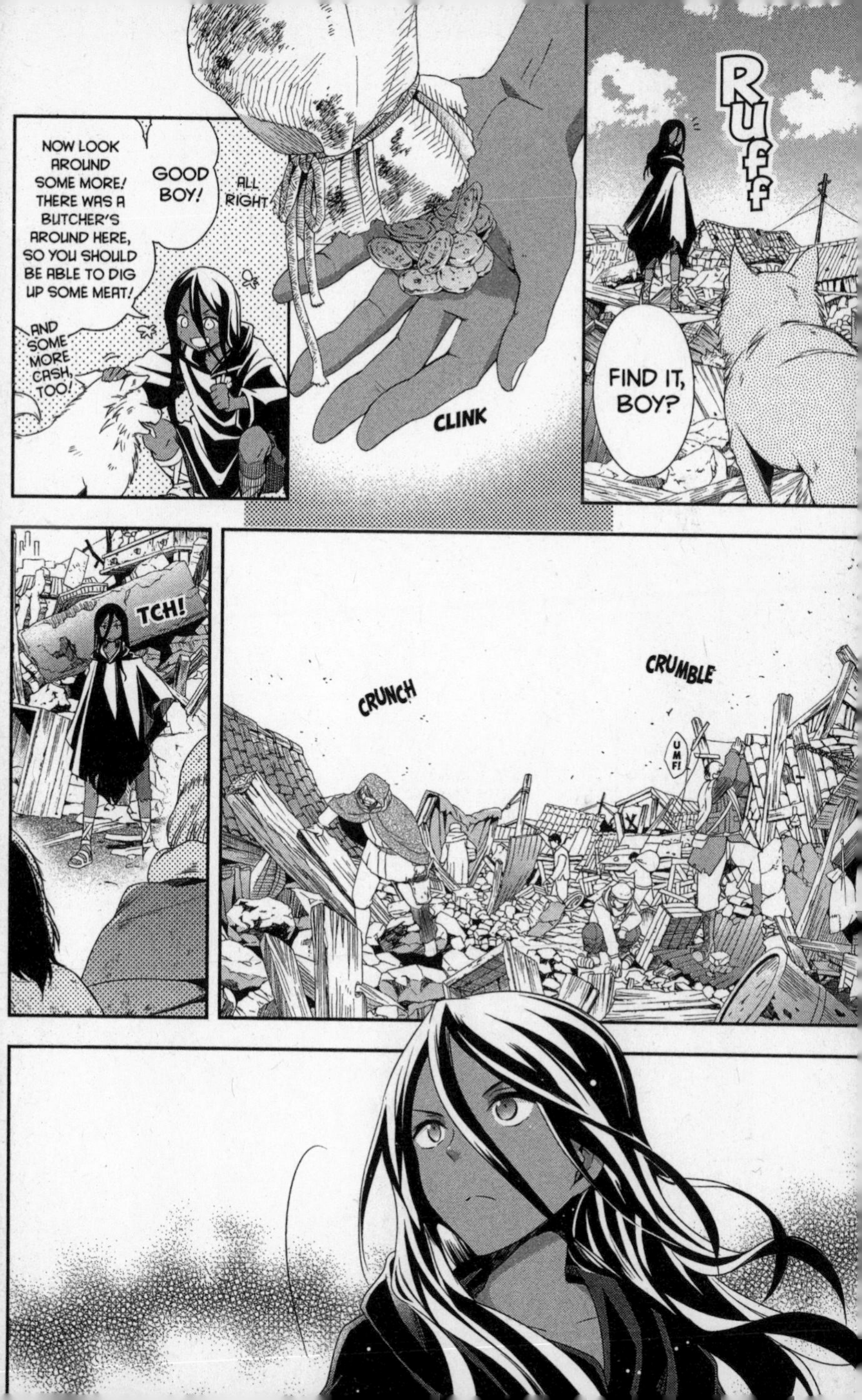

Ruff
FIND IT, BOY?
CLINK
ALL RIGHT
GOOD BOY!
NOW LOOK AROUND SOME MORE! THERE WAS A BUTCHER'S AROUND HERE, SO YOU SHOULD BE ABLE TO DIG UP SOME MEAT!
AND SOME MORE CASH, TOO!
CRUMBLE
UMF!
CRUNCH
TCH!

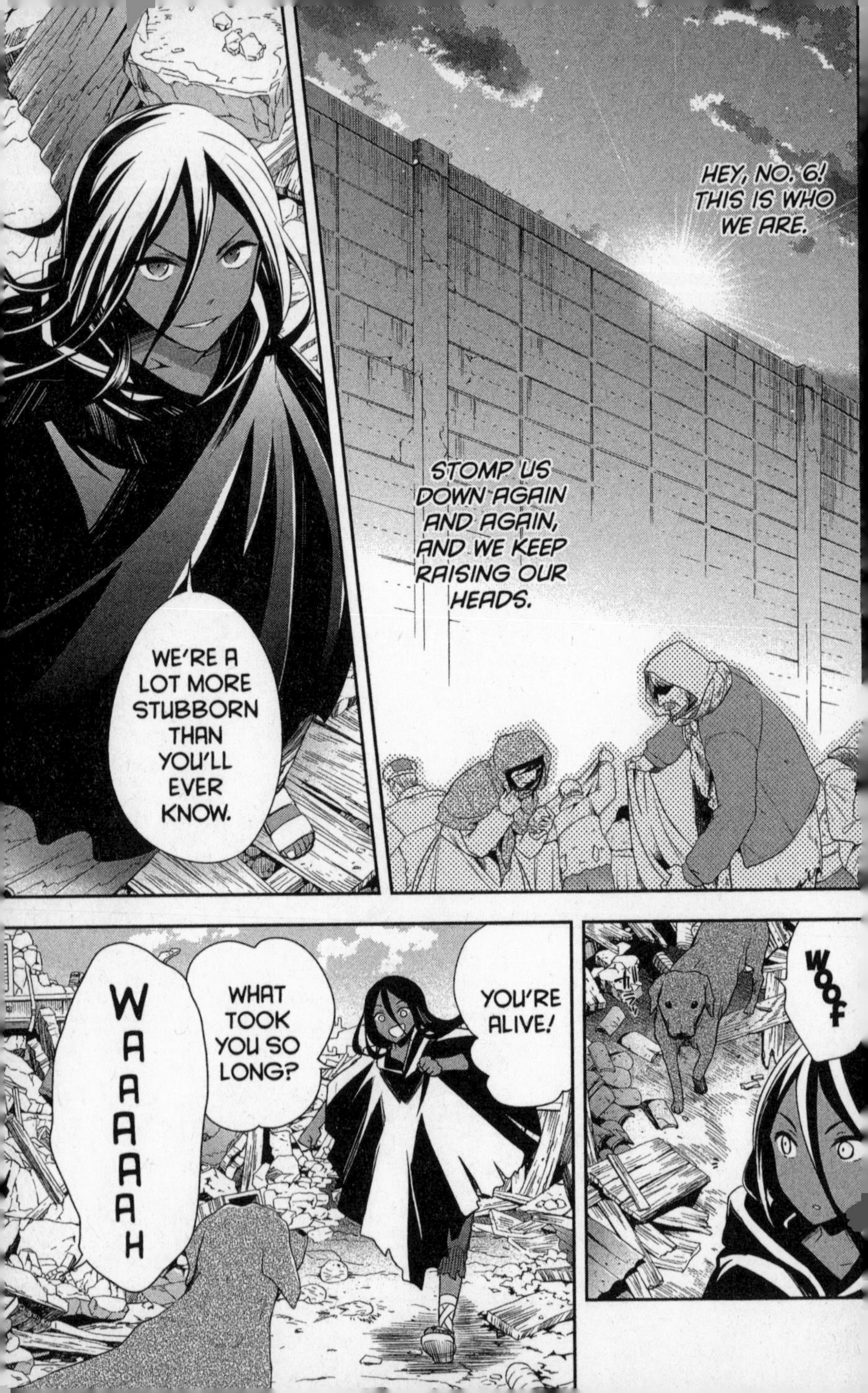
HEY, NO. 6! THIS IS WHO WE ARE.
STOMP US DOWN AGAIN AND AGAIN, AND WE KEEP RAISING OUR HEADS.
WE'RE A LOT MORE STUBBORN THAN YOU'LL EVER KNOW.
WOOF
YOU'RE ALIVE!
WHAT TOOK YOU SO LONG?
WAAAAAAH

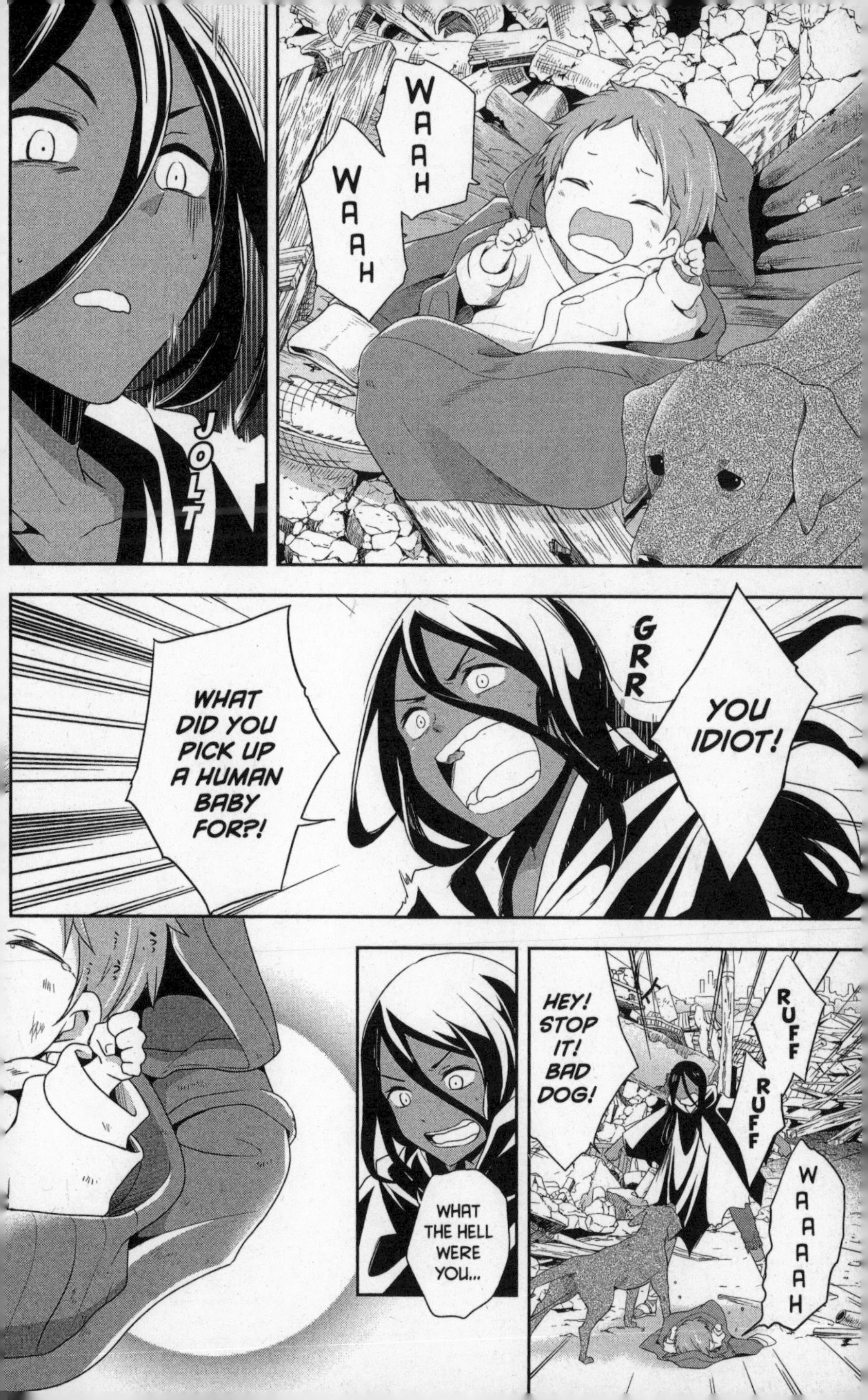
WAAH
WAAH
JOLT
GRR
YOU IDIOT!
WHAT DID YOU PICK UP A HUMAN BABY FOR?!
RUFF
RUFF
HEY! STOP IT! BAD DOG!
WAAAAH
WHAT THE HELL WERE YOU...

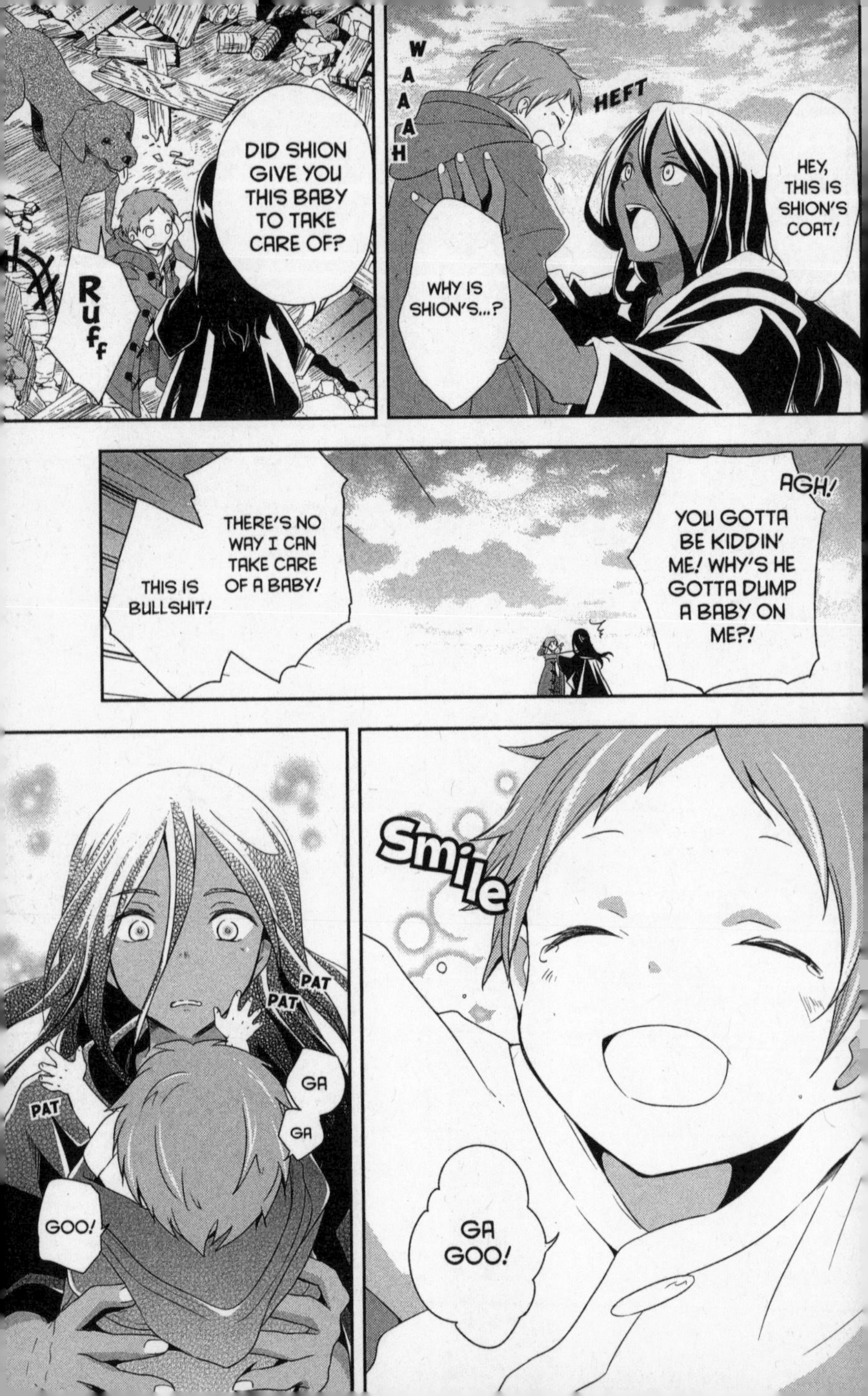
WAAAAH
HEFT
HEY, THIS IS SHION'S COAT!
WHY IS SHION'S...?
DID SHION GIVE YOU THIS BABY TO TAKE CARE OF?
Ruff
AGH!
YOU GOTTA BE KIDDIN' ME! WHY'S HE GOTTA DUMP A BABY ON ME?!
THERE'S NO WAY I CAN TAKE CARE OF A BABY!
THIS IS BULLSHIT!
Smile
GA GOO!
PAT
PAT
GA
GA
PAT
GOO!

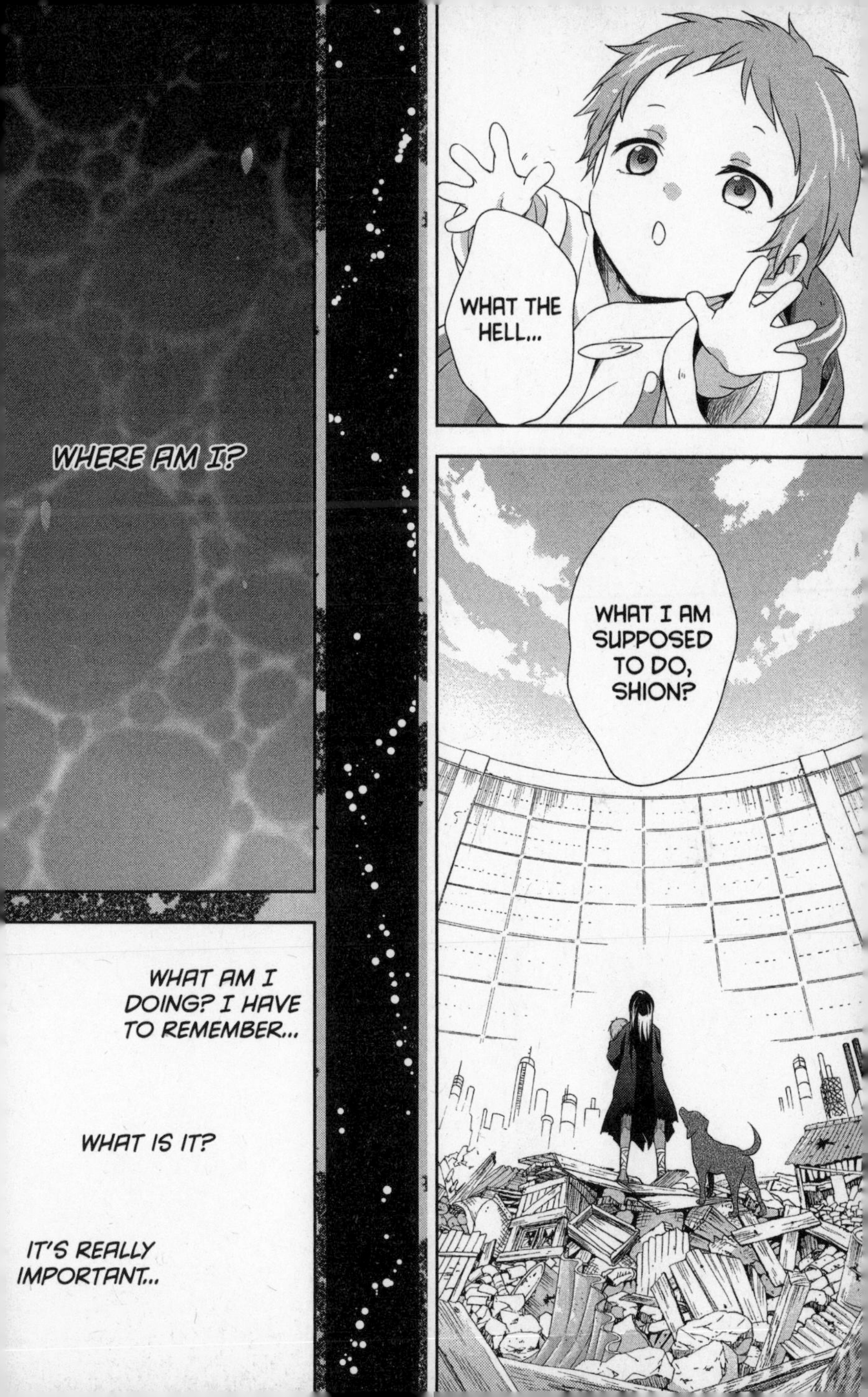
WHAT THE HELL...
WHAT I AM SUPPOSED TO DO, SHION?
WHERE AM I?
WHAT AM I DOING? I HAVE TO REMEMBER...
WHAT IS IT?
IT'S REALLY IMPORTANT...

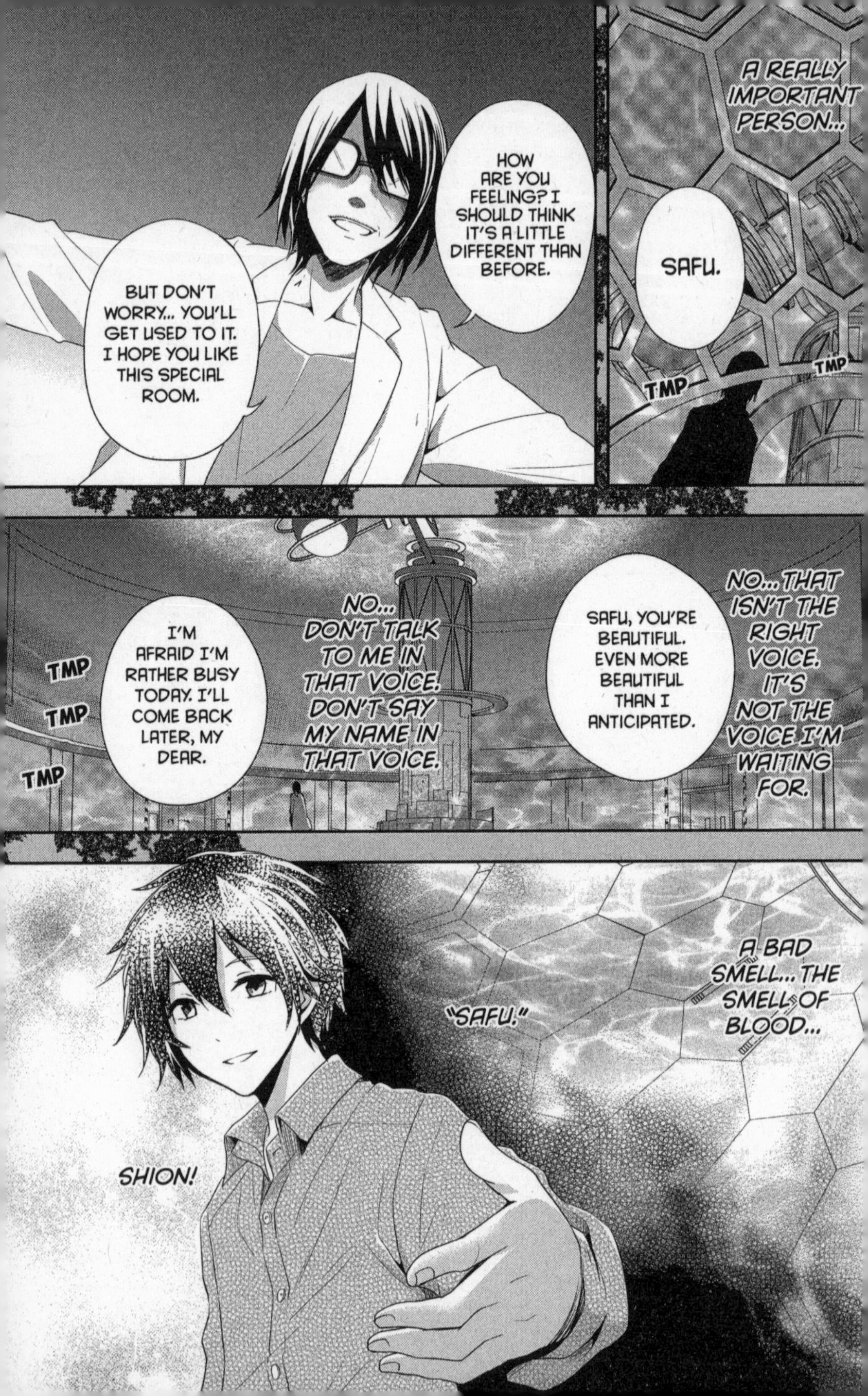
A REALLY IMPORTANT PERSON...
SAFU.
TMP
TMP
HOW ARE YOU FEELING? I SHOULD THINK IT'S A LITTLE DIFFERENT THAN BEFORE.
BUT DON'T WORRY... YOU'LL GET USED TO IT. I HOPE YOU LIKE THIS SPECIAL ROOM.
NO... THAT ISN'T THE RIGHT VOICE. IT'S NOT THE VOICE I'M WAITING FOR.
SAFU, YOU'RE BEAUTIFUL. EVEN MORE BEAUTIFUL THAN I ANTICIPATED.
NO... DON'T TALK TO ME IN THAT VOICE. DON'T SAY MY NAME IN THAT VOICE.
I'M AFRAID I'M RATHER BUSY TODAY. I'LL COME BACK LATER, MY DEAR.
TMP
TMP
TMP
A BAD SMELL... THE SMELL OF BLOOD...
"SAFU."
SHION!

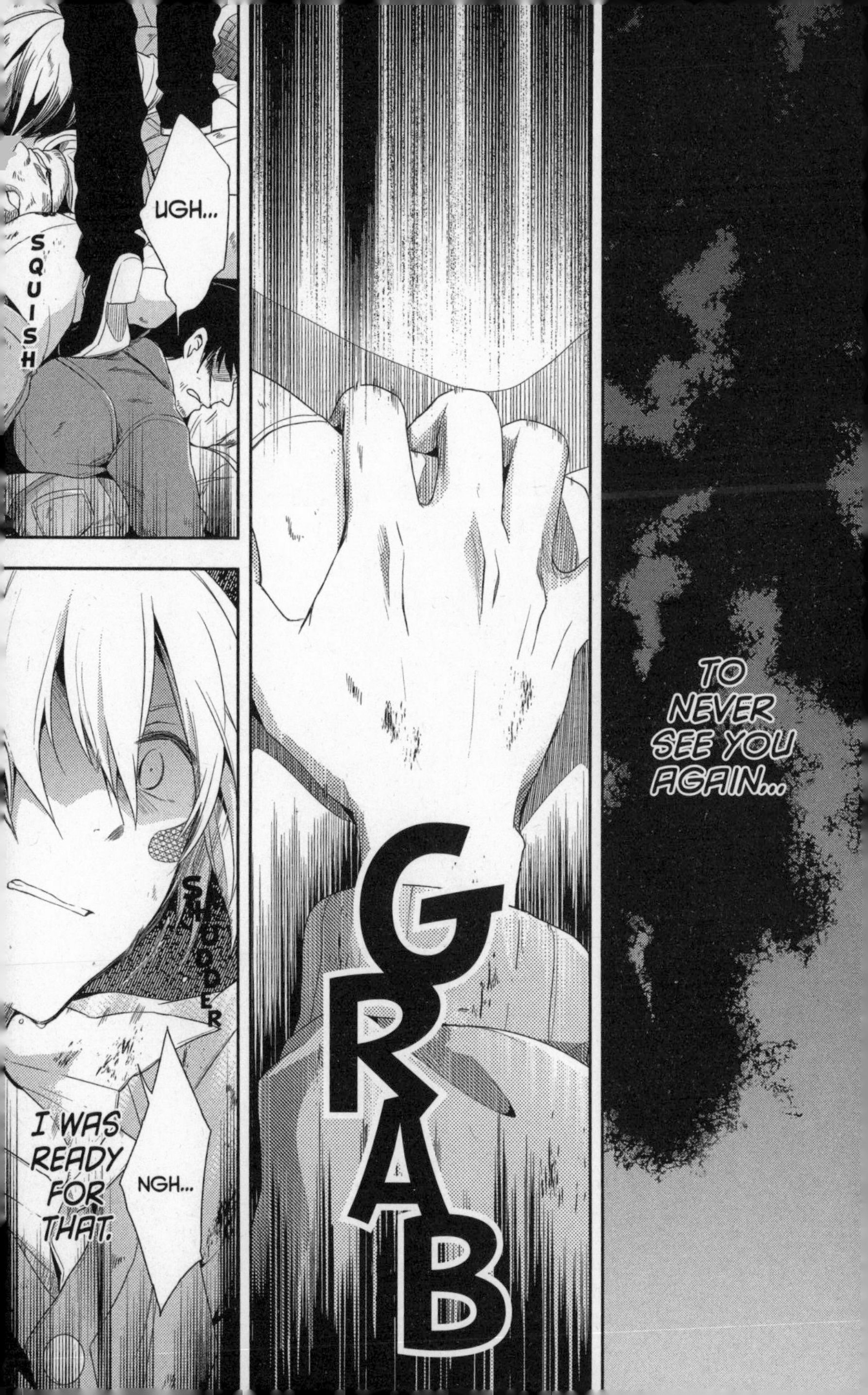
TO NEVER SEE YOU AGAIN...
GRAB
UGH...
SQUISH
SHUDDER
NGH...
I WAS READY FOR THAT.

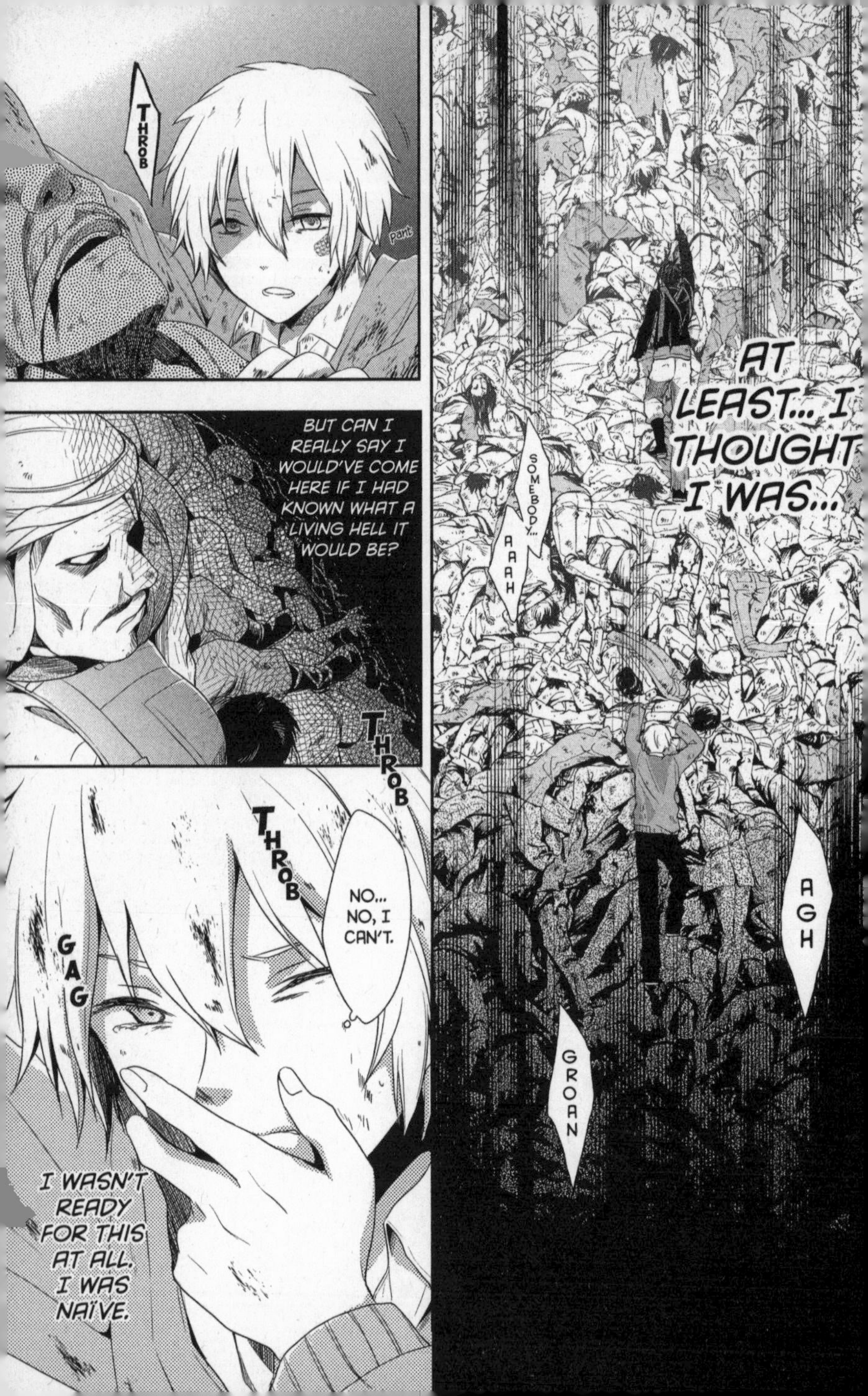
AT LEAST... I THOUGHT I WAS...
SOMEBODY...
AAAH
AGH
GROAN
THROB
pant
BUT CAN I REALLY SAY I WOULD'VE COME HERE IF I HAD KNOWN WHAT A LIVING HELL IT WOULD BE?
THROB
THROB
NO... NO, I CAN'T.
GAG
I WASN'T READY FOR THIS AT ALL. I WAS NAÏVE.

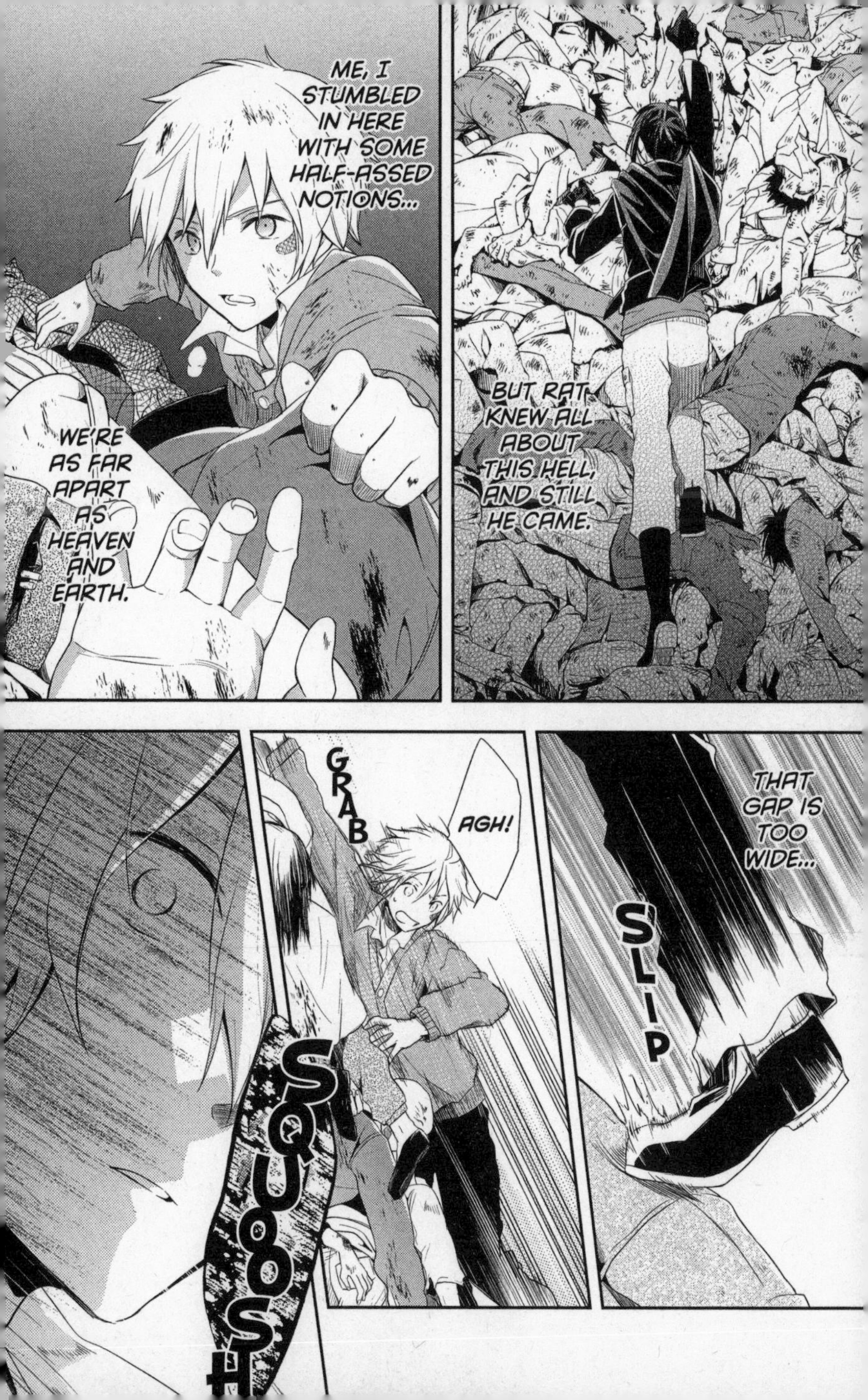
BUT RAT KNEW ALL ABOUT THIS HELL, AND STILL HE CAME.
ME, I STUMBLED IN HERE WITH SOME HALF-ASSED NOTIONS...
WE'RE AS FAR APART AS HEAVEN AND EARTH.
THAT GAP IS TOO WIDE...
SLIP
GRAB
AGH!
SQUOOSH

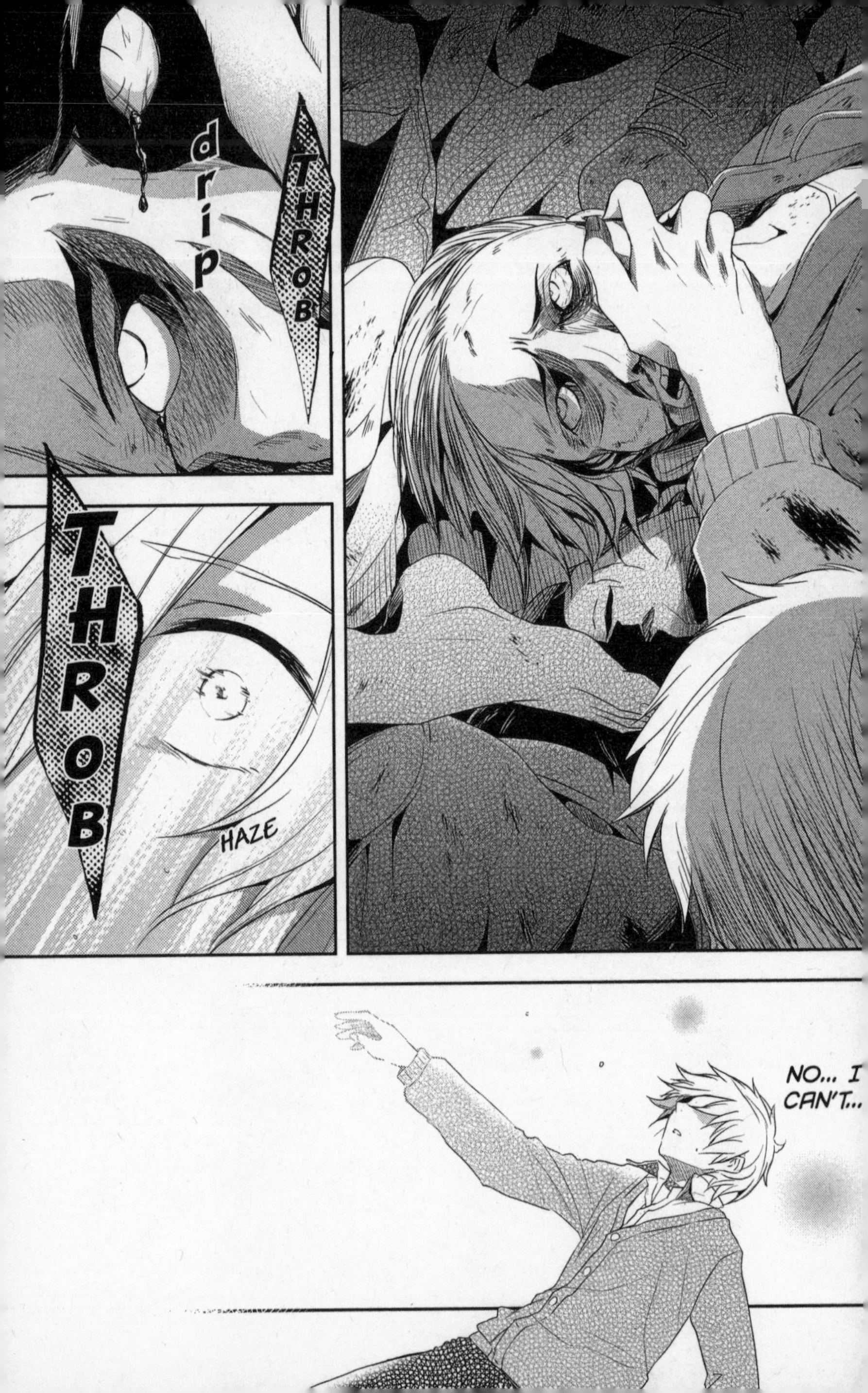
THROB
drip
THROB
HAZE
NO... I CAN'T...

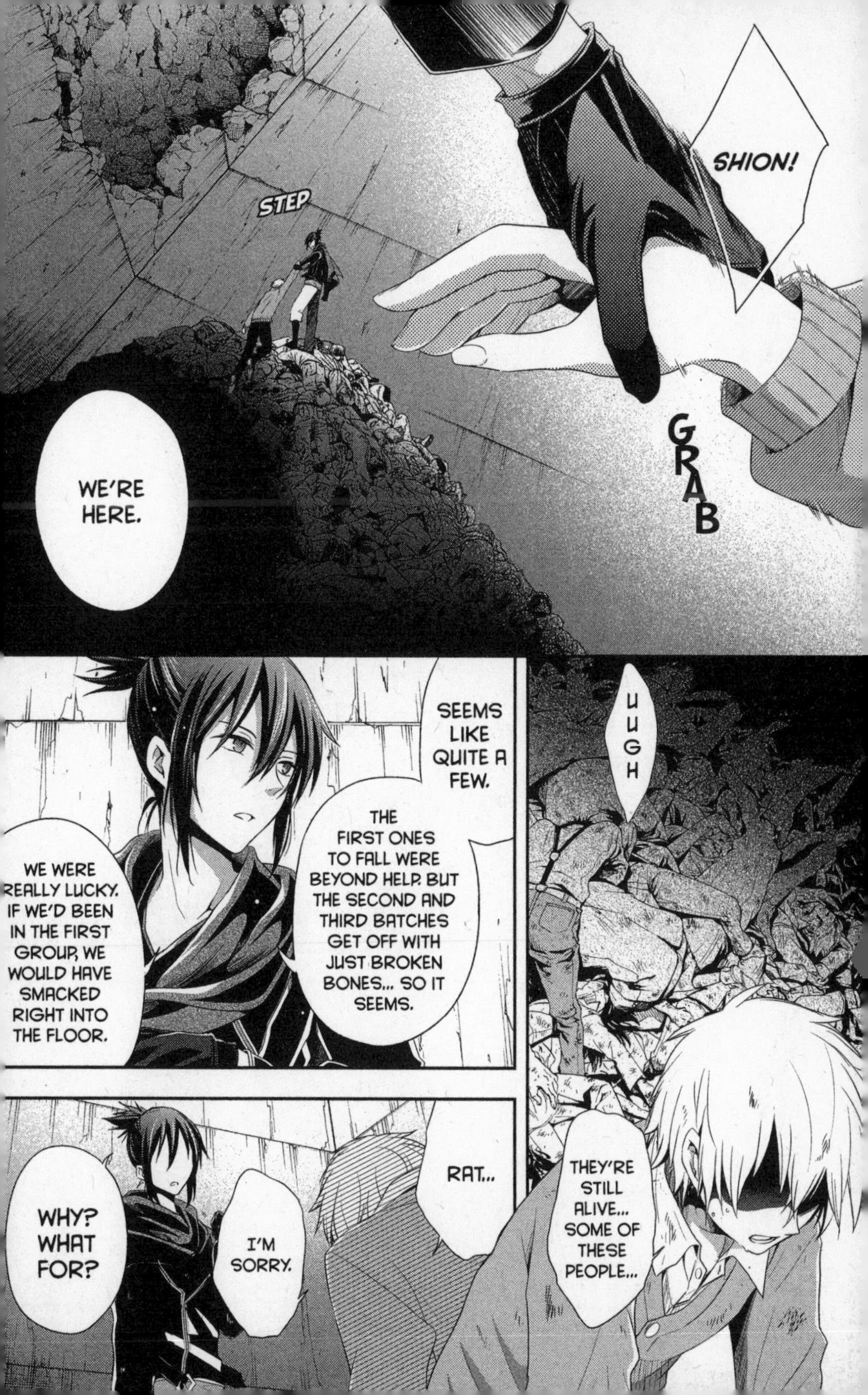
SHION!
GRAB
STEP
WE'RE HERE.
UUGH
SEEMS LIKE QUITE A FEW.
THE FIRST ONES TO FALL WERE BEYOND HELP. BUT THE SECOND AND THIRD BATCHES GET OFF WITH JUST BROKEN BONES... SO IT SEEMS.
WE WERE REALLY LUCKY. IF WE'D BEEN IN THE FIRST GROUP, WE WOULD HAVE SMACKED RIGHT INTO THE FLOOR.
THEY'RE STILL ALIVE... SOME OF THESE PEOPLE...
RAT...
I'M SORRY.
WHY? WHAT FOR?

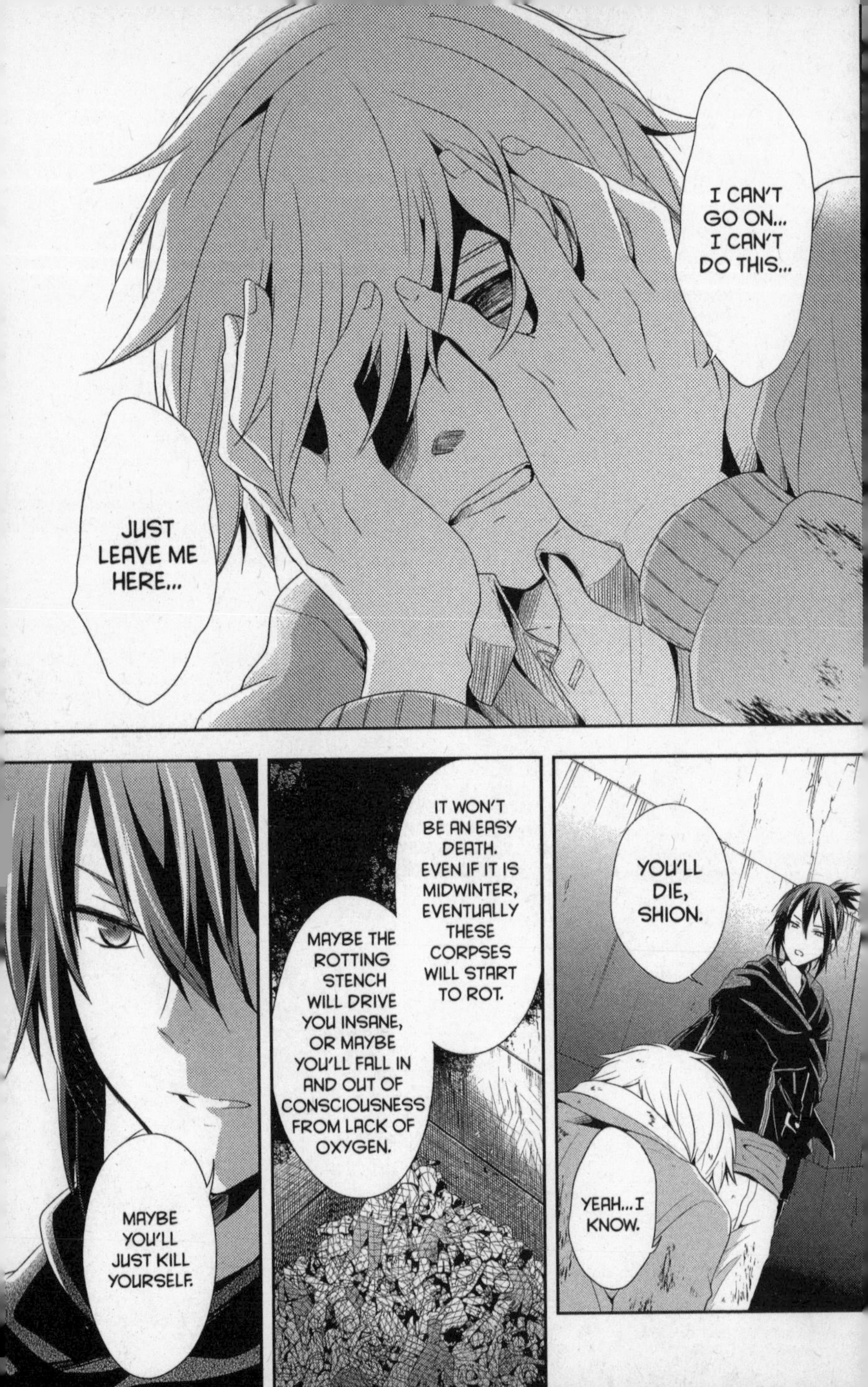
I CAN'T GO ON... I CAN'T DO THIS...
JUST LEAVE ME HERE...
YOU'LL DIE, SHION.
YEAH...I KNOW.
IT WON'T BE AN EASY DEATH. EVEN IF IT IS MIDWINTER, EVENTUALLY THESE CORPSES WILL START TO ROT.
MAYBE THE ROTTING STENCH WILL DRIVE YOU INSANE, OR MAYBE YOU'LL FALL IN AND OUT OF CONSCIOUSNESS FROM LACK OF OXYGEN.
MAYBE YOU'LL JUST KILL YOURSELF.

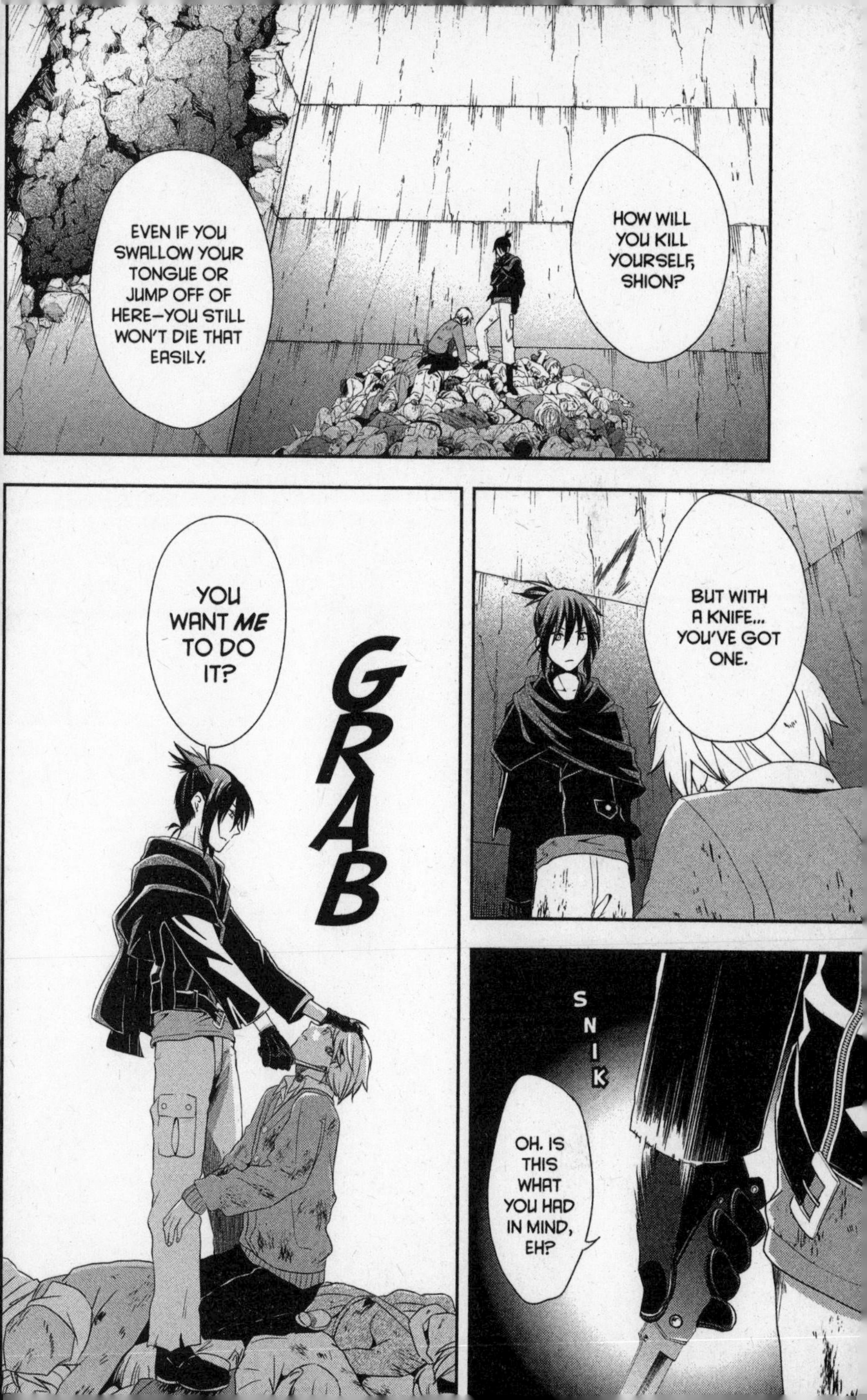
HOW WILL YOU KILL YOURSELF, SHION?
EVEN IF YOU SWALLOW YOUR TONGUE OR JUMP OFF OF HERE—YOU STILL WON'T DIE THAT EASILY.
BUT WITH A KNIFE... YOU'VE GOT ONE.
SNIK
OH. IS THIS WHAT YOU HAD IN MIND, EH?
YOU WANT *ME* TO DO IT?
GRAB

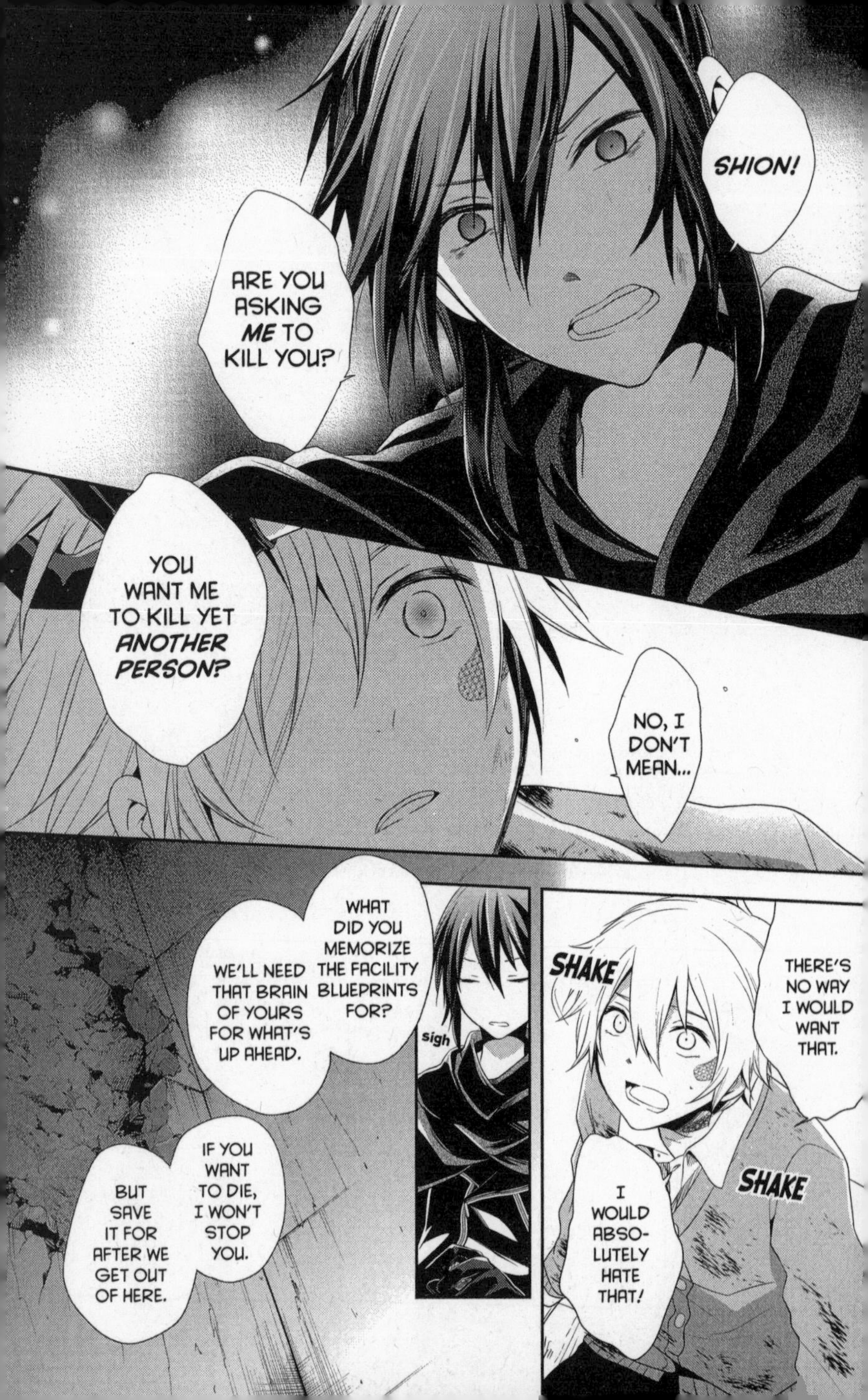
SHION!
ARE YOU ASKING *ME* TO KILL YOU?
YOU WANT ME TO KILL YET *ANOTHER PERSON?*
NO, I DON'T MEAN...
SHAKE
THERE'S NO WAY I WOULD WANT THAT.
SHAKE
I WOULD ABSO-LUTELY HATE THAT!
sigh
WHAT DID YOU MEMORIZE THE FACILITY BLUEPRINTS FOR?
WE'LL NEED THAT BRAIN OF YOURS FOR WHAT'S UP AHEAD.
IF YOU WANT TO DIE, I WON'T STOP YOU.
BUT SAVE IT FOR AFTER WE GET OUT OF HERE.

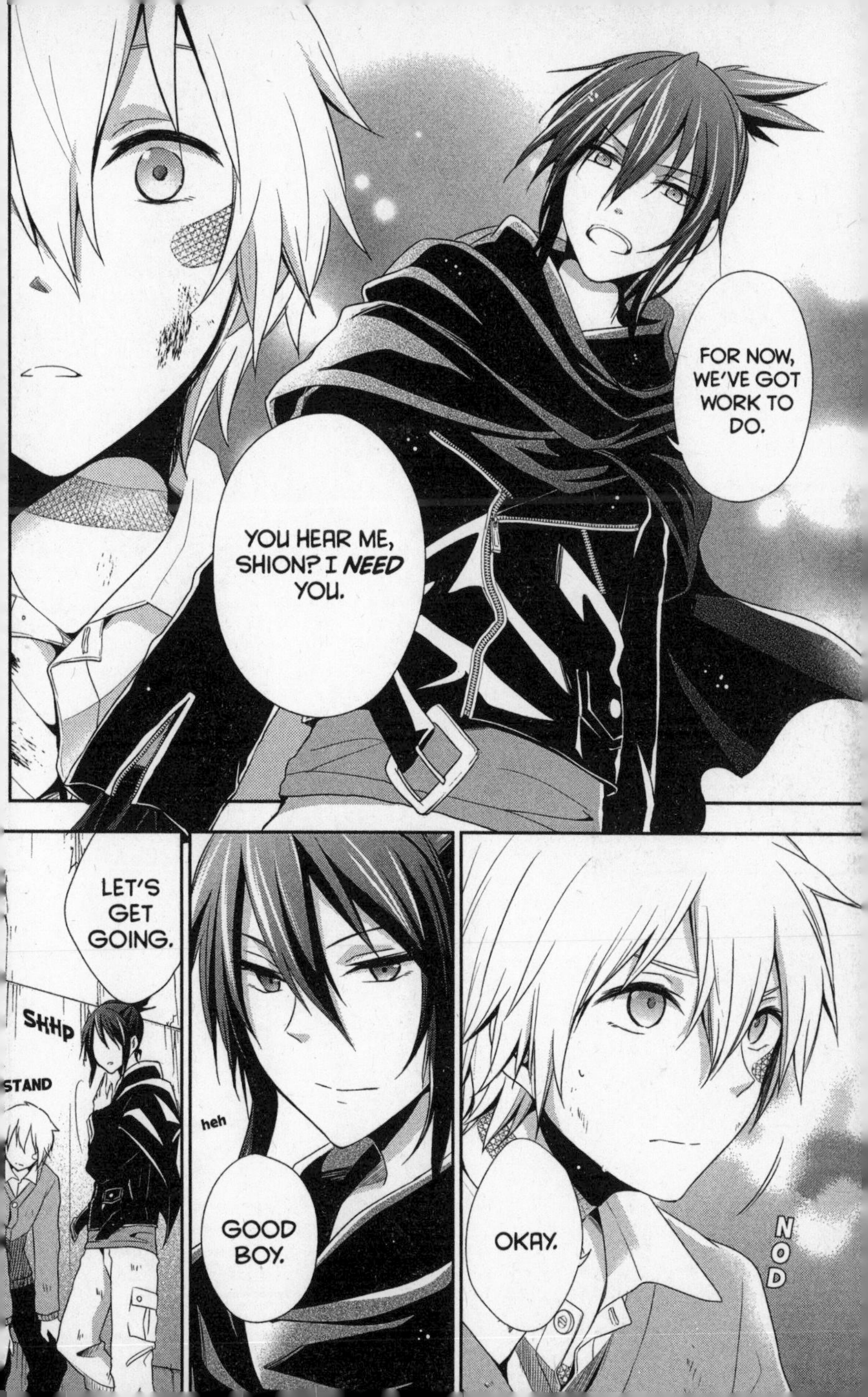
FOR NOW, WE'VE GOT WORK TO DO.
YOU HEAR ME, SHION? I *NEED* YOU.
NOD
OKAY.
heh
GOOD BOY.
LET'S GET GOING.
SHHP
STAND

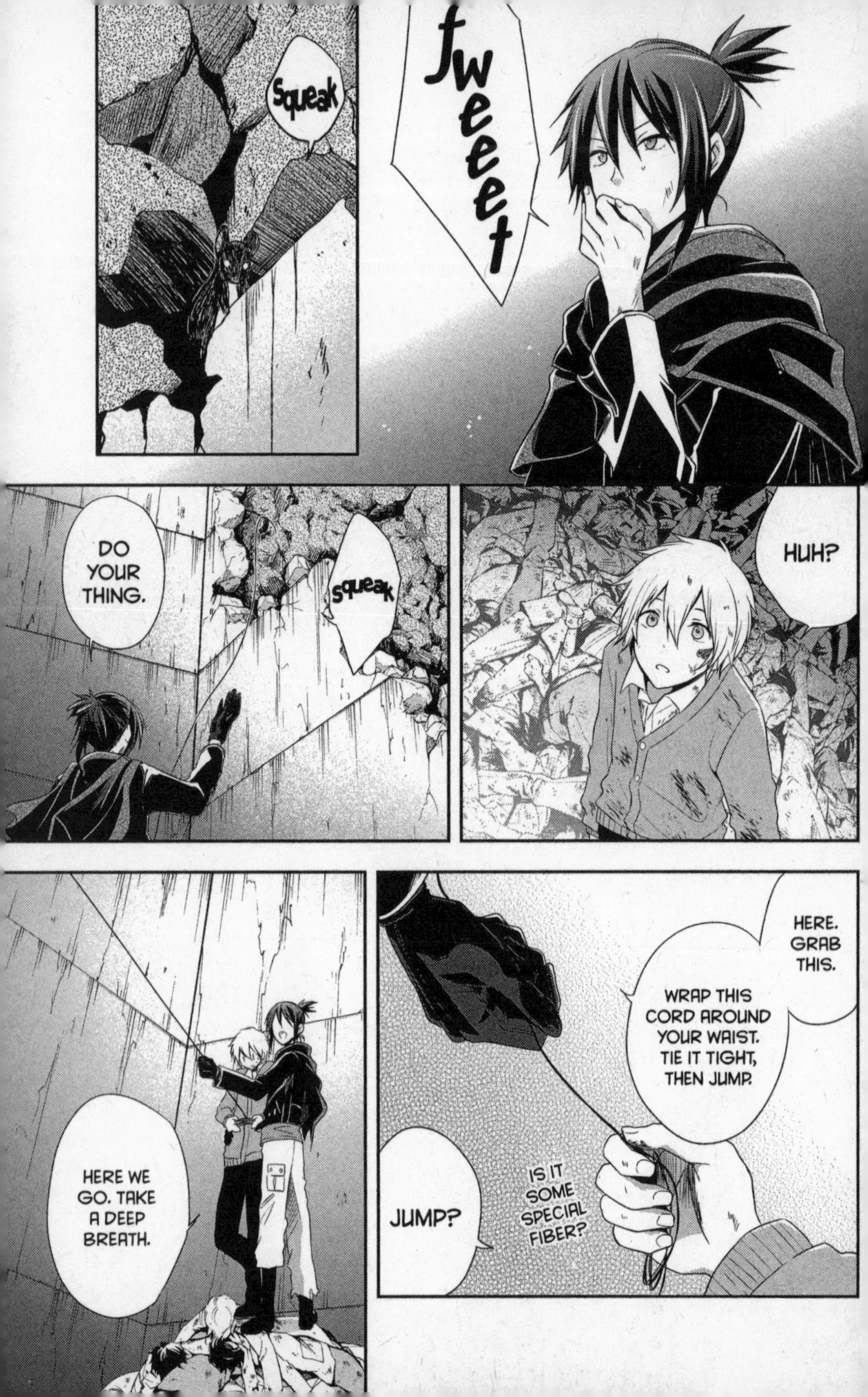
tweeet
Squeak
HUH?
squeak
DO YOUR THING.
HERE. GRAB THIS.
WRAP THIS CORD AROUND YOUR WAIST. TIE IT TIGHT, THEN JUMP.
IS IT SOME SPECIAL FIBER?
JUMP?
HERE WE GO. TAKE A DEEP BREATH.

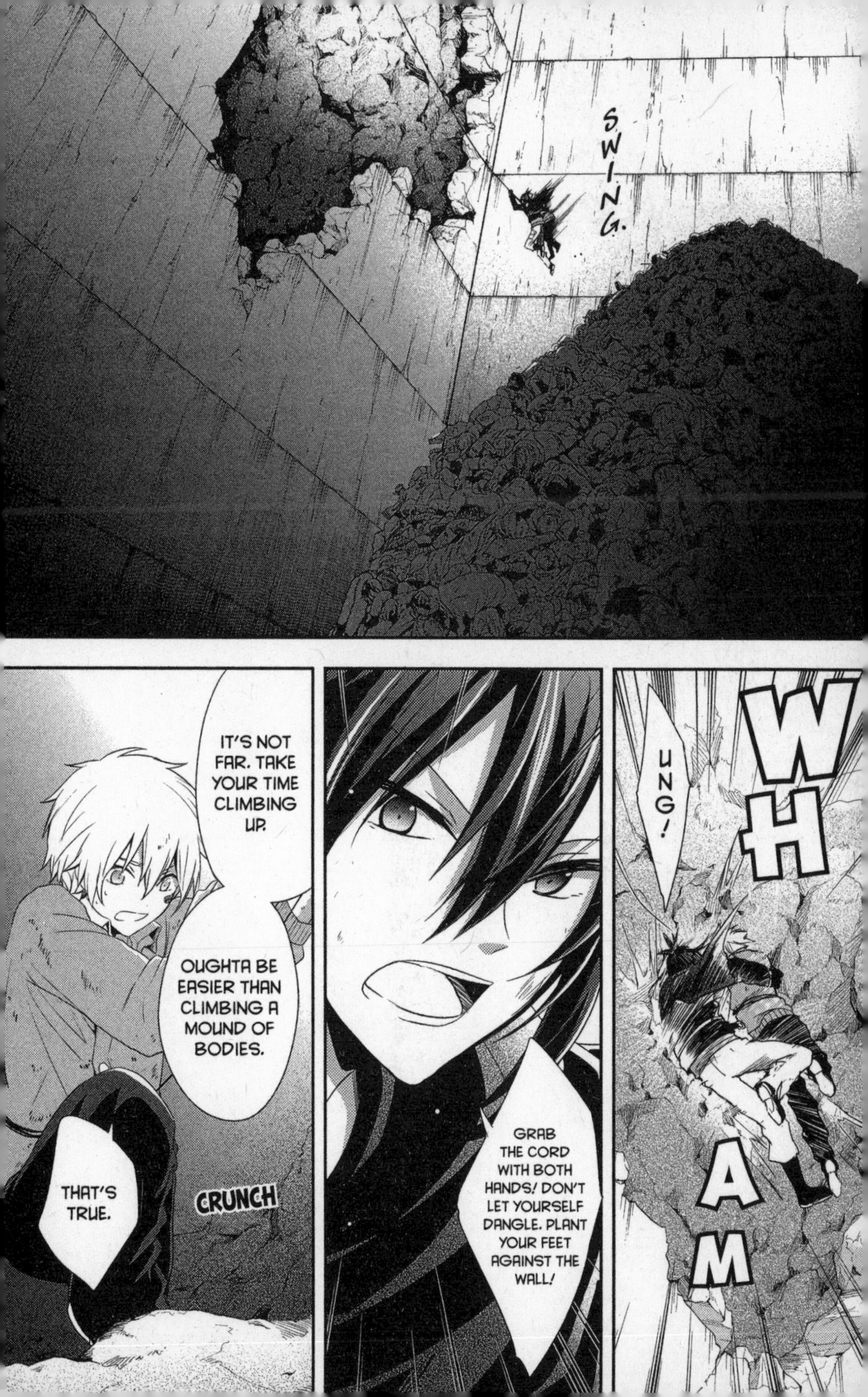
SWING.
UNG!
WHAM
GRAB THE CORD WITH BOTH HANDS! DON'T LET YOURSELF DANGLE. PLANT YOUR FEET AGAINST THE WALL!
IT'S NOT FAR. TAKE YOUR TIME CLIMBING UP.
OUGHTA BE EASIER THAN CLIMBING A MOUND OF BODIES.
CRUNCH
THAT'S TRUE.

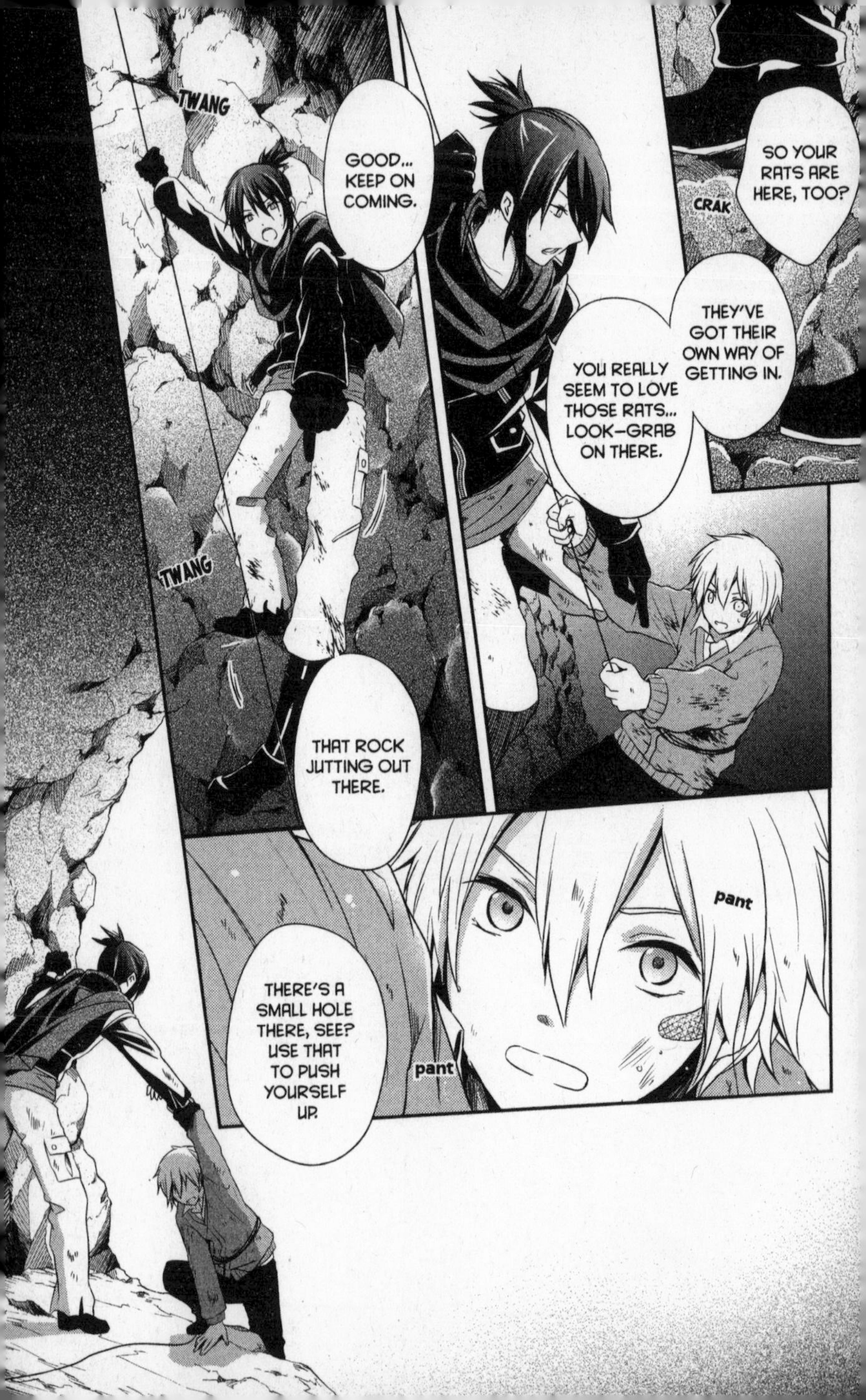
SO YOUR RATS ARE HERE, TOO?
CRAK
THEY'VE GOT THEIR OWN WAY OF GETTING IN.
YOU REALLY SEEM TO LOVE THOSE RATS... LOOK—GRAB ON THERE.
TWANG
GOOD... KEEP ON COMING.
TWANG
THAT ROCK JUTTING OUT THERE.
pant
THERE'S A SMALL HOLE THERE, SEE? USE THAT TO PUSH YOURSELF UP.
pant

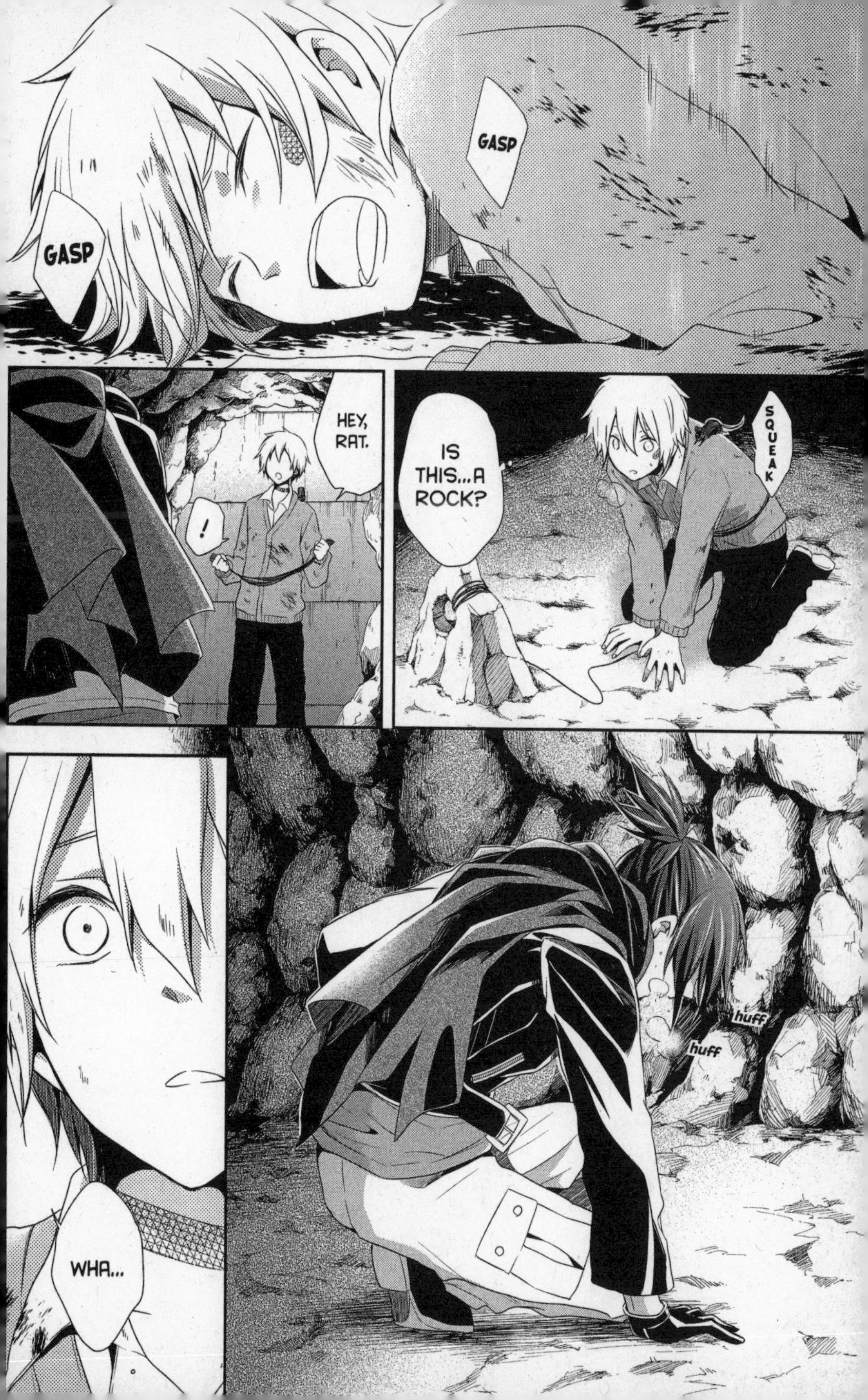
GASP
GASP
SQUEAK
IS THIS...A ROCK?
HEY, RAT.
!
huff
huff
WHA...

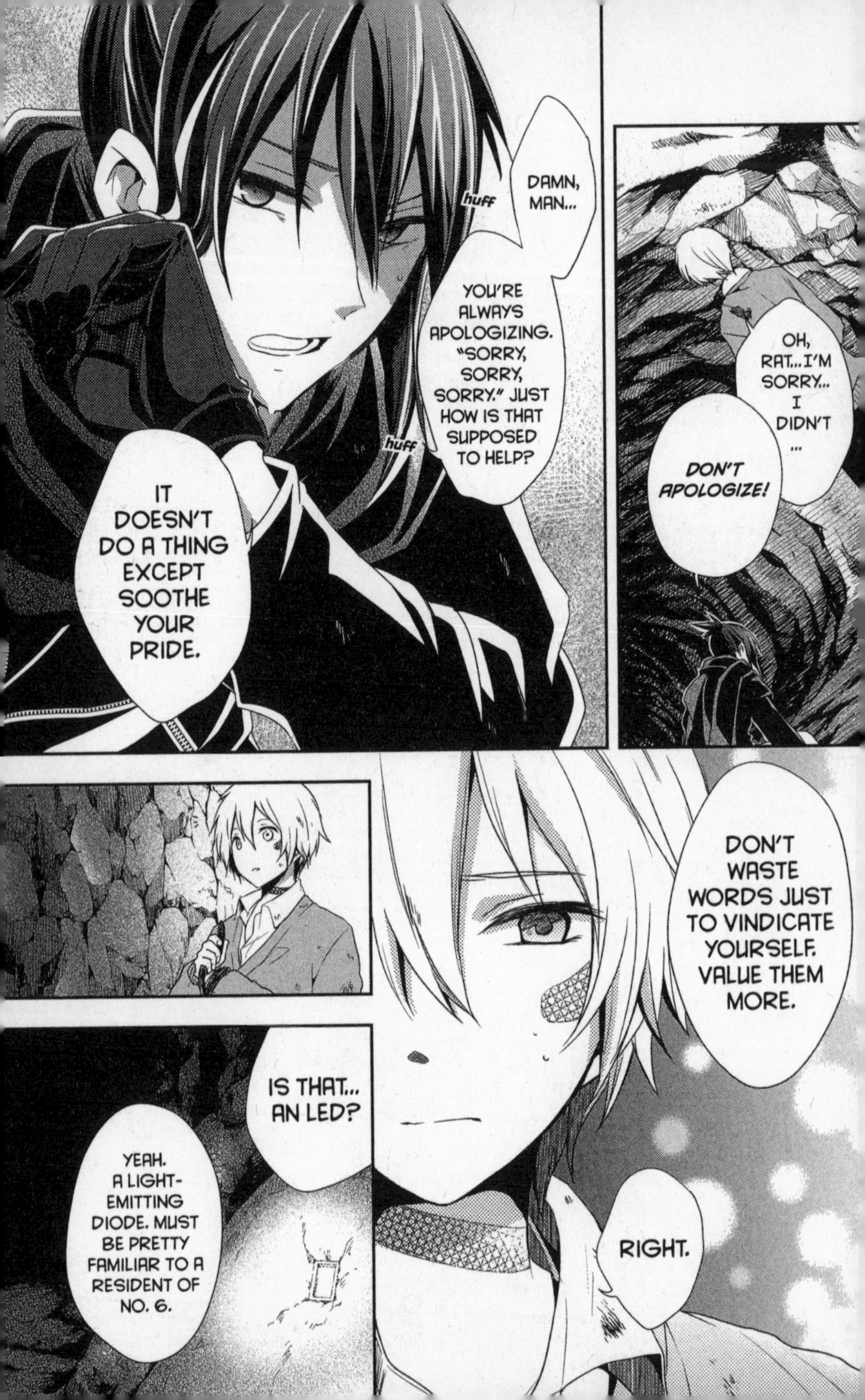
OH, RAT...I'M SORRY... I DIDN'T ...
DON'T APOLOGIZE!
huff
DAMN, MAN...
YOU'RE ALWAYS APOLOGIZING. "SORRY, SORRY, SORRY." JUST HOW IS THAT SUPPOSED TO HELP?
huff
IT DOESN'T DO A THING EXCEPT SOOTHE YOUR PRIDE.
DON'T WASTE WORDS JUST TO VINDICATE YOURSELF. VALUE THEM MORE.
RIGHT.
IS THAT... AN LED?
YEAH. A LIGHT-EMITTING DIODE. MUST BE PRETTY FAMILIAR TO A RESIDENT OF NO. 6.

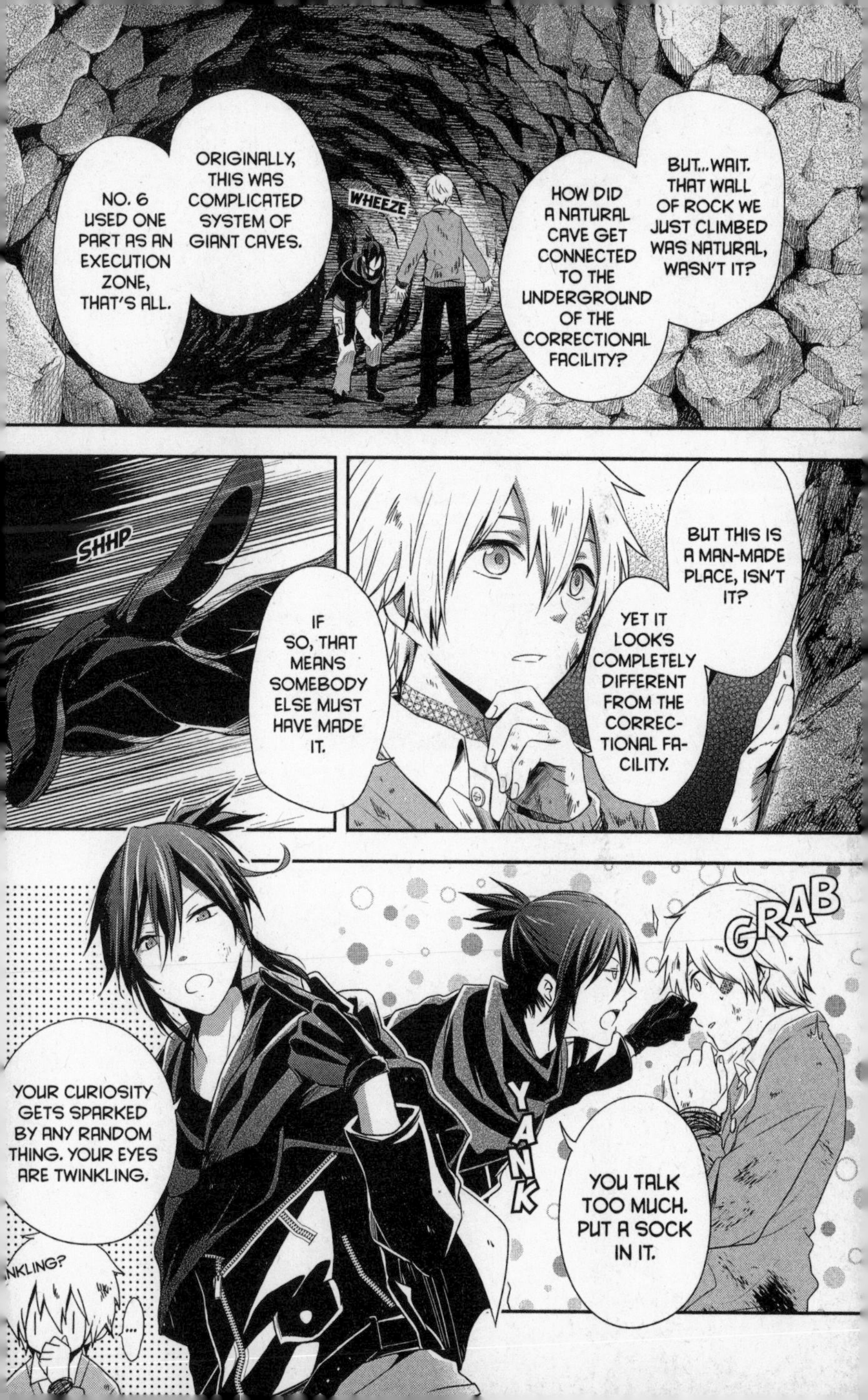
BUT...WAIT. THAT WALL OF ROCK WE JUST CLIMBED WAS NATURAL, WASN'T IT?
HOW DID A NATURAL CAVE GET CONNECTED TO THE UNDERGROUND OF THE CORRECTIONAL FACILITY?
WHEEZE
ORIGINALLY, THIS WAS COMPLICATED SYSTEM OF GIANT CAVES.
NO. 6 USED ONE PART AS AN EXECUTION ZONE, THAT'S ALL.
BUT THIS IS A MAN-MADE PLACE, ISN'T IT?
YET IT LOOKS COMPLETELY DIFFERENT FROM THE CORREC-TIONAL FA-CILITY.
IF SO, THAT MEANS SOMEBODY ELSE MUST HAVE MADE IT.
SHHP
GRAB
YOU TALK TOO MUCH. PUT A SOCK IN IT.
YANK
YOUR CURIOSITY GETS SPARKED BY ANY RANDOM THING. YOUR EYES ARE TWINKLING.
NKLING?
...

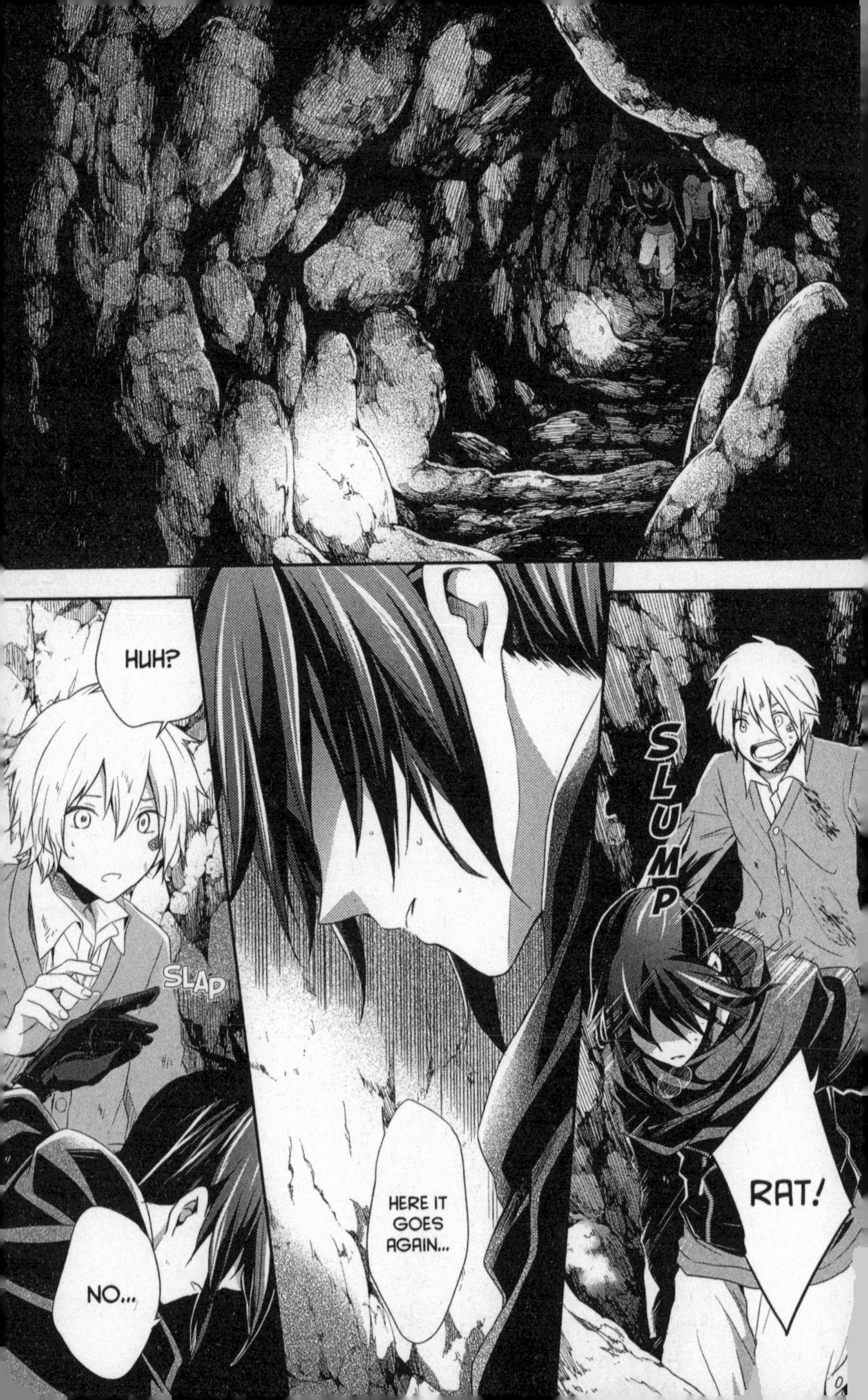
SLUMP
RAT!
HERE IT GOES AGAIN...
HUH?
SLAP
NO...

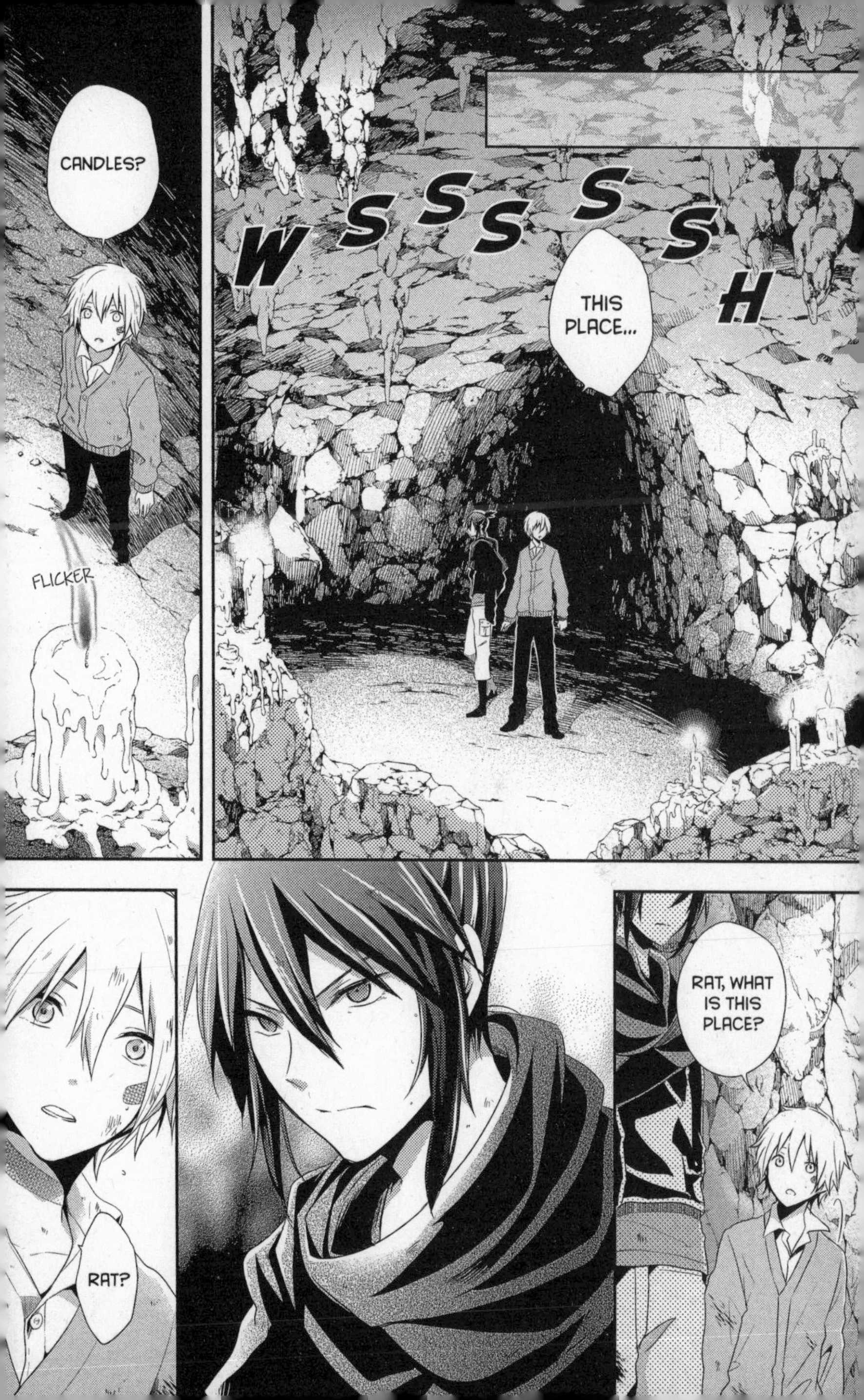
WSSSSSH
THIS PLACE...
CANDLES?
FLICKER
RAT, WHAT IS THIS PLACE?
RAT?

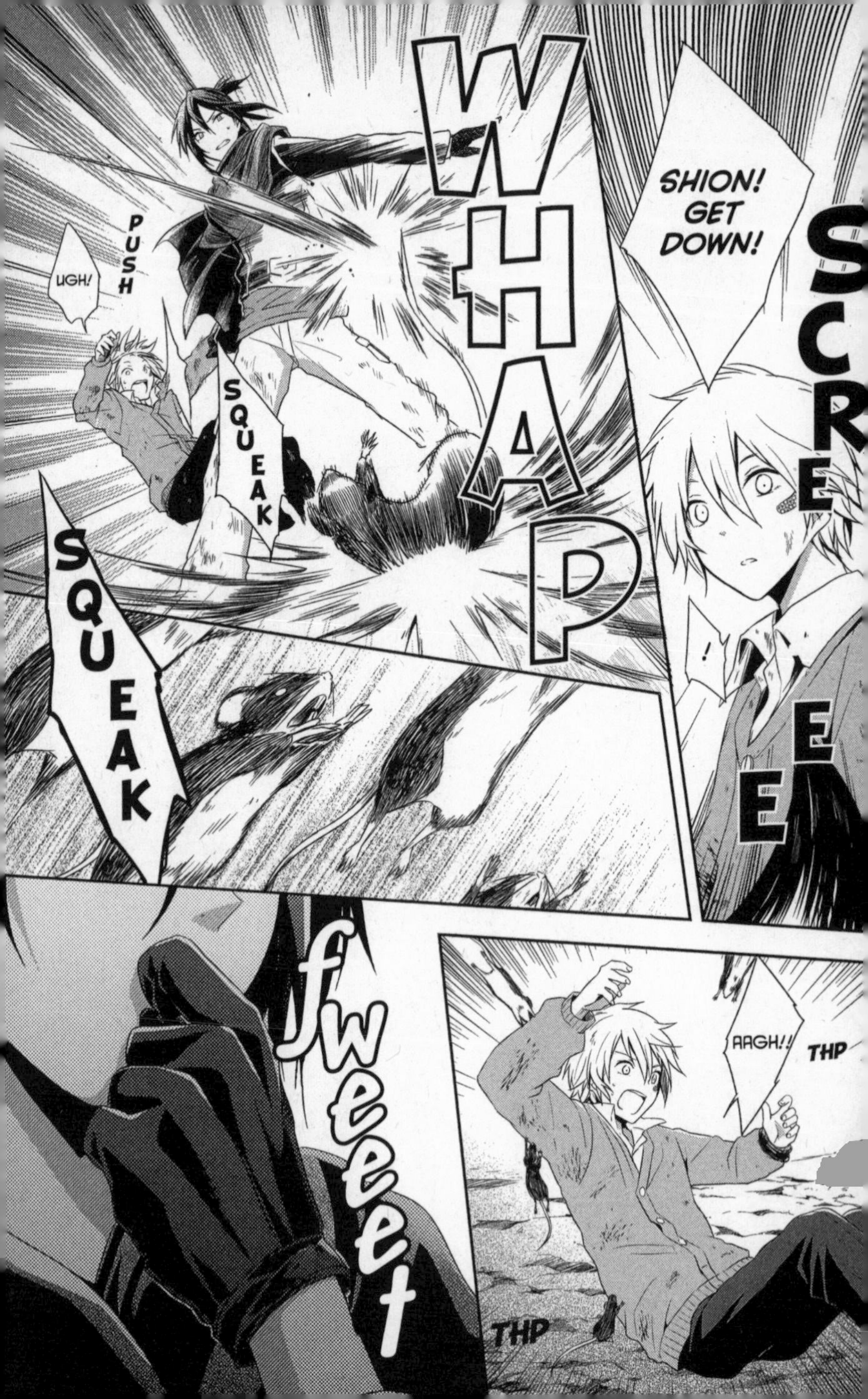
SHION! GET DOWN!
SCREEEE
WHAP
PUSH
UGH!
SQUEAK
SQUEAK
AAGH!!
THP
THP
fweeet

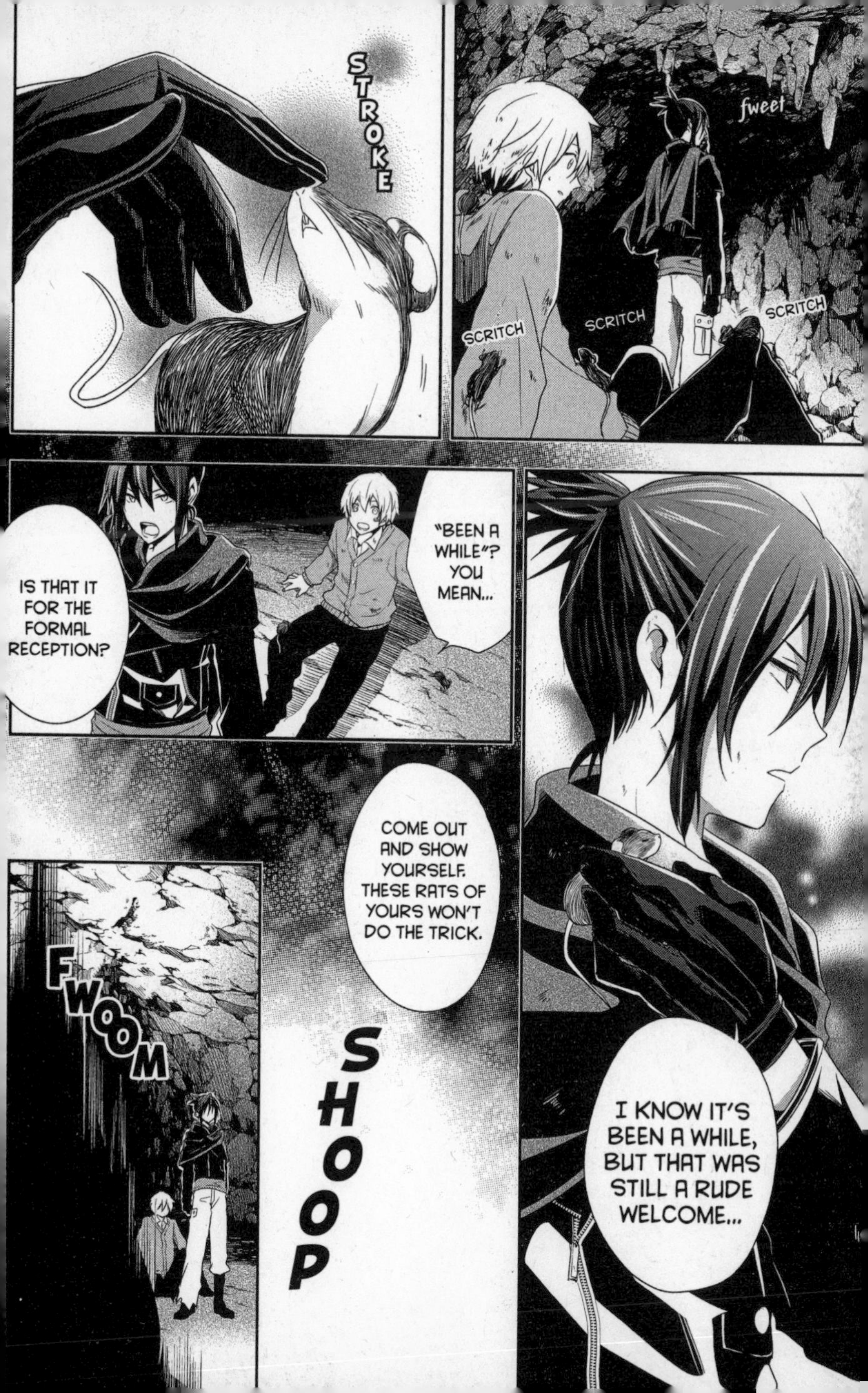
fweet
SCRITCH
SCRITCH
SCRITCH
STROKE
I KNOW IT'S BEEN A WHILE, BUT THAT WAS STILL A RUDE WELCOME...
"BEEN A WHILE"? YOU MEAN...
IS THAT IT FOR THE FORMAL RECEPTION?
COME OUT AND SHOW YOURSELF. THESE RATS OF YOURS WON'T DO THE TRICK.
SHOOP
FWOOM

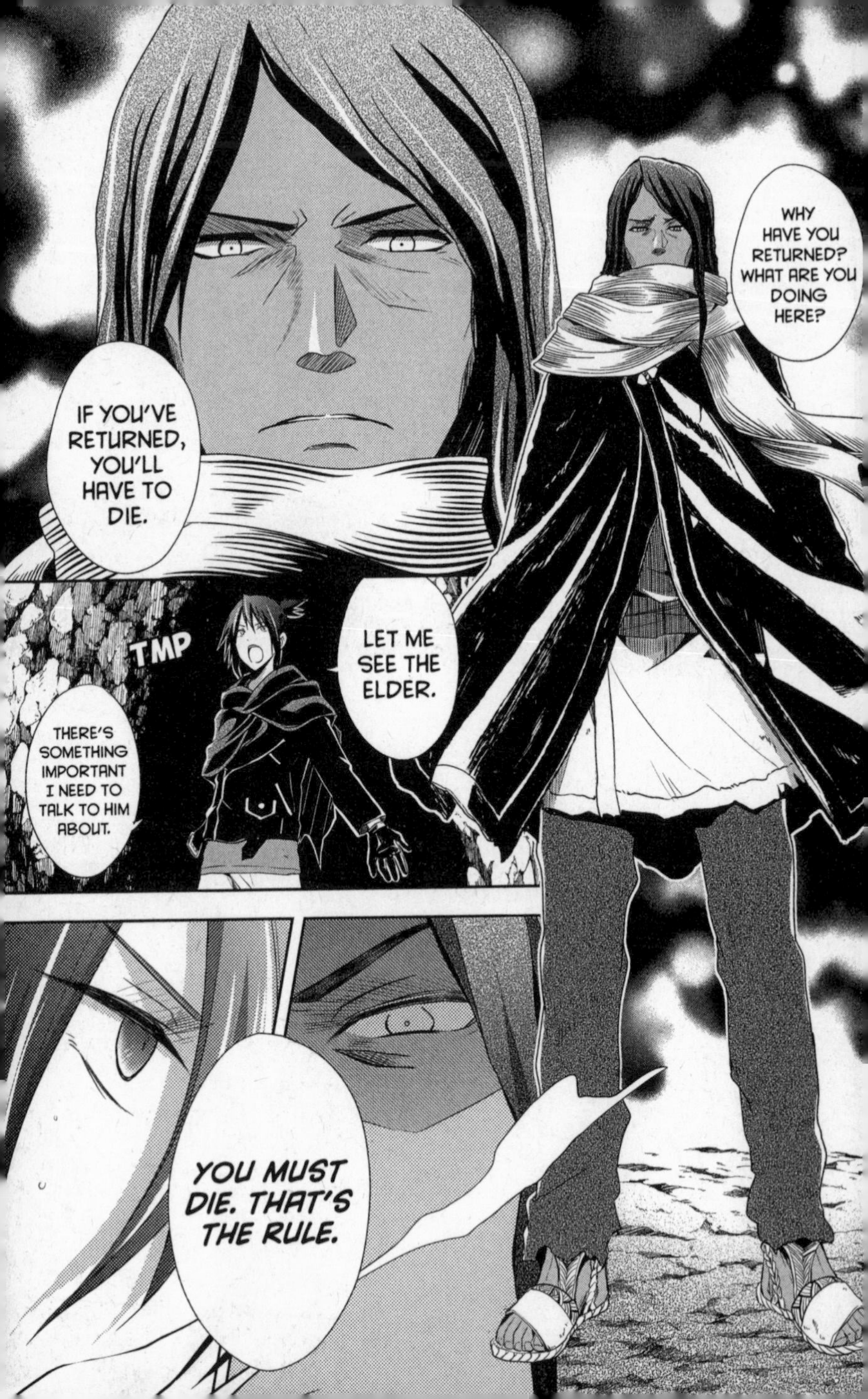
WHY HAVE YOU RETURNED? WHAT ARE YOU DOING HERE?
IF YOU'VE RETURNED, YOU'LL HAVE TO DIE.
LET ME SEE THE ELDER.
TMP
THERE'S SOMETHING IMPORTANT I NEED TO TALK TO HIM ABOUT.
YOU MUST DIE. THAT'S THE RULE.

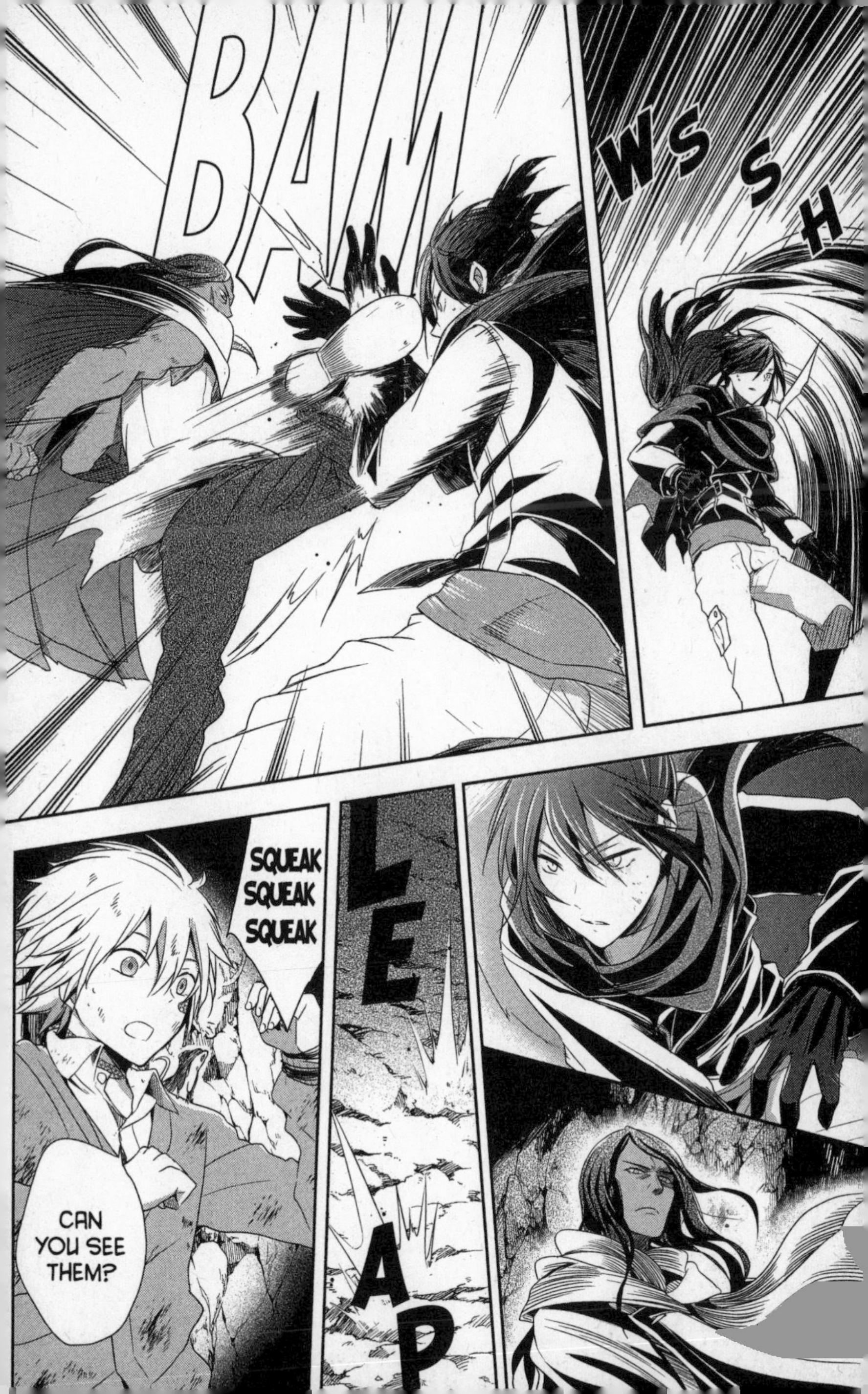
WSSH
BAM
LEAP
SQUEAK SQUEAK SQUEAK
CAN YOU SEE THEM?

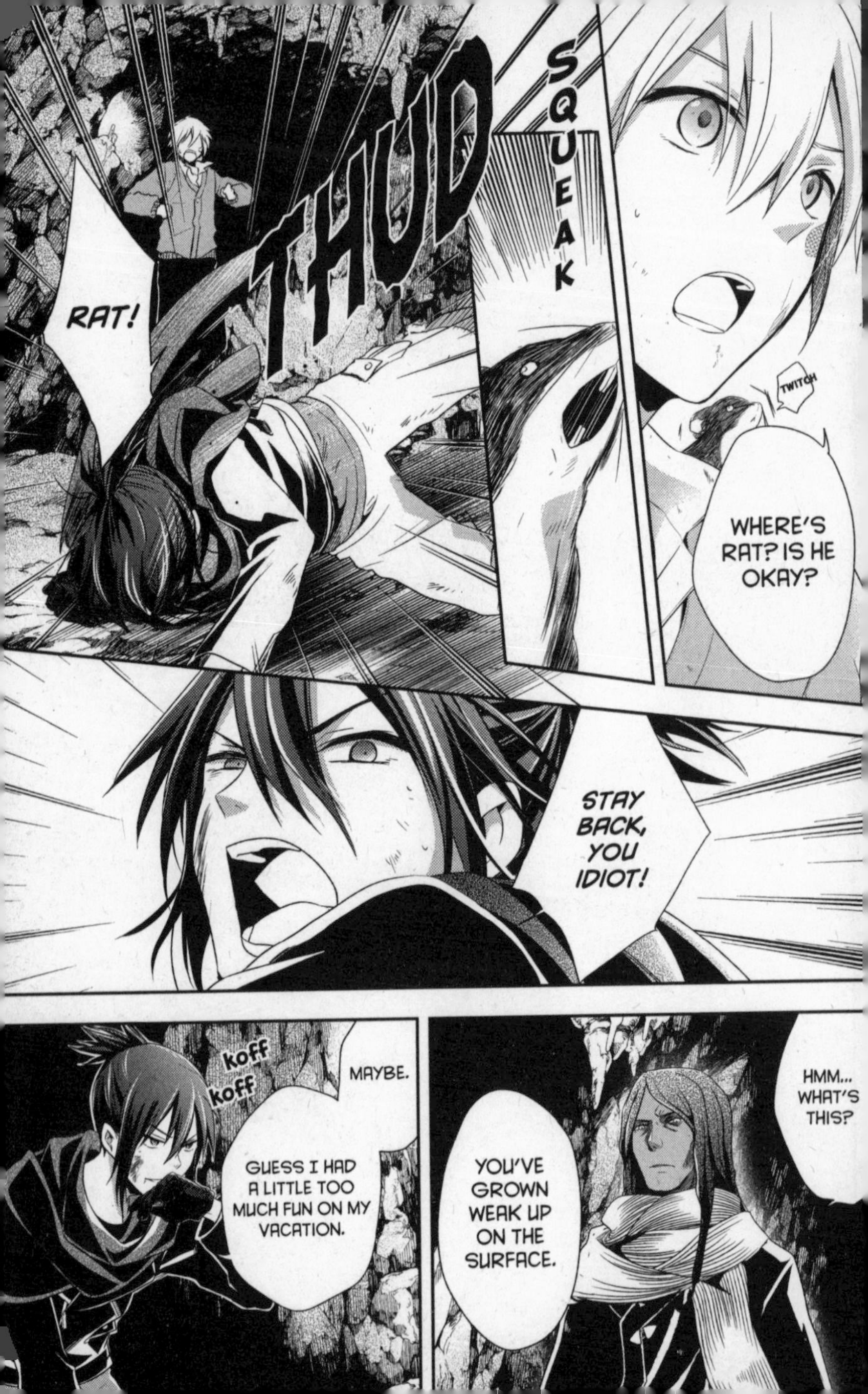
TWITCH
WHERE'S RAT? IS HE OKAY?
SQUEAK
THUD
RAT!
STAY BACK, YOU IDIOT!
HMM... WHAT'S THIS?
YOU'VE GROWN WEAK UP ON THE SURFACE.
MAYBE.
koff koff
GUESS I HAD A LITTLE TOO MUCH FUN ON MY VACATION.

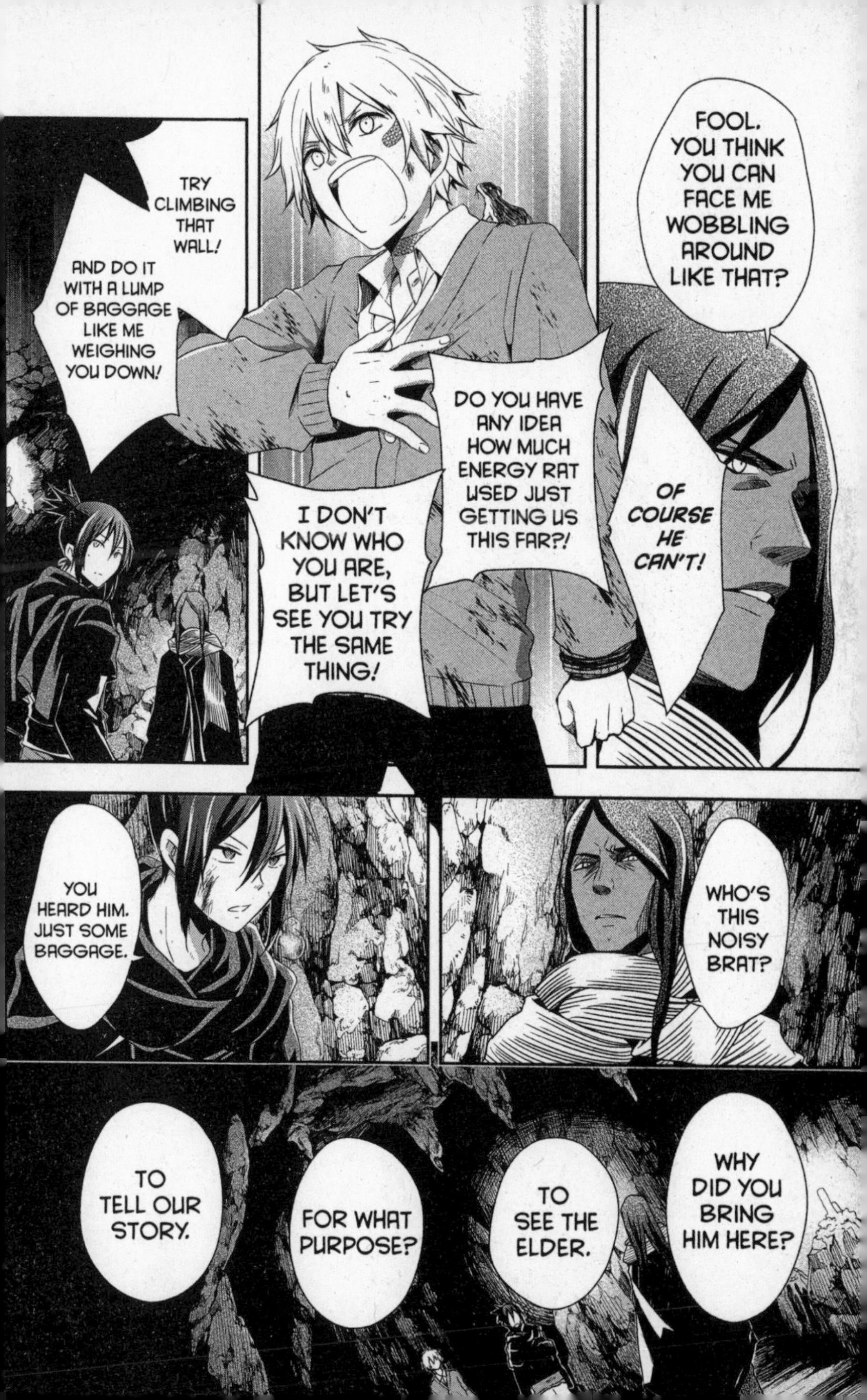
FOOL. YOU THINK YOU CAN FACE ME WOBBLING AROUND LIKE THAT?
OF COURSE HE CAN'T!
DO YOU HAVE ANY IDEA HOW MUCH ENERGY RAT USED JUST GETTING US THIS FAR?!
I DON'T KNOW WHO YOU ARE, BUT LET'S SEE YOU TRY THE SAME THING!
TRY CLIMBING THAT WALL!
AND DO IT WITH A LUMP OF BAGGAGE LIKE ME WEIGHING YOU DOWN!
WHO'S THIS NOISY BRAT?
YOU HEARD HIM. JUST SOME BAGGAGE.
WHY DID YOU BRING HIM HERE?
TO SEE THE ELDER.
FOR WHAT PURPOSE?
TO TELL OUR STORY.

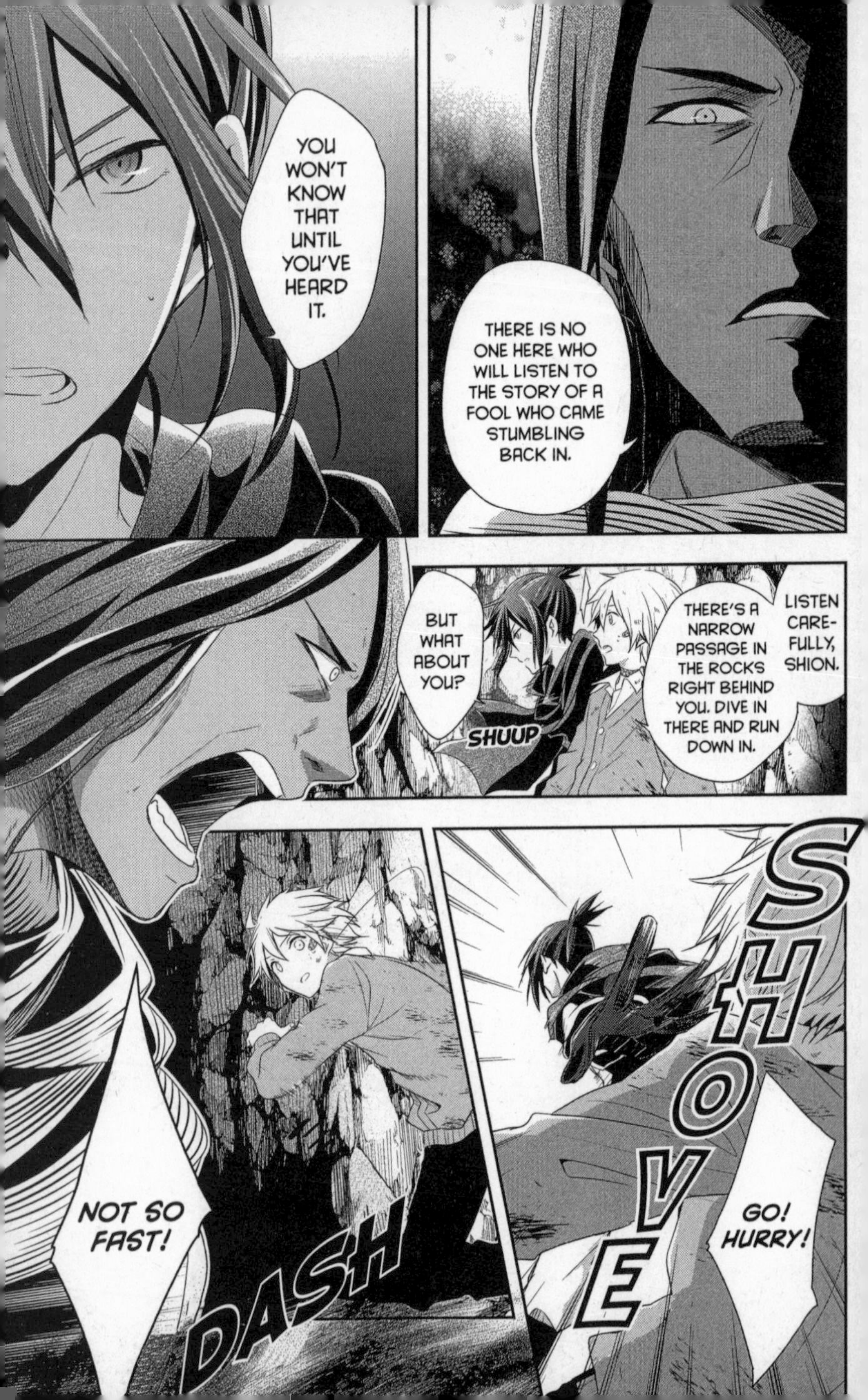
THERE IS NO ONE HERE WHO WILL LISTEN TO THE STORY OF A FOOL WHO CAME STUMBLING BACK IN.
YOU WON'T KNOW THAT UNTIL YOU'VE HEARD IT.
LISTEN CARE-FULLY, SHION.
THERE'S A NARROW PASSAGE IN THE ROCKS RIGHT BEHIND YOU. DIVE IN THERE AND RUN DOWN IN.
BUT WHAT ABOUT YOU?
SHUUP
SHOVE
GO! HURRY!
NOT SO FAST!
DASH

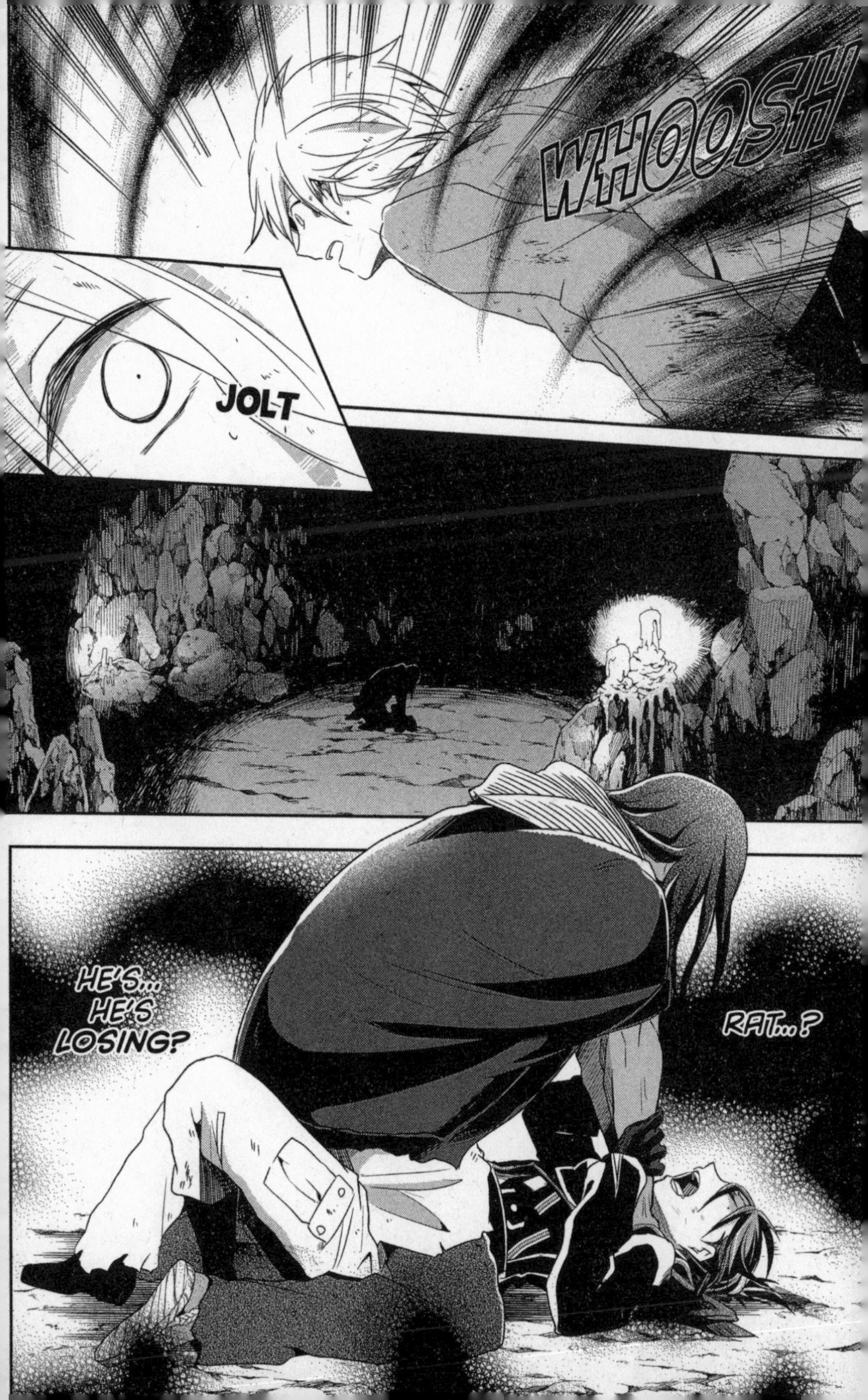
WHOOSH
JOLT
RAT...?
HE'S... HE'S LOSING?

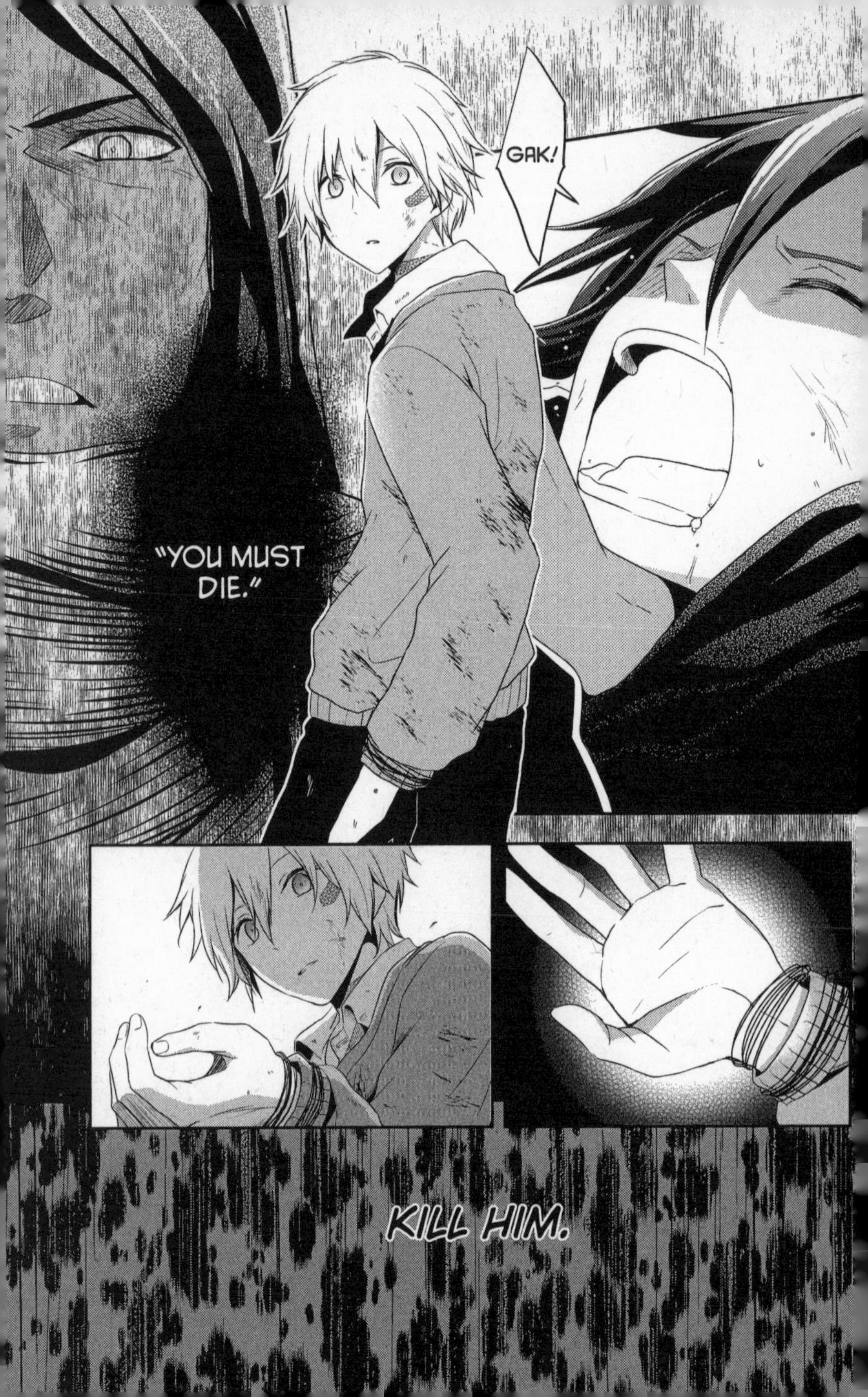
GAK!
"YOU MUST DIE."
KILL HIM.

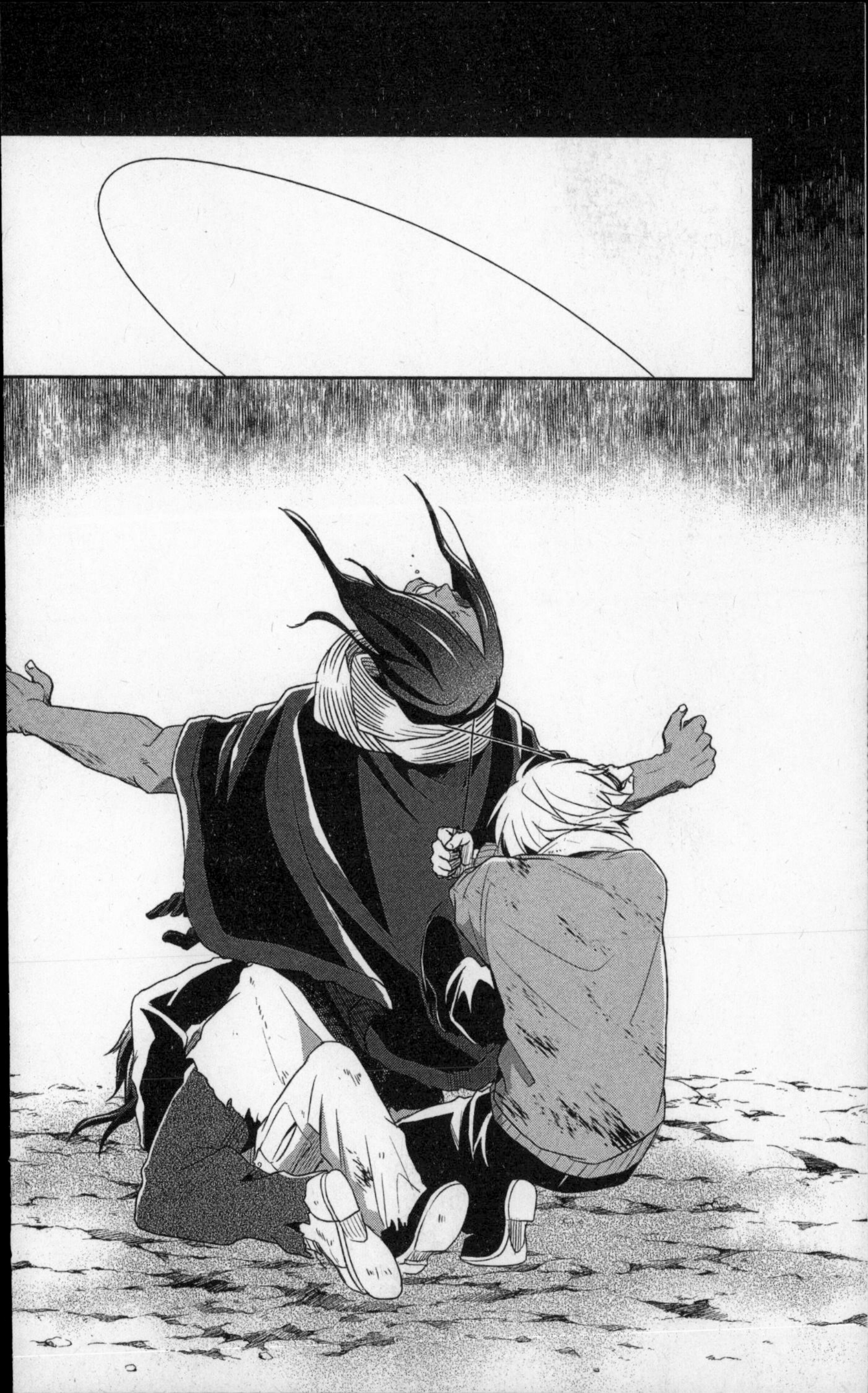

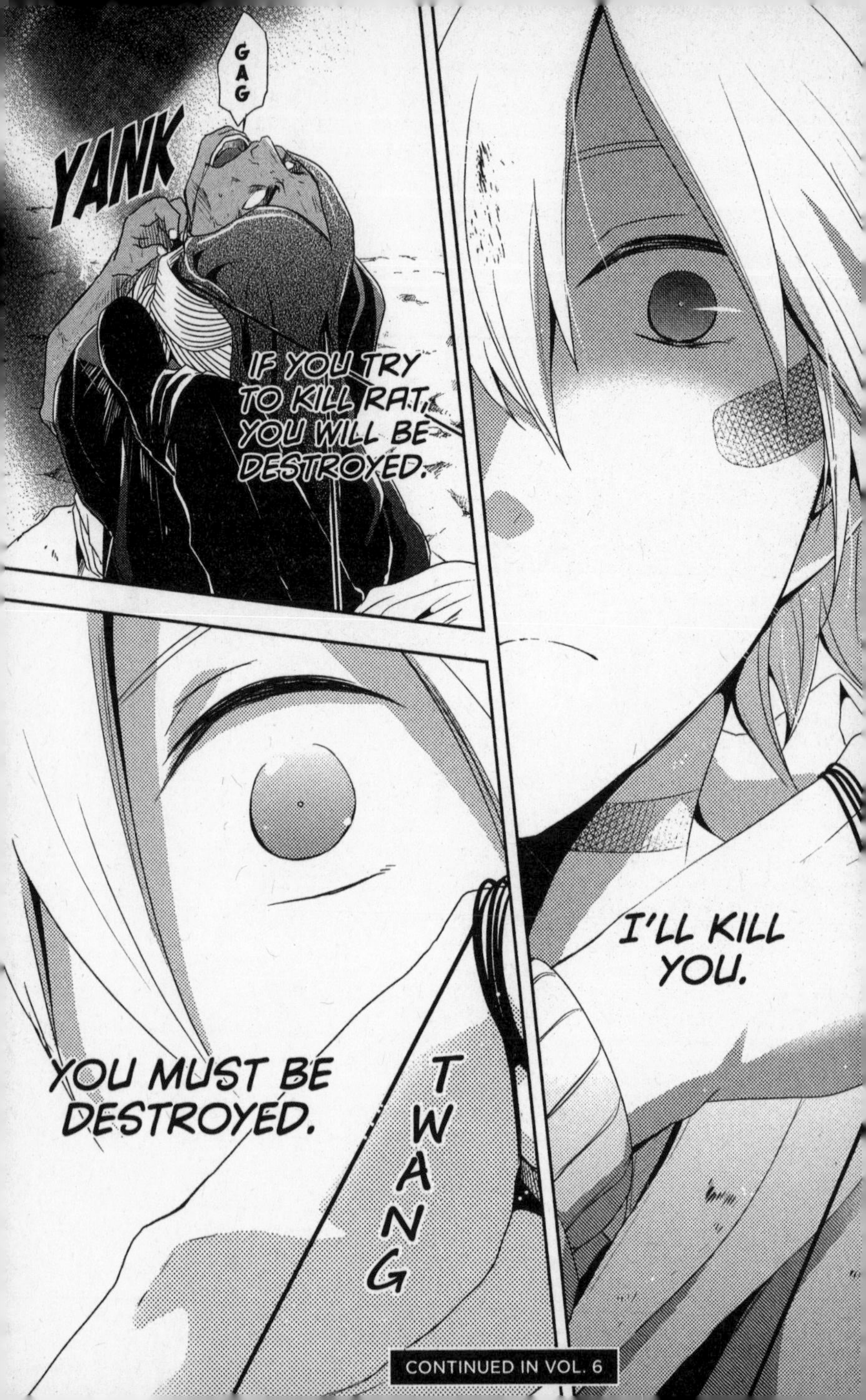GAG
YANK
IF YOU TRY TO KILL RAT, YOU WILL BE DESTROYED.
I'LL KILL YOU.
YOU MUST BE DESTROYED.
TWANG

CONTINUED IN VOL. 6

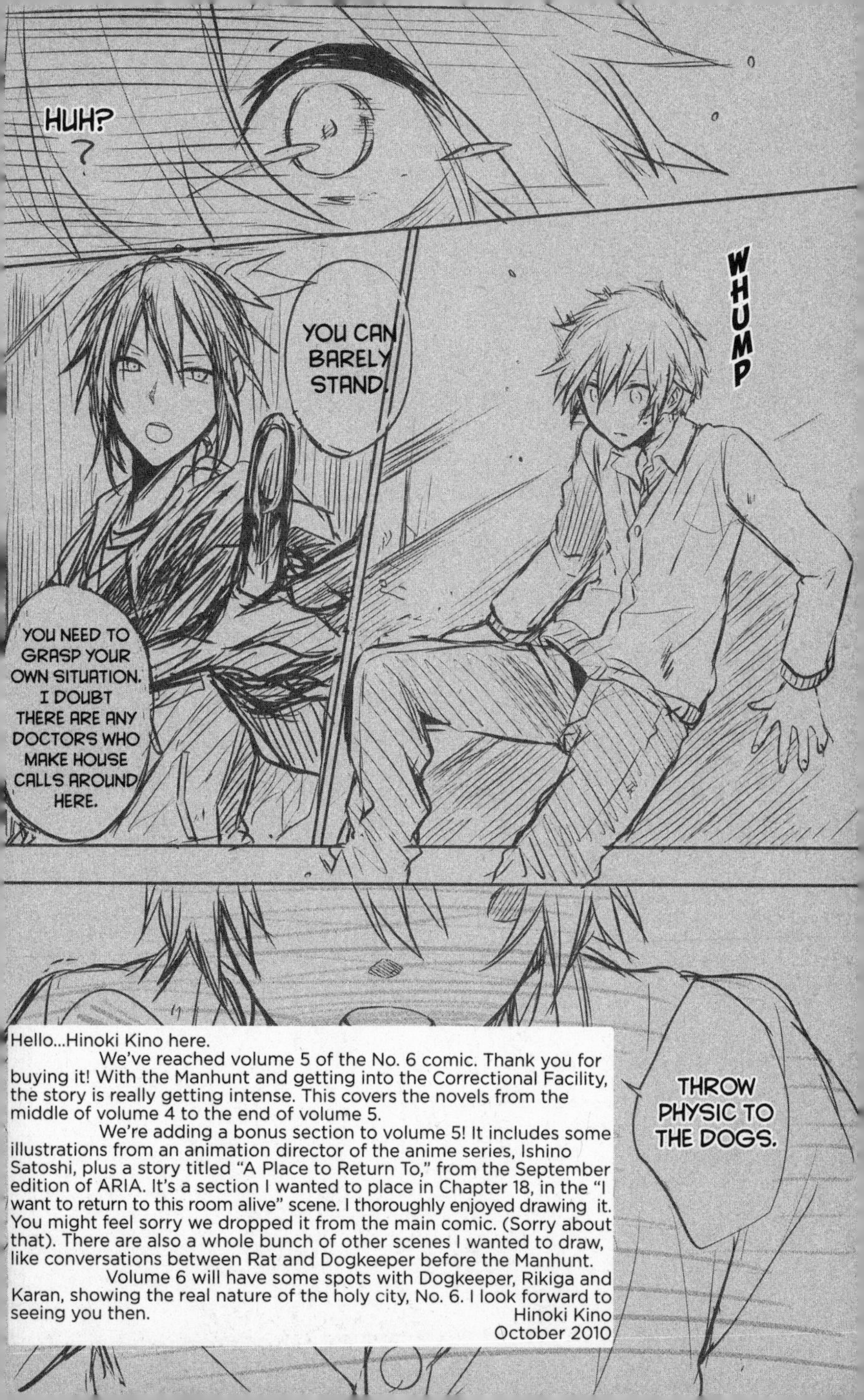
HUH?
?
WHUMP
YOU CAN BARELY STAND.
YOU NEED TO GRASP YOUR OWN SITUATION. I DOUBT THERE ARE ANY DOCTORS WHO MAKE HOUSE CALLS AROUND HERE.
THROW PHYSIC TO THE DOGS.

Hello...Hinoki Kino here.

We've reached volume 5 of the No. 6 comic. Thank you for buying it! With the Manhunt and getting into the Correctional Facility, the story is really getting intense. This covers the novels from the middle of volume 4 to the end of volume 5.

We're adding a bonus section to volume 5! It includes some illustrations from an animation director of the anime series, Ishino Satoshi, plus a story titled "A Place to Return To," from the September edition of ARIA. It's a section I wanted to place in Chapter 18, in the "I want to return to this room alive" scene. I thoroughly enjoyed drawing it. You might feel sorry we dropped it from the main comic. (Sorry about that). There are also a whole bunch of other scenes I wanted to draw, like conversations between Rat and Dogkeeper before the Manhunt.

Volume 6 will have some spots with Dogkeeper, Rikiga and Karan, showing the real nature of the holy city, No. 6. I look forward to seeing you then.

Hinoki Kino
October 2010

SPECIAL THANKS!

Atsuko Asano Sensei

Everyone in the Kodansha Aria Editorial Department

Everyone on the No. 6 Team
Editor K
toi8-sensei
Satoshi Ishino
Everyone on the anime staff
Everyone at NARTi;S
Ginkyo-sensei

* Production Cooperation
Honma
Megi
Netanon
Sayuri Noguchi

* Finishing
Tsunocchi

* 3D
Kei Rinkan

* Color Backgrounds
Mr. dominori (Big Brother)

Family (Mom, Dad, siblings, Granny, the dog)

And everyone else who helped out

Also, all you readers!

Thank you all so very much!

CONTINUING...

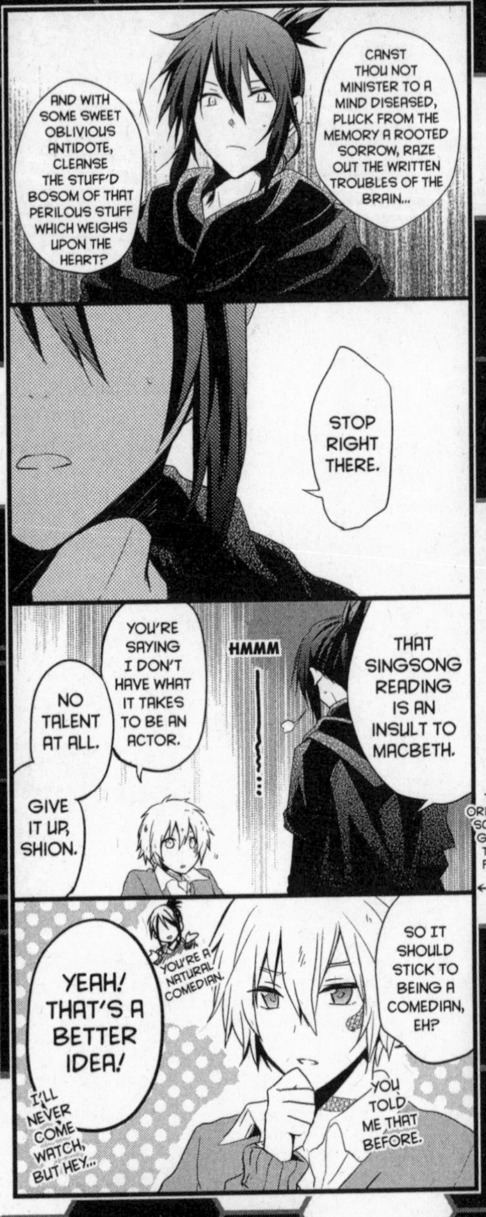
CANST THOU NOT MINISTER TO A MIND DISEASED, PLUCK FROM THE MEMORY A ROOTED SORROW, RAZE OUT THE WRITTEN TROUBLES OF THE BRAIN...
AND WITH SOME SWEET OBLIVIOUS ANTIDOTE, CLEANSE THE STUFF'D BOSOM OF THAT PERILOUS STUFF WHICH WEIGHS UPON THE HEART?
STOP RIGHT THERE.
THAT SINGSONG READING IS AN INSULT TO MACBETH.
HMMM
YOU'RE SAYING I DON'T HAVE WHAT IT TAKES TO BE AN ACTOR.
NO TALENT AT ALL.
GIVE IT UP, SHION.
SO IT SHOULD STICK TO BEING A COMEDIAN, EH?
YOU'RE A NATURAL COMEDIAN.
YEAH! THAT'S A BETTER IDEA!
YOU TOLD ME THAT BEFORE.
I'LL NEVER COME WATCH, BUT HEY...

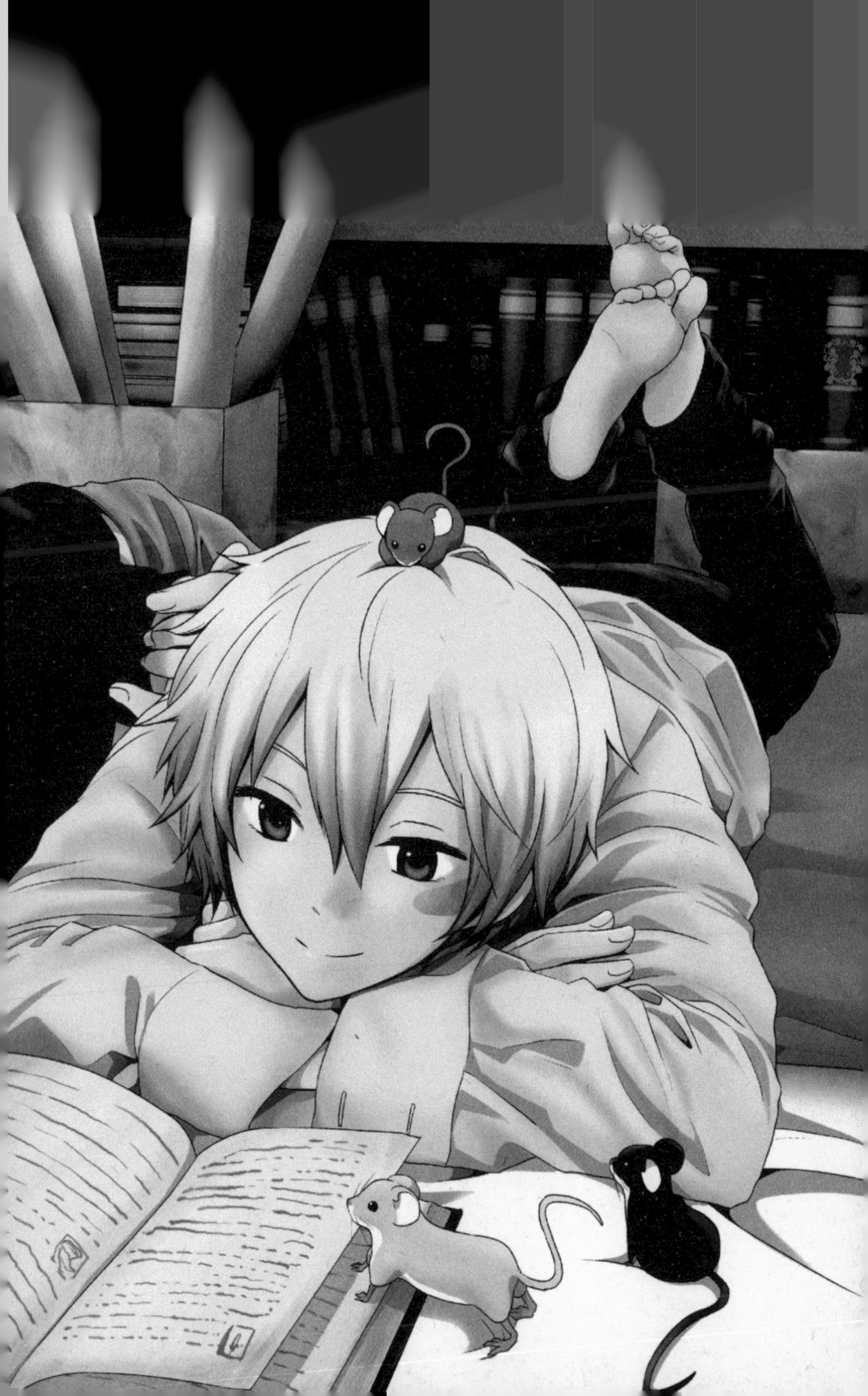

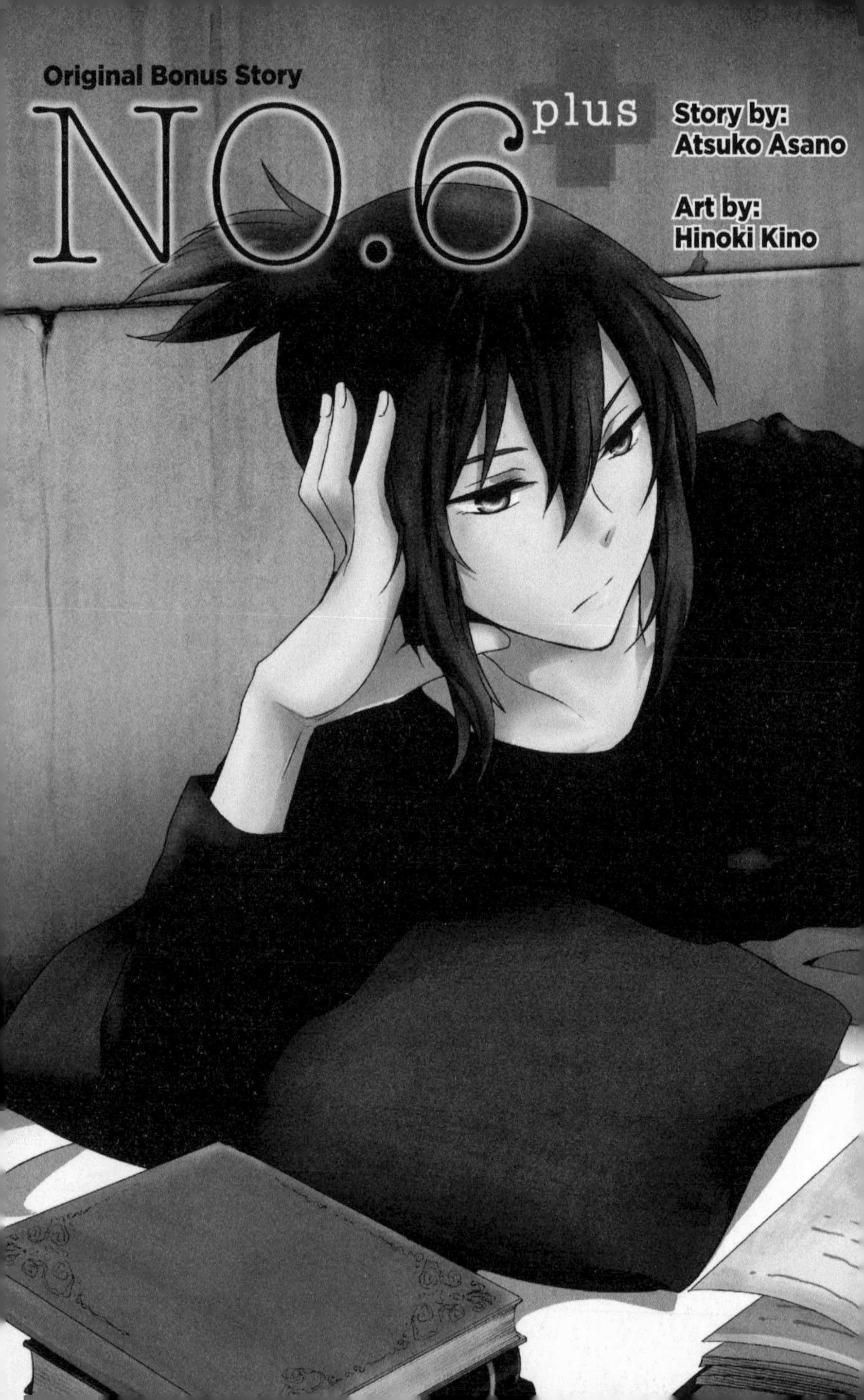
Original Bonus Story
NO.6 plus
Story by:
Atsuko Asano
Art by:
Hinoki Kino

NO.6

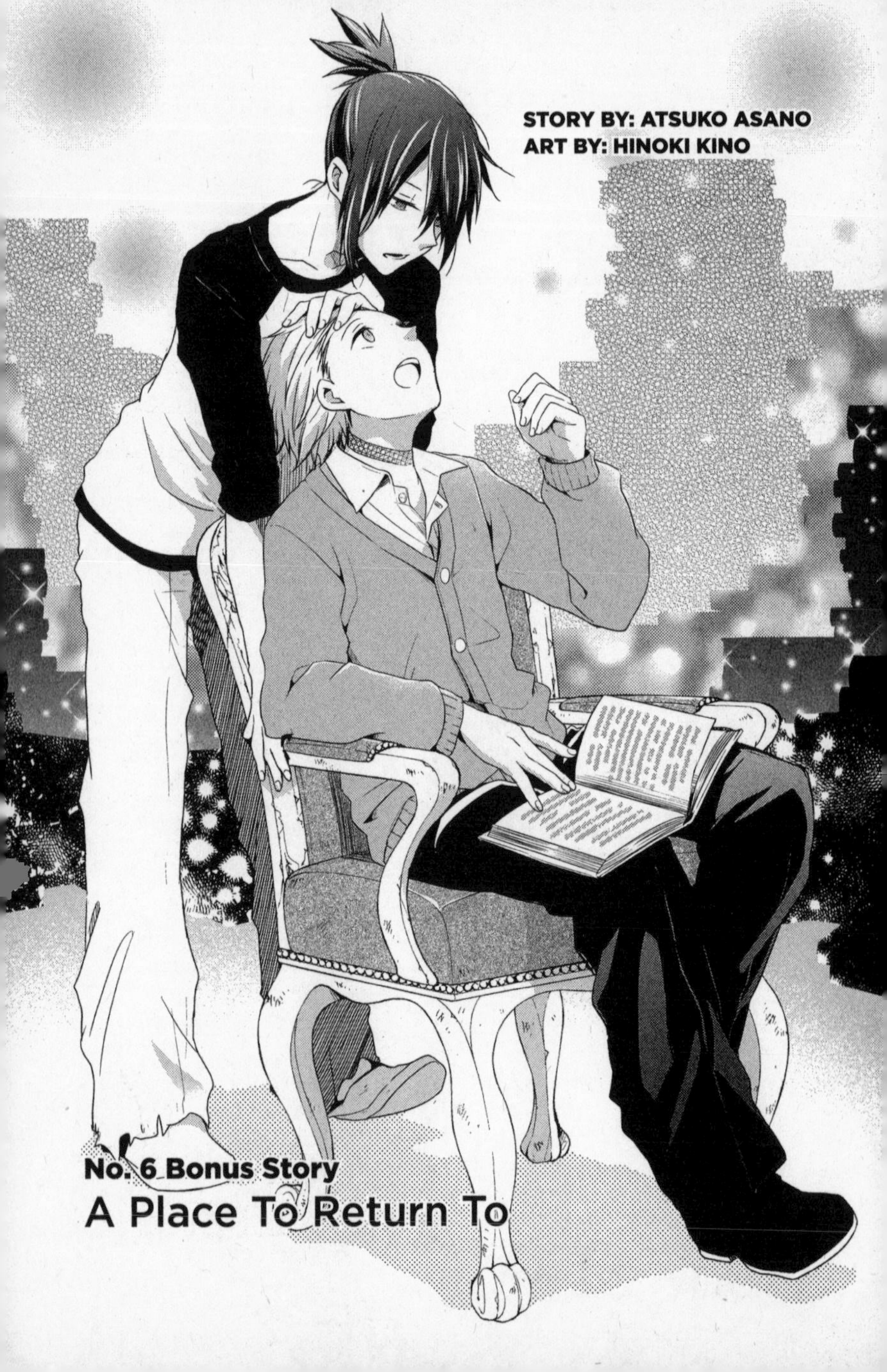
STORY BY: ATSUKO ASANO
ART BY: HINOKI KINO
No. 6 Bonus Story
A Place To Return To

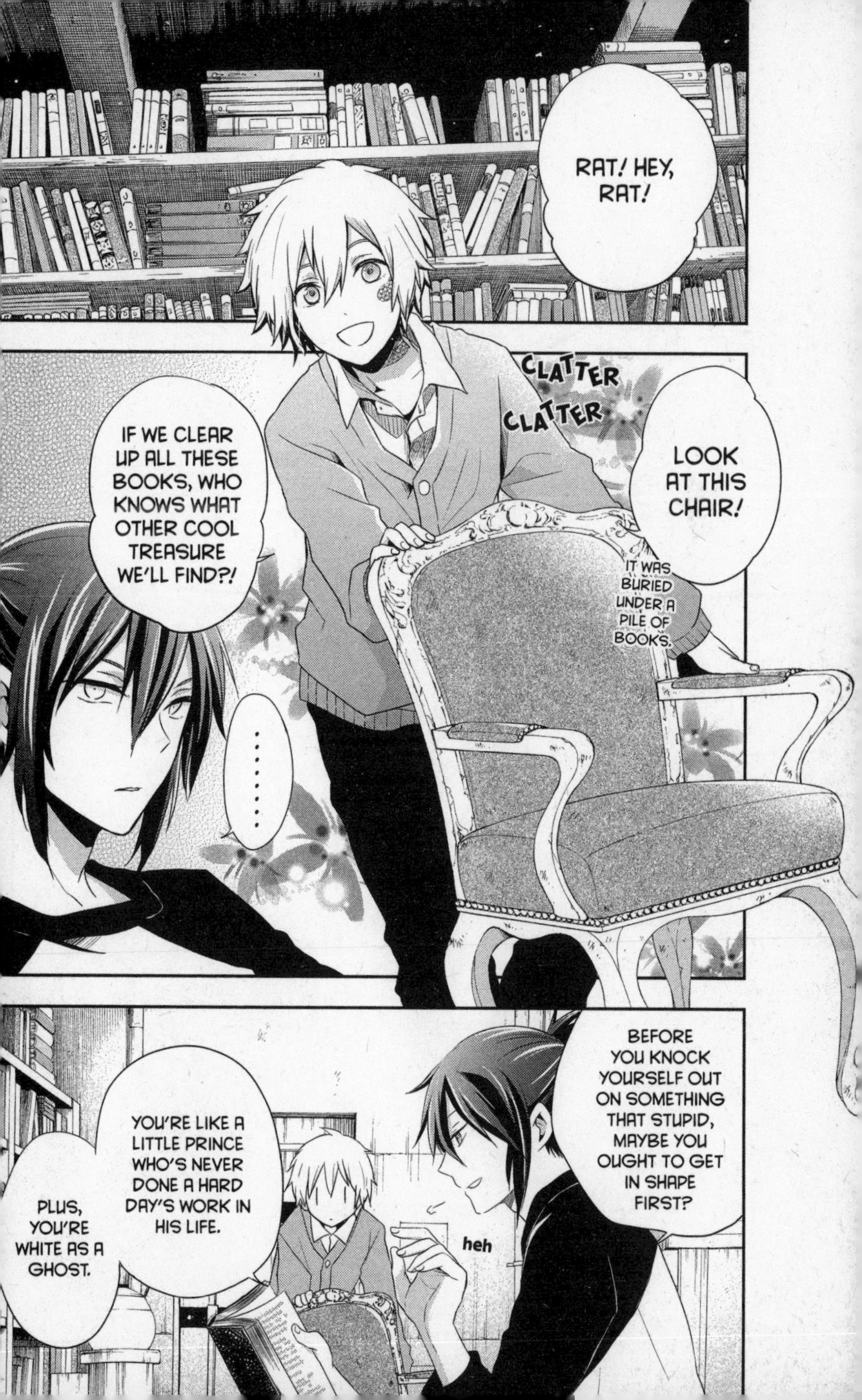
RAT! HEY, RAT!
CLATTER CLATTER
LOOK AT THIS CHAIR!
IT WAS BURIED UNDER A PILE OF BOOKS.
IF WE CLEAR UP ALL THESE BOOKS, WHO KNOWS WHAT OTHER COOL TREASURE WE'LL FIND?!
......
BEFORE YOU KNOCK YOURSELF OUT ON SOMETHING THAT STUPID, MAYBE YOU OUGHT TO GET IN SHAPE FIRST?
heh
YOU'RE LIKE A LITTLE PRINCE WHO'S NEVER DONE A HARD DAY'S WORK IN HIS LIFE.
PLUS, YOU'RE WHITE AS A GHOST.

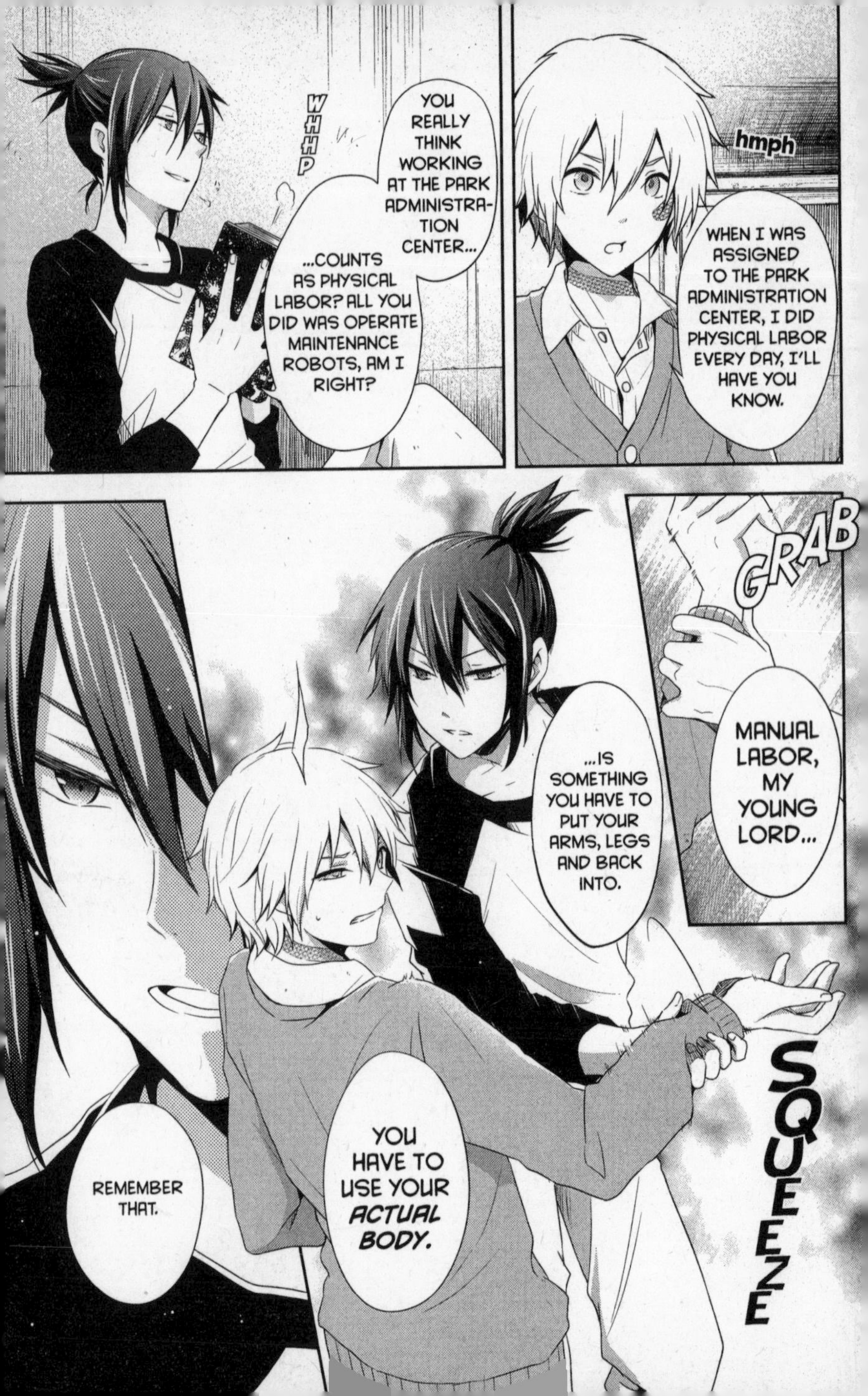
hmph
WHEN I WAS ASSIGNED TO THE PARK ADMINISTRATION CENTER, I DID PHYSICAL LABOR EVERY DAY, I'LL HAVE YOU KNOW.
WHHP
YOU REALLY THINK WORKING AT THE PARK ADMINISTRA-TION CENTER...
...COUNTS AS PHYSICAL LABOR? ALL YOU DID WAS OPERATE MAINTENANCE ROBOTS, AM I RIGHT?
GRAB
MANUAL LABOR, MY YOUNG LORD...
...IS SOMETHING YOU HAVE TO PUT YOUR ARMS, LEGS AND BACK INTO.
SQUEEZE
YOU HAVE TO USE YOUR *ACTUAL* *BODY.*
REMEMBER THAT.

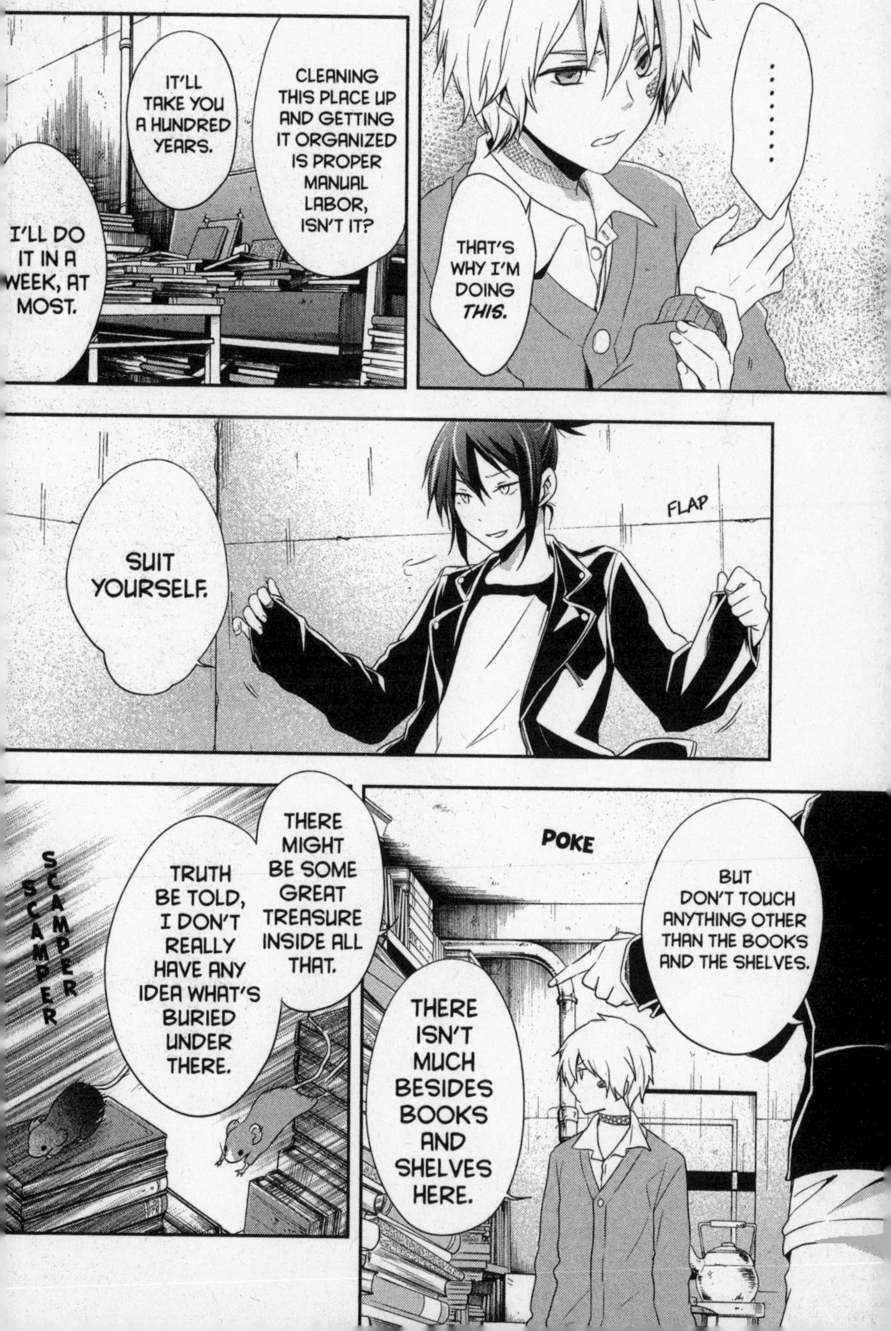
……
THAT'S WHY I'M DOING *THIS.*
CLEANING THIS PLACE UP AND GETTING IT ORGANIZED IS PROPER MANUAL LABOR, ISN'T IT?
IT'LL TAKE YOU A HUNDRED YEARS.
I'LL DO IT IN A WEEK, AT MOST.
FLAP
SUIT YOURSELF.
POKE
BUT DON'T TOUCH ANYTHING OTHER THAN THE BOOKS AND THE SHELVES.
THERE ISN'T MUCH BESIDES BOOKS AND SHELVES HERE.
THERE MIGHT BE SOME GREAT TREASURE INSIDE ALL THAT.
TRUTH BE TOLD, I DON'T REALLY HAVE ANY IDEA WHAT'S BURIED UNDER THERE.
SCAMPER
SCAMPER

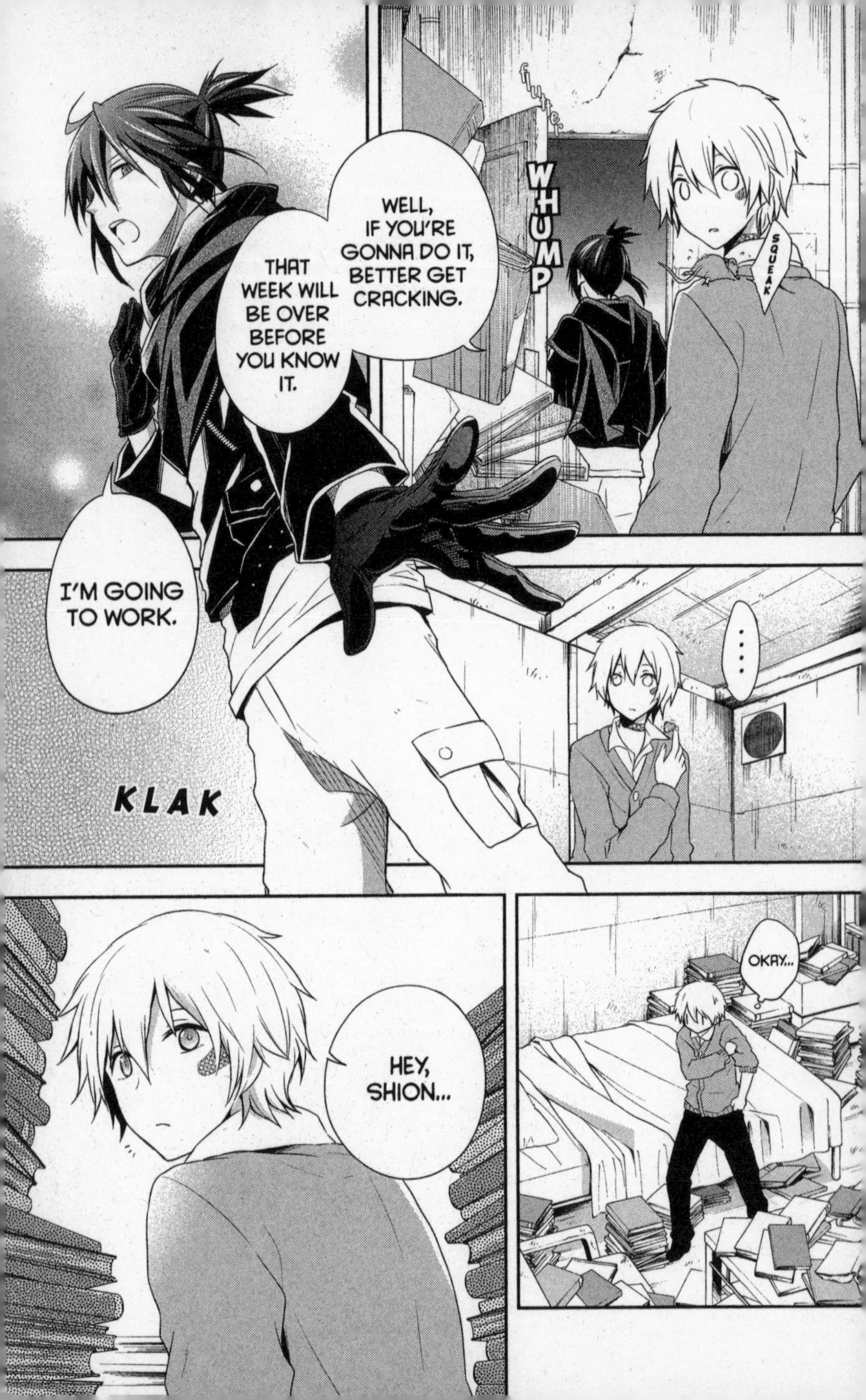
flutter
WHUMP
SQUEAK
WELL, IF YOU'RE GONNA DO IT, BETTER GET CRACKING.
THAT WEEK WILL BE OVER BEFORE YOU KNOW IT.
I'M GOING TO WORK.
KLAK
....
OKAY...
HEY, SHION...

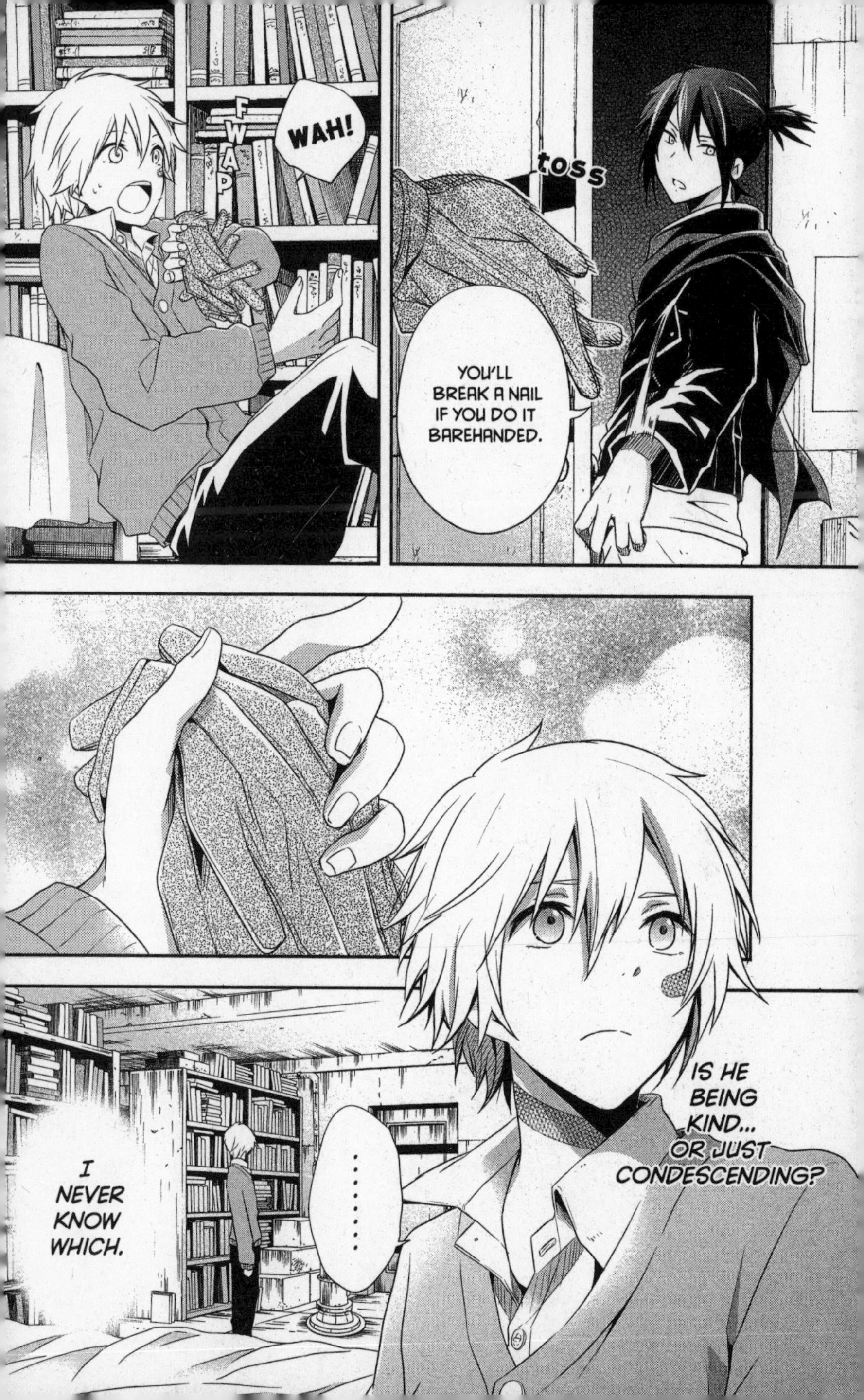
toss
YOU'LL BREAK A NAIL IF YOU DO IT BAREHANDED.
FWAP
WAH!
IS HE BEING KIND... OR JUST CONDESCENDING?
......
I NEVER KNOW WHICH.

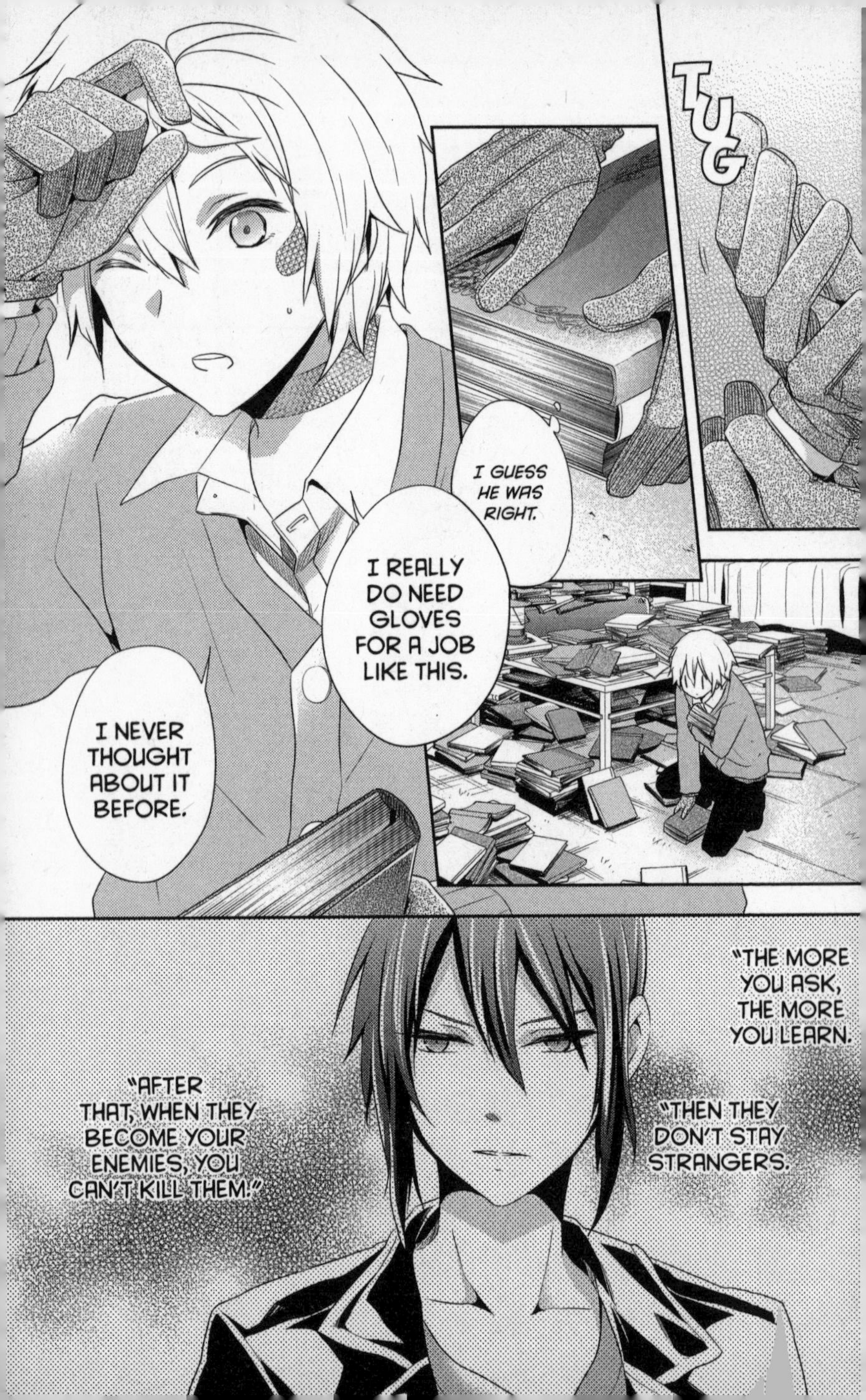
TUG
I GUESS HE WAS RIGHT.
I REALLY DO NEED GLOVES FOR A JOB LIKE THIS.
I NEVER THOUGHT ABOUT IT BEFORE.
"THE MORE YOU ASK, THE MORE YOU LEARN.
"THEN THEY DON'T STAY STRANGERS.
"AFTER THAT, WHEN THEY BECOME YOUR ENEMIES, YOU CAN'T KILL THEM."

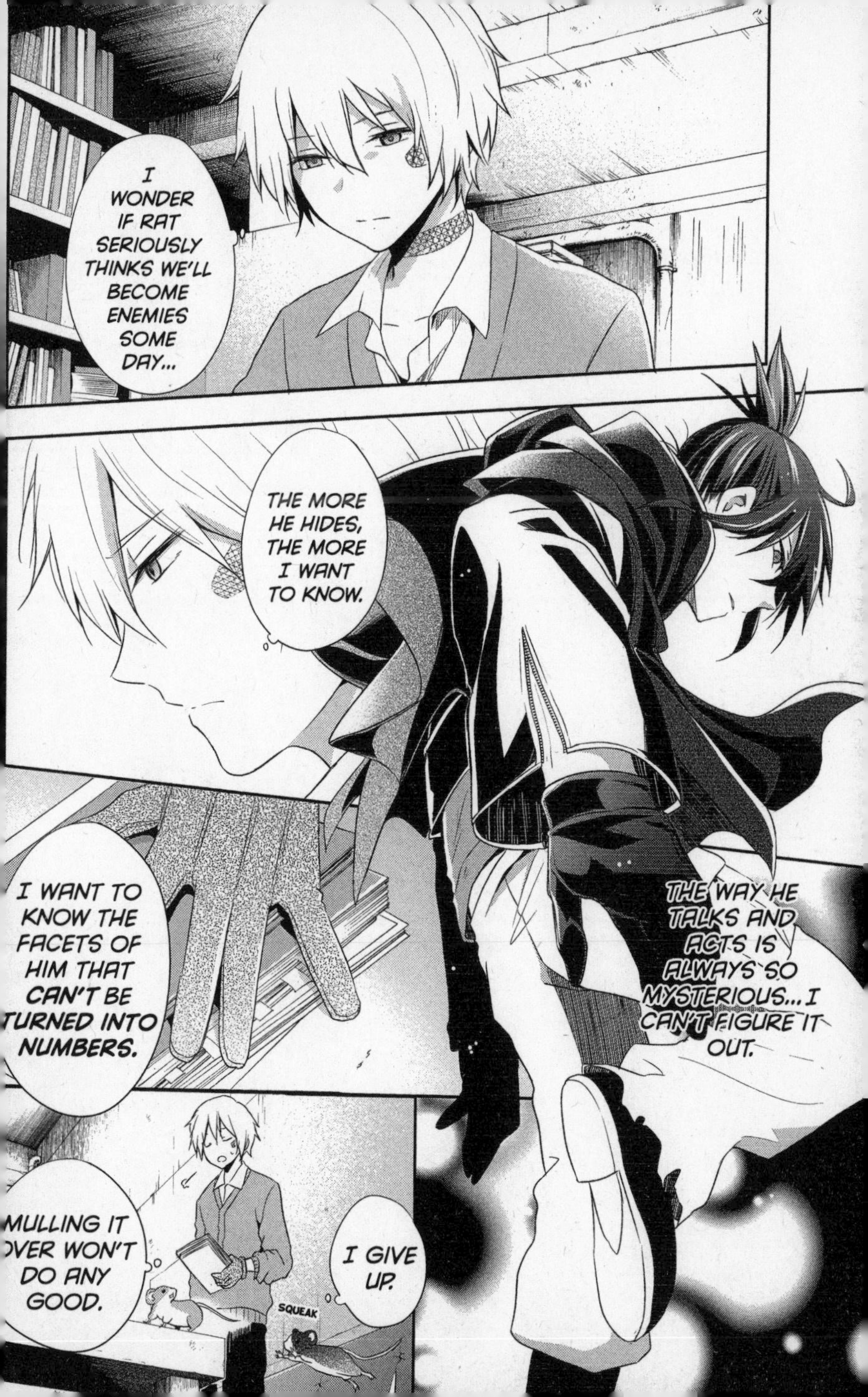
I WONDER IF RAT SERIOUSLY THINKS WE'LL BECOME ENEMIES SOME DAY...
THE MORE HE HIDES, THE MORE I WANT TO KNOW.
THE WAY HE TALKS AND ACTS IS ALWAYS SO MYSTERIOUS... I CAN'T FIGURE IT OUT.
I WANT TO KNOW THE FACETS OF HIM THAT CAN'T BE TURNED INTO NUMBERS.
MULLING IT OVER WON'T DO ANY GOOD.
I GIVE UP.
SQUEAK

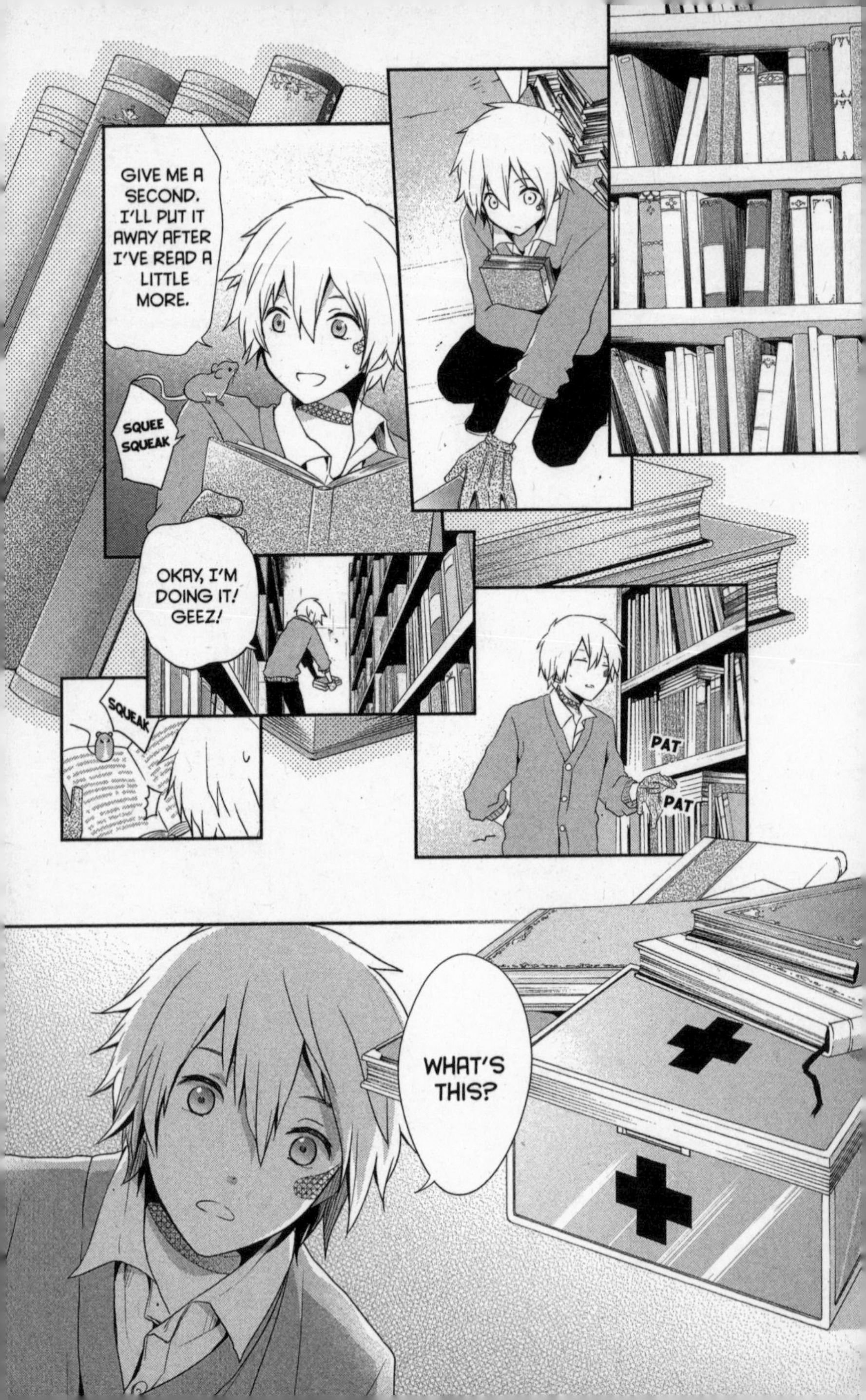
GIVE ME A SECOND. I'LL PUT IT AWAY AFTER I'VE READ A LITTLE MORE.
SQUEE SQUEAK
PAT
PAT
OKAY, I'M DOING IT! GEEZ!
SQUEAK
WHAT'S THIS?

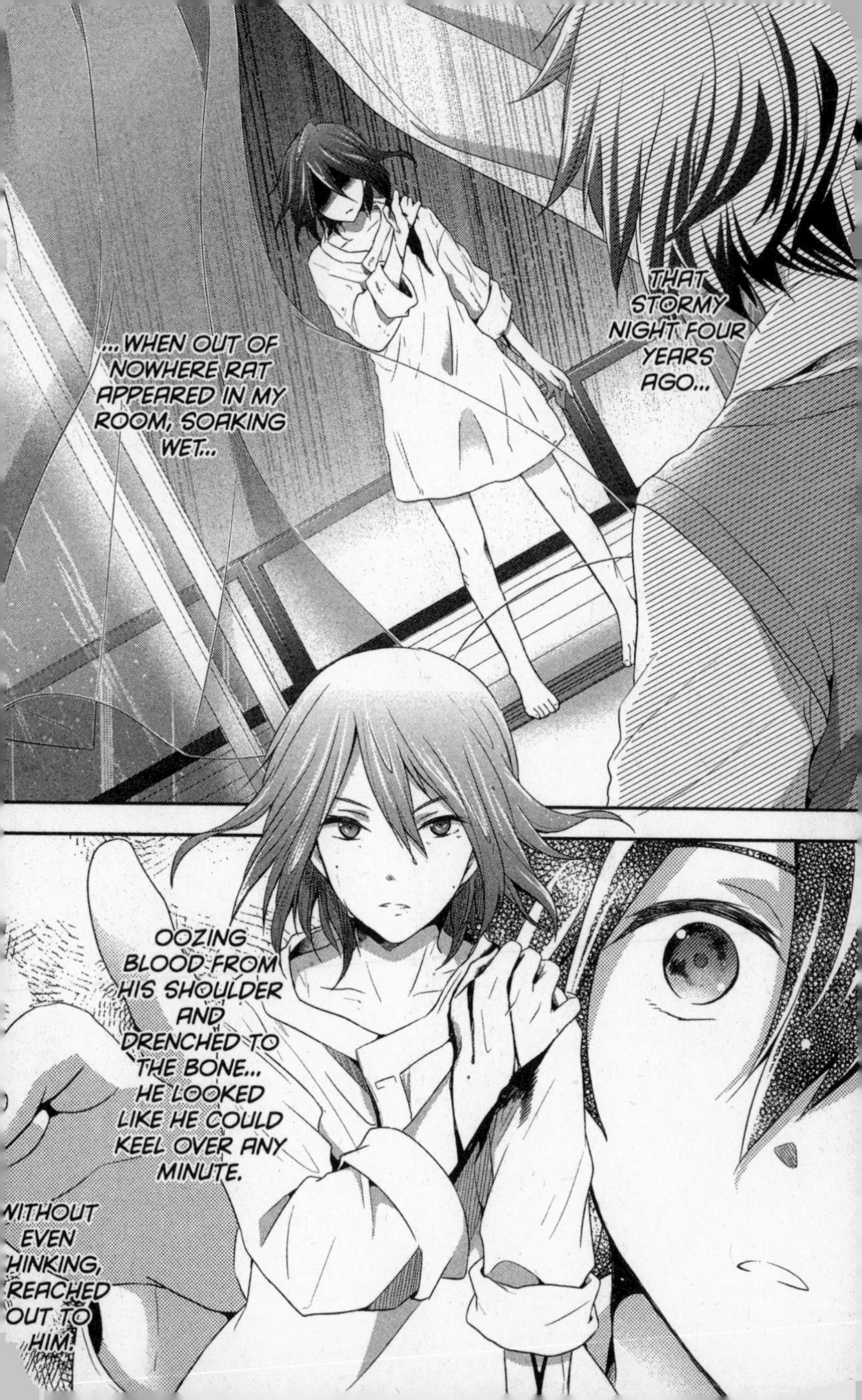
THAT STORMY NIGHT FOUR YEARS AGO...
...WHEN OUT OF NOWHERE RAT APPEARED IN MY ROOM, SOAKING WET...
OOZING BLOOD FROM HIS SHOULDER AND DRENCHED TO THE BONE... HE LOOKED LIKE HE COULD KEEL OVER ANY MINUTE.
WITHOUT EVEN THINKING, REACHED OUT TO HIM.

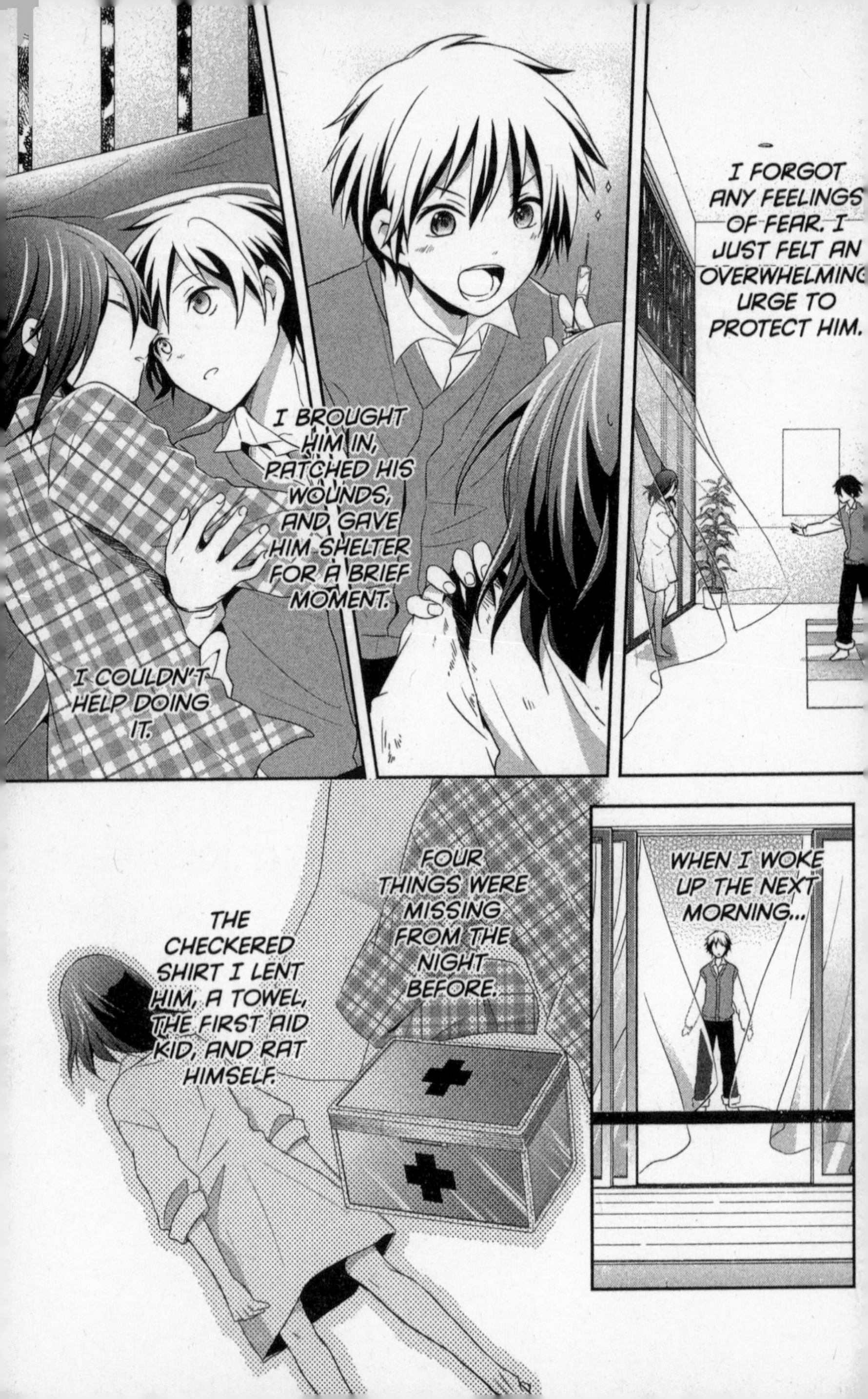
I FORGOT ANY FEELINGS OF FEAR. I JUST FELT AN OVERWHELMING URGE TO PROTECT HIM.
I BROUGHT HIM IN, PATCHED HIS WOUNDS, AND GAVE HIM SHELTER FOR A BRIEF MOMENT.
I COULDN'T HELP DOING IT.
WHEN I WOKE UP THE NEXT MORNING...
FOUR THINGS WERE MISSING FROM THE NIGHT BEFORE.
THE CHECKERED SHIRT I LENT HIM, A TOWEL, THE FIRST AID KID, AND RAT HIMSELF.

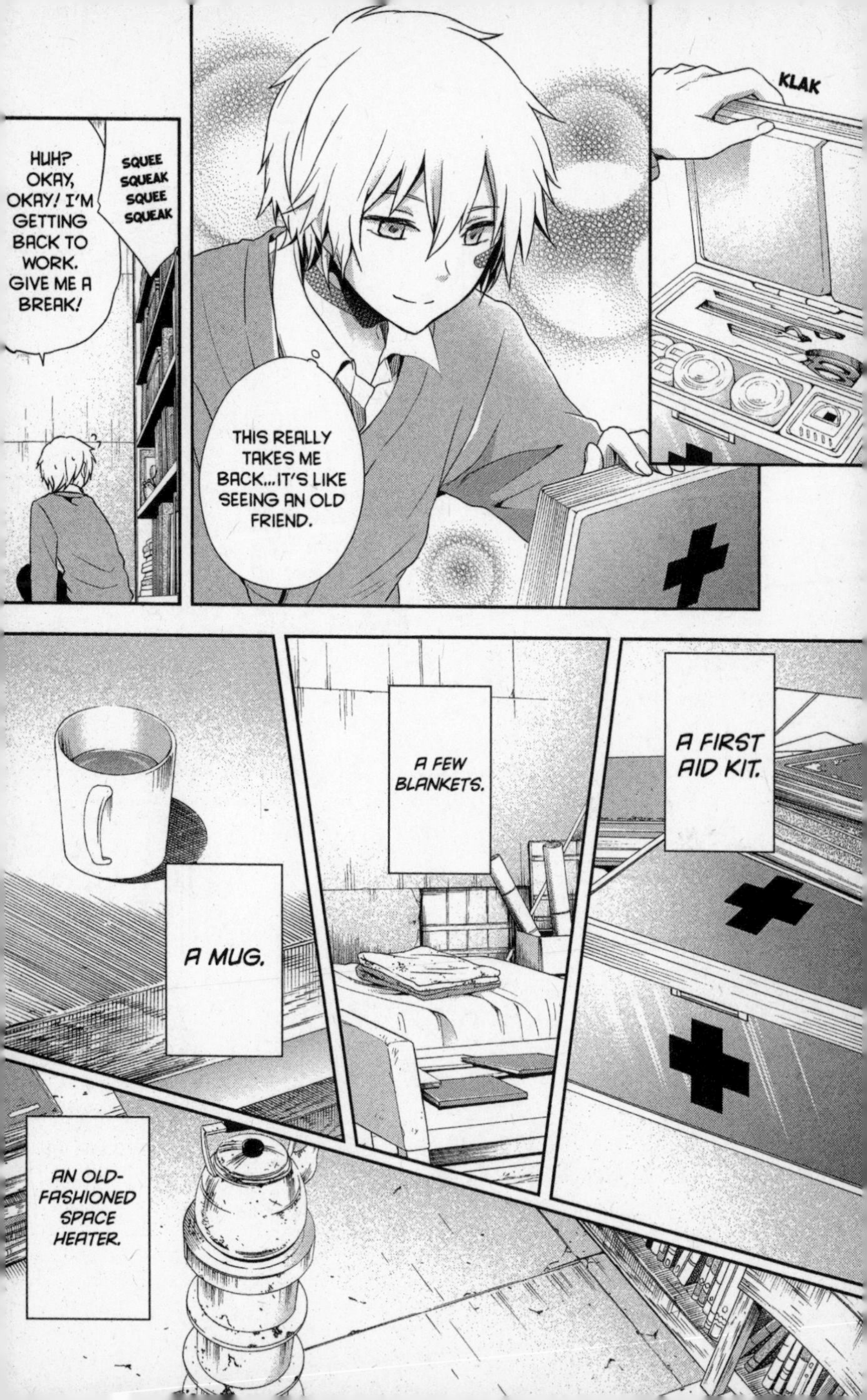
KLAK
THIS REALLY TAKES ME BACK...IT'S LIKE SEEING AN OLD FRIEND.
SQUEE SQUEAK SQUEE SQUEAK
HUH? OKAY, OKAY! I'M GETTING BACK TO WORK. GIVE ME A BREAK!
A FIRST AID KIT.
A FEW BLANKETS.
A MUG.
AN OLD-FASHIONED SPACE HEATER.

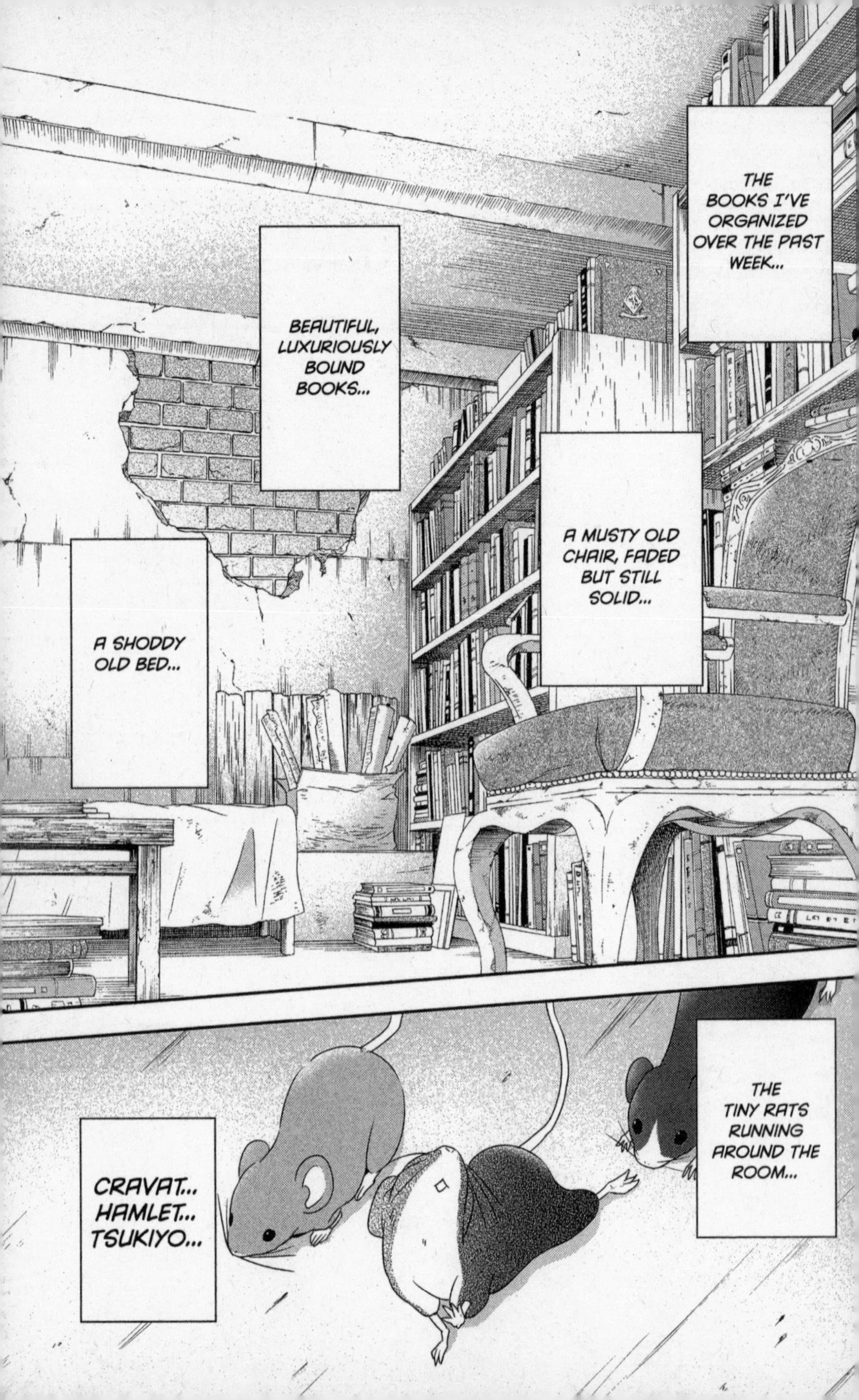

THE BOOKS I'VE ORGANIZED OVER THE PAST WEEK...
BEAUTIFUL, LUXURIOUSLY BOUND BOOKS...
A MUSTY OLD CHAIR, FADED BUT STILL SOLID...
A SHODDY OLD BED...
THE TINY RATS RUNNING AROUND THE ROOM...
CRAVAT... HAMLET... TSUKIYO...

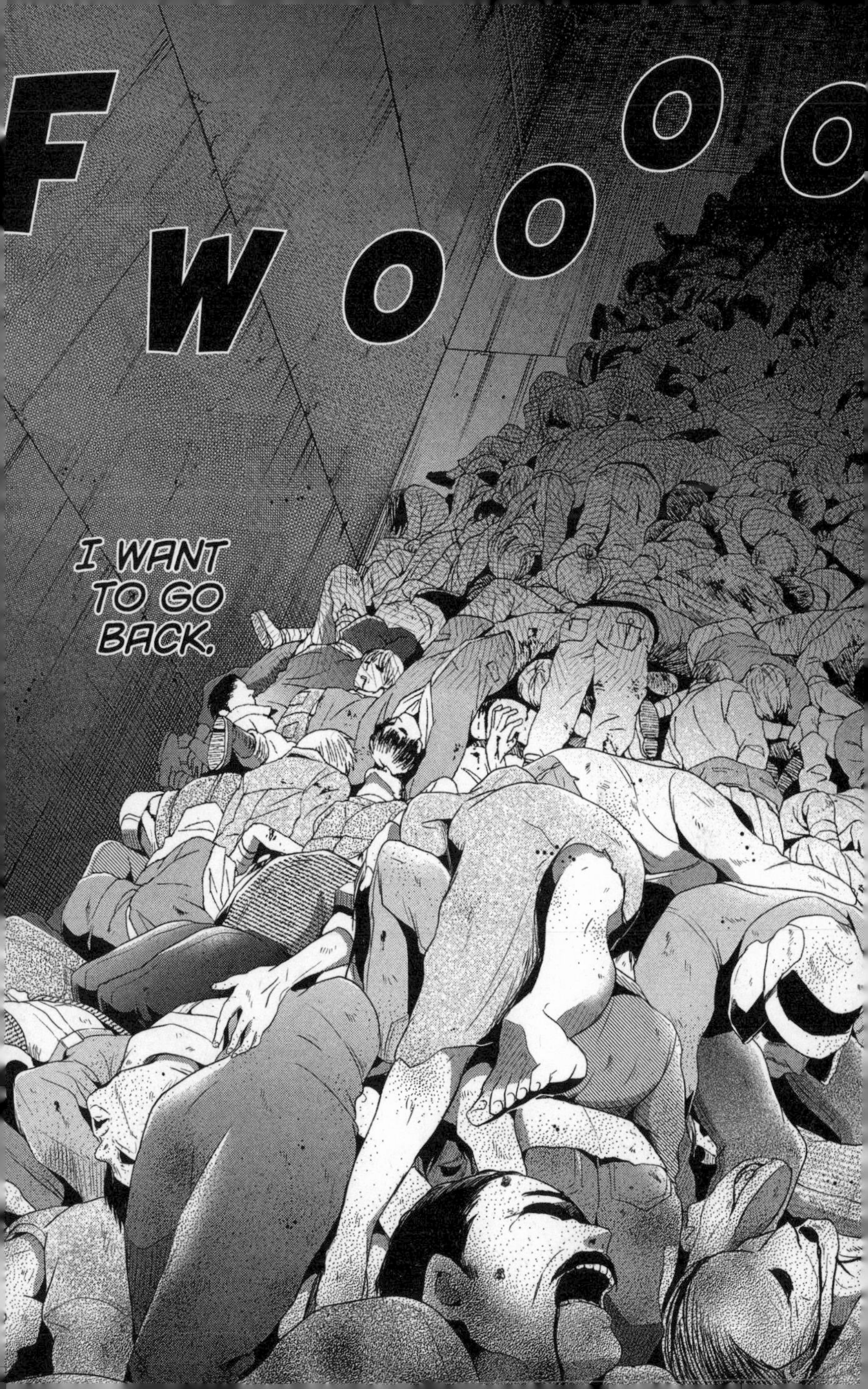
FWOOOO
I WANT TO GO BACK.

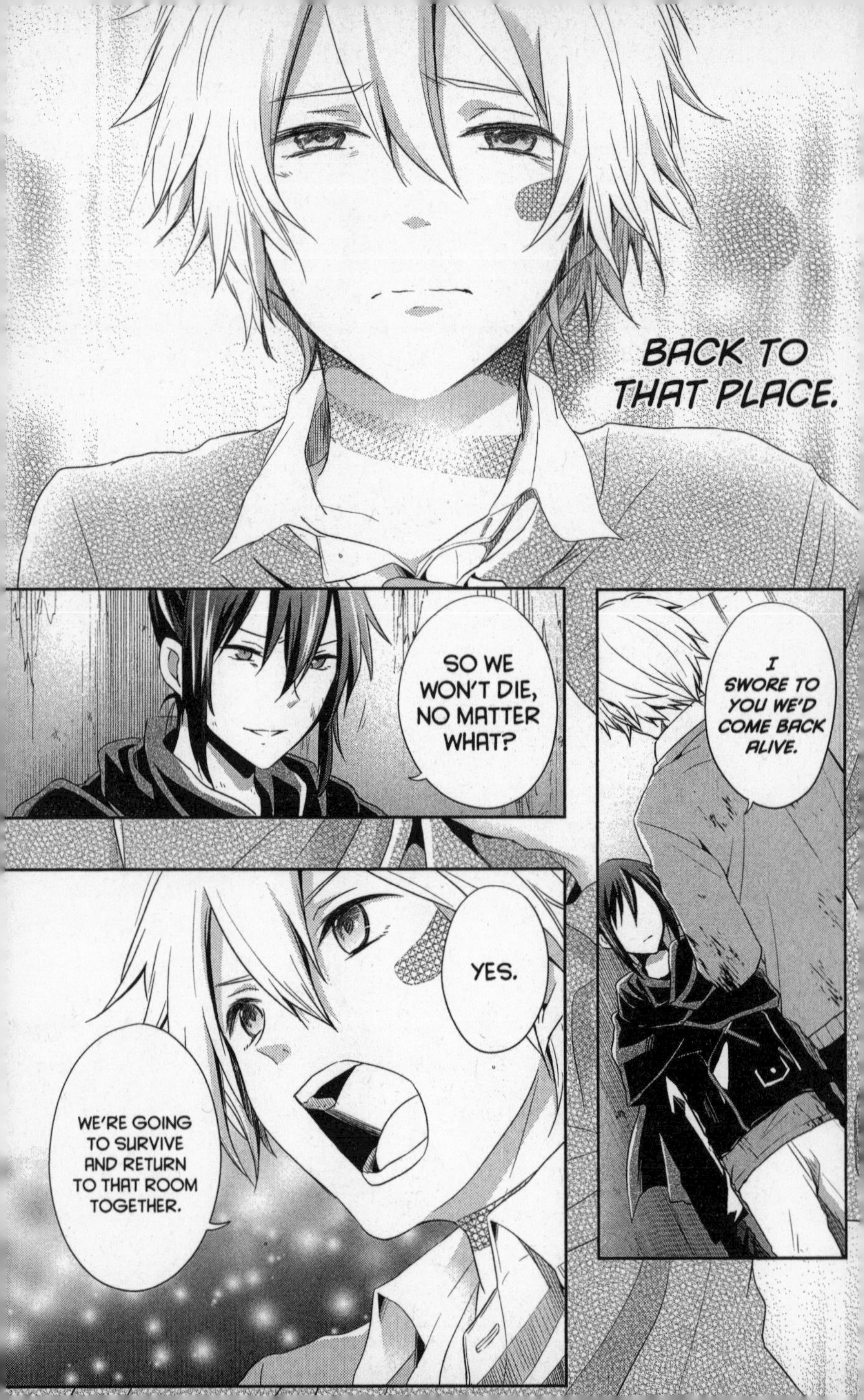
BACK TO THAT PLACE.
I SWORE TO YOU WE'D COME BACK ALIVE.
SO WE WON'T DIE, NO MATTER WHAT?
YES.
WE'RE GOING TO SURVIVE AND RETURN TO THAT ROOM TOGETHER.

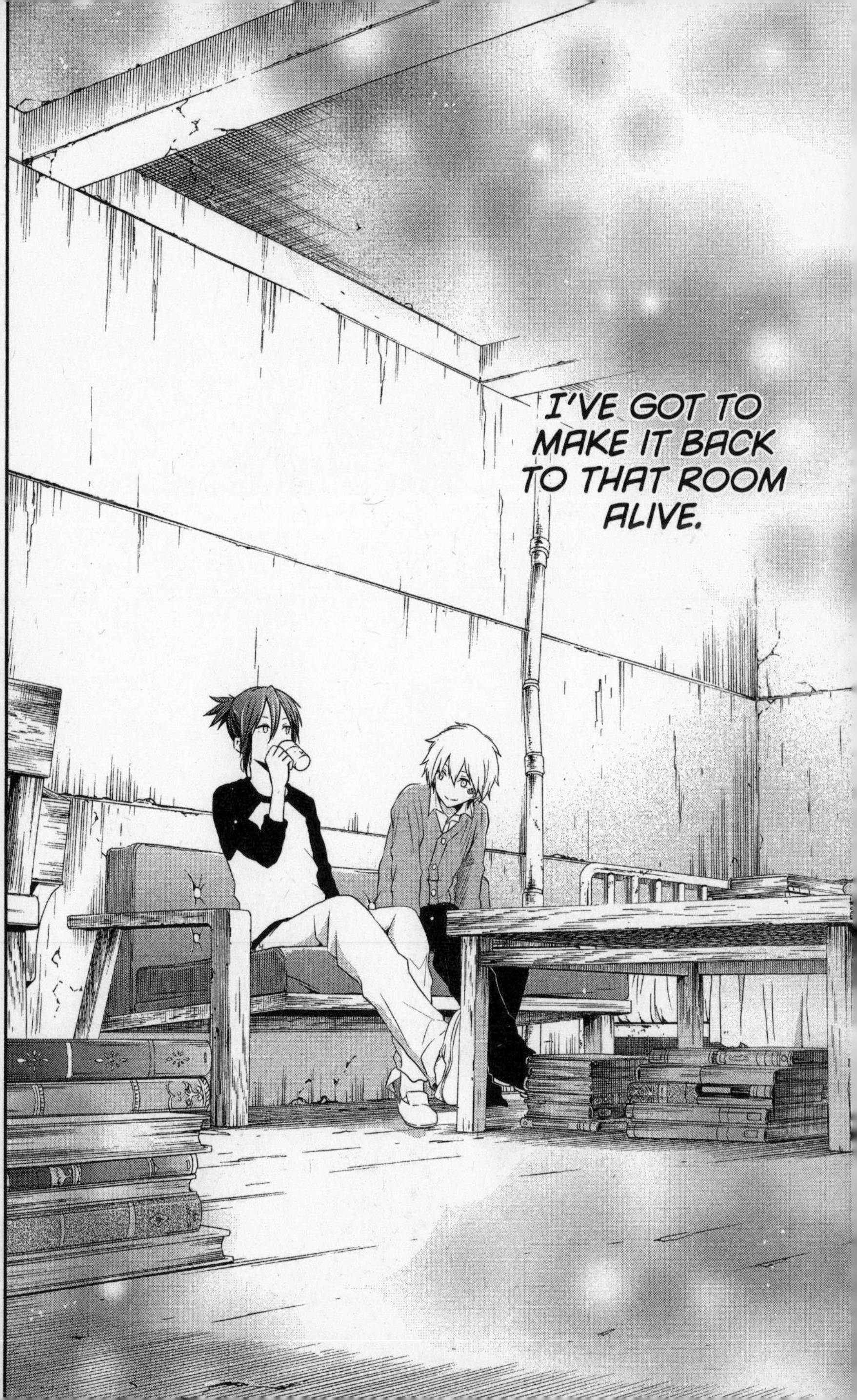
I'VE GOT TO MAKE IT BACK TO THAT ROOM ALIVE.

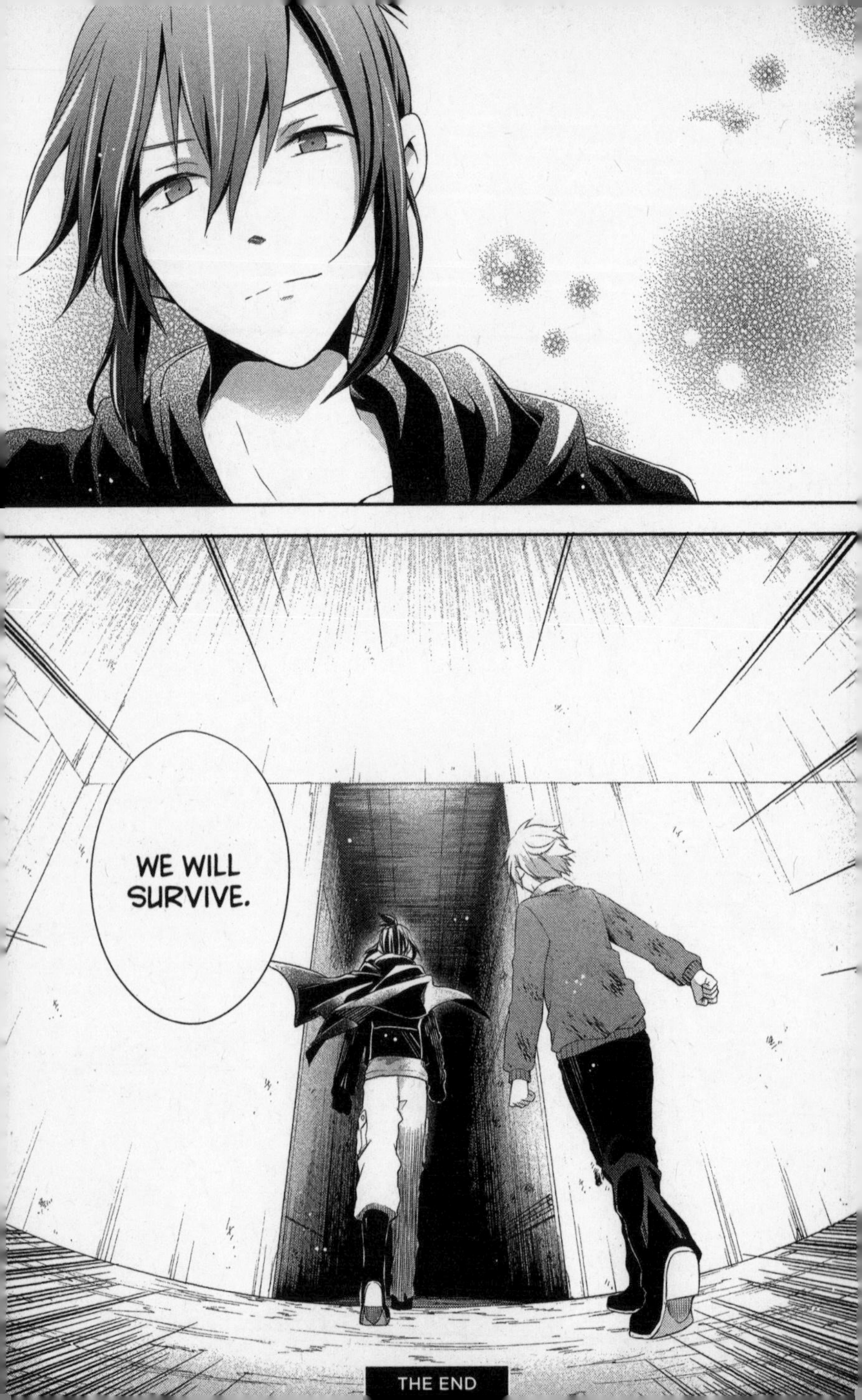
WE WILL SURVIVE.
THE END

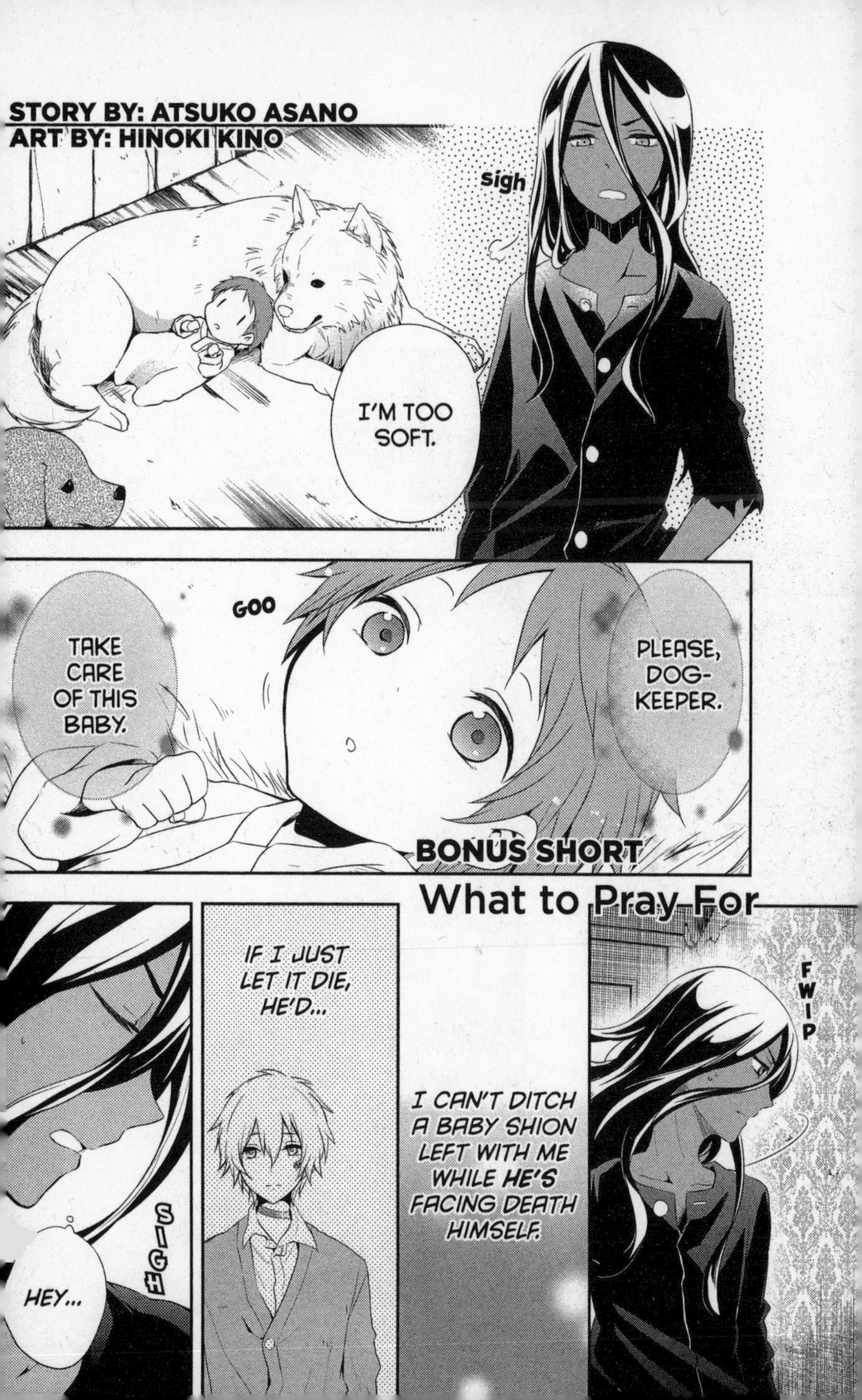
STORY BY: ATSUKO ASANO
ART BY: HINOKI KINO
sigh
I'M TOO SOFT.
PLEASE, DOG-KEEPER.
GOO
TAKE CARE OF THIS BABY.
BONUS SHORT
What to Pray For
FWIP
IF I JUST LET IT DIE, HE'D...
I CAN'T DITCH A BABY SHION LEFT WITH ME WHILE HE'S FACING DEATH HIMSELF.
SIGH
HEY...

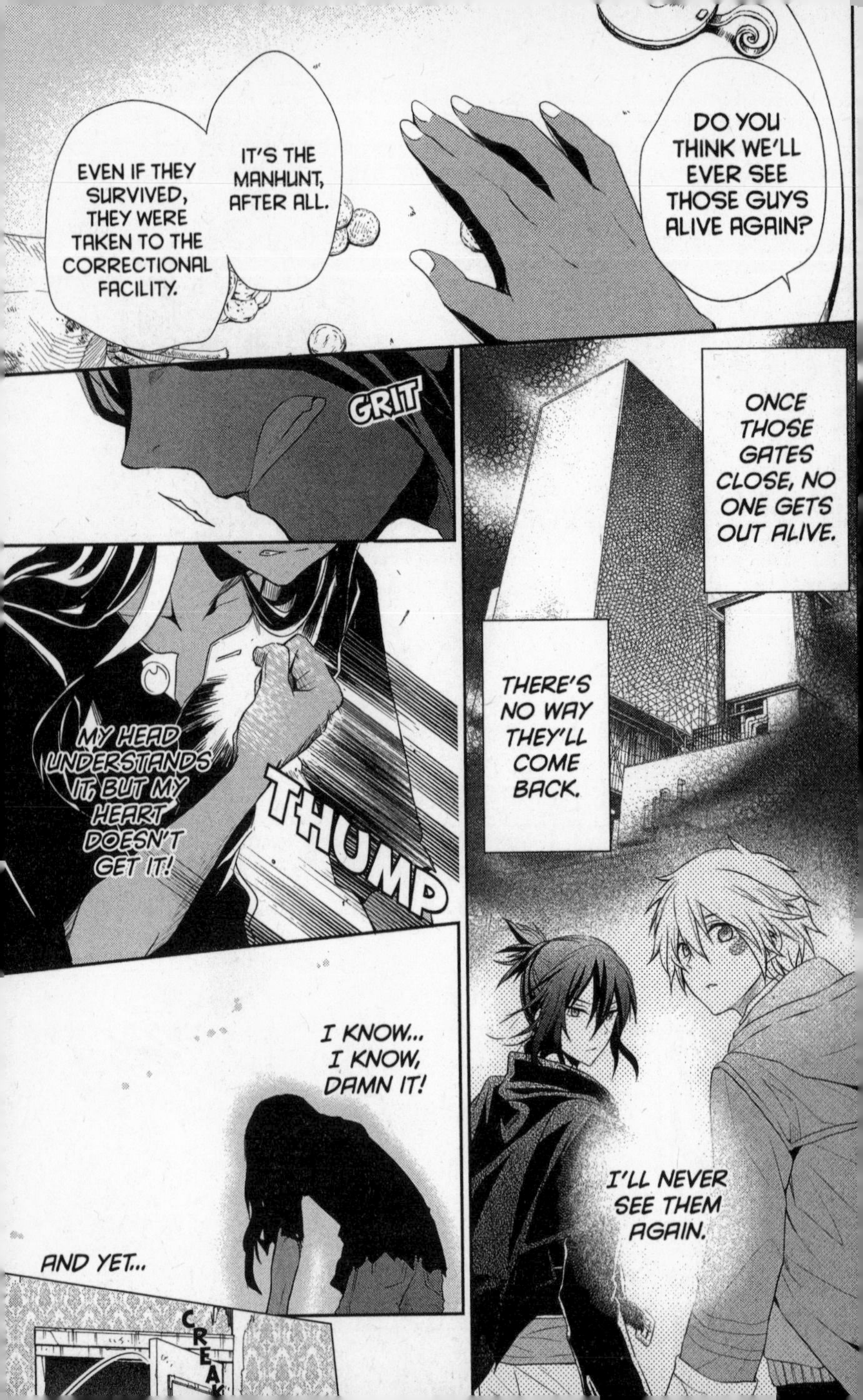
DO YOU THINK WE'LL EVER SEE THOSE GUYS ALIVE AGAIN?
IT'S THE MANHUNT, AFTER ALL.
EVEN IF THEY SURVIVED, THEY WERE TAKEN TO THE CORRECTIONAL FACILITY.
ONCE THOSE GATES CLOSE, NO ONE GETS OUT ALIVE.
THERE'S NO WAY THEY'LL COME BACK.
I'LL NEVER SEE THEM AGAIN.
GRIT
THUMP
MY HEAD UNDERSTANDS IT, BUT MY HEART DOESN'T GET IT!
I KNOW... I KNOW, DAMN IT!
AND YET...
CREAK

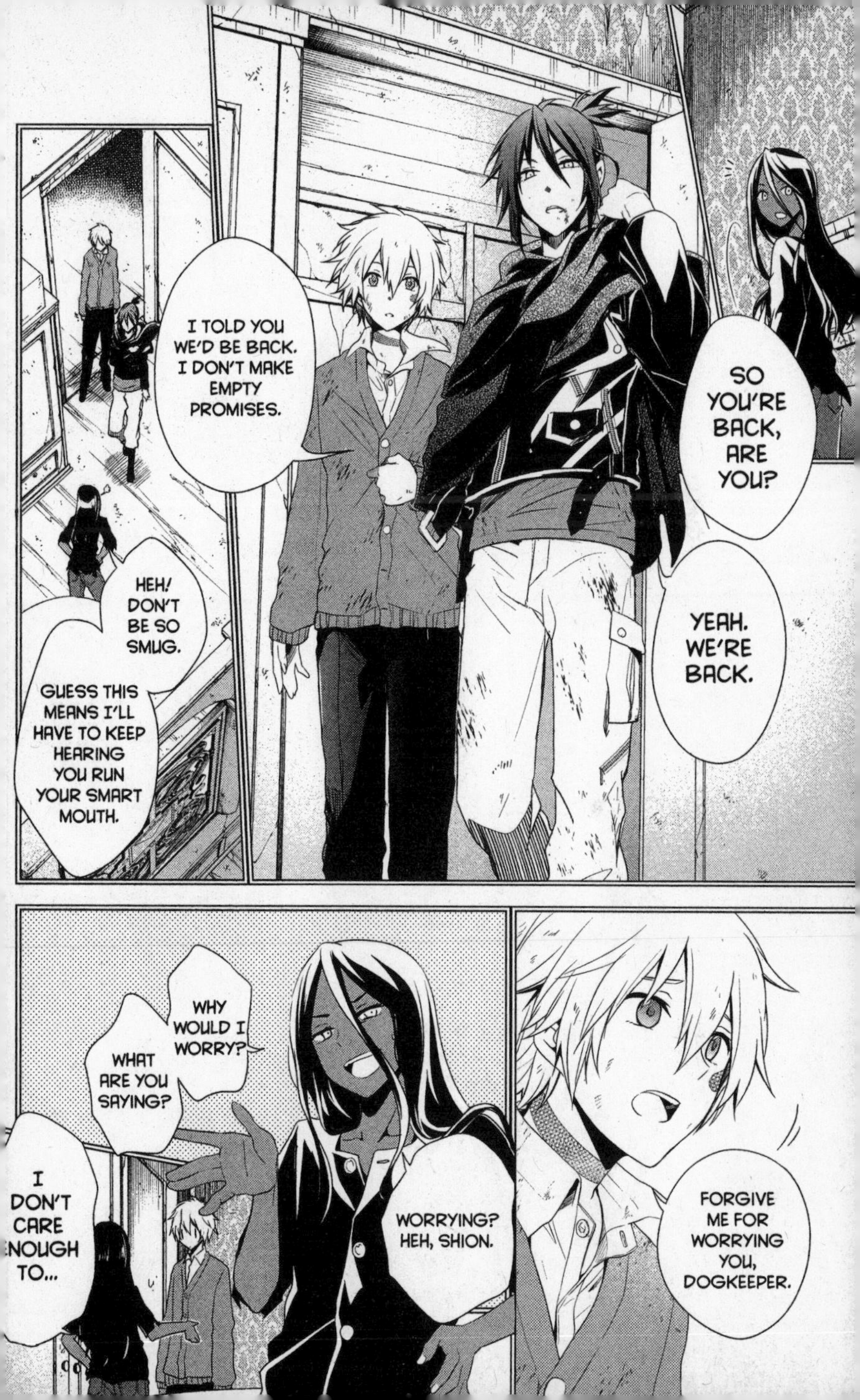
SO YOU'RE BACK, ARE YOU?
YEAH. WE'RE BACK.
I TOLD YOU WE'D BE BACK. I DON'T MAKE EMPTY PROMISES.
HEH! DON'T BE SO SMUG.
GUESS THIS MEANS I'LL HAVE TO KEEP HEARING YOU RUN YOUR SMART MOUTH.
FORGIVE ME FOR WORRYING YOU, DOGKEEPER.
WORRYING? HEH, SHION.
WHY WOULD I WORRY?
WHAT ARE YOU SAYING?
I DON'T CARE ENOUGH TO...

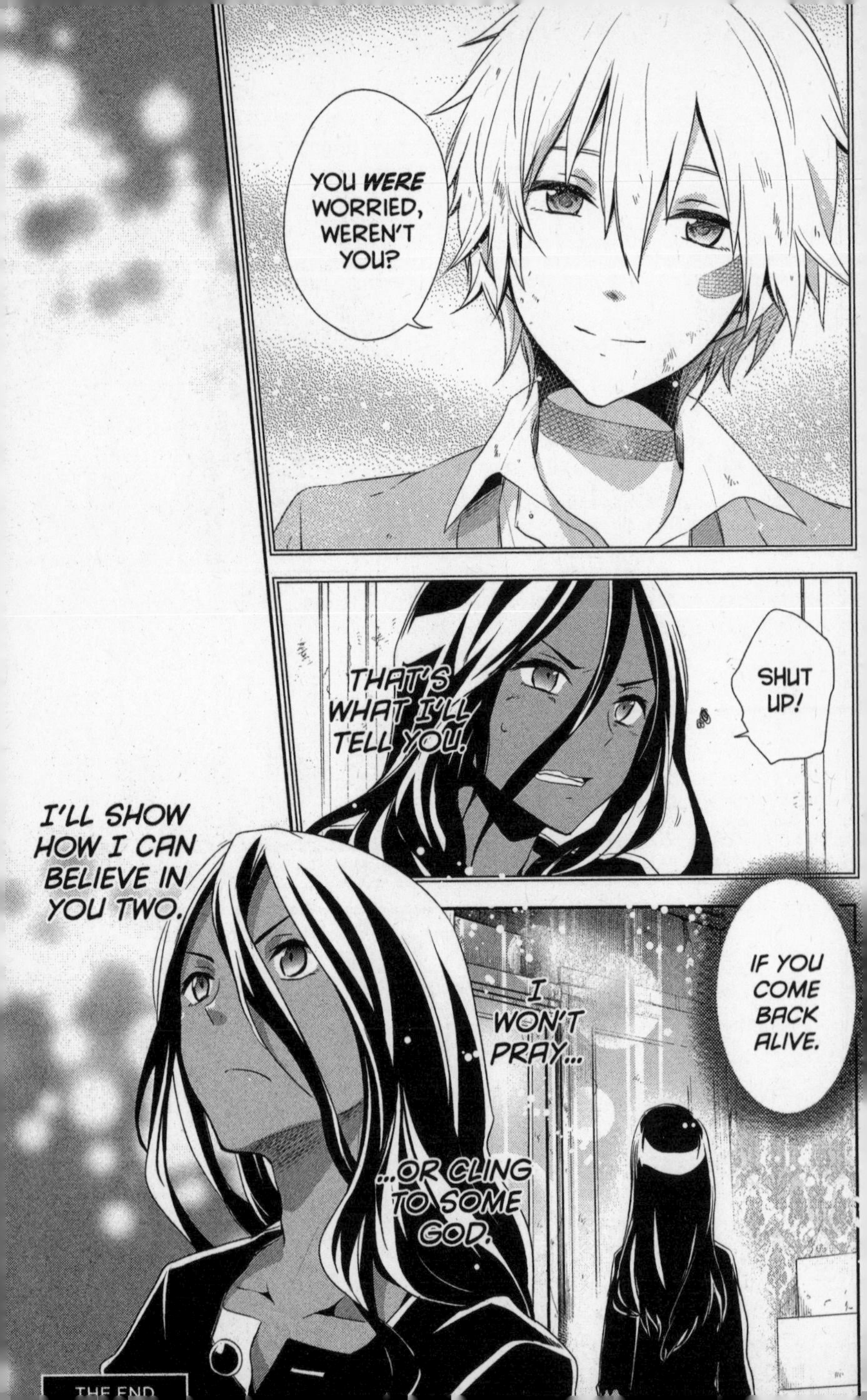
YOU WERE WORRIED, WEREN'T YOU?
SHUT UP!
THAT'S WHAT I'LL TELL YOU.
IF YOU COME BACK ALIVE.
I WON'T PRAY...
...OR CLING TO SOME GOD.
I'LL SHOW HOW I CAN BELIEVE IN YOU TWO.
THE END

I drew this short scene "A Place to Return To" as a combination of the chapter "That Which Is in the Abyss" from Vol. 5 and the room cleaning scene from Vol. 2.

I have a real love for the cleaning scene. I remember crying as I read the scenes of Shion and Rat living together. I thought that over as I carefully drew the scenes of life with Rat, and I'm so glad to draw it in a bonus section.

I also drew a bonus scene with Dogkeeper. It was so satisfying to draw lots of scenes with Dogkeeper. There are a lot more scenes I couldn't draw. I'm always trying to figure out where I can squeeze one in. I really want to draw them!

I hope you all enjoy it. Thank you so much for getting this book.

Rat really likes Shion's hair, doesn't he?

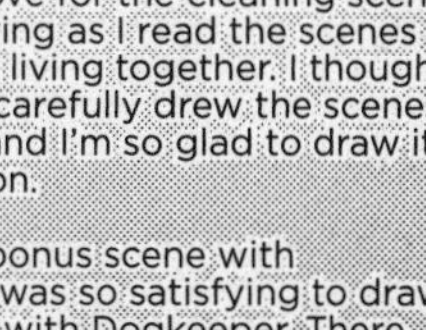

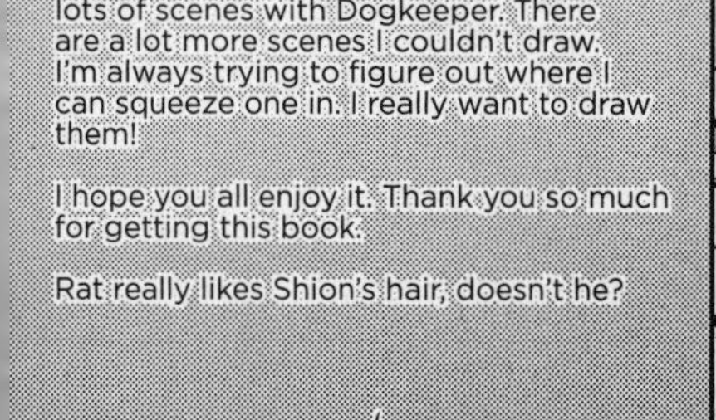

AND SO THE MICE SCAMPER OFF THE PAGE AND ONTO THE COVER. (SEE PAGE 164.)

SHERLOCK BONES

KC
KODANSHA
COMICS

DEDUCTIVE DOG DETECTIVE

When Takeru adopts a new pet, he's in for a surprise—the dog is none other than the reincarnation of Sherlock Holmes. With no one else able to communicate with Holmes, Takeru is roped into becoming Sherdog's assistant, John Watson. Using his sleuthing skills, Holmes uncovers clues to solve the trickiest crimes.

 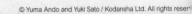

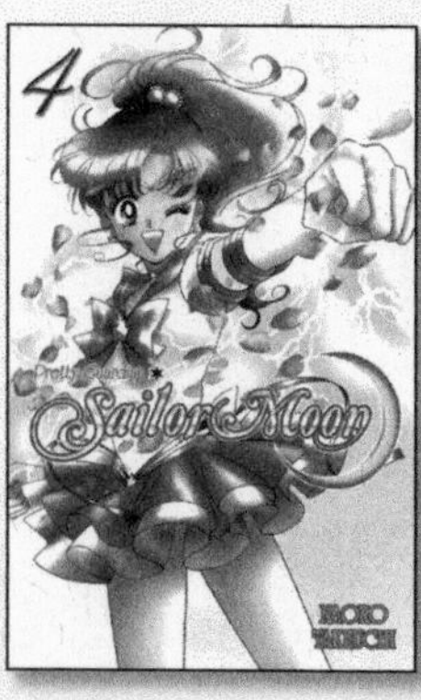
4
Sailor Moon
NAOKO TAKEUCHI

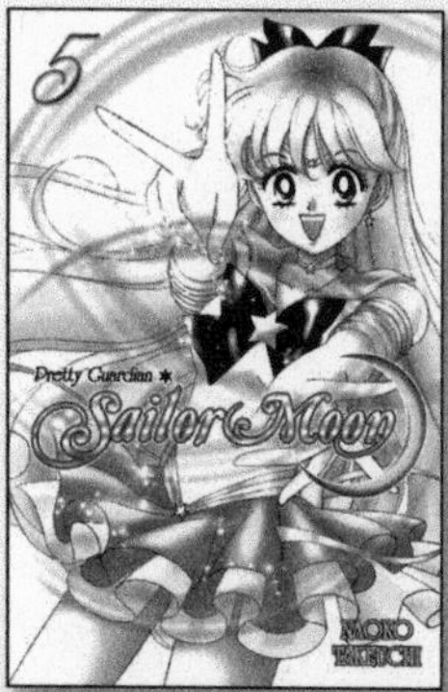
5
Pretty Guardian
Sailor Moon
NAOKO TAKEUCHI

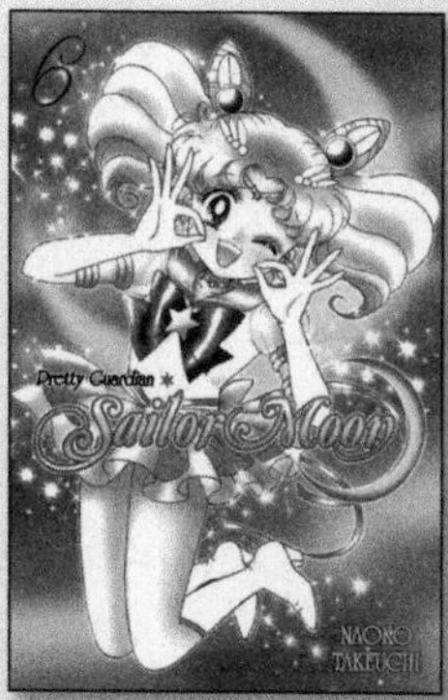
6
Pretty Guardian
Sailor Moon
NAOKO TAKEUCHI

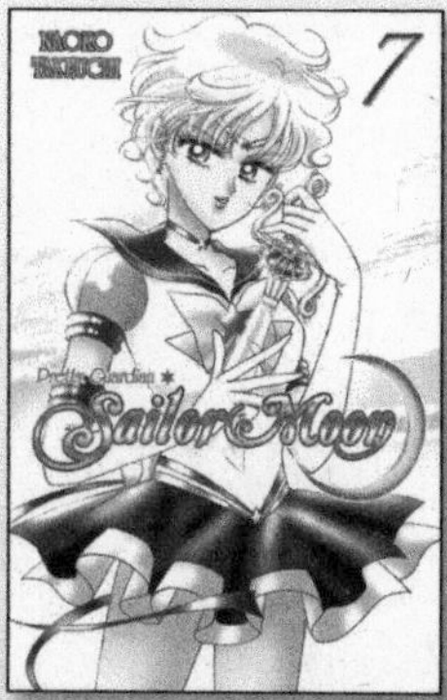
NAOKO TAKEUCHI
7
Pretty Guardian
Sailor Moon

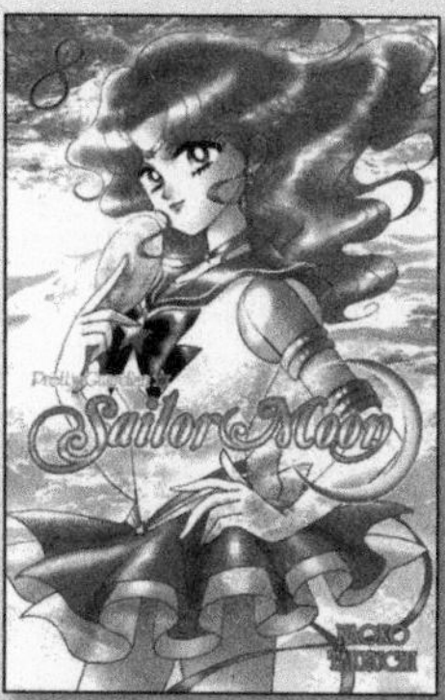
8
Sailor Moon
NAOKO TAKEUCHI

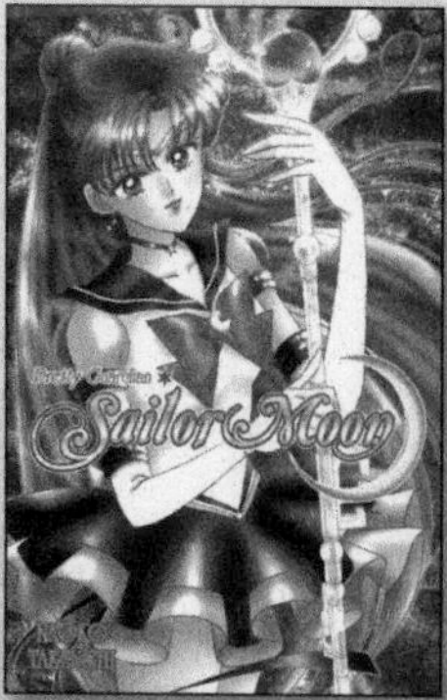
Sailor Moon

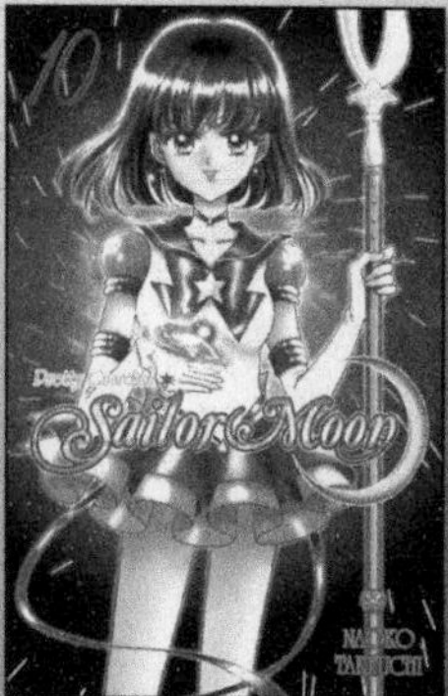
10
Sailor Moon
NAOKO TAKEUCHI

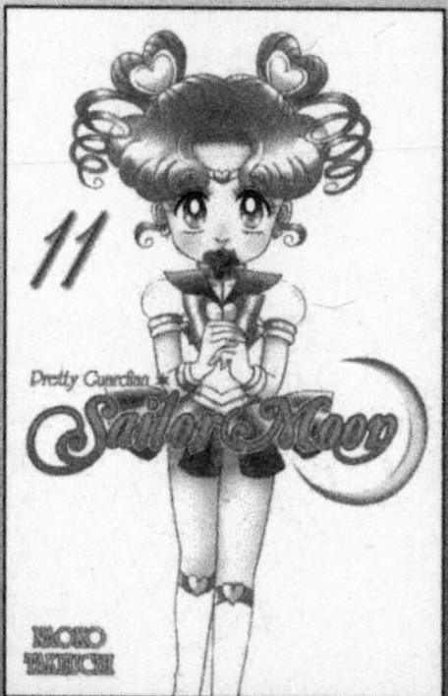
11
Pretty Guardian
Sailor Moon
NAOKO TAKEUCHI

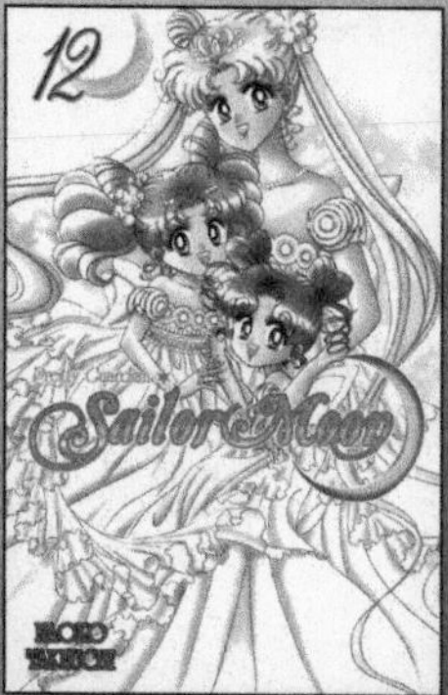
12
Sailor Moon
NAOKO TAKEUCHI

The Pretty Guardians are back!

*

Kodansha Comics is proud to present *Sailor Moon* with all new translations.

For more information, go to **www.kodanshacomics.com**

. *6* volume 5 is a work of fiction. Names, characters, places, and incidents e the products of the author's imagination or are used fictitiously. Any semblance to actual events, locales, or persons, living or dead, is entirely incidental.

Kodansha Comics Trade Paperback Original.

ublished in the United States by Kodansha Comics, an imprint of Kodansha
JSA Publishing, LLC, New York.

ublication rights for this English edition arranged through Kodansha Ltd.,
okyo.

irst published in Japan in 2012 by Kodansha Ltd., Tokyo
SBN 978-1-61262-359-7

rinted in the United States of America.

vww.kodanshacomics.com

 8 7 6 5 4 3 2 1

ranslation: Jonathan Tarbox/Arashi Productions
ettering: Christy Sawyer
diting: Ben Applegate